Vehicle Body Fitting and Repair

Vehicle Body Fitting and Repair

NVQ Levels 2 and 3

Alan Robinson RTechEng, MInstBE, MIBCAM, AWeldI, MISME

Section Leader for Vehicle Bodywork and Vehicle Body Repair Course, Coordinator for CGLI 3440 Vehicle Body Repair, Coordinator for CGLI 398 Vehicle Body Competences Course, Coordinator for CGLI 385 Vehicle Bodywork, Gateshead College

NEWNES

Newnes
An imprint of Butterworth-Heinemann Ltd
Linacre House, Jordan Hill, Oxford OX2 8DP

ℛ A member of the Reed Elsevier plc group

OXFORD   LONDON   BOSTON
NEW DELHI   SINGAPORE   SYDNEY
TOKYO   TORONTO   WELLINGTON

First published 1995

British Library Cataloguing in Publication Data
A catalogue record for this book is available from the
British Library

ISBN 0 7506 2271 7

Library of Congress Cataloguing in Publication Data
A catalogue record for this book is available from the
library of congress

Printed in Great Britain

Contents

Foreword

The Vehicle Builders and Repairers Association Ltd has always pioneered the need for well-trained staff and the highest standards of workmanship in the motor vehicle repair industry. It has become increasingly important, with the revolution in materials technology bringing major changes in vehicle repair equipment and techniques, that those who work in the body repair industry receive the proper skills training.

Over the last few years we have also seen a revolution in vocational training, with the advent of the NVQ establishing new standards for the industry.

Vehicle Body Fitting and Repair has been written specifically to provide a textbook for the level 2 NVQ in Vehicle Body Fitting and the level 3 NVQ in Vehicle Body Repair. It contains all the information that students at these levels will need, and provides step-by-step guidance aimed at a wide audience of part-time students working in firms of all sizes. *Vehicle Body Fitting and Repair* is an important training manual for all those studying for, or teaching, National Vocational Qualifications in vehicle repair.

R. D. Nicholson FIMI
Director of Operations
Vehicle Builders and
Repairs Association Ltd

Preface

This book covers the underpinning knowledge to support the evidence of competency within NVQ qualifications and is intended for apprentices entering the trade, students already in the trade, and mature tradesmen wishing to further their qualifications, by studying for the City and Guilds of London Institute, National Vocational Qualifications (NVQs).

National Vocational Qualifications (NVQs) for the motor industry are part of a new structure of qualifications being put in place to support the efforts of employers and employees to raise the standards of performance and competence in the workplace.

The qualifications are based on a new approach to describing and assessing a person's performance while engaged at work. This involves identification of the competence and the definition of standards in the workplace to which a person is expected to perform.

The Motor Industry Training Standards Council (MITSC) was established in 1990 as a lead body for the United Kingdom retail motor industry and its associated sectors. The Council is committed to the development of occupational standards for the motor industry especially in the areas of vehicle body repair, vehicle body fitting, vehicle body refinishing and the coordination of the award of NVQ.

The NVQ awards are at five levels, so there are qualifications for those just starting their career (levels 1 and 2), those carrying out skilled work (level 3), and those at supervisory and management positions (levels 4 and 5).

In order for candidates to be awarded NVQ they must prove ability in a number of units of occupational competency, each unit being certified upon its successful completion and building up a portfolio of evidence for accreditation in Vehicle Body Work to Level 2 and/or Level 3 within the NVQ framework.

Within the motor industry the following vehicle body units are necessary to achieve an NVQ qualification:

CGLI 3440 Vehicle Body Fitting Level 2 (the following six units are required for this level) (see Figure 1)

A2-LH   Replace vehicle body panels, panel sections and ancillary fittings.
A9-L2   Remove and replace vehicle components/units.
A10-L   Augment vehicle body work to meet customer's requirements.
A11-L   Prepare new, used or repaired vehicles for customer's use.
A12-G   Maintain effective working relationships.
A13-G   Maintain the health, safety and security of the working environment.

CGLI 3440 Vehicle Body Repair Level 3 (the following six units are required for this level) (see Figure 2)

A2-LH   Replace vehicle body panels, panel sections and ancillary fittings.
A3-LH   Repair body panels.
A10-L   Augment vehicle body work to meet customer's requirements.
A12-G   Maintain effective working relationships.
A13-G   Maintain the health, safety and security of the working environment.

A4-L   Rectify body misalignment and repair/replace body sections.
OR
A4-LH   Rectify chassis frame misalignment and repair/replace chassis sections.

(*Note*: Figures 1 and 2 include the unit A6-G, Reinstate the cleanliness of the vehicle, as an additional unit. Further information about these units is available from MITSC or CGLI.)

NVQs for Vehicle Bodywork
This book is intended to supply underpinning knowledge for students working to achieve National Vocational Qualifications (NVQs) in Vehicle Body Repair through the Motor Industry Training Standards Council (MITSC).

Figure 1   Route plan to NVQ Level 2

CGLI has been accredited by NCVQ as one of the awarding bodies for these qualifications under the following schemes:

Scheme No. 3440 Vehicle Body Fitting – Level 2 NVQ
Scheme No. 3440 Vehicle Body Repair – Level 3 NVQ

The book begins by giving an insight into health, safety and personal protection which are essential parts of the employee's safe working environment, and covers personal hygiene, protective clothing, fire precautions, safety signs and general workshop safety.

ROUTE to NVQ 3 in VEHICLE BODY REPAIR

CGLI 3440 NVQ Level 3

A13-G
Maintain the health, safety and security of the working environment

---

UNITS A2-A3-A4-A10

A4-L
Rectify body misalignment & repair/replace body sections

OR

A4-LH
Rectify chassis frame misalignment and repair/replace chassis sections

A2-LH
Replace vehicle body panels, panel sections & ancillary fittings

A3-LH
Repair vehicle body panels

A10-L
Augment vehicle bodywork to meet customer's requirements

A6-G
Reinstate the cleanliness of the vehicle

A12-G
Maintain effective working relationships

ASSESSMENTS

NVQ 3

Figure 2   Route plan to NVQ Level 3

NVQ Level 2 UNIT REFERENCE	√			√	√	√	√	√	√
	A2	A3	A4	A6	A9	A10	A11	A12	A13
Chap 1 Health and Safety in the Workshop	√			√	√	√			√
Chap 2 Design & Construction of car body	√				√	√			
Chap 3 Hand and Power Tools	√			√	√	√			
Chap 4 Materials used in Vehicle Bodies	√								
Chap 5 Methods of Joining Materials	√								
Chap 6 Cutting and Plasma Arc Cutting									
Chap 7 Electric Resistance Welding									
Chap 8 TIG/MIG/MAG Welding									
Chap 9 Minor Accident Damage				√	√				
Chap 10 Major Accident Damage				√	√		√	√	
Chap 11 Company Admin. & Personnel						√	√	√	
NOTE: Tick denotes element information may be found in this chapter									

Figure 3 NVQ Level 2 – unit reference chart

It continues with a brief description of the history and development of the motor car and the evolution of design, and then goes on to explain the early types of construction, explaining styling forms and vehicle classification leading up to that of the present day. Hand tools, power tools and simple machines used by the body repair worker are fully described and explained, and there is a comprehensive study of the various materials which are used in the manufacture and repair of vehicles.

Basic craft techniques are studied, beginning with the panel beater, who in the early days formed hand-made panels for coach-built vehicles, and advancing to the present-day repair worker, who supplements his hand tools by the use of portable hydraulic equipment.

Nowadays, the repair of minor and major accident damage requires the use of precision equipment such as laser measuring equipment linked electronically to computers to give instant digital display, recording and printouts of any measurements and deviations. In addition, precision alignment repair jig equipment and hydraulic pulling and pushing equipment are needed to enable a first-class repair to be carried out. The use of these systems has been made essential by the current safety design concept of monocoque construction, with its strong passenger compartment and front and rear crumple zones, which absorb energy through deformation of panel structures on impact. Consequently, precision diagnostic and repair equipment is required to enable the repairer to restore the vehicle to its original manufacturer's specifications. The development of modern methods has been encouraged by the research carried out at the Motor Insurance Repair Research Centre and by the involvement of the Vehicle Builders and Repairers Association and the Automobile Association in updating and improving standards throughout the vehicle body repair trade.

While the joining of materials used in the motor industry is very complicated, a selection is included of established methods. The vehicle of today is assembled using resistance welding techniques; therefore it is important for the body repair worker to understand these techniques as used in both the manufacture and repair of vehicles. Gas shielded arc welding (TIG/MIG/MAG welding) is now used in both the construction and the repair of vehicle bodies.

As a large proportion of repair work is financed through insurance claims, a simple explanation is given

NVQ Level 3 UNIT REFERENCE	√	√	√	√	√		√	√
	A2	A3	A4	A6	A10	A11	A12	A13
Chap 1 Health and Safety in the Workshop	√	√	√	√	√			√
Chap 2 Design & Construction of car body	√	√	√		√			
Chap 3 Hand and Power Tools	√	√	√	√	√			
Chap 4 Materials used in Vehicle Bodies	√	√	√					
Chap 5 Methods of Joining Materials	√	√	√					
Chap 6 Cutting and Plasma Arc Cutting		√	√					
Chap 7 Electric Resistance Welding		√	√					
Chap 8 TIG/MIG/MAG Welding		√	√					
Chap 9 Minor Accident Damage		√	√	√				
Chap 10 Major Accident Damage			√	√	√		√	
Chap 11 Company Admin. & Personnel					√		√	
NOTE: Tick denotes element information may be found in this chapter								

Figure 4   NVQ Level 3 – unit reference chart

of correct insurance procedures, together with the assessment of costing and estimating for repairs using computer technology so that workshops are capable of carrying out repairs which are of an acceptably high quality and meet the requirements of customers and insurance companies.

Company structure, staff duties and responsibilities are dealt with in addition to staff appointments and staff training. Different types of customer and customer relationships, together with the handling of customer complaints, are important parts of any bodyshop's activities.

Relevant Regulations and Acts which influence the administration of any company are included. These include *Construction and Use Regulations*, *Vehicle Type Approval*, *Trades Description Act*, *Law of Contract*, *Supply of Goods and Services Act*, and warranties given by manufacturers, VBRA and individual bodyshops.

A. Robinson

Acknowledgements

I wish to express my appreciation of assistance given by my colleagues in the Body Work and Painting Section at Gateshead College. I am also grateful for the efficient help given by the library staff of the college.

I wish to thank my wife Norma for the many hours spent working at the computer to assist me. Also I would like to take this opportunity to thank my son Andrew for the production of some of the photographs taken especially for this edition.

I would also like to take this opportunity of offering my sincere thanks to the following firms and/or their representatives who have so readily cooperated with me by permitting the reproduction of data, illustrations and photographs:

AGA Ltd
AI Welders Ltd
Akzo Coatings PLC
Alcan Design and Development
Alkor Plastics (UK) Ltd
Aluminium Federation Ltd
Ambi-Rad Ltd
ARO Welding Ltd
Aston Martin Lagonda Ltd
Auchard Development Co. Ltd
Autoglym
Autokraft Ltd
Auto-Quote
Avdel Ltd
Bayer UK Ltd
Berger Industrial Coatings
Black and Decker Ltd
Blackhawk Automotive Ltd
BOC Ltd
Bodyshop Magazine
Bodymaster UK
Bondaglass-Voss Ltd
Bostick Ltd
BP Chemicals (UK) Ltd
British Motor Industry Heritage Trust
British Standards Institution
British Steel Stainless
BSC Strip Product Group
Callow & Maddox Bros Ltd
Car Bench
Car-O-Liner UK Ltd
Celette UK Ltd
Cengar Universal Tool Company Ltd
Chicago Pneumatic Tool Co. Ltd
Chief Automotive Ltd
Chubb Fire Ltd
Citroen UK Ltd
City and Guilds of London Institute
Dana Distribution Ltd, Martyn Ferguson

ACKNOWLEDGEMENTS

Dataliner, Geotronics Ltd
Desoutter Automotive Ltd
DeVilbiss Automotive Refinishing Products
Dinol-Protectol Ltd
DRG Kwikseal Products
Du Pont (UK) Ltd
Duramix
Dunlop Adhesives
East Coast Traders
Edwards Pearson Ltd
ESAB Ltd
European Industrial Services
Facom Tools Ltd
Farécla Products Ltd
Fifth Generation Technology Ltd
Fire Extinguishing Trades Association
Ford Motor Company Ltd
Forest Fasteners
Frost Auto Restoration Techniques Ltd
Fry's Metals Ltd
George Marshall (Power Tools) Ltd
GE Plastics Ltd
GKN Screws and Fasteners Ltd
Glasurit Automotive Refinish
Glas-Weld Systems (UK) Ltd
Go-Jo Industries Europe Ltd
Gramos Chemicals International Ltd
Gray Campling Ltd
Harboran Ltd
Herberts
Hooper & Co. (Coachbuilders) Ltd
Huck UK Ltd
IBCAM Journal
ICI Autocolor
ICI Chemicals and Polymers Group
ICI Paints
Industrial and Trade Fairs Ltd
Jack Sealey Ltd
Jaguar Cars Ltd
John Cotton (Colne) Ltd
Kärcher
Kenmore Computing Services Ltd
Kroll (UK) Ltd
Land Rover Ltd
Lotus Engineering
Migatronic Welding Equipment Ltd
Minden Industrial Ltd
Morgan Motor Company Ltd
Motor Industry Training Standards Council (MITSC)
Murex Welding Products Ltd
3M Automotive Trades
National Adhesives & Resins Ltd
Nederman Ltd
Neill Tools Ltd

Nettlefolds Ltd
Olympus Welding & Cutting Technology Ltd
Owens-Corning Fiberglas (GB) Ltd
Parkway Consultancy (S. Hamill)
Partco Engineering
Permabond
Pickles Godfrey Design Partnership, Ernest W.
    Godfrey
Plastics and Rubber Institute
Racal Safety Ltd
Reliant Motors Ltd
Renault UK Ltd
Rolls-Royce Motor Cars Ltd
Rover Group Ltd
Saab-Scania
Schlegel (UK) Ltd
Scott Bader Co. Ltd
Selson Machine Tool Co. Ltd
SIP (Industrial Products) Ltd
Spraybake Ltd
Standard Forms Ltd
Stanners Ltd
Sun Electric UK Ltd
Sykes-Pickavant Ltd
Teroson UK
The Institute of Materials
The Motor Insurance Repair Research Centre
The National Motor Museum
Thornley and Knight Ltd
Triplex Safety Glass
Tri-Sphere Ltd
TRW United-Car Ltd
Tucker Fasteners Ltd
UK Fire International Ltd
United Continental Steels Ltd
Vauxhall Motors Ltd
Vitamol Ltd
Volkswagen-Audi
Volvo Concessionaires Ltd
W. David and Sons Limited
Welding & Metal Fabrication
Welwyn Tool Co. Ltd
Wheelforce V. L. Churchill
Wholesale Welding Supplies Ltd

Abbreviations and symbols

ABS	acrylonitrile butadiene styrene
ABS	anti-lock braking system
AF	across flats (bolt size)
AC	alternating current
A	ampere
AFFF	aqueous film forming foam (fire fighting)
bar	10^6 dyn/cm^2; 10^5 N/m^2; 0.98682 atm; 14.505 psi
BATNEEC	best available techniques not enabling excessive costs
BS	British Standard
BSI	British Standards Institution
BCF	bromochlorodifluoromethane (fire extinguishers)
C_d	aerodynamic drag coefficient
CO	carbon monoxide
CO_2	carbon dioxide
C	centigrade (Celsius)
cm	centimetre
CAD	computer-aided design
CAE	computer-aided engineering
CAM	computer-aided manufacturing
CIM	computer-integrated manufacturing
COSHH	Control of Substances Hazardous to Health (Regulations)
cm^3	cubic centimetres
°	degree (angle or temperature)
dB(A)	noise level at the ear
DTI	dial test indicator
dia.	diameter
DC	direct current
dB	decibel
ECU	electronic control unit
EPA	Environmental Protection Act
EC	European Community
F	fahrenheit
ft	foot
ft/min	feet per minute
gal	gallon (imperial)
GLS	general lighting service (lamp)
GRP	glass fibre reinforced plastic
g	gram (mass)
HASAWA	Health and Safety at Work Act
HSE	Health and Safety Executive

HT	high tension (electrical)
HVLP	high velocity low pressure (spray guns)
in	inch
in^2	square inches
in^3	cubic inches
IFS	independent front suspension
IR	infrared
ID	internal diameter
ISO	International Organization for Standardization
kg	kilogram (mass)
kW	kilowatt
LH	left hand
LHD	left-hand drive
LHThd	left-hand thread
l	litre
LT	low tension
lumen	light energy radiated per second per unit solid angle by a uniform point source of 1 candela intensity
lux	unit of illumination equal to 1 lumen/m^2
max.	maximum
MAG	metal active gas (welding)
MIG	metal inert gas (welding)
m	metre
mm	millimetre
min.	minimum
−	minus (of tolerance)
′	minute (of angle)
(−)	negative (electrical)
N m	newton metre
no.	number
lbf	pound force
lb	pound (mass)
lbf ft	pound force foot (torque)
lbf/in^2	pound force per square inch
$L_{ep, d}$	noise exposure level, personal (daily)
$L_{cp, w}$	noise exposure level, personal (weekly)
ozf	ounce (force)
oz	ounce (mass)
OD	outside diameter
part no.	part number
%	percentage
PPE	Personal Protection Equipment (Regulations)
pt	pint (imperial)
+	plus (tolerance)
±	plus or minus
PVA	polyvinyl acetate

PVC	polyvinyl chloride
+	positive (electrical)
r	radius
ref.	reference
rev/min	revolutions per minute
RH	right hand
RHD	right-hand drive
″	second (angle)
SAE	Society of Automobile Engineers
cm^2	square centimetres
std	standard
TIG	tungsten inert gas (welding)
VIN	vehicle identification number
VOCs	volatile organic compounds
V	volt

1

Health and safety in the working environment

The main responsibility for occupational health and safety lies with the employer. It is the employer who must provide a safe working environment, safe equipment and safety protection, and must also ensure that all work methods are carried out safely.

The Health and Safety at Work Act (HASAWA) 1974 is a major piece of occupational legislation which requires the employer to ensure, as far as is reasonably practicable, the health and safety of all staff and any other personnel who may be affected by the work carried out. The other two important regulations affecting bodyshops are the Control of Substances Hazardous to Health (COSHH) Regulations 1988 and the Environmental Protection Act (EPA) 1990.

1.1 PERSONAL SAFETY AND HEALTH PRACTICES

1.1.1 Skin care (personal hygiene) systems

All employees should be aware of the importance of personal hygiene and should follow correct procedures to clean and protect the skin in order to avoid irritants causing skin infections and dermatitis. All personnel should use a suitable barrier cream before starting work and again when recommencing work after a break. There are waterless hand cleaners available which will remove heavy dirt on skin prior to thorough washing. When the skin has been washed, after-work creams will help to restore its natural moisture.

Many paints, refinishing chemicals and bodyshop materials will cause irritation on contact with the skin and must be removed promptly with a suitable cleansing material. Paint solvents may cause dermatitis, particularly where skin has been in contact with peroxide hardeners or acid catalysts: these have a drying effect which removes the natural oils in the skin. There are specialist products available for the bodyshop which will remove these types of materials from the skin quickly, safely and effectively.

1.1.2 Hand protection

Body technicians and painters are constantly handling substances which are harmful to health. The harmful effect of liquids, chemicals and materials on the hands can be prevented, in many cases, by wearing the correct type of gloves. To comply with COSHH Regulations, vinyl disposable gloves must be used by painters to give skin protection against toxic substances. Other specialist gloves available are: rubber and PVC gloves for protection against solvents, oil and acids; leather gloves for hard wear and general repair work in the bodyshop; and welding gauntlets, which are made from specially treated leather and are longer than normal gloves to give adequate protection to the welder's forearms.

1.1.3 Protective clothing

Protective clothing is worn to protect the worker and his clothes from contact with dirt, extremes of temperature, falling objects and chemical substances. The most common form of protective clothing for the body repairer is the overall, a one-piece boiler suit made from good quality cotton, preferably flameproof. Worn and torn materials should be avoided as they can catch in moving machinery. Where it is necessary to protect the skin, closely fitted sleeves should be worn down to the wrist with the cuffs fastened. All overall buttons must be kept fastened, and any loose items such as ties and scarves should not be worn.

Protective clothing worn in the paint shop by the spray painters should be either good quality washable nylon garments, anti-static, and complete with hood, elasticated wrists and ankles, or low-linting disposable coveralls, which offer a liquid barrier protection from splashes, airborne dusts and paint overspray. The coveralls must withstand continuous exposure to a variety of chemicals and must be suitable for protection when using isocyanate-based two-pack paints; they also prevent the environment being contaminated by particles from the operator's clothing and hair.

1

(a)

(b)

Figure 1.1 (a) Disposable protective coverall
(b) protective coverall and face mask in use (*Gramos Chemicals International Ltd*)

They can be of the one-piece variety or can have separate disposable hoods (Figure 1.1a, b).

1.1.4 Head protection

Head protection is very important to the body worker when working underneath a vehicle or under its bonnet while it is being repaired. A light safety helmet, normally made from aluminium, fibreglass or plastic, should be worn if there is any danger from falling objects, and will protect the head from damage when working below vehicles. Hats and other forms of fabric headwear keep out dust, dirt and overspray and also prevent long hair (tied back) becoming entangled in moving equipment.

1.1.5 Eye and face protection

Eye protection is required where there is a possibility of eye injury from flying particles when using a grinder, disc sander, power drill or pneumatic chisel, or when removing glass windscreens or working underneath vehicles. Many employers are now requiring all employees to wear some form of safety glasses when they are in either the repair or the paint areas of the

Figure 1.2 Lightweight safety spectacles (*Racal Safety Ltd*)

Figure 1.3 General-purpose safety goggles (*Racal Safety Ltd*)

bodyshop, because in any bodyshop location there is always the possibility of flying objects, dust particles or splashing liquids entering the eyes. Not only is this painful but it can, in extreme cases, cause loss of sight. Eyes are irreplaceable: therefore it is advisable to wear safety goggles, glasses or face shields in all

working areas. The following types of eye protection are available:

Lightweight safety spectacles with adjustable arms and side shields for extra protection. There is a choice of impact grades for the lenses (Figure 1.2).

General purpose safety goggles with a moulded PVC frame which is resistant to oils chemicals and water. These have either a clear acetate or a polycarbonate lens with BS impact grades 1 and 2 (Figure 1.3).

Face shields with an adjustable head harness and deep polycarbonate brow guard with replaceable swivel-up clear or anti-glare polycarbonate visor BS grade 1, which gives protection against sparks, molten metal and chemicals (Figure 1.4a, b).

Welding helmet or welding goggles with appropriate shaded lens to BS regulations. These must be worn at all times when welding. They will protect the eyes and face from flying molten particles of steel when gas welding and brazing, and from the harmful light rays generated by the arc when MIG/MAG, TIG or MMA welding (Figure 1.5a, b).

1.1.6 Foot protection

Safety footwear is essential in the bodyshop environment. Boots or shoes with steel toecaps will protect the toes from falling objects. Rubber boots will give protection from acids or wet conditions. Never wear defective footwear as this becomes a hazard in any workshop environment.

1.1.7 Respiratory protection (lungs)

One of the most important hazards faced by the bodyshop worker is that of potential damage to the lungs. Respirators are usually needed in body repair shops even though adequate ventilation is provided for the working areas. During welding, metal or paint preparation, or spraying, some form of protection is necessary. Under the COSHH Regulations, respiratory protection is essential and therefore must be used.

Respirators give protection against abrasive dusts, gases, vapours from caustic solutions and solvents, and spray mist from undercoats and finishing paint by filtering the contaminated atmosphere before it is inhaled by the wearer. They may be either simple filtering devices, where the operator's lungs are used to draw air through the filter, or powered devices incorporating a battery-driven fan to draw contaminated air through the filters and deliver a flow of clean air to the wearer's face. There are four primary types of respirator available to protect bodyshop technicians:

3

(b)

(a)

Figure 1.4 (a) Face shield (*Racal Safety Ltd*) (b) face shield with protective hood (*DeVilbiss Automotive Refinishing Products*)

(a) (b)

Figure 1.5 (a) Standard visor-type welding helmet (b) standard welding goggles with hinged lenses (*Racal Safety Ltd*) dust respirators, cartridge filter respirators, powered respirators and constant flow air line breathing apparatus.

Dust respirators (masks)

The most basic form of respiratory protection is the disposable filtering half-mask, typically used when preparing or finishing bodywork such as by rubbing down or buffing, and where dust, mist and fumes are a problem. This face mask provides an excellent face seal while at the same time allowing the wearer to speak freely without breaking the seal. Breathing resistance is minimal, offering cool and comfortable use. Various types of mask are available for use in a variety of environments where contaminants vary from nuisance dust particles to fine dusts and toxic mists. These masks can only be used in atmospheres containing less than the occupational exposure limit of the contaminant (Figure 1.6a, b).

Cartridge filter mask

The cartridge filter or organic vapour type of respirator, which covers the nose and mouth, is equipped with a replacement cartridge that removes the organic vapours by chemical absorption. Some of these are also designed with a pre-filter to remove solid particles from the air before the air passes through the chemical cartridge. They are used in finishing operations with non-toxic paints, but not with isocyanate paints. For the vapour/particle respirator to function correctly it is essential that it fits properly against the face. Follow the manufacturer's instructions for changing the cartridges when spraying over a continuous period (Figure 1.7a, b).

Powered respirators

Powered respirators using canister filters offer protection against toxic dusts and gases. The respirator draws contaminated air through filters with a motor fan powered by a rechargeable battery and supplies clean air to the wearer's face. This avoids discomfort and fatigue caused by the effort of having to inhale air through filters, permitting longer working periods. These devices find great use both in the spray shop and in the repair shop when carrying out welding (Figure 1.8a, b).

Constant-flow air line breathing apparatus

The constant-flow compressed air line breathing apparatus is designed to operate from an industrial compressed air system in conjunction with the spray gun. Using a waist-belt-mounted miniature fixed-pressure regulator and a pre-filter, the equipment supplies breathing quality air through a small-bore hose to a

(a)

(b)

Figure 1.6 (a) Dust mask (b) dust mask in use (*Racal Safety Ltd*)

5

(a)

(b)

Figure 1.7 (a) Standard cartridge mask with filters (*Racal Safety Ltd*) (b) cartridge mask and protective coveralls being used while spraying (*Gramos Chemicals International Ltd*)

variety of face masks and visors to provide respiratory protection for paint spraying (such as with isocyanates), cleaning and grinding (Figure 1.9a, b). The COSHH Regulations have made it mandatory for all respiratory protection equipment to be both approved and suitable for the purpose, for the operatives to be correctly trained in the equipment's use and maintenance, and for proper records to be kept.

1.1.8 Ear protection

The Noise at Work Regulations 1989 define three action levels for exposure to noise at work:

1 A daily personal exposure of up to 85 dB(A). Where exposure exceeds this level, suitable hearing protection must be provided on request (Figure 1.10).
2 A daily personal exposure of up to 90 dB(A). Above this second level of provision, hearing protection is mandatory.
3 A peal; sound pressure of 200 pascals (140 dB).

Where the second or third levels are reached, employers must designate ear protection zones and require all who enter these zones to wear ear protection. Where the third level is exceeded, steps must be taken to reduce noise levels as far as is reasonably practicable. In every case where there is a risk of significant exposure to noise, assessment must be carried out and action taken to minimize hearing damage.

The first two noise action levels relate to exposure over a period (one day) and are intended to cater for the risks of prolonged work in noisy surroundings. The third level is related to sudden impact noises like those occurring in metal working procedures.

1.2 FIRE PRECAUTIONS

The Fire Precautions (Places of Work) Regulations 1992 replaced and extended the old Fire Precautions Act 1971 as from 1 January 1993. These Regulations are aligned with standard practice in EC Directives in placing the responsibility for compliance on the employers. They require employers not only to assess risks from fire, but now to include the preparation of an evacuation plan, to train staff in fire precautions and to keep records. Workplaces with fewer than 20 employees may require emergency lighting points and fire warning systems. The self-employed who do not employ anyone but whose premises are regularly open to the public may only require fire extinguishers and warning signs; they will, however, need to be able to demonstrate that there is a means of escape in case of fire. Where five or more persons work on the premises as employees, all assessments need to be recorded in writing.

Most of these requirements were already covered by existing legislation. The prime differences are the

(a)   (b)

Figure 1.8   (a) Airstream welding helmet (powered respirator) (b) powered respirator in use in welding
(*Racal Safety Ltd*)

recording of assessments, the provision of training and the requirement that means of fighting fire, detecting fire and giving warning in case of fire be maintained in good working order.

1.2.1   What is fire?

Fire is a chemical reaction called combustion (usually oxidation resulting in the release of heat and light). To initiate and maintain this chemical reaction, or in other words for an outbreak of fire to occur and continue, the following elements are essential (Figure 1.11):

Fuel A combination substance, either solid, liquid or gas.
Oxygen Usually air, which contains 21 per cent oxygen.
Heat The attainment of a certain temperature (once a fire has started it normally maintains its own heat supply).

1.2.2   Methods of extinction

Because three ingredients are necessary for fire to occur, it follows logically that if one or more of these ingredients is removed, fire will be extinguished. Basically three methods are employed to extinguish a fire: removal of heat (cooling); removal of fuel (starving); and removal or limitation of oxygen (blanketing or smothering).

Removal of heat
If the rate of heat generation is less than the rate of dissipation, combustion cannot continue. For example, if cooling water can absorb heat to a point where more heat is being absorbed than generated, the fire will go out.

Removal of fuel
This is not a method that can be applied to fire extinguishers. The subdividing of risks can starve a fire, prevent large losses and enable portable extinguishers

(a)

(b)

Figure 1.9 (a) Visionair constant-flow breathing apparatus (b) operator wearing complete constant-flow breathing apparatus (*Racal Safety Ltd*)

Figure 1.10 Ear protectors (*Racal Safety Ltd*)

Figure 1.11 The fire triangle (*Chubb Fire Ltd*)

to retain control; for example, part of a building may be demolished to provide a fire stop.

The following advice can contribute to a company's fire protection programme:

1 What can cause fire in this location, and how can it be prevented?
2 If fire starts, regardless of cause, can it spread?
3 If so, where to?

4 Can anything be divided or moved to prevent such spread?

Removal or limitation of oxygen

It is not necessary to prevent the contact of oxygen with the heated fuel to achieve extinguishment. It will be found that where most flammable liquids are concerned, reducing the oxygen in the air from 21 to 15 per cent or less will extinguish the fire. Combustion becomes impossible even though a considerable proportion of oxygen remains in the atmosphere. This rule applies to most solid fuels although the degree to which the oxygen content must be reduced may vary. Where solid materials are involved they may continue to burn or smoulder until the oxygen in the air is reduced to 6 per cent. There are also substances which carry within their own structures sufficient oxygen to sustain combustion.

1.2.3 Fire risks in the workshop

Fire risks in the vehicle body repair shop cover all classes of fire: class A, i.e. paper, wood and cloth; class B, i.e. flammable liquids such as oils, spirits, alcohols, solvents and grease; class C, i.e. flammable gases such as acetylene, propane, butane; and also electrical risks. It is essential that fire is detected and extinguished in the early stages. Workshop staff must know the risks involved and should be aware of the procedures necessary to combat fire. Bodyshop personnel should be aware of the various classes of fire and how they relate to common workshop practice.

Class A fires: wood, paper and cloth

Today wood is not used in cars, although there are exceptions. Cloth materials are used for some main trim items and are therefore a potential fire hazard. The paper used for masking purposes is a prime area of concern. Once it has done its job and is covered in overspray it is important that it is correctly disposed of, ideally in a metal container with a lid, and not scrunched up and thrown on the floor to form the potential start of a deep seated fire.

Class B fires: flammable liquids

Flammable liquids are the stock materials used in the trade for all body refinishing processes: gun cleaner to clear finish coats, cellulose to the more modern finishes, can all burn and produce acrid smoke.

Class C fires: gases

Not many cars run on liquid propane gas (LPG), but welding gases or propane space heaters not only burn but can be the source of ignition for A or B fires.

Electrical hazards

Electricity is not of itself a class of fire. It is, however, a potential source of ignition for all of the fire classes mentioned above.

The Electricity at Work Regulations cover the care of cables, plugs and wiring. In addition, in the bodyshop the use of welding and cutting equipment produces sparks which can, in the absence of good housekeeping, start a big fire. Training in how to use fire fighting equipment can stop a fire in its early stages. Another hazard is the electrical energy present in all car batteries. A short-circuit across the terminals of a battery can produce sufficient energy to form a weld and, in turn, heating, a prime source of ignition. When tackling a car fire a fireman will always try to disconnect the battery, as otherwise any attempt to extinguish a fire can result in the re-ignition of flammable vapours.

Body filler

A further possible source of ignition to be aware of is the mixing of two materials to use as a body filler. The result of mixing in the wrong proportions can give rise to an exothermic (heat releasing) reaction; in extreme cases the mix can ignite.

1.2.4 General precautions to reduce fire risk

1 Good housekeeping means putting rubbish away rather than letting it accumulate.
2 Read the manufacturer's material safety data sheets so that the dangers of flammable liquids are known.
3 Only take from the stores sufficient flammable material for the job in hand.
4 Materials left over from a specific job should be put back into a labelled container so that not only you but anyone (and this may be a fireman) can tell what the potential risk may be.
5 Take care when welding that sparks or burning underseal do not cause a problem, especially when working in confined areas of vehicles.
6 Be extremely careful when working close to plastic fuel lines.
7 Petrol tanks are a potential hazard: supposedly empty tanks may be full of vapour. To give some idea of the potential problem, consider one gallon of petrol: it will evaporate into 33 ft^3 of neat vapour, which will mix with air to form 2140 ft^3 of flammable vapour. Thus the average petrol tank needs only a small amount of petrol to give a tank full of vapour waiting to ignite and explode.

The key to fire safety is:

1 Take care.
2 Think.
3 Train staff in the correct procedures before things go wrong.
4 Ensure that these procedures are written down, understood and followed by all personnel in the workshop.

1.2.5 Portable extinguishers: types and uses

The colour codes for each type of appliance are as follows:

Red for water.
Cream for foam.
Black for CO_2.
Blue for powder.
Green for halon (BCF).

Figures 1.12a–c show various types of extinguisher.

Water
Water is the most widely used extinguisher agent.

With portable extinguishers, a limited quantity of water can be expelled under pressure and its direction controlled by a nozzle.

There are basically two types of water extinguishers. The gas (CO_2) cartridge-operated extinguisher, when pierced by a plunger, pressurizes the body of the extinguisher, thus expelling the water and producing a powerful jet capable of rapidly extinguishing class A fires. In stored pressure extinguishers the main body is constantly under pressure from dry air or nitrogen, and the extinguisher is operated by opening the squeeze grip discharge valve. These extinguishers are available with 6 litre or 9 litre capacity bodies and thus provide alternatives of weight and accessibility.

Foam
Foam is an agent most suitable for dealing with flammable liquid fires. Foam is produced when a solution of foam liquid and water is expelled under pressure through a foam-making branch pipe at which point air is entrained, converting the solution into a foam.

Foam extinguishers can be pressurized either by a CO_2 gas cartridge or by stored pressure. The standard capacities are 6 and 9 litres.

Spray foam
Unlike conventional foams, aqueous film forming foam (AFFF) does not require to be fully aspirated in order to extinguish fires. Spray foam extinguishers expel an AFFF solution in an atomized form which is suitable for use on class A and class B fires. AFFF is a fast and powerful means of tackling a fire and seals the surfaces of the material, preventing re-ignition. The capacity can be 6 or 9 litres, and operation can be by CO_2 cartridge or stored pressure.

Carbon dioxide
Designed specifically to deal with class B, class C and electrical fire risks, these extinguishers deliver a powerful concentration of carbon dioxide gas under great pressure. This not only smothers the fire very rapidly, but is also non-toxic and is harmless to most delicate mechanisms and materials.

Dry powder
This type of extinguisher is highly effective against flammable gases, open or running fires involving flammable liquids such as oils, spirits, alcohols, solvents and waxes, and electrical risks. The powder is contained in the metal body of the extinguisher from which it is supplied either by a sealed gas cartridge or by dry air or nitrogen stored under pressure in the body of the extinguisher in contact with the powder.

Dry powder extinguishers are usually made in sizes containing 1 to 9 kg of either standard powder or (preferably and more generally) all-purpose powder, which is suitable for mixed risk areas.

Vaporizing liquid (halon 1211, BCF)
Portable extinguishers of this type are manufactured in sizes ranging from 1 to 15 kg. They are particularly effective for dealing with class B fires and with fires started by an electrical source.

Halon 1211 (bromochlorodifluoromethane, BCF) has a low toxicity level, is considered to be non-corrosive and has a long storage life. It is clean to use and leaves no residue, thus rendering it harmless to delicate fabrics and machinery. However, owing to the contribution of halons to atmospheric ozone depletion most companies have decided to cease production of halon 1211.

Choosing and siting portable extinguishers
Because there is such a variety of fire risks in bodyshops, it is important to analyse these risks separately and (with the help of experts such as fire officers) to choose the correct fire fighting medium to deal with each possible fire situation. It should be noted that portable fire extinguishers are classified as first-aid fire fighting and are designed for ease of operation in an emergency. It is important to realise that because they are portable they have only a limited discharge. Therefore their siting, together with an appreciation of their individual characteristics, is fundamental to their success in fighting fire (Figure 1.13).

Types of modern fire extinguishers
B.S.I.DD48:1976

Water	Foam	Fire blanket	Powder	CO$_2$	BCF
Use for wood, paper, fabrics etc	Use for flammable liquids, oils, fats, spirits etc	Use for smothering	Use for all fires, flammable liquids and gases	Use for electrical and flammable liquid fires	Use for electrical and flammable liquid fires
Do not use on electrical or flammable liquid fires	Do not use on electrical fires				

(a)

(b)

(c)

Figure 1.12 (a) Types of portable fire extinguisher (b) types of fire fighting equipment (*UK Fire International Ltd*) (c) portable fire extinguishers suitable for a bodyshop (*Chubb Fire Ltd*)

Class of fire	Water	Foam (AFFF)	CO$_2$ gas	Powder
A Paper Wood Textile Fabric	✓	✓		✓
B Flammable liquids		✓	✓	✓
C Flammable gases			✓	✓
Electrical hazards			✓	✓
Vehicle protection		✓		✓

Figure 1.13 Which extinguisher to use (*Chubb Fire Ltd*)

1.3 SAFETY SIGNS IN THE WORKSHOP

It is a legal requirement that all safety signs used in a bodyshop comply with BS 5378:Part 1. Each of these signs is a combination of colour and design, within which the symbol is inserted. If additional information is required, supplementary text may be used in conjunction with the relevant symbol, provided that it does not interfere with the symbol. The text can be in an oblong or square box of the same colour as the sign, with the text in the relevant contrasting colour, or the box can be white and the text black.

BS 5378 divides signs into four categories (Figure 1.14):

Prohibition Prohibition signs have a red circular outline and crossbar running from top left to bottom right on a white background (Figure 1.15a). The symbol displayed on the sign must be black and placed centrally on the background, without obliterating the crossbar. The colour red is associated with 'stop' or 'do not'.

Warning Warning signs have a yellow triangle with a black outline (Figure 1.15b). The symbol or text used on the sign must be black and placed centrally on the background. This combination of black and yellow identifies caution.

Mandatory Mandatory signs have a blue circular background (Figure 1.15c). The symbol or text used must be white and placed centrally on the background. Mandatory signs indicate that a specific course of action is to be taken.

Safe condition The safe condition signs provide information for a particular facility (Figure 1.15d) and have a green square or rectangular background to accommodate the symbol or text, which must be in white. The safety colour green indicates 'access' or 'permission'.

Fire safety signs are specified by BS 5499, which gives the characteristics of signs for fire equipment, precautions and means of escape in case of fire (Figure 1.16). It uses the basic framework concerning safety colours and design adopted by BS 5378.

1.4 GENERAL SAFETY PRECAUTIONS IN THE WORKSHOP

The Health and Safety at Work Act imposes on employers a statutory duty to ensure safe working conditions and an absence of risk in the use of equipment and the handling of materials, and to comply with Regulations regarding safe working practices in order to reduce to a minimum the hazards to health and safety associated with vehicle body repair work. To skilled and experienced operators this does not mean that any additional restrictions are imposed on their activities, but merely that they should carry out their tasks with constant regard for the health and safety of themselves and their fellow workers.

Particular hazards may be encountered in the bodyshop, and safety precautions associated with them are as follows:

1 Do wash before eating, drinking or using toilet facilities to avoid transferring the residues of sealers, pigments, solvents, filings of steel, lead and other metals from the hands to the inner parts and other sensitive areas of the body.

Key to British and European Standard safety signs

Prohibition   Warning   Safe condition   Mandatory
Don't do   Risk of danger   The safe way   Must do

Figure 1.14 Standard safety signs

2 Do not use kerosene, thinners or solvents to wash the skin. They remove the skin's natural protective oils and can cause dryness and irritation or have serious toxic effects.

3 Do not overuse waterless hand cleaners, soaps or detergents, as they can remove the skin's protective barrier oils.

4 Always use barrier cream to protect the hands, especially against fuels, oils, greases, hydrocarbon solvents and solvent-based sealers.

5 Do follow work practices that minimize the contact of exposed skin and the length of time liquids or substances stay on the skin.

6 Do thoroughly wash contaminants such as used engine oil from the skin as soon as possible with soap and water. A waterless hand cleaner can be used when soap and water are not available. Always apply skin cream after using waterless hand cleaner.

7 Do not put contaminated or oily rags in pockets or tuck them under a belt, as this can cause continuous skin contact.

8 Do not dispose of dangerous fluids by pouring them on the ground, or down drains or sewers.

9 Do not continue to wear overalls which have become badly soiled or which have acid, oil, grease, fuel or toxic solvents spilt over them. The effect of prolonged contact from heavily soiled overalls with the skin can be cumulative and life threatening. If the soilants are or become flammable from the effect of body temperature, a spark from welding or grinding could envelop the wearer in flames with disastrous consequences.

10 Do not clean dusty overalls with an air line: it is more likely to blow the dust into the skin, with possible serious or even fatal results.

11 Do wash contaminated or oily clothing before wearing it again.

12 Do disguard contaminated shoes.

13 Wear only shoes which afford adequate protection to the feet from the effect of dropping tools and sharp and/or heavy objects on them, and also from red hot and burning materials. Sharp or hot objects could easily penetrate unsuitable footwear such as canvas plimsolls or trainers. The soles of the shoes should also be maintained in good condition to guard against upward penetration by sharp or hot pieces of metal.

14 Ensure gloves are free from holes and are clean on the inside. Always wear them when handling materials of a hazardous or toxic nature.

15 Keep goggles clean and in good condition. The front of the glasses or eyepieces can become obscured by welding spatter adhering to them. Renew the glass or goggles as necessary. Never use goggles with cracked glasses.

16 Always wear goggles when using a bench grindstone or portable grinders, disc sanders, power saws and chisels.

17 When welding, always wear adequate eye protection for the process being used. MIG/MAG welding is particularly high in ultraviolet radiation which can seriously affect the eyes.

18 Glasses, when worn, should have 'safety' or 'splinterproof' glass or plastic lenses.

19 Always keep a suitable mask for use when dry flatting or working in dusty environments and when spraying adhesive, sealers, solvent carried waxes, and paints.

20 In particularly hostile environments such as when using volatile solvents or isocyanate materials, respirators or fresh air-fed masks must be worn.

21 Electric shock can result from the use of faulty and poorly maintained electrical equipment or misuse of equipment. All electrical equipment must be frequently checked and maintained in good condition. Flexes, cables and plugs must not be frayed, cracked, cut or damaged in any way. Equipment must be protected by the correctly rated fuse.

22 Use low-voltage equipment wherever possible (110 volts).

23 In case of electric shock:
   (a) Avoid physical contact with the victim.
   (b) Switch off the electricity.

Figure 1.15   (a) Prohibition signs (b) warning signs (c) mandatory signs (d) safe condition signs

Mandatory signs

 Eye protection must be worn

 First aid

 Head protection must be worn

 Indication of direction (may be used in conjunction with A.4.1)

 Hearing protection must be worn

 Emergency eye wash

 Respiratory protection must be worn

 Emergency telephone

 Foot protection must be worn

 Emergency stop push-button

(d)

 Hand protection must be worn

(c)

Figure 1.15 (continued)

Figure 1.16 Fire signs

Figure 1.17 Portable dust extraction system used in the workshop (*Nederman Ltd*)

(c) If this is not possible, drag or push the victim away from the source of the electricity using non-conductive material.

(d) Commence resuscitation if trained to do so.

(e) Summon medical assistance as soon as possible.

1.5 DUST AND FUME EXTRACTION (EXTRACTION AND ARRESTMENT SYSTEMS)

Polluted air is often invisible to the naked eye. However, the effect it can have on the health of a workforce and the overall efficiency of an organization can be dramatic. The most effective way to purify air is to capture airborne pollutants at source and, depending on individual applications, either to recirculate fresh and preheated air or to vent the pollutants away from the working environment to a safe collection point. The systems should actually be extraction and arrestment systems and should extract the pollutant materials and collect them in a safe and manageable form (Figure 1.17).

In the context of bodyshops, the main problems are fillers and paint dust from the rubbing down and flatting processes, paint and solvent fumes from the wiping down and painting processes, and welding fumes.

Filler and paint dust generated in the preparation area is best collected as soon as it is produced by using off-the-tool extraction (Figure 1.18). This can be either by portable units serving one or two operators, or by fixed systems with a central extraction unit serving a number of fixed extraction points located in the workshop (Figure 1.19).

Specially designed extraction equipment can be tailor-made to an individual bodyshop for the removal of dust and fumes. Gases, powders and chemical vapours are all types of hazardous elements to which fume extraction can be applied. The range of self-supporting arms, combined with the versatility to mount the system on ceilings, floors, benches and walls, make the access to applications unlimited. Furthermore, the easily manoeuvred suction hoods create extraction right at the source of the problem. The fans are designed to draw the polluted air through the extraction arms, dispersing the fumes via the assembly ducting. Alternatively, to recirculate the purified air, an electrostatic unit can be employed to eliminate harmful particles and utilize existing preheated air.

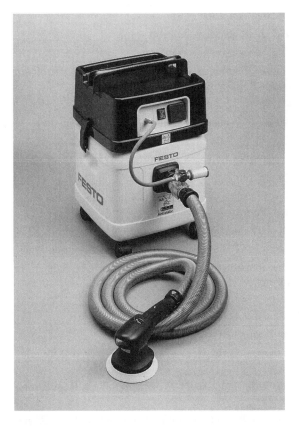

Figure 1.18 Tool extraction system (*Minden Industrial Ltd*)

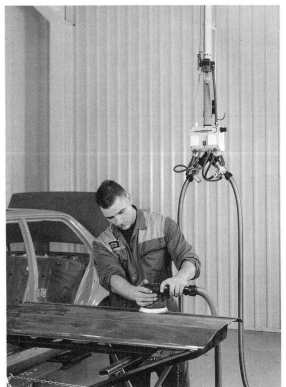

Figure 1.19 Central extraction unit (*Minden Industrial Ltd*)

A range of vehicle exhaust extraction systems is available: a choice can be made from a simple drop system through to the rail system (Figure 1.20), which allows vehicles to be driven whilst maintaining at-source extraction with both advanced infrared remote-controlled and electrically motor-driven reels.

At-source extraction of welding fumes is far more energy efficient than using central ventilation systems.

Harmful fumes can be captured and disposed of in a safe and simple way regardless of the welding environment. Irritation, fever, poisoning and fibrosis are a few of the effects that can be minimized with the extraction of fumes from the welding operations. Many welding processes create noxious and harmful fumes which can be eliminated with portable welding smoke eliminators (Figure 1.21). These provide complete extraction where confined areas pose a problem, especially in body repair workshops. There is a wide range of lightweight smoke eliminators which take up very little floor space and can be carried from job to job. The filters in these portable extraction systems can be changed very quickly, and some have an alarm

Figure 1.20 Vehicle exhaust extraction using a rail system (*Nederman Ltd*)

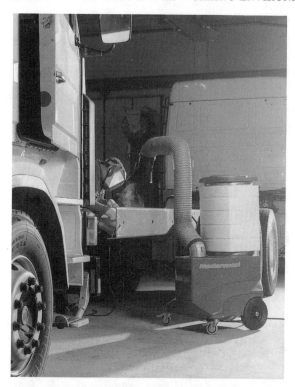

Figure 1.21 Portable fume and smoke extraction system (*Nederman Ltd*)

light fitted to warn the user that the filter needs replacing.

It is a specific requirement of the COSHH Regulations that equipment is maintained in efficient working order. The physical system must be regarded as part of a broader health and safety housekeeping policy aimed at keeping the whole area dust and fume free.

1.6 BODYSHOPS AND LEGAL REQUIREMENTS

Health and safety legislation has made the vehicle body repair industry increasingly aware of the need to provide adequate facilities for employees, both as a legal duty and to improve the working environment. Within this framework of a safe working environment the employer must also promote efficient work methods, which together should result in improved productivity.

1.6.1 Statutory legislation

Petroleum (Consolidation) Act 1928

Petroleum (Mixtures) Orders 1929 and 1947

Factory Act 1961

Weights and Measures Act 1963

Fire Precautions Act 1971

Highly Flammable Liquids and Liquefied Petroleum Gases Regulations 1972

Road Traffic Act 1972 (MOT)

Abrasive Wheel Regulations 1974

Control of Pollution Act 1974

Protection of Eyes Regulations 1974

Health and Safety at Work Act 1974

Fire Precautions (Factories, Offices, Shops and Railway Premises) Order 1976

Motor Vehicle Construction and Use Regulations 1978

Control of Pollution (Special Wastes) Regulations 1980

Classification, Packaging and Labelling of Dangerous Substances Regulations 1984

Control of Substances Hazardous to Health (COSHH) Regulations 1988

Environment Protection Act 1990

Management of Health and Safety at Work Regulations 1992

Provision and Use of Work Equipment Regulations 1992

Personal Protection Equipment at Work (PPE) Regulations 1992

Manual Handling Operation Regulations 1992

Workplace (Health, Safety and Welfare) Regulations 1992

The bodyshop is most affected by the legislation described in the following sections.

1.6.2 Regulations covering paint storage, fire precautions and fire fighting

The storage of paints with a flashpoint below 22°C is governed by the Petroleum (Consolidation) Act and the statutory rules and orders 1929. Those with a flash point of 22–32°C are governed by the Highly Flammable Liquids and Liquefied Petroleum Gases Regulations 1972.

Requirements of the Petroleum (Consolidation) Act 1928

Paints, thinners, and other products governed by this Act will either be labelled 'Petroleum mixture giving off an inflammable heavy vapour' or have a flame symbol and the words 'Highly flammable', indicating a flashpoint below 22°C.

.The Act requires that the storeroom should be licensed and constructed to approved standards.

Requirements of the Highly Flammable Liquids Regulations 1972

Paints governed by these Regulations will be labelled 'Flammable'. More precise flashpoint details can be obtained from the relevant product data sheet, which indicates products with a flashpoint range between 22 and 32°C.

Products with a flashpoint greater than 32°C do not fall within the Regulations, but other Regulations require that products with a flashpoint up to 55°C have a 'Flammable' warning.

1.6.3 Health and safety legislation

The Health and Safety at Work Act 1974 places a duty upon employers to ensure, so far as is reasonably practicable, safe working conditions and the absence of risks to health in connection with the use, handling, storage and transport of articles and substances.

The Act places a statutory duty on employers to have a declared safety policy for a business in which more than five persons are employed. The Act does not specify what you should do; it merely provides the framework in which you should operate, together with establishing the Health and Safety Executive and the Health and Safety Commission. The Act regulates all working methods. The importance of this Act cannot be overemphasized; no working methods may be employed that can be seen to be a health or safety hazard to employees.

First, a company safety policy must be established and a safety committee formed. The committee should consist of members with specialized knowledge of the risks of a particular area, i.e. bodyshop, paint shop, parts department, offices. The chairman of the committee should be a senior member of the company.

Safety committee's main objectives

1 To ensure that the company's premises outside and inside are safe and healthy.
2 To set up an administrative system to maintain a safe working environment.
3 To set up some kind of information system on all matters relating to health and safety.
4 To ensure that employees receive adequate training in health and safety matters.

Regular inspections of all equipment as outlined in the safety practice code are now a legal requirement. Failure to meet this requirement can result in imprisonment or unlimited fines or both.

Employer's duties
To provide and maintain:

1 Safe equipment.
2 Safe place of work with safe access and exit.
3 Safe systems of work.
4 Healthy working environment.
5 Welfare arrangements (washing facilities, eating facilities, first aid).
6 Proper training with time off for this purpose.

Employee's duties

1 To take reasonable care for his/her own safety and the safety of others who may be affected by his/her acts.
2 To cooperate with his/her employer or any person on whom a duty or requirement is imposed.

The company should establish, in conjunction with the safety committee, its own code of practice on safety procedures within its establishment, and all personnel should receive a copy.

Objectives of the Act

1 To repeal, replace or modify existing regulations.
2 To maintain or improve standards of health and welfare of people at work.
3 To protect people or other workers against any risk to health or safety arising out of the activities of people at work.
4 To control the keeping and use of dangerous substances including explosive and highly flammable materials (paints, solvents, resins).
5 To control the emissions of toxic substances into the atmosphere (dust, fumes, smoke, gases).

1.6.4 Control of Substances Hazardous to Health (COSHH) Regulations 1988

Since 1974 a number of Regulations have been introduced which describe in detail the requirements for specific safe working practices. One of the most important is the Control of Substances Hazardous to Health (COSHH) Regulations 1988.

COSHH is a major piece of health and safety legislation. It tightens the general obligations of an employer under Section 2 of the Health and Safety at Work Act by specifying comprehensive rules on how substances should be controlled. COSHH applies to all substances in all forms, including gases, vapours, solids, dusts, liquids, and even micro-organisms. It also covers mixtures and preparations.

A substance may be a 'hazard to health' if the substance itself is harmful or if:

1 There are hazards from impurities.
2 Dust or fumes are generated during use.
3 It is dangerous when used in combination with other materials.

COSHH attempts to follow the principle of good occupational hygiene practice:

1 Assess the hazard (Regulation 6).
2 Control it (Regulations 7, 8, 12).
3 Maintain the control (Regulations 9, 10, 11).

Assessment: Regulation 6
An employer shall not carry on any work which is liable to expose any employees to any substance hazardous to health unless he has made a suitable and sufficient assessment of the risk created, and the steps needed to achieve and maintain control.

Control of exposure: Regulation 7
Exposure must be prevented or adequately controlled. 'Adequately controlled' means that repeated exposure must not cause damage to health. Maximum exposure limits must not be exceeded or employers may be prosecuted.

Use of controls: Regulation 8
Employers should take all reasonable steps to ensure that control measures are properly used, and employees shall make full and proper use of the controls provided.

Maintenance of controls: Regulation 9
Controls must be maintained in efficient working order and good repair. Thorough examinations and tests must be made at suitable intervals. Records of tests and repairs must be kept for five years.

Exposed monitoring: Regulation 10
Air sampling is required to monitor exposure every 12 months if:

1 It is needed to maintain control.
2 It is needed to protect health.
3 Listed carcinogens are in use.

Health surveillance: Regulation 11
Health surveillance is required at least every 12 months if:

1 Valid health surveillance techniques exist.
2 Specified substances are in use.

Surveillance may include biological monitoring, clinical examinations and review of health records. Records must be kept for 30 years (Figure 1.22).

HEALTH SURVEILLANCE RECORD

EMPLOYEE'S NAME	TYPE OF SURVEILLANCE	RESULT	DATE CARRIED OUT
MR JOHN SMITH	RESPIRATORY FUNCTION SCREENING.	WITHIN NORMAL LIMITS.	30-1-93
MR DEREK BROWN	CHEST X-RAY	WITHIN NORMAL LIMITS.	6-3-93
MR WILLIAM BLACK	AUDIOMETRIC HEARING TEST.	CATEGORY 5 (NORMAL)	20-4-93

Figure 1.22 Health surveillance record (*Akzo Coatings PLC*)

TRAINING RECORD

EMPLOYEE'S NAME	TYPE OF TRAINING	DATE CARRIED OUT
MR JOHN SMITH	SAFETY TRAINING ON THE USE OF AIR-FED MASKS	1-3-93
MR DEREK BROWN	TRAINING IN THE USE OF PORTABLE FIRE-FIGHTING EQUIPMENT FOR THE WORKSHOP.	10-4-93
MR WILLIAM BLACK	TRAINING IN THE SAFE USAGE OF MIG WELDING EQUIPMENT.	5-5-93

Figure 1.23 Training record (*Akzo Coatings PLC*)

Information, instruction and training: Regulation 12
The employees must be told:

1 The risk to health.
2 The results of the tests.
3 The control measures to be used.

They must be given appropriate instruction and training. Any person carrying out work under the Regulations must be competent to do so (Figure 1.23).

Carrying out a COSHH assessment.
Gather information

1 What is used, handled, stored.
2 Intermediates, by-products, wastes.

Identify hazards (a hazard is the potential to cause harm)

1 Nature of hazard.
2 Route of exposure.
3 Possible interactions.

Evaluate the risk (risk is the likelihood that a substance will cause harm in the actual circumstances of use)

1 How is the substance used?
2 How is it controlled?
3 What is the level of exposure?

Decide on controls

1 Type of controls (substitution, local exhaust ventilation (LEV)).
2 Maintenance and testing procedures.
3 Air monitoring.
4 Health surveillance.
5 Record keeping.

Record assessment A record must be kept of all assessments other than in the most simple cases that can be easily repeated (Table 1.1, Figure 1.24).

Review Assessments should be reviewed, for example, when:

1 There are any significant changes to the process, e.g. plant changes, volume of production.
2 New substances are introduced.
3 Ill-health occurs.
4 New information becomes available on hazards or risks.

1.6.5 Environmental Protection Act 1990

The Environmental Protection Act 1990, like the Health and Safety at Work Act, allows the Secretary of State to introduce Regulations to control, among other things, the release of harmful substances to air, water and land. The legislation is wide in scope, with the long-term aim of minimizing environment pollution. The paint application industry is among the third largest group of environment polluters, and it is because of this that the EPA introduces many refinishing industry specific controls. The object of the Act is to reduce and eventually eliminate the use of volatile organic compounds (VOCs) in surface coatings, using the best available techniques not entailing excessive costs (BATNEECs). VOCs are substances which react with nitrous oxides in sunlight to create low-level ozone. This photochemical air pollution causes damage to vegetation and can also cause serious breathing difficulties in humans and animals. All users will have to use BATNEECs to prevent, minimize and render harmless any release of VOCs. If there is alleged contravention, the user will have to prove that no better techniques were available.

Bodyshops purchasing more than 2 tonnes of solvent per year will be required to register under the classification of Part B, 'The Respraying of Motor Vehicles', of the Act. Any bodyshop currently operating below these levels is not required to register.

Existing bodyshops which registered by the deadline set for their area of the country (in England and Wales by 30 September 1992, and in Scotland by 31 March 1993) have until October 1998 to fulfil all their legal obligations under the Act.

Two separate pollution control regimes are established in Part I of the Act to control industrial processes falling into categories A and B. Category A is integrated pollution control (IPC) operated by HMIP in England and Wales and HMIPI in Scotland. Category B is local authority air pollution control.

Environmental Protection (Prescribed Processes and Substances) Regulations 1991
These identify the respraying of road vehicles as a category B process (local authority air pollution control) if the process may result in the release into the air of any particular matter or of any volatile organic compound (solvents) where the process is likely to involve the use of 2 tonnes or more of organic solvents in any 12 month period. Cleaning agents, fillers, stoppers, primers, gunwash and many other products in the refinishing of motor vehicles all contribute to this figure. The figure should represent the amount consumed in the process, i.e. lost through evaporation, spillage and transfer.

If the process involves the use of 2 tonnes of organic solvents in any 12 month period then the bodyshop operator must seek authorization from his or her local authority to carry out the process. If the operator of the bodyshop calculates the solvent usage to be less than 2 tonnes, then the best advice would be to monitor solvent usage in order to demonstrate the fact to the local authority.

First, check with the local authority, which will require information about your operation such as:

1 Who and where you are.
2 What you do and how you do it.
3 What is released to air, how much, and where from.
4 What you do to prevent, control and monitor such releases.
5 Evidence or proposals that the objectives of BATNEEC will be met.

Upgrading of existing bodyshops to comply with the Act
The engineering controls that the EPA imposes upon equipment are very significant, particularly regarding spray booths if emission exceeds the 2 tonnes VOCs limit. For spray booths already working there is a

Table 1.1   Guide to safe working practices: to be filled in by the bodyshop. The example gives a typical process carried out in most paint shops every day. The initial assessment has identified there is a serious risk to people's health from the way the hazardous substance is being used. Immediate steps must be introduced to control and reduce the risks. Failure to comply to the approved code of practice by an employer may lead to prosecution

Activity	Hazard	Risk	Precautions		Products used	Products contain	Remarks
			Personal	General			
Wet sanding of fillers and stoppers	Wet sludges of unknown composition	Skin contact with unknown materials	Gloves	Carry out in a properly ventilated area			
		Eye contact with splashes of unknown materials	Goggles or visor				
		Remarks:	Conclusions:	Conclusions:			
Priming Mixing (hardener addition and or thinning)	Solvents and, depending on the particular product, isocyanates, acids or polyamides may be present	Inhalation of solvent vapours	Respirator suitable for solvent vapours where extraction inadequate	Carrying out in a well ventilated area or with local exhaust ventilation to minimize vapour build-up. NB air-fed respirators are not required when mixing isocyanate containing products at ambient temperatures under conditions of good ventilation	Washfiller 580	Zinc chromate <5% MEL Butyl acetate 10–25% OES Plus blends of additional solvents	Product substitution not possible. Issue staff with respirator and eye protection Arrange for extraction to be installed in mixing room
		Skin contact with solvents	Gloves				
		Eye contact with vapours, solvents or paint splashes	Goggles or visor	Conclusions: No LEA in mixing area			
		Remarks: High risk Carried out three times daily	Conclusions: Strong smell of solvent from acid hardener No respirator or eye protection used whilst mixing		Washfiller phosphoric hardener	Ethanol 15–30% OES Methyl isobutyl ketone 30–45% OES + Plus blend of additional solvents including phosphoric acid	Reduce mixing from three times a day to once daily

Table 1.1 Continued

Activity	Hazard	Risk	Precautions			Products used	Products contain	Remarks
			Personal	General				
Application	Spray mist containing solvent and, depending on the particular product, isocyanates, zinc or strontium chromates, polyamides or acids	Inhalation of solvent vapours or spray mists	Respirator suitable for solvent vapours and particulates Air-fed respirators *must* be worn (i) whenever isocyanates are present or (ii) when zinc or strontium chromate containing primers are used and the ventilation in the spray enclosure is inadequate for the particular job	All spraying *must* be carried out in a properly ventilated spray enclosure		As above	As above	Issue replacement charcoal respirator, set up inspection and maintenance records. No spraying to be done outside spray booth
		Skin contact with solvent vapour or spray mists	Gloves					
		Eye contact with solvent vapour or spray mists	Goggles or visor					
		Remarks: High risk Process carried out daily	Conclusions: Cartridge mask used but in poor condition	Conclusions: Spraying in open workshop Poor extraction				

23

COSHH ASSESSMENT RECORD

RECORD No.

PROCESS IDENTIFICATION ....

PROCESS LOCATIONS ....

FREQUENCY OF USE ....

NUMBER OF OPERATORS ....

SUBSTANCES/PRODUCTS USED	SUPPLIER	HAZARDS	OES	MEL

CONTROLS

PRECAUTIONS CURRENTLY USED ....

HOW EFFECTIVE ARE THEY ....

LIKELY HAZARD ....

– INHALATION ....

– SKIN CONTAMINATION ....

– EYE CONTACT ....

ACTION REQUIRED

NEW CONTROLS INTRODUCED

IS A MAINTENANCE SCHEDULE REQUIRED	YES	NO

HEALTH SURVEILLANCE REQUIRED	YES	NO

CARRIED OUT BY ....

SIGNATURE .... DATE ....

Figure 1.24 COSHH assessment record (*Akzo Coatings PLC*)

24

requirement to submit an upgrading programme to the local authority within 12 months of the initial registration. That programme must be implemented by 1 April 1998.

The requirements for upgrading are as follows:

1 Filtration systems have to ensure that the concentration of paint particulate matter in the final discharge to atmosphere from the spray booth does not exceed 10 mg/m³.
2 Manufacturers or companies upgrading booths will be required to provide a guarantee confirming that the equipment conforms to the emissions limit.
3 The vent velocity of the extract duct must achieve a minimum of 15 m/s for dry filter systems.
4 The vent velocity of the extract duct must achieve a maximum of 9 m/s where a wet method is used.
5 Pressure control systems must be provided which will shut down the spray booth if it is over-pressurized and activate an audio alarm.
6 Exhaust duct openings must not be fitted with plates, caps or cowls that could act as restrictors or deflectors.
7 Exhaust ducting (the chimney) must be a minimum of 8 metres above ground level, but it also has to be minimum of 3 metres higher than the roof height of any nearby building which is within a distance of five times the uncorrected chimney height.
8 Preventive measures must be taken for fugitive emissions of odour, fumes and particulate matter from mechanical operations like welding, grinding or sanding. All these activities should take place in a building.
9 Shot blasting emissions must not exceed 50 mg/m³.
10 Paint mixing and equipment cleaning are to take place in an adequately ventilated area.
11 An automatic totally enclosed machine for cleaning spray guns and equipment must be provided.
12 Spray gun testing must be into an extracted area.

Waste management: EPA Part II
Section 34 of the EPA makes it a criminal offence to 'treat, keep or dispose of controlled waste in a manner likely to cause pollution of the environment or to harm human health'. In order to meet this stated aim, the Part II provisions impose a 'duty of care' on everybody involved in the chain of waste management. This means that if you are involved in the creation of waste, then you are responsible for its safe and proper disposal. Typical relevant bodyshop waste includes dirty solvent, paint residues, empty cans and dirty rags. Those subject to the duty of care must try to achieve the following four things:

1 To prevent any other person committing the offence of disposing of 'controlled waste', or treating it, or storing it without a waste management licence; or breaking the conditions of a licence; or in a manner likely to cause pollution or harm to health.
2 To prevent the escape of waste which is, or at any time has been, under their control (this has implications for waste storage facilities and waste containment).
3 To ensure that if waste is transferred it goes only to an 'authorised person' or to a person for 'authorised transport purposes'.
4 When waste is transferred, to make sure that there is also transferred a written description of the waste, which is good enough to enable each person receiving it to avoid committing any offence under 1, and to comply with the duty at 2 to prevent the escape of waste.

Under the code of practice, the waste must be:

1 Identified (paint, solvent, paper and tape, dust, loaded extract filter media, scrap metal, tyres and batteries).
2 Categorized.
3 Kept in appropriate containers (external skip, internal container, paper baler, can crusher, solvent/paint 'closed loop' system, parts for recycling).
4 Collected and disposed of by a registered operator (transfer note signed by the disposer and collector, and a written description of the waste).
5 Documented at all stages.

1.6.6 Management of Health and Safety at Work Regulations 1992

These Regulations set out broad general duties which apply to almost all work activities in Great Britain. They are aimed mainly at improving health and safety management, and can be seen as a way of making more explicit what is required of employers under the HSW Act. The main provisions are designed to encourage a more systematic and better organized approach to deal with health and safety.

The Regulations require that employers should:

1 Assess the risk to health and safety of employees and of anyone else who may be affected by the company's work activity. This is so that the necessary preventive and protective measures can be identified. Employers with five or more employees will have to record the significant findings of the assessment.
2 Make arrangements for putting into practice the health and safety measures that follow from the assessment.

3 Provide appropriate health surveillance for employees where the risk assessment shows it to be necessary.

4 Appoint competent people either from inside the organization or from outside to help devise and apply measures needed to comply with duties under health and safety law.

5 Set up emergency procedures.

6 Provide employees with information they can understand about health and safety matters.

7 Cooperate with other employers sharing the work site.

8 Make sure that employees have adequate health and safety training and are capable enough at their jobs to avoid risk.

9 Provide temporary workers with some particular health and safety information to meet special needs.

The Regulations will also:

1 Place duties on the employees to follow health and safety instructions and report danger.

2 Extend the current law which requires the employer to consult employees' safety representatives and provide facilities for them.

1.6.7 Provision and Use of Work Equipment Regulations 1992

These regulations will place general duties on employers, and list minimum requirements for work equipment to deal with selected hazards whatever the industry.

In general the Regulations will make explicit what is already somewhere in the law or is good practice. If equipment has been well chosen and well maintained there should be little need to do more than follow the guidance on the Regulations. Some older equipment may need to be upgraded to meet the minimum requirements, but the company will have until 1997 to do any necessary work.

Work equipment will be broadly defined to include everything from a hand tool, through machines of all kinds, to a complete plant. Use of the equipment will include starting, stopping, repairing, modifying, installing, dismantling, programming, setting, transporting, maintaining, servicing and cleaning.

The general duties will require the employer to:

1 Make sure that equipment is suitable for the use that will be made of it.

2 Take into account the working conditions and hazards in the workplace when selecting equipment.

3 Ensure that equipment is used only for operations for which and under conditions for which it is suitable.

4 Ensure the equipment is maintained in an efficient state, in efficient working order and in good repair.

5 Give adequate information, instruction and training.

6 Provide equipment that conforms with EC product safety Directives (see below).

Specific requirements will cover:

1 Guarding of dangerous parts of machinery (replacing the current law on this).

2 Protection against specific hazards, i.e. falling/ejected articles and substances, rupture/disintegration of work equipment parts, equipment catching fire or overheating, unintended or premature discharge of articles and substances, explosion.

3 Working equipment parts and substances at high or very low temperatures.

4 Control systems and control devices.

5 Isolation of equipment from the source of energy.

6 Stability of equipment.

7 Lighting.

8 Maintaining operations.

9 Warnings and markings.

The Regulations implement an EC Directive aimed at the protection of workers. There are other Directives setting out conditions which much new equipment (especially machinery) will have to satisfy before it can be sold in the EC member states. They will be implemented in the UK by Regulations made by the Department of Trade and Industry.

1.6.8 Personal Protective Equipment (PPE) at Work Regulations 1992

These Regulations set out in legislation sound principles for selecting, providing, maintaining and using PPE. They do not replace recently introduced law dealing with PPE, for example COSHH or noise at work regulations.

PPE is defined as all equipment designed to be worn or held to protect against a risk to health or safety. This includes most types of protective clothing and equipment such as eye, foot and head protection, safety harnesses, life jackets and high-visibility clothing. PPE should be relied upon only as a last resort, but where risks are not adequately controlled by other means the employer will have a duty to ensure that suitable PPE is provided free of charge for employees exposed to these risks. The Regulations say what is meant by suitable PPE, a key point in making sure that it effectively protects the wearer. PPE will only be suitable if it is appropriate for the risks and the working conditions, takes account of workers' needs, fits properly, gives adequate protection, and is compatible with any other item of PPE worn.

Employers also have duties to:

1 Assess the risks and PPE intended for issue, to ensure that it is suitable.
2 Maintain, clean and replace PPE.
3 Provide storage for PPE when it is not being used.
4 Ensure that PPE is properly used.
5 Give training, information and instruction to employees on its use and how to look after it.

PPE is also subject to a separate EC Directive on design, certification and testing, and will be marked by the manufacturer with a CE mark.

1.6.9 Manual Handling Operations Regulations 1992

These will apply to any manual handling operations which may cause injury at work. These operations will be identified by the risk assessment carried out under the Management of Health and Safety at Work Regulations 1992. They will include not only lifting of loads, but also lowering, pushing, pulling, carrying, or moving them, whether by hand or other bodily force.

Employers will have to take three key steps:

1 Avoid hazardous manual handling operations wherever reasonably practicable. Consider whether the load must be moved at all and, if it must, whether it can be moved mechanically.
2 Assess adequately any hazardous operations that cannot be avoided. An ergonomic assessment should look at more than just the weight of the load. Employers should consider the shape and size of the load, the way the task is carried out, the handler's posture, the working environment (cramped or hot), the individual's capacity, and the strength required. Unless the assessment is very simple, a written record will be needed.
3 Reduce the risk of injury as far as reasonably practicable. A good assessment will not only show whether there is a problem but will also point to where the problem lies.

1.6.10 Workplace (Health, Safety and Welfare) Regulations 1992

The Regulations will cover many aspects of health, safety and welfare in the workplace. Some of them are not explicitly mentioned in the current law, though they are implied in the general duties of the Health and Safety at Work Act.

The Regulations will set out general requirements in four broad areas.

Working environment

1 Temperature in indoor workplaces.
2 Ventilation.
3 Lighting including emergency lighting.
4 Room dimensions and space.
5 Suitability of workstations and seating.

Safety

1 Safe passage of pedestrians and vehicles (traffic routes must be wide enough and marked where necessary, and there must be enough of them).
2 Windows and skylights (safe opening, closing and cleaning).
3 Transparent and translucent doors and partitions (use of safety material and marking).
4 Doors, gates, escalators (safety devices).
5 Floors (construction and maintenance, obstructions and slipping and tripping hazards).
6 Falling a distance into a dangerous substance.
7 Falling objects.

Facilities

1 Toilets.
2 Washing, eating and changing facilities.
3 Clothing storage.
4 Drinking water.
5 Rest area (and arrangements to protect people from the discomfort of tobacco smoke).
6 Rest facilities for pregnant women and nursing mothers.

Housekeeping

1 Maintenance of workplace, equipment and facilities.
2 Cleanliness.
3 Removal of waste materials.

Employers will have to make sure that any workplace within their control complies with the Regulations. Existing workplaces will have until 1996 to comply.

QUESTIONS

1 State five basic rules concerning dress and behaviour which demonstrate personal safety in the workshop environment.
2 List five necessary precautions for safety in the workshop and describe each one briefly.
3 What is meant by a skin care system as used in the workshop?

4 Explain the importance of eye and face protection in the workshop environment.

5 Explain the importance of protective clothing for a body repairer and a paint sprayer.

6 Explain the significance of headwear and footwear while working in the workshop.

7 Name the four types of respirator used in a bodyshop.

8 Why have the COSHH Regulations made the use of respiratory equipment mandatory?

9 State the minimum noise level at which ear protection must be used.

10 With the aid of a diagram, explain the fire triangle.

11 Name the three methods of fire extinction.

12 Explain the three classifications of fire.

13 Identify the correct colour code for the following fire extinguishers: water, foam, CO_2, powder, halon.

14 Name the four categories of safety signs used in the workshop.

15 Sketch and identify a safety sign used in a bodyshop.

16 Name the items of personal safety equipment that should be used when operating the following power tools: power saw, power chisel, disc sander.

17 State the essential personal safety precautions to be taken before working under a vehicle which is on a hoist.

18 Give practical reasons for wearing safety gloves in the workshop.

19 Identify the type of fire extinguisher that must be used when dealing with a solvent fire.

20 Explain the precautions which must be taken when handling toxic substances in a workshop environment.

21 When dealing with a petrol fire, which would be the correct type of fire extinguisher to use?

22 Explain the importance of the use of a barrier cream.

23 Explain the following abbreviations: COSHH, EPA, HASAWA.

24 State the health hazards associated with the use of GRP for repairs.

25 Explain the importance of dust and fume extraction systems.

26 Name five of the main health and safety legislation Acts which affect the workshop.

27 Discuss volatile organic compounds (VOCs) and their effect on the environment.

28 Which Act applies to waste management?

29 Explain the importance of the Personal Protective Equipment (PPE) at Work Regulations 1992.

30 Explain what is meant by the Manual Handling Operation Regulations 1992.

2

The design and construction of the car body

2.1 DEVELOPMENT OF THE MOTOR CAR BODY

2.1.1 Brief history

The first motor car bodies and chassis frames, made between 1896 and 1910, were similar in design to horse-drawn carriages and, like the carriages, were made almost entirely of wood.

The frames were generally made from heavy ash, and the joints were reinforced by wrought iron brackets which were individually fitted. The panels were either cedar or Honduras mahogany about 9.5 mm thick, glued, pinned or screwed to the framework. The tops, on cars which had them, were of rubberized canvas or other fabrics. Some bodies were built with closed cabs, and the tops were held in place by strips of wood bent to form a solid frame. About 1921 the Weymann construction was introduced, in which the floor structure carried all the weight of the seating, and the body shell, which was of very light construction, was attached to the floor unit. Each joint in the shell and between the shell and the floor was made by a pair of steel plates, one on each side of the joint and bolted through both pieces of timber, leaving a slight gap between the two pieces. The panelling was of fabric, first canvas, then a layer of wadding calico and finally a covering of leather cloth. This form of construction allowed flexibility in the framing and made a very light and quiet body frame, but the outer covering had a very short life.

As the demand for vehicles increased it became necessary to find a quicker method of production. Up to that time steel had been shaped by hand, but it was known that metal in large sheets could be shaped using simple die tools in presses, and machine presses were introduced to the steel industry to form steel sheets into body panels. Initially the sheets were not formed into complex shapes or contours, and the first bodies were very square and angular with few curves. The frame and inner construction was still for the most part made of wood, as shown in Figure 2.1.

About 1923 the first attempts were made to build all-steel bodies, but these were not satisfactory as the design principles used were similar to those which had been adopted for the timber-framed body. The real beginning of the all-steel body shell came in 1927, when presses became capable of producing a greater number of panels and in more complex shapes; this was the dawn of the mass production era. During the 1930s most of the large companies which manufactured motor vehicles adopted the use of metal for the complete construction of the body shell, and motor cars began to be produced in even greater quantities.

Owing to the ever-increasing demand for private transport, competition increased between rival firms, and in consequence their body engineers began to incorporate features which added to the comfort of the driver and passengers. This brought about the development of the closed cars or saloons as we know them today. The gradual development of the shape of the motor car body can be clearly seen in Figure 2.2, which shows a selection of Austin vehicles from 1909 to 1992.

The inner construction of the head roof of these saloons was concealed by a headlining. Up to and including the immediate post-war years, this headlining was made from a woollen fabric stitched together and tacked into position on wooden frames. However, the more recently developed plastic and vinyl materials were found to be more suitable than fabric, being cheaper and easier to clean and fit. They are fitted by stretching over self-tensioning frames which are clipped into position for easy removal, or alternatively the headlining is fastened into position with adhesives.

Comfort improved tremendously with the use of latex foam rubber together with coil springs in the seating, instead of the original plain springing. The general interior finish has also been improved by the introduction of door trim pads, fully trimmed dash panels and a floor covering of either removable rubber or carpeting.

Then came the general use of celluloid for windows

Figure 2.1 Timber constructed bodies: (a) De Dion Works bodyshop, Finchley, *c.*1923 (b) Gordon England Ltd, 1922 (*National Motor Museum, Beaulieu*)

instead of side curtains, and next a raising and lowering mechanism for the windows. Nowadays the windscreen and door glasses are made of laminated and/or toughened safety glass. The window mechanism in use today did not begin to develop until well into the 1920s.

Mudguards, which began as wooden or leather protections against splattered mud, grew into wide splayed deflectors in the early part of the twentieth century and then gradually receded into the body work, becoming gracefully moulded into the streamlining of the modern motor car and taking the name of wings. Carriage steps retained on earlier models gave place to running boards which in their turn disappeared altogether.

Between 1890 and 1906 steering was operated by a tiller (Figure 2.3). This was followed by the steering

wheel which is in current use. The position of the gear lever made an early change from the floor to the steering column, only to return to some convenient place on the floor.

Some of the first vehicles, or horseless carriages as they were known, carried no lights at all; then carriage candle lamps made their appearance. Later came oil lamps, acetylene lamps and finally the electric lighting system, first fitted as a luxury extra and ultimately becoming standard and finally obligatory equipment which must conform with legislation of the day.

When windscreens were first introduced such accessories as windscreen wipers and washers were unknown. Then came the single hand-operated wiper, followed by the suction wiper and finally electrically driven wipers.

The design of the wheels was at first dictated by fashion. It was considered necessary for the rear wheels to be larger than the front, a legacy from the elegant horse-drawn carriages. Wooden spokes and iron tyres were the first wheels to appear, and with both rear and front wheels of the same dimensions. Then came the wooden-spoked artillery wheel with pneumatic tyre (Figure 2.4). The artillery wheel gave way to the wire-spoked wheel, and this in turn to the modern disc wheel with tubeless tyres.

Great strides have been made in the evolution of the motor car since 1770, when Cugnot's steam wagon travelled at 3 mile/h (4.8 km/h), to the modern vehicle which can carry driver and passengers in silence, comfort and safety at speeds which at one time were thought to be beyond human endurance: indeed, special vehicles on prepared tracks are now approaching the speed of sound.

It must be borne in mind that the speed of the vehicle is governed by (a) the type of power unit, (b) its stability and manoeuvring capabilities, and (c) its shape which is perhaps at present one of the most important features in high-speed travel. Whatever the mechanical future of the car, we may rest assured that the shape of the motor car body will continue to change as technical progress is made (Figure 2.5).

2.1.2 Highlights of motor vehicle history

The idea of a self-propelled vehicle occurs in Homer's *Iliad*. Vulcan, the blacksmith of the gods, in one day made 20 tricycles which 'self-moved obedient to the beck of the gods'. The landmarks in more modern motor vehicle history are as follows:

1688 Ferdinand Verbiest, missionary in China, made a model steam carriage using the steam turbine principle.

1909 The first Baby Austin

1922 Austin Tourer

1932 Austin Saloon

1946 Austin 16

1948 Austin A–70

1952 Austin Seven

1959 Austin Princess

1960 Austin Mini

1963 Austin 1100

1964 Austin 1800

Figure 2.2 Development of the Austin car body 1909 to 1992

1970 Austin Maxi 1800

1973 Austin Allegro

1975 Austin Princess

1976 Austin Rover SDI

1983 Austin Maestro

1980 Austin Metro

1986 Austin Rover 200

1984 Austin Montego

1987 Austin Rover Sterling

Figure 2.2   (continued)

1988 Rover 820 Fastback

1989 Mini Flame

1992 Rover 220 Coupé

Figure 2.2   (continued)

1992 MG RV8

Figure 2.2 (continued)

Figure 2.3 First Vauxhall, tiller operated, 1903 (*Vauxhall Motors Ltd*)

1740 Jacques de Vaucansen showed a clockwork carriage in Paris.

1765 Watt developed the steam engine.

1765 Nicholas Joseph Cugnot, a French artillery officer, built a steam wagon which carried four people at a speed of 2.25 mile/h. It overturned in the streets of Paris and Cugnot was thrown into prison for endangering the populace.

1803 Richard Trevithick built a steam carriage and drove it in Cornwall.

1831 Sir Charles Dance ran a steam coach (built by Sir Goldsworthy Gurney) on a regular service from Gloucester to Cheltenham.
Sometimes they did four round trips a day, doing 9 miles in 45 minutes. The steam coaches were driven off the road by the vested interests of the stage coach companies, who increased toll charges and piled heaps of stones on the roads along which the steam coaches passed. This, combined with the problems of boilers bursting and mechanical breakdowns and the advent of

the railways, contributed to the withdrawal of the steam coaches.

1859 Oil was discovered in the USA.

1865 The Locomotive Act of 1865 (the Red Flag Act) was pushed through by the railway and coach owners. One of the stipulations was that at least three people must be employed to conduct the locomotive through the streets, one of whom had to walk 60 yards in front carrying a red flag. Speeds were restricted to 2–4 mile/h. This legislation held back the development of the motor vehicle in Great Britain for 31 years, allowing the continental countries to take the lead in this field.

1885 Karl Benz produced his first car. This is recognized as being the first car with an internal combustion engine as we know it.

1886 Gottlieb Daimler also produced a car.

1890 Panhard and Levasser began making cars in France.

1892 Charles and Frank Duryea built the first American petrol-driven car, although steam cars had been in use long before this.

1895 First motor race in Paris.
First Automobile Club formed in Paris.

1896 The repeal of the Red Flag Act. This is commemorated by the London to Brighton veteran car run. The speed limit was raised to 12 mile/h and remained at that until 1903, when the 20 mile/h limit in built-up areas was introduced. There was much persecution of motorists by police at this time, which led to the formation of the RAC and the AA.

1897 The RAC was formed, largely through the efforts of F. R. Simms, who also founded the SMMT in 1902.

1899 Jenatzy set the world speed record of 66 mile/h.

1900 Steering wheel replaces tiller.
Frederick Lanchester produced his first car, a 10 hp model. He had built an experimental phaeton in 1895.

Figure 2.4 1905 and 1909 Vauxhalls with wooden spoked artillery wheels with pneumatic tyres (*Vauxhall Motors Ltd*)

Figure 2.5 Twin concept car with interchangeable engines (petrol/electric motor drive module) (*Vauxhall Motors Ltd*)

1901 Front-mounted engine.
Mercedes car produced.
1902 Running board.
Serpollet did a speed of 74 km/h in a steam car.
1903 Pressed steel frames.
First windshield.
The Motor Car Act resulted in considerable persecution of the motorist for speeding, number plates and lights, so much so that the motoring organizations paid cyclists to find police speed traps.
1904 Folding windshield.
Closed saloon-type body.
A petrol car reached 100 mile/h and, in the same year, a Stanley steam car achieved a speed of 127 mile/h. Stanley steam cars used paraffin

35

in a multitube boiler and had a chassis made from hickory.

Rolls-Royce exhibited their first car in Paris. The motoring press were impressed with its reliability.

Veteran cars are cars up to and including this year.

2.1.3 Terms used to describe early vehicle body styles

In the history of the motor car there has been some ambiguity in the names used to describe various types of body styles, built by coach builders from different countries. The following terms relate to the vehicles produced during the period 1895 to 1915, and show the derivation of the terminology used to describe the modern vehicle.

Berlina Rarely used before the First World War. A closed luxury car with small windows which allowed the occupants to see without being seen.

Cab A term taken directly from the days of the horse-drawn carriages. Used to describe an enclosed vehicle which carried two passengers, while the driver was situated in front of this compartment and unprotected.

Cabriolet Used towards the end of the period. Describes a car with a collapsible hood and seating two or four people.

Coupé A vehicle divided by a fixed or movable glass partition behind the front seat. The driver's position was only partially protected by the roof whilst the rear compartment was totally enclosed and very luxurious.

Coupé cabriolet or double cabriolet A long vehicle having the front part designed as a coupé and the rear part designed as a cabriolet. There were often two supplementary seats.

Coupé chauffeur A coupé with the driving position completely covered by an extension of the rear roof.

Coupé de ville A coupé having the driving position completely open.

Coupé limousine A vehicle having a totally enclosed rear compartment and the front driving position closed on the sides only.

Double Berlina A longer version of the Berlina but having the driving position separated from the rear part of the vehicle.

Double landaulet A longer version of the landaulet. It had two permanent seats plus two occasional seats in the rear and a driving position in front.

Double phaeton A phaeton which had two double seats including the driver's seat.

Double tonneau A longer version of the tonneau in which the front seats were completely separated from the rear seats.

Glass saloon A large closed vehicle similar to a double Berlina but with enlarged windows.

Landau A cabriolet limousine having only the roof behind the rear windows collapsible.

Landaulet or landaulette A small landau having only two seats in the closed collapsible roof portion.

Limousine A longer version of the coupé with double side windows in the rear compartment.

Limousine chauffeur A limousine with an extended rear roof to cover the driving position.

Phaeton A term from the days of the horse-drawn carriage. In early motoring it was used to describe a lightweight car with large spoked wheels, one double seat and usually a hood.

Runabout An open sporting type of vehicle with simple bodywork and two seats only.

Saloon A vehicle having the driving seat inside the enclosed car but not separated from the rear seat by a partition.

Tonneau An open vehicle having a front bench seat and a semicircular rear seat which was built into the rear doors.

Torpedo A long sports vehicle having its hood attached to the windscreen.

Victoria Another term derived from the era of horses. The Victoria was a long, luxurious vehicle with a separate driving position and a large rear seat. It was equipped with hoods and side screens.

Wagon saloon A particularly luxurious saloon used for official purposes.

2.1.4 Vehicle classification

There are many ways in which motor vehicles may be classified into convenient groups for recognition. Much depends on such factors as the manufacturer, the make of the car, the series and the body type or style. Distinctive groups of passenger vehicle bodies include the following:

1 Small-bodied mass-produced vehicles.
2 Medium-bodied mass-produced vehicles.
3 Large-bodied mass-produced vehicles.
4 Modified mass-produced bodywork to give a standard production model a more distinctive appearance.

5 Specially built vehicles using the major components of mass produced models.

6 High-quality coach-built limousines (handmade).

7 Sports and GT bodywork (mass-produced).

8 Specially coach-built sports cars (handmade).

Styling forms include the following:

Saloon The most popular style for passenger vehicles is the two-door or four-door saloon. It has a fully enclosed, fixed-roof body for four or more people. This body style also has a separate luggage or boot compartment (Figure 2.6a).

Hatchback This body style is identified by its characteristic sloping rear tailgate, which is classed as one of the three or five doors. With the rear seats down there is no division between the passenger and luggage compartments and this increases the luggage carrying capacity of the vehicle (Figure 2.6b).

Estate This type of vehicle is styled so that the roof extends to the rear to give more luggage space, especially when the rear seats are lowered (Figure 2.6c).

Sports coupé and coupé A sports coupé is a two-seater sports car with a fixed roof and a high performance engine. A coupé is a two-door, fixed-roof, high-performance vehicle with similar styling but with two extra seats at the rear, and is sometimes referred to as a '2-plus-2' (Figure 2.6d).

Convertible or cabriolet This can have either two or four doors. It has a soft-top folding roof (hood) and wind-up windows, together with fully enclosed or open bodywork (Figure 2.6e).

Sports This is a two-seater vehicle with a high performance engine and a folding or removable roof (hood) (Figure 2.6f).

Limousine This vehicle is characterized by its extended length, a high roofline to allow better headroom for seating five passengers comfortably behind the driver, a high-quality finish and luxurious interiors (Figure 2.6g).

2.1.5 The evolution of design

When the first motor cars appeared, little attention was paid to their appearance; it was enough that they ran. Consequently the cars initially sold to the public mostly resembled horse-drawn carriages with engines added. Henry Ford launched his Model T in 1908, and it sold on its low price and utility rather than its looks. However, the body design of this car had to be changed over its 19 year production span to reflect changes in customer taste.

The 1930s saw greater emphasis on streamlining design. Manufacturers began to use wind tunnels to eliminate unnecessary drag-inducing projections from their cars. One of the dominant styling features of the 1950s and 1960s was the tail fin, inspired by the twin tail fins of the wartime Lockhead Lightning fighter aircraft. Eventually a reaction set in against such excesses and the trend returned to more streamlined styling.

In creating cars for today's highly competitive car market, designers have to do far more than just achieve a pleasing shape. National legal requirements determine the positions of lamps, direction indicators and other safety-related items, while the buying market has become much more sophisticated than before. Fuel economy, comfort, function and versatility are now extremely important.

2.2 CREATION OF A NEW DESIGN FROM CONCEPT TO REALIZATION

The planning, design, engineering and development of a new motor car are extremely complex processes. With approximately 15 000 separate parts, the car is the most complicated piece of equipment built using mass production methods.

Every major design project has its own design team led by a design manager, and they stay with the project throughout. The size of the team varies according to the progress and status of the project. The skill and judgement of the trained and experienced automotive designer is vital to the creation of any design concept.

To assist in the speed and accuracy of the ensuing stages of the design process (the implementation), some of the most advanced computer-assisted design equipment is used by the large vehicle manufacturers. For example, computer-controlled measuring bridges that can automatically scan model surfaces, or machines that can mill surfaces, are linked to a computer centre through a highly sophisticated satellite communication network. The key terms in computer equipment are as follows:

Computer-aided design (CAD) Computer-assisted design work, basically using graphics.

Computer-aided engineering (CAE) All computer-aided activities with respect to technical data processing, from idea to preparation for production, integrated in an optimum way.

Computer-aided manufacturing (CAM) Preparation of production and analysis of production processes.

Computer-integrated manufacturing (CIM) All computer-aided activities from idea to serial production.

Figure 2.6 Vehicle styling forms: (a) saloon (b) hatchback (c) estate (d) coupé (e) convertible (f) sports (g) limousine

The use of CAE is growing in the automotive industry and will probably result in further widespread changes. Historically, the aerospace industry was the leader in CAE development. The three major motor companies of GM, Ford and Chrysler started their CAE activities as soon as computers became readily available in the early 1960s. The larger automotive companies in Europe started CAE activities in the early 1970s – about the same time as the Japanese companies.

Each new project starts with a series of detailed paper studies, aimed at identifying the most competitive and innovative product in whichever part of the market is under review. Original research into systems and concepts is then balanced against careful analysis of operating characteristics, features performance and economy targets, the projected cost of ownership and essential dimensional requirements. Research into competitors' vehicles, market research to judge tastes in future years and possible changes in legislation are all factors that have to be taken into account by the product planners when determining the specification of a new vehicle.

The various stages of the design process are as follows:

1 Vehicle styling, ergonomics and safety.
2 Production of scale and full-size models.
3 Engine performance and testing.
4 Wind tunnel testing.
5 Prototype production.
6 Prototype testing.
7 Body engineering for production.

2.2.1 Vehicle styling

Styling
Styling has existed from early times. However, the terms 'stylist' and 'styling' originally came into common usage in the automotive industry during the first part of the twentieth century.

The automotive stylist needs to be a combination of artist, inventor, craftsman and engineer, with the ability to conceive new and imaginative ideas and to bring these ideas to economic reality by using up-to-date techniques and facilities. He must have a complete understanding of the vehicle and its functions, and a thorough knowledge of the materials available, the costs involved, the capabilities of the production machinery, the sources of supply and the directions of worldwide changes. His responsibilities include the conception, detail, design and development of all new products, both visual and mechanical. This includes the exterior form, all applied facias, the complete

Figure 2.7 Style artist at work (*Ford Motor Company Ltd*)

interior, controls, instrumentation, seating, and the colours and textures of everything visible outside and inside the vehicle.

Styling departments vary enormously in size and facilities, ranging from the individual consultant stylist to the comprehensive resources of major American motor corporations like General Motors, which has more than 2000 staff in their styling department at Detroit. The individual consultant designer usually provides designs for organizations which are too small to employ full time stylists. Some act as an additional brain for organizations who want to inject new ideas into their own production. Among the famous designers are the Italians Pininfarina (Lancia, Ferrari, Alfa), Bertone (Lamborghini), Ghia (Ford) and Issigonis (Mini).

The work of the modern car stylist is governed by the compromise between his creativity and the world of production engineering. Every specification, vehicle type, payload, overall dimensions, engine power and vehicle image inspire the stylist and the design proposals he will make. Initially he makes freehand sketches of all the fundamental components placed in their correct positions. If the drawing does not reduce the potential of the original ideas, he then produces more comprehensive sketches of this design, using colours to indicate more clearly to the senior executives the initial thinking of the design (Figure 2.7). Usually the highly successful classic designs are the work of one outstanding individual stylist rather than of a team.

The main aim of the designer is to improve passenger comfort and protection, vision, heating and ventilation. The styling team may consider the transverse engine as a means of reducing the space occupied by the mechanical elements of the car. Front-wheel drive eliminates the driveshaft and tunnel and the occupants can sit more comfortably. Certain minimum standards are laid down with regard to seat widths, knee room and headroom. The interior dimensions of the car are part of the initial specifications and not subject to much modification. Every centimetre of space is considered in the attempt to provide the maximum interior capacity for the design. The final dimensions of the interior and luggage space are shown in a drawing, together with provision for the engine and remaining mechanical assemblies.

Ergonomics
Ergonomics is a fundamental component of the process of vehicle design. It is the consideration of human factors in the efficient layout of controls in the driver's environment. In the design of instrument panels, factors such as the driver's reach zones and his field of vision, together with international standards, all have to be considered. Legal standards include material performance in relation to energy absorption and deformation under impact. The vision and reach zones are geometrically defined, and allow for the elimination of instrument reflections in the windshield.

Basic elements affecting the driver's relationship to the instrument panel controls, instruments, steering wheel, pedals, seats and other vital elements in the car are positioned for initial evaluation using the 'manikin', which is a two- and three-dimensional measuring tool developed as a result of numerous anthropometric surveys and representing the human figure. Changes are recorded until the designer is satisfied that an optimum layout has been achieved.

2.2.2 Safety

With regard to bodywork, the vehicle designer must take into account the safety of the driver, passengers and other road users. Although the vehicle cannot be expected to withstand collision with obstacles or other vehicles, much can be done to reduce the effects of collision by the use of careful design of the overall shape, the selection of suitable materials and the design of the components. The chances of injury can be reduced both outside and inside the vehicle by avoiding sharp-edged, projecting elements.

Every car should be designed with the following crash safety principles in mind:

1 The impact from a collision is absorbed gradually by controlled deformation of the outer parts of the car body.
2 The passenger area is kept intact as long as possible.
3 The interior is designed to reduce the risk of injury.

Safety-related vehicle laws cover design, performance levels and the associated testing procedures; requirements for tests, inspections, documentation and records for the process of approval; checks that standards are being maintained during production; the issue of safety-related documentation; and many other requirements throughout the vehicle's service life.

Primary or active safety
This refers to the features designed into the vehicle which reduce the possibility of an accident. These include primary design elements such as dual-circuit braking systems, anti-lock braking systems, high aerodynamic stability and efficient bad weather equipment, together with features that make the driver's environment safer, such as efficient through-ventilation, orthopaedic seating, improved all-round vision, easy-to-read instruments and ergonomic controls.

An anti-lock braking system (ABS) enhances a driver's ability to steer the vehicle during hard braking. Sensors monitor how fast the wheels are rotating and feed data continuously to a microprocessor in the vehicle to signal that a wheel is approaching lockup. The computer responds by sending a signal to apply and release brake pressure as required. This pumping action continues as long as the driver maintains adequate force on the brake pedal and impending wheel lock condition is sensed.

The stability and handling of the vehicle are affected by the width of the track and the position of the centre of gravity. Therefore the lower the centre of gravity and the wider the track the more stable is the vehicle.

Secondary or passive safety
If a crash does happen, secondary safety design should protect the passengers by:

1 Making sure that, in the event of an accident, the occupants stay inside the car.
2 Minimizing the magnitude and duration of the deceleration to which they are subjected.
3 Restraining the occupants so that they are not injured by secondary impacts within the car, and, if they do strike parts of the inside of the vehicle, making sure that there is sufficient padding to prevent serious injury.
4 Designing the outside of the vehicle so that the least possible injury is caused to pedestrians and others who may come into contact with the outside of the vehicle.

The primary concern is to develop efficient restraint systems which are comfortable to wear and easy to use. Manufacturers are now fitting automatic seatbelt

Figure 2.8 Automatic seat belt tensioner (*Vauxhall Motors Ltd*)

tensioners. These automatic 'body lock' front seatbelt tensioners reduce the severity of head injuries by 20 per cent, with similar gains in chest protection. In impacts over 12 mile/h (20 km/h) the extra tension in the seatbelt buckle triggers a sensor which tightens the lap and diagonal belts in 22 milliseconds, that is before the occupant even starts to move. In addition, because it operates at low speeds, it covers a broad spectrum of accident situations. Anti-submarining ramps built into the front seats further aid safety by reducing the possibility of occupants sliding under the belt (Figure 2.8). There are also engineering features such as impact energy-absorbing steering columns, head restraints, bumpers, anti-burst door locks, and self-aligning steering wheels. Anti-burst door locks prevent unrestrained occupants from falling out of the vehicle, especially during rollover. The chances of survival are much reduced if the occupant is thrown out. Broad padded steering wheels are used to prevent head or chest damage. Collapsible steering columns also prevent damage to the chest and abdomen

and are designed to prevent the steering column being pushed back into the passenger compartment while the front end is crumpling. The self-aligning steering wheel is designed to distribute force more evenly if the driver comes into contact with the steering wheel during a crash. This steering wheel has an energy-absorbing hub which incorporates six deformable metal legs. In a crash, the wheel deforms at the hub and the metal legs align the wheel parallel to the chest of the driver to help spread the impact and reduce chest, abdomen and facial injuries.

Body shells are now designed to withstand major collision and rollover impacts while absorbing shock by controlled deformation of structure in the front and rear of the vehicle. Vehicle design and accident prevention is based on the kinetic energy relationship of damage to a vehicle during a collision. Energy is absorbed by work done on the vehicle's materials by elastic deformation. This indicates that, to be effective, bumpers and other collision-absorbing parts of a vehicle should be made of materials such as foam-filled plastics and heavy rubber sections. Data indicate that long energy-absorbing distances should be provided in vehicle design, and the panel assemblies used for this purpose should have a lower stiffness than the central section or passenger compartment of the vehicle. The crumple zones are designed to help decelerate the car by absorbing the force of collision at a controlled rate, thereby cushioning the passengers and reducing the risk of injury (Figure 2.9). The safety cage (or safety cell) is the central section of the car body which acts as the passenger compartment. To ensure passenger safety, all body apertures around the passenger area should be reinforced by box-type profiles; seats should be secured rigidly to the floor; and heavy interior padding should be used around the dashboard areas. A strengthened roof construction, together with an anti-roll bar, afford additional protection in case of overturning (Figure 2.10).

Figure 2.9 Crumple zones (*Volvo Concessionaires Ltd*)

Narrow but strong roof
pillar section

Closed section profiles form a
safety cage for the passengers

Strong door pillar
attachment

Extra protection against
side impact

Upper attachment of spring
struts is extra strong

Safety cage protects the
occupants of the car

Figure 2.10 Safety cage (*Volvo Concessionaires Ltd*)

To counteract side impact manufacturers are now fitting, in both front and rear doors, lateral side supports in the form of twin high-strength steel tubular beams, which are set 90 mm apart to reduce the risk of the vehicle riding over the beams during side collision. These beams absorb the kinetic energy produced when the vehicle is struck from the side. To further improve the body structure the BC-pillars are being reinforced at the points of attachment to the sill and roof, again giving more strength to the safety cage and making it stronger and safer when the vehicle is involved in a collision (Figure 2.11a, b).

Visibility in design is the ability to see and be seen. In poor visibility and after dark, light sources must be relied on. The lights on vehicles now are much more efficient than on earlier models. The old tungsten filament lamp has given way to quartz-halogen lamps which provide much better illumination. The quartz-halogen lamp is able to produce a more powerful beam because the filament can be made hotter without

Seatbelt Tensioners

Full Size Airbag

Safety Cage

Twin Door Beams

(a)

Improvements to a conventional uni-body.
Shaded areas indicate reinforcements

(b)

Figure 2.11 (a) Safety features included in the safety cage (*Vauxhall Motors Ltd*) (b) reinforced BC-pillar and anti-roll bar (*Volvo Concessionaires Ltd*) shortening its lifespan. Hazard, reversing and fog lights are now fitted to most vehicles to improve safe driving.

In daylight, colour is probably the most important factor in enabling cars to be seen. If a vehicle is coloured towards the red end of the spectrum, it can be less obvious to other road users than a yellow one, especially in sodium vapour street lights: a red car absorbs yellow light from the street light and reflects little, and so appears to be dark in colour, whereas a yellow car reflects the yellow light and appears more obvious. Silver vehicles will blend into mist and fog and become difficult to see.

Blind spots can be diminished first by good design of front pillars, making them slim and strong, and second by reducing the area of rear quarter sections. This elimination of blind spots is now being achieved by using bigger windscreens which wrap round the front A-post, and rear windows which wrap round the rear quarter section, giving a wider field of vision.

Many automotive manufacturers now believe that a seatbelt/airbag combination provides the best possible interior safety system. Airbags play an important safety role in the USA since the wearing of seatbelts is not compulsory in many states. As competition to manufacture Europe's safest car increases, more manufacturers including those in the UK are starting to fit airbags. These Eurobags, or facebags as they are now called, since their main function in Europe and the UK is to protect the face rather than the entire body in the event of a collision, are less complex than their USA counterparts.

The first automotive airbags were made more than 20 years ago using nylon-based woven fabrics, and these remain the preferred materials among manufacturers. Nylon fabrics for airbags are supplied in two basic designs depending on whether the airbag is to protect the driver or the front passenger. The driver's airbag is housed in the steering wheel and requires special attention because of the confined space (Figure 2.12). The passenger's airbag system has a compartment door, located in front of the passenger in the dash area, which must open within 10 milliseconds and deploy the airbag within 30 milliseconds. The vehicle has a crash sensor which signals the airbags to deploy on impact (Figure 2.13).

2.2.3 Production of models

Scale models
Once the initial designs have been accepted, scale models are produced for wind-tunnel testing to determine the aerodynamic values of such a design. These models are usually constructed of wood and clay to allow for modifications to be made easily. At the same

Figure 2.12 Driver's airbag system (*Du Pont (UK) Ltd*)

Figure 2.13 Driver and front passenger airbag systems in use (*Du Pont (UK) Ltd*)

Figure 2.14 Scale model maker at work (*Ford Motor Company Ltd*)

time, design engineering personnel construct models of alternative interiors so that locations of instruments can be determined.

A one-quarter or three-eighth scale model is produced from the stylist's drawings to enable the stylist designer to evaluate the three-dimensional aspect of the vehicle. These scale models can look convincingly real (Figure 2.14). The clay surfaces are covered with a thin coloured plastic sheet which closely resembles genuine painted metal. Bumpers, door handles and trim strips are all cleverly made-up dummies, and the windows are made of Plexiglass. The scale models are examined critically and tested. Changes to the design can be made at this stage.

Full-size models

A full-size clay model is begun when the scale model has been satisfactorily modified. It is constructed in a similar way to the scale model but uses a metal, wood and plastic frame called a buck. The clay is placed on to the framework by professional model makers, who create the final outside shape of the body to an accuracy of 0.375 mm. The high standard of finish and detail results in an exact replica of the future full-size vehicle (Figure 2.15). This replica is then evaluated by the styling management and submitted to top management for their approval. The accurate life-size model is used for further wind-tunnel testing and also to provide measurements for the engineering and production departments. A scanner, linked to a computer, passes over the entire body and records each and every dimension (Figure 2.16). These are stored and can be produced on an automatic drafting machine. The same dimensions can also be projected on the screen of a graphics station; this is a sophisticated computer-controlled video system showing three-dimensional illustrations, allowing design engineers either to smooth the lines or to make detail alterations. The use of computers or CAD allows more flexibility and saves a lot of time compared with the more conventional drafting systems.

At the same time as the exterior model is being made, the interior model is also being produced accurately in every detail (Figure 2.17). It shows the seating arrangement, instrumentation, steering wheel, control unit location and pedal arrangements. Colours

45

Figure 2.15 Full-size clay model (*Ford Motor Company Ltd*)

Figure 2.16 Checking dimensional accuracy of the full-size model (*Ford Motor Company Ltd*)

Figure 2.17 Interior styling model (*Ford Motor Company Ltd*)

and fabrics are tried out on this mock-up until the interior styling is complete and ready for approval.

2.2.4 Engine performance and testing

Development engineers prepare to test an engine in a computer-linked test cell to establish the optimum settings for best performance, economy and emission levels. With the increasing emphasis on performance with economy, computers are used to obtain the best possible compromise. They are also used to monitor and control prolonged engine testing to establish reliability characteristics. If current engines and transmissions are to be used for a new model, a programme of refining and adapting for the new installation has to be initiated. However, if a completely new engine, transmission or driveline configuration is to be adopted, development work must be well in hand by this time.

2.2.5 Aerodynamics and wind-tunnel testing

Aerodynamics is an experimental science whose aim is the study of the relative motions of a solid body and the surrounding air. Its application to the design of a car body constitutes one of the chief lines of the search for energy economy in motor vehicles.

In order to move over flat ground, a car must overcome two forces:

1 Resistance to tyre tread motion, which varies with the coefficient of tyre friction over the ground and with the vehicle's mass.
2 Aerodynamic resistance, which depends on the shape of the car, on its frontal area, on the density of the air and on the square of the speed.

One of the objects of aerodynamic research is to reduce the latter: in other words to design a shape that will, for identical performance, require lower energy production. An aerodynamic or streamlined body allows faster running for the same consumption of energy, or lower consumption for the same speed. Research for the ideal shape is done on reduced-scale models of the vehicle. The models are placed in a wind tunnel, an experimental installation producing wind of a certain quality and fitted with the means for measuring the various forces due to the action of the wind on the model or the vehicle. Moreover, at a given cruising speed, the more streamlined vehicle has more power left available for acceleration: this is a safety factor.

The design of a motor car body must, however, remain compatible with imperatives of production, of

Figure 2.18 Theoretical drag curves for four types of vehicle, all reduced for comparison purposes to a front section of 2 m². Since air resistance increases in proportion to the square of the speed, a truck with C_d 1.0 requires 35 bhp at 100 km/h, whereas a coupé with C_d 0.2 requires only 7 bhp

overall measurements and of inside spaciousness. It is also a matter of style, for the coachwork must be attractive to the public. This makes it impossible to apply the laws of aerodynamics literally. The evolution of the motor car nevertheless tends towards a gradual reduction in aerodynamic resistance.

Aerodynamic drag
The force which opposes the forward movement of an automobile is aerodynamic drag, in which air rubs against the exterior vehicle surfaces and forms disturbances about the body, thereby retarding forward movement. Aerodynamic drag increases with speed; thus if the speed of a vehicle is doubled, the corresponding engine power must be increased by eight times. Engineers express the magnitude of aerodynamic drag using the drag coefficient Cd. The coefficient expresses the aerodynamic efficiency of the vehicle: the smaller the value of the coefficient, the smaller the aerodynamic drag.

Figure 2.18 illustrates the improvements in aerodynamic drag coefficient achieved by alterations to the shape of vehicles. Over the years the value of Cd has been reduced roughly as follows:

1910	0.95	1960	0.40
1920	0.82	1970	0.36
1930	0.56	1980	0.30
1940	0.45	1990	0.22
1950	0.42	1995	0.20 (probable)

During the wind-tunnel test all four wheels of the car rest on floating scales connected to a floor balance, which has a concrete foundation below the main floor area. The vehicle is then subjected to an air stream of up to 112 mile/h; the sensitive balances register the effect of the headwind on the vehicle as it is either pressed down or lifted up from the floor, pushed to the left or right, or rotated about its longitudinal axis. The manner in which the forces affect the vehicle body and the location at which the forces are exerted depends on the body shape, underbody contours and projecting parts. The fewer disturbances which occur as air moves past the vehicle, the lower its drag. Threads on the vehicle exterior as well as smoke streams indicate the air flow, and enable test engineers to see where disturbance exists and where air flows are interrupted or redirected, and therefore where reshaping of the body is necessary in order to produce better aerodynamics (Figures 2.19 and 2.20).

2.2.6 Prototype production

The new model now enters the prototype phase. The mock-ups give way to the first genuine road-going vehicle, produced with the aid of accurate drawings and without complex tooling and machinery. The prototype must accurately reproduce the exact shape, construction and assembly conditions of the final production body it represents if it is to be of any value in illustrating possible manufacturing problems and accurate test data. The process begins with the issue of drawing office instructions to the experimental prototype workshop. Details of skin panels and other large pressings are provided in the form of tracings or as photographic reproductions of the master body drafts. As the various detailed parts are made, by either simple press tools or traditional hand methods, they are spot welded into minor assemblies or subassemblies; these later become part of a major assembly to form the completed vehicle body.

2.2.7 Prototype testing

While still in the prototype stage, the new car has to face a number of arduous tests. For these tests a mobile laboratory is connected to the vehicle by a cable, which transmits signals from various sensors on the vehicle back to the onboard computer for collation and analysis. The prototype will also be placed on a computer-linked simulated rig to monitor, through controlled vibrations, the stresses and strains experienced by the driveline, suspension and body.

Crash testing (Figure 2.21) is undertaken to establish that the vehicle will suffer the minimum of damage

Figure 2.19   Wind-tunnel testing of a prototype: front view (*Ford Motor Company Ltd*)

Figure 2.20   Wind-tunnel testing of a prototype: side view (*Ford Motor Company Ltd*)

(a)

(b)

(c)

(d)

Figure 2.21 Basic frontal crash and side impact (angled sideswipe) tests (*Vauxhall Motors Ltd*)

or distortion in the event of an impact and that the occupants are safely installed within the strong passenger compartment or safety cell. The basic crash test is a frontal crash at 30 mile/h (48 km/h) into a fixed barrier set perpendicularly to the car's longitudinal axis. The collision is termed 100 per cent overlap, as the complete front of the car strikes the barrier and there is no offset (Figure 2.22). The main requirement is that the steering wheel must not be moved back by more than 120 mm, but there is no requirement to measure the force to which the occupants will be subjected in a collision. The manufacturers use

anthropometric dummies suitably instrumented with decelerometers and strain gauges which collect relevant data on the effect of the collision on the dummies. A passenger car side impact test aimed at reducing chest and pelvic injuries has been legal in the USA from 1993. This stricter standard requires that a new vehicle must pass a full-scale crash test designed to simulate a collision at an intersection in which a car travelling at 15 mile/h is hit in the side by another car travelling at 30 mile/h. This test is called an angled sideswipe: the displacement is 27 degrees forward from the perpendicular of the test vehicle's main axis.

Figure 2.22 Standard frontal impact test

Figure 2.24 Road testing a prototype (*Ford Motor Company Ltd*)

Figure 2.23 Volvo crash test (*Volvo Concessionaires Ltd*)

The test is conducted by propelling a movable deformable barrier at 33.5 mile/h into the side of a test car occupied by dummies in the front and rear seats. The dummies are wired with instruments to predict the risk potential of human injury. Volvo do a very unusual promotional crash test which involves propelling a car from the top of a tall building (Figure 2.23).

Extensive durability tests are undertaken on a variety of road surfaces in all conditions (Figure 2.24) Vehicles are also run through water tests (Figure 2.25) and subjected to extreme climatic temperature changes to confirm their durability.

The final stages are now being reached: mechanical specifications, trim levels, engine options, body styles and the feature lists are confirmed.

Figure 2.25 Water testing a prototype (*Ford Motor Company Ltd*)

Figure 2.26 (Three-dimensional graphics display of a scale model (*Ford Motor Company Ltd*)

2.2.8 Body engineering for production

The body engineering responsibilities are to simulate the styling model and overall requirements laid down by the management in terms of drawings and specification. The engineering structures are designed for production, at a given date, at the lowest possible tooling cost and to a high standard of quality and reliability.

As competition between the major car manufacturers increases, so does the need for lighter and more effective body structures. Until recently the choice of section, size and metal gauges was based on previous experience. However, methods have now been evolved which allow engineers to solve problems with complicated geometry on a graphical display computer which can be constructed to resemble a body shape (Figure 2.26). The stiffness and stress can then be computed from its geometry, and calculations made of the load bearing of the structures using finite-element methods (Figure 2.27).

With the final specifications approved, the new car is ready for production. At this stage an initial batch of cars is built (a pilot run) to ensure that the plant facilities and the workforce are ready for the start of full production. When the production line begins to turn out the brand new model, every stage of production is carefully scrutinized to ensure quality in all the vehicles to be built.

2.3 METHODS OF CONSTRUCTION

The steel body can be divided into two main types: those which are mounted on a separate chassis frame, and those in which the underframe or floor forms an integral part of the body. The construction of today's mass-produced motor car has changed almost completely from the composite, that is conventional separate chassis and body, to the integral or mono unit. This change is the result of the need to reduce body weight and cost per unit of the total vehicle.

2.3.1 Composite construction (conventional separate chassis)

The chassis and body are built as two separate units (Figure 2.28). The body is then assembled on to the chassis with mounting brackets, which have rubber-bushed bolts to hold the body to the rigid chassis. These flexible mountings allow the body to move slightly when the car is in motion. This means that the car can be dismantled into the two units of the body and chassis. The chassis assembly is built up of engine, wheels, springs and transmission. On to this assembly is added the body, which has been preassembled in units to form a complete body shell (Figure 2.29).

2.3.2 Integral (mono or unity) construction

Integral body construction employs the same principles of design that have been used for years in the aircraft industry. The main aim is to strengthen without unnecessary weight, and the construction does not employ a conventional separate chassis frame for attachment of suspension, engine and other chassis and transmission components (Figure 2.30). The major difference between composite and integral construction is the design and construction of the floor (Figure 2.31). In integral bodies the floor pan area is generally called the underbody. The underbody is made up of formed floor sections, channels, boxed sections, formed rails and numerous reinforcements. In most integral underbodies a suspension member is incorporated in both the front and rear of the body. The suspension members have very much the same appearance as the conventional chassis frame from the

SIERRA

MODEL 6 (DEZ 81)

GRID POINTS : 10078 (X2)
ELEMENTS : 11574 (X2)
PARTS : 109

FINITE ELEMENT STRUCTURAL ANALYSIS

Figure 2.27 Finite-element structural analysis (*Ford Motor Company Ltd*)

underside, but the front suspension members end at the cowl or bulkhead and the rear suspension members end just forward of the rear boot floor. With the floor pan, side rails and reinforcements welded to them, the suspension members become an integral part of the underbody and form the supports for engine, front and rear suspension units and other chassis components. In the integral body the floor pan area is usually of heavier gauge metal than in the composite body, and has one or more box sections and several channel sections which may run across the floor either from side to side or from front to rear; this variety of underbody construction is due largely to the difference in wheelbase, length and weight of the car involved. A typical upper body for an integral constructed car is very much the same as the conventional composite body shell; the major differences lie in the rear seat area and the construction which joins the front wings to the front bulkhead or cowl assembly. The construction in the area to the rear of the back seat is much heavier in an integral body than in a composite body. The same is true of the attaching members for the front wings, front bulkhead and floor

assembly, as these constructions give great strength and stability to the overall body structure.

2.3.3 Semi-integral methods of construction

In some forms of integral or mono assemblies, the entire front end or subframe forward of the bulkhead is joined to the cowl assembly with bolts. With this construction, the bolts can be easily removed and the entire front (or in some cases rear) subframe can be replaced as one assembly in the event of extensive damage.

2.3.4 Glass fibre composite construction

This method of producing complex shapes involves applying layers of glass fibre and resin in a prepared mould. After hardening, a strong moulding is produced with a smooth outer surface requiring little maintenance. Among the many shapes available in this composite material are lorry cabs, bus front canopies, container vehicles, and the bodies of cars such as the Lotus. The designers have styled the GRP body

Figure 2.28 Composite construction (conventional separate chassis)

so that separately moulded body panels could be used and overlapped to hide the attachment points. This allows the panels to be bolted directly to the supporting square-section steel tube armatures located on the main chassis frame. The inner body, which rests directly on the chassis frame and which forms the base for all internal trim equipment, is a complex GRP moulding. The windscreen aperture is moulded as a part of the inner body, and incorporates steel reinforcing hoops which are braced directly to the chassis. The boot compartment is also a separate hand-laid GRP moulding, as are the doors and some of the other panels. Most of the body panels are secured by self-tapping bolts which offer very positive location

and a useful saving in assembly time (Figures 2.32 and 2.33).

2.3.5 Galvanized body shell clad entirely with composite skin panels

Renault have designed a high-rise car which has a skeletal steel body shell (Figure 2.34), clad entirely with composite panels. After assembly the complete body shell is immersed in a bath of molten zinc, which applies an all-over 6.5 micron (millionth of a metre) coating. The process gives anti-rust protection, while the chemical reaction causes a molecular change in the steel which strengthens it. Lighter-gauge steel can

53

Figure 2.29 Composite construction showing a Lotus Elan chassis before fitting the body (*Lotus Engineering*)

Figure 2.30 Complete body assembly of Austin Maestro (*Austin Rover Group Ltd*)

Figure 2.31 Front end construction: (a) Integral or mono (b) composite

Figure 2.32 Motor body panel assembly using GRP: Lotus Elan (*Lotus Engineering*)

Figure 2.33 Complete Lotus Elan SE body shell (*Lotus Engineering*)

Figure 2.35 Espace high-rise car showing composite panel cladding (*Renault UK Ltd*). Plastic parts are made from a composite material based on polyester resin: pre-impregnated type (SMC) for parts 1, 4, 5, 6, 7, 8, 9, 10; injected resin type for parts 2, 3

Parts bonded to chassis:	Detachable parts:
1 Body top	3 Tailgate lining
2 Roof	4 Tailgate outer panel
5 Rear wing	6 Rear door panel
9 Front wing	8 Front door panel
7 Sill	10 Bonnet

Figure 2.34 Espace high-rise car with galvanized skeletal steel body shell (*Renault UK Ltd*)

therefore be used without sacrificing strength, resulting in a substantial weight saving even with the zinc added.

Skin panels are formed in reinforced polyester sheet, made of equal parts of resin, fibreglass and mineral filler. The panels are joined to the galvanized frame and doors by rivets or bonding as appropriate. The one-piece high-rise tailgate is fabricated entirely from polyester with internal steel reinforcements (Figure 2.35). Damage to panels through impact shocks is contained locally and absorbed through destruction of the material, unlike the steel sheet which transmits deformation. Accident damage and consequent repair costs are thus reduced.

2.3.6 Variations in body shape

Among the motor car manufacturers there are variations in constructional methods which result in different body types and styles. Figure 2.36 illustrates four

types of body shell – a saloon with a boot, a hatchback, an estate car and a light van. Figure 2.37 shows a coach-built limousine of extremely high quality, built on a Rolls-Royce Silver Spirit chassis by the coachbuilders Hooper & Co. This vehicle has been designed for the use of heads of state and world-ranking VIPs.

2.4 BASIC BODY CONSTRUCTION

A typical four-door saloon body can be likened to a hollow tube with holes cut in the sides. The bulkhead towards the front and rear completes the box-like form and assists in providing torsional stability. The roof, even if it has to accommodate a sunshine roof, is usually a quite straightforward and stable structure; the curved shape of the roof panel prevents lozenging (going out of alignment in a diamond shape). The floor is a complete panel from front to rear when assembled, and is usually fitted with integral straightening ribs to prevent lozenging. With its bottom sides or sill panels, wheel arches, cross members and heelboard, it is the strongest part of the whole body.

Figure 2.36 Body shell variations: (a) saloon with boot (b) hatchback (c) estate car (d) light van (*Rover Group Ltd*)

Figure 2.37 Coach-built limousine: Emperor State Landaulette (*Hooper & Co (Coach-builders) Ltd*)

The rear bulkhead, mainly in the form of a rear squab panel, is again a very stable structure. However, the scuttle or forward bulkhead is a complex structure in a private motor car. Owing to the awkward shape of the scuttle and the accommodation required for much of the vehicle's equipment, it requires careful designing to obtain sufficient strength. Body sides with thin pillars, large windows and door openings are inherently weak, requiring reinforcing with radiusing corners to the apertures to give them sufficient constructional strength.

A designer in a small coach-building firm will consider methods necessary to build the body complete with trim and other finishing processes. The same job in a mass production factory may be done by a team of designers and engineers all expert in their own particular branch of the project. The small manufacturer produces bodies with skilled labour and a minimum number of jigs, while the mass producer uses many jigs and automatic processes to achieve the necessary output. However, the problems are basically the same: to maintain strength and stability, a good standard of finish and ease of production.

Figure 2.38 shows the build-up details of a four-door saloon, from the main floor assembly to the complete shell assembly. In the figure the main floor unit (1), commencing at the front, comprises a toeboard or pedal panel, although in some cases this may become a part of the scuttle or bulkhead. Apart from providing a rest for the front passengers' feet, it seals off the engine and gearbox from the body and connects the scuttle to the main floor. The main centre floor panel (2) should be sufficiently reinforced to carry the weight of the front seats and passengers. It may be necessary to have a tunnel running the length of the floor in the centre to clear the transmission system from the engine to the rear axle, and holes

57

Panel windshield scuttle assembly

Sectional view A–A

may have to be cut into the floor to allow access to the gearbox, oil filler, and dipstick, in which case removable panels or large grommets would be fitted in these access holes (3).

The front end of the main floor is fixed to the toeboard panel and the sides of the main centre floor are strengthened by the bottom sills (4) and/or some form of side members which provide the necessary longitudinal strength. The transverse strength is provided by the cross members. The floor panel itself prevents lozenging, and the joints between side members and cross members are designed to resist torsional stresses.

The rear end of the floor is stiffened transversely by the rear seat heelboard (5). This heelboard also stiffens the front edges of the rear seat panel. In addition, it often provides the retaining lip for the rear seat cushion, which is usually made detachable from the body. The heelboard together with the rear panel and rear squab panel forms the platform for the rear seat.

The rear seat panel (6) is reinforced or swaged if necessary to gain enough strength to support the rear passengers. Usually the rear seat panel has to be raised to provide sufficient clearance for the deflection of the rear axle differential housing. The front edge of the rear seat panel is stiffened by the rear seat heelboard, and the rear edge of the seat panel is stiffened by the rear squab panel. The rear squab panel completes this unit and provides the rear bulkhead across the car. It seals off the boot or luggage compartment from the main body or passenger compartment.

The boot floor (7), which extends from the back of the rear squab panel to the extreme back of the body, completes the floor unit. In addition to the luggage, the spare wheel has to be accommodated here. The front edge of the boot floor is reinforced by the rear squab panel and the rear end by a cross member of some form (8). The sides of the floor are stiffened by vertical boot side panels at the rear, while the wheel arch panels complete the floor structure by joining the rear end of the main floor and its side members.

The wheel arch panels (9) themselves seal the rear road wheels from the body.

In general the floor unit is made up from a series of panels with suitable cross members or reinforcements. The edges of the panels are stiffened either by flanging reinforcing members, or by joining to the adjacent panels. The boot framing is joined at the back to the rear end of the boot floor, at the sides to the boot side panels and at the top to the shelf panel behind the rear squab (10). It has to be sufficiently strong at the point where the boot lid hinges are fitted to carry the weight of the boot lid when this is opened. Surrounding the boot lid opening there is a gutter to carry away rain and water to prevent it entering the boot; opposite the hinges, provision is made for the boot lid lock striking plate (11) to be fixed. From the forward edge of the boot, the next unit is the back light and roof structure (12), and this extends to the top of the windscreen or canopy rail (13). The roof is usually connected to the body side frames, which comprise longitudinal rails or stringers and a pair of cantrails which form the door openings (14). Provision in the roof should be made for the interior lights and wiring and also the fixing of the interior trimming. The scuttle and windscreen unit, including the front standing pillar or A-post (15), provides the front bulkhead and seals the engine from the passenger compartment.

Accommodation has to be made for the instrumentation of the car, the wiring, radio, windscreen wipers and driving cable, demisters and ducting, steering column support, handbrake support and pedals. The scuttle (16) is a complicated structure which needs to be very strong. When the front door is hinged at the forward edge, provision has to be made in the front pillar for the door hinges, door check and courtesy light switches.

The centre standing pillar or BC-post (17) is fixed to the side members of the main floor unit and supports the cantrails of the roof unit. It provides a shut face for the front door, a position for the door lock striking plate and buffers or dovetail, and also a hinge

---

(Facing page)

Figure 2.38 Body constructional details of Austin Rover Maestro (*Austin Rover*)

1 Main floor unit	11 Boot lid lock striking plate
2 Main centre floor panel	12 Roof structure
3 Access holes	13 Windscreen or canopy rail
4 Bottom sills	14 Cantrails
5 Rear seat heelboard	15 Front standing pillar (A-post)
6 Rear seat panel	16 Scuttle
7 Boot floor	17 Centre standing pillar (BC-post)
8 Cross member	18 Rear standing pillar (D-post)
9 Wheel arch panel	19 Quarter panels
10 Rear squabs	

Figure 2.39 Major body panels

1 Roof panel	8 Sidelamps
2 Bonnet panel	9 Sill panel
3 Boot lid	10 Front door
4 Front wing	11 Rear door
5 Radiator grille	12 Centre pillar
6 Front bumper bar	13 Rear quarter panel
7 Headlamps	14 Rear bumper bar

face for the rear door; as with the front standing pillar, provision is made for the door hinges and door check. The rear standing pillar or D-post (18) provides the shut face for the rear end of the floor side members at the bottom, while the top is fixed to the roof cantrails and forms the front of the quarters.

The quarters (19) are the areas of the body sides between the rear standing pillars and the back light and boot. If the body is a six-light saloon there will be a quarter window here with its necessary surrounding framing, but in the case of a four-light saloon this portion will be more simply constructed. Apart from the doors, bonnet, boot lid and front wings this completes the structure of the average body shell.

2.5 IDENTIFICATION OF MAJOR BODY PRESSINGS

The passenger-carrying compartment of a car is called the body, and to it is attached all the doors, wings and such parts required to form a complete body shell assembly (Figure 2.39).

2.5.1 Outer construction

This can be likened to the skin of the body, and is usually considered as that portion of a panel or panels which is visible from the outside of the car.

2.5.2 Inner construction

This is considered as all the brackets, braces and panel assemblies that are used to give the car strength (Figure 2.40). In some cases the entire panels are inner construction on one make of car and a combination of inner and outer on another.

2.5.3 Front-end assembly including cowl or dash panel

The front-end assembly (Figure 2.41) is made up from the two front side member assemblies which are designed to carry the weight of the engine, suspension, steering gear and radiator. The suspension system used will affect the design of the panels, but whatever system is used the loads must be transmitted to the wing valances and on to the body panels. The front cross member assembly braces the front of the car and carries the radiator and headlamp units. The side valance assemblies form a housing for the wheels, a mating edge for the bonnet and a strong box section for attachment of front wings. Both the side frames and valance assemblies are connected to the cowl or dash panel. The front-end assembly is attached to the main floor at the toe panel.

The cowl or dash panel forms the front bulkhead of the body (Figure 2.41) and is usually formed by joining smaller panels (the cowl upper panel and the cowl side panel) by welds to form an integral unit. In some cases the windscreen frame is integral with the cowl panel. The cowl extends upwards around the entire windscreen opening so that the upper edge of the cowl panel forms the front edge of the roof panel. In this case the windscreen pillars, i.e. the narrow sloping construction at either side of the windscreen opening, are merely part of the cowl panel. In other constructions, only a portion of the windscreen pillar is formed as part of the cowl. The cowl is sometimes called the fire wall because it is the partition between the passenger and engine compartments, and openings in the cowl accommodate the necessary controls, wiring and tubing that extend from one compartment to the other. The instrument panel, which is usually considered as part of the cowl panel although it is a complex panel in itself, provides a mounting for the instruments necessary to check the performance of the vehicle during operation. Cowl panels usually have both inner and outer construction, but in certain constructions only the upper portion of the cowl around the windscreen is visible. On many vehicles the front door hinge pillar is also an integral part of the cowl.

2.5.4 Front side member assembly

This is an integral part of the front-end assembly; it connects the front wing valances to the cowl or dash assembly. It is designed to strengthen the front end; it is part of the crumple zone, giving lateral strength on impact and absorbing energy by deformation during a collision. It also helps to support the engine and suspension units (see Figure 2.41; key figure references 13, 15, 16, 20, 22).

2.5.5 A-post assembly

This is an integral part of the body side frame. It is connected to the front-end assembly and forms the front door pillar or hinge post. It is designed to carry the weight of the front door and helps to strengthen the front bulkhead assembly (Figure 2.41).

2.5.6 Main floor assembly

This is the passenger-carrying section of the main floor. It runs backwards from the toe panel to the heelboard or back seat assembly. It is strengthened to carry the two front seats, and in some cases may have a transmission tunnel running through its centre. Strength is built into the floor by the transmission tunnel acting like an inverted channel section. The body sill panels provide extra reinforcement in the form of lateral strength. Transverse strength is provided by box

sections at right angles to the transmission tunnel, generally in the areas of the front seat and in front of the rear seat. The remaining areas of flat floor are ribbed below the seats and in the foot wells to add stiffness (Figure 2.42).

2.5.7 Boot floor assembly

This is a section of the floor between the seat panel and the extreme back of the boot. It is strengthened by the use of cross members to carry the rear seat passengers. This area forms the rear bulkhead between the two rear wheel arches, forming the rear seat panel or heelboard, and in a saloon body shell can incorporate back seat supports and parcel shelf. The boot floor is also strengthened to become the luggage compartment, carrying the spare wheel and petrol tank. At the extreme back it becomes the panel on to which the door or tailgate closes (Figure 2.42).

2.5.8 Complete underbody assembly

This is commonly called the floor pan assembly, and is usually composed of several smaller panels welded together to form a single floor unit. All floor panels are reinforced on the underside by stiffening members or cross members. Most floor pans are irregular in shape for several reasons. They are formed with indentations or heavily swaged areas to strengthen the floor sections between the cross members, and foot room for the passengers is often provided by these recessed areas in the floor. Figure 2.42 shows a complete underbody assembly.

2.5.9 Body side frame assembly

On a four-door saloon this incorporates the A-post, the BC-post, the D-post and the rear quarter section. The side frames reinforce the floor pan along the sill sections. The hinge pillar or A-post extends forward to meet the dash panel and front bulkhead to provide strength at this point. The centre pillars or BC-posts connect the body sills to the roof cantrails. They are usually assembled as box sections using a top-hat section and flat plate. These are the flanges which form the attachments for the door weather seals and provide the four door openings. The D-post and rear quarter section are integral with the rear wheel arch and can include a rear quarter window (Figure 2.43).

2.5.10 Roof panel

The roof panel is one of the largest of all major body panels, and it is also one of the simplest in construc-

tion. The area which the roof covers varies between different makes and models of cars. On some cars, the roof panel ends at the windscreen. On others it extends downwards around the windscreen so that the windscreen opening is actually in the roof. On some cars the roof ends above the rear window, while on others it extends downwards so that the rear window opening is in the lower rear roof. When this is the case the roof panel forms the top panel around the rear boot opening. Some special body designs incorporate different methods of rear window construction, which affects the roof panel; this is particularly true for estate cars, hatchbacks and hardtop convertibles. Alternatively the top is joined to the rear quarter panel by another smaller panel which is part of the roof assembly.

The stiffness of the roof is built in by the curvature given to it by the forming presses, while the reinforcements, consisting of small metal strips placed crosswise to the roof at intervals along the inside surface, serve to stiffen the front and rear edges of the windscreen and rear window frames. In some designs the roof panel may have a sliding roof built in (Figure 2.43) or a flip-up detachable sunroof incorporated.

2.5.11 Rear quarter panel or tonneau assembly

This is integral with the side frame assembly and has both inner and outer construction. The inner construction comprises the rear wheel arch and the rear seat heelboard assembly. This provides the support for the rear seat squab in a saloon car; if the vehicle is a hatchback or estate car, the two back seats will fold flat and the seat squabs will not need support. This area is known as the rear bulkhead of the car; it gives additional transverse strength between the wheel arch sections and provides support for the rear seat. The rear bulkhead also acts as a partition between the luggage and passenger compartments (Figure 2.43).

2.5.12 Rear wheel arch assembly

This assembly is constructed as an integral part of the inner construction of the rear quarter panel. It is usually a two-piece construction comprising the wheel arch and the quarter panel, which are welded together (Figure 2.42).

2.5.13 Wings

A wing is a part of the body which covers the wheel. Apart from covering the suspension construction, the wing prevents water and mud from being thrown up on to the body by the wheels. The front wings (or the fender assembly) are usually attached to the wing valance of the front-end assembly (see Figure 2.41) by means of a flange the length of the wing, which is turned inwards from the outer surface and secured by either welding or bolts. Adjustment for the front wing is usually provided for by slotting the bolt holes so that the wing can be moved either forwards or backwards by loosening the attaching bolts. This adjustment cannot be made if the wing is welded to the main body structure.

In some models the headlights and sidelights are recessed into the front wing and fastened in place by flanges and reinforcement rims on the wing. Any trim or chrome which appears on the side of the wing is usually held in place by special clips or fasteners which allow easy removal of the trim.

The unsupported edges of the wing are swaged edges known as beads. The bead is merely a flange which is turned inwards on some cars and then up to form a U-section with a rounded bottom. It not only gives strength but prevents cracks developing in the edges of the wing due to vibration, and it provides a smooth finished appearance to the edge of the wing.

In general the rear wing is an integral part of the body side frame assembly and rear quarter panel. When the wing forms an integral part of the quarter

---

(Facing page)
Figure 2.40 Body shell assembly (*Austin Rover Group Ltd*)

1 Underbody assembly	13 Back window upper rail panel assembly
2 Body side frame assembly	14 Rear-end upper panel assembly
3 Windscreen upper rail assembly	15 Radiator panel complete assembly
4 Cowl and dash panel assembly	16 Centre pillar (BC-post)
5 Front wheel house complete panel	17 D-post
6 Instrument panel assembly	18 Rear quarter assembly
7 Cowl side lower brace	19 Sill panel
8 Front body hinge pillar (A-post)	20 Front side member assembly
9 Roof panel assembly	21 Rear wheel arch assembly
10 Roof bow assembly	22 Main floor assembly
11 Bulkhead brace assembly	23 Front valance complete assembly
12 Rear quarter centre panel assembly (back window)	

Figure 2.41 Complete front-end assemblies (*Rover Group Ltd*)

1 Headlamp panel RH and LH
2 Front cross member closing panel
3 Front cross member
4 Bonnet lock panel
5 headlamp panel reinforcement RH and LH
6 Front wing corner piece RH and LH
7 Bonnet frame extension
8 Bonnet skin
9 Bonnet frame
10 Dash panel
11 Scuttle panel
12 Front bulkhead
13 Chassis leg reinforcement RH and LH
14 Front inner wing RH and LH
15 Front chassis leg RH and LH
16 Subframe mounting RH and LH
17 Front wheel arch RH and LH
18 Front wing RH and LH
19 Battery tray
20 Chassis leg gusset RH and LH
21 Bumper mounting reinforcement RH and LH
22 Chassis leg extention RH and LH
23 A-post rear reinforcement RH and LH
24 A-post front reinforcement RH and LH

Figure 2.42 Main floor assemblies and boot floor assemblies (*Rover Group Ltd*)

42 Boot lid skin
43 Boot lid frame
44 Boot lid lower skin
45 Boot lid striker reinforcement
46 Outer rear panel
47 Rear panel reinforcement
48 Boot floor
49 Rear chassis leg RH and LH
50 Inner sill rear extension RH and LH
51 Chassis leg reinforcement RH and LH
52 Rear suspension mounting
53 Centre chassis leg RH and LH

54 Inner sill RH and LH
55 Centre cross member
56 Main floor centre reinforcement
57 Centre tunnel reinforcement
58 Main floor
59 Heelboard
60 Rear suspension cross member
61 Rear seatbelt upper mounting RH and LH
62 Outer rear wheel arch RH and LH
63 Wheel arch gusset RH and LH
64 Inner rear wheel arch RH and LH
65 Rear suspension turret capping RH and LH

Figure 2.43 Body side assemblies, roof, BC-post, front and rear doors (*Rover Group Ltd*)

25 A-post RH and LH
26 A-post lower reinforcement RH and LH
27 A-post upper reinforcement RH and LH
28 Header rail
29 Roof panel
30 Sunroof frame
31 Roof rear cross member
32 Cantrail RH and LH
33 Body side assembly RH and LH

34 Front door frame RH and LH
35 Front door skin RH and LH
36 Front door crash rail RH and LH
37 Rear door frame RH and LH
38 Rear door skin RH and LH
39 Rear door crash rail RH and LH
40 Intermediate sill RH and LH
41 B-post reinforcement RH and LH

panel, the inner construction is used to form part of the housing around the wheel arch. The wheel arch is welded to the rear floor section and is totally concealed by the rear quarter panel, while the outer side of the wheel arch is usually attached to the quarter panel around the wheel opening. This assembly prevents road dirt being thrown upwards between the outer panel and inner panel construction.

2.5.14 Doors

Several types of door are used on each vehicle, although the construction of the various doors is similar regardless of the location of the door on the vehicle, as indicated on Figure 2.43. The door is composed of two main panels, an outer and an inner panel, both being of all-steel construction. The door derives most of its strength from the inner panel since this is constructed mainly to act as a frame for the door. The outer panel flanges over the inner panel around all its edges to form a single unit, which is then spot welded or, in some cases, bonded with adhesives to the frame.

The inner panel has holes or apertures for the attachment of door trim. This trim consists of the window regulator assembly and the door locking mechanism. These assemblies are installed through the large apertures in the middle of the inner panel. Most of the thickness of the door is due to the depth of the inner panel which is necessary to accommodate the door catch and window mechanism. The inner panel forms the lock pillar and also the hinge pillar section of the door. Small reinforcement angles are usually used between the outer and inner panel, both where the lock is inserted through the door and where the hinges are attached to the door. The outer panel is either provided with an opening through which the outside door handle protrudes, or is recessed to give a more streamlined effect and so to create better aerodynamics.

The upper portion of the door has a large opening which is closed by glass. The glass is held rigidly by the window regulator assembly, and when raised it slides in a channel in the opening between the outer and inner panels in the upper portion of the door. When fully closed the window seats tightly in this channel, effectively sealing out the weather.

2.5.15 Boot lid or tailgate

This is really another door which allows access to the luggage compartment in the rear of the car (Figure 2.42). A boot lid is composed of an outer and an inner panel. These panels are spot welded along their flanged edges to form a single unit in the same manner as an ordinary door. Hatchback and estate cars have a rear window built into the boot lid, which is then known as a tailgate. Some manufacturers use external hinges, while others use concealed hinges attached to the inner panel only. A catch is provided at the lower rear edge of the boot lid or tailgate and is controlled by an external handle or locking mechanism. This mechanism may be concealed from the eye under a moulding or some type of trim. In some models there is no handle or external locking mechanism; instead the hinges are spring loaded or use gas-filled piston supports, so that when the lid is unlocked internally it automatically rises and is held in the open position by these mechanisms.

2.5.16 Bonnet

The bonnet (Figure 2.41) is the panel which covers the engine compartment where this is situated at the front of the vehicle, or the boot compartment of a rear-engined vehicle. Several kinds of bonnet are in use on different makes of car. The bonnet consists of an outer panel and an inner reinforcement constructed in the H or cruciform pattern, which is spot welded to the outer skin panel at the flanged edges of the panels. The reinforcement is basically a top-hat section, to give rigidity to the bonnet. In some cases the outer panel is bonded to the inner panel using epoxy resins. This system avoids the dimpling effect on the outer surface of the bonnet skin which occurs in spot welding.

Early models used a jointed type of bonnet which was held in place by bolts through the centre section of the top of the bonnet into the body of the cowl and into the radiator. A piano-type hinge was used where the bonnet hinged both at the centre and at the side.

The most commonly used bonnet on later constructions is known as the mono or one-piece type, and can be opened by a variety of methods. On some types it is hinged at the front so that the rear end swings up when the bonnet is open. Others are designed so that they can be opened from either side, or unlatched from both sides and removed altogether. Most bonnets, however, are of the alligator pattern, which is hinged at the rear so that the front end swings up when opened.

The type of bonnet catch mechanism depends on the type of bonnet used. When a bonnet opens from the rear the catch mechanism is also at the rear. When it opens from either side the combination hinge and catch are provided at each side. Alligator bonnets have their catches at the front, and in most cases the catches are controlled from inside the car.

Bonnets are quite large, and to make opening easier

Figure 2.44 Exterior trim (*Rover Group Ltd*)

73 Lower front grille
74 Front spoiler
75 Front bumper
76 Front bumper insert
77 Front grille
78 Motif
81 Door mirror assembly
82 Scuttle grille

83 Scuttle moulding
84 Lower screen moulding
85 Rear bumper insert
86 Rear bumper
87 Rear wing waist moulding
88 Rear door waist moulding
89 Front door waist moulding
90 Front wing waist moulding

the hinges are usually counterbalanced by means of tension or torsion springs. Where smaller bonnets are used the hinges are not counterbalanced and the bonnet is held in place by a bonnet stay from the side of the wing to the bonnet. Adjustment of the bonnet position is sometimes possible by moving the hinges.

2.5.17 Trims

Some details of exterior and interior trims are shown in Figures 2.44 and 2.45.

2.5.18 Complete body shell

A contemporary vehicle embracing all the techniques of panel assembly is shown in Figures 2.46 and 2.47.

Figure 2.46 illustrates the completed structure with all panel assemblies in place. Figure 2.47 shows the completely finished vehicle ready for the road.

2.5.19 Comparative terms in common use by British, American and European car manufacturers

As manufacturers use differing terms for the various body panel assemblies and individual panels, difficulties may arise when identifying specific panels. The following are the terms in most common use:

Bonnet, hood
Boot lid, deck lid, trunk lid, tailgate

Figure 2.45 Interior trim (*Rover Group Ltd*)
 91 Front seat headrest
 92 Front seatbelt assembly
 93 Front seat cushion
 94 Front seatbelt centre stalk
 95 Front seat back rest
 96 Front seat head rest
 97 Rear seat back rest small section
 98 Rear seat centre aim rest
 99 Rear seatbelt buckle assembly
100 Rear seat back rest large section
101 Rear seat side bolster
102 Rear seatbelt lap assembly
103 Rear seat cushion
104 Rear seatbelt assembly
105 Main floor carpet

Cantrail, roof side rail, drip rail
Centre pillar, BC-post
Courtesy light, interior light
Cowl, scuttle, bulkhead, fire wall
Dash panel, facia panel
Door opening plates, scuff plates
Door skin, outside door panel
Face bar, bumper bar
Front pillar, A-post, windscreen pillar
Light, window
Quarter panel, tonneau assembly
Roof, turret
Roof lining, headlining
Sill panel, rocker panel
Squab, seat back
Underbody, floor pan assembly
Valance of front wing, fender side shield
Vent window, flipper window
Waist rail, belt rail
Wheel arch, wheel house
Windscreen, windshield
Wing, fender.

2.5.20 Vehicle identification numbers

The vehicle identification number (VIN) is stamped
on a plate located typically inside the engine compartment or on a door pillar. A VIN system is shown
in Figure 2.48. The figure also shows the paint and
trim codes which are usually included on the VIN
plate.

Figure 2.46 Complete body shell (*Rover Group Ltd*)

Figure 2.47 Rover 800 series (*Rover Group Ltd*)

Figure 2.48 Vehicle identification number

The car body number is provided separately in the engine or boot compartments.

QUESTIONS

1 Why were the earliest motor vehicle bodies made almost entirely of wood?
2 When and why did manufacturers commence to use metal for the construction of vehicle bodies?
3 Give a brief history of the development of the vehicle body style, illustrating the significant changes which have taken place.
4 What is meant by monocoque construction, and why has it become so popular in motor vehicle manufacture?
5 With the aid of sketches, describe the general principles of monocoque construction.
6 Describe, with the aid of sketches, the general principles of composite and integral methods of body construction.
7 Draw a sketch of a vehicle body shell and name all the major body panels.
8 State the location and function on a vehicle body of the following sections: (a) BC-post, (b) quarter panel, (c) wheel arch, (d) bonnet.
9 What is the most common form of vehicle body construction?
10 What are the alternatives to integral construction?
11 What is a load-bearing stressed panel assembly? Give examples.
12 What is a non-load-bearing panel assembly? Give examples.
13 Explain how rigidity and strength are achieved in monoconstruction.
14 Describe the location and function of the front and rear bulkheads.
15 Give a brief description of the following early vehicle body styles: coupé, cabriolet, limousine, saloon.
16 What is meant by a veteran vehicle? Name and describe three such vehicles.
17 Name two people who were associated with the early development of the motor vehicle, and state their involvement.
18 Explain what is meant by the semi-integral method of construction.
19 Explain why it is difficult to mass produce composite constructed vehicles.
20 In integral construction, what section of the body possesses the greatest amount of strength?
21 What is the front section of the body shell called, and what are its principal panel assemblies?
22 Explain the role of the stylist in the design organization.
23 Name one vehicle design stylist who has become well known during the last 25 years.
24 List the stages of development in the creation of a new vehicle body design.
25 State the definition of the symbol Cd.
26 Define the term CAD-CAM.
27 Explain the role of the clay modeller in the structure of the styling department.
28 With the aid of a sketch, explain what is meant by profile aerodynamic drag.

29 Explain the necessity for prototype testing.

30 Explain the use of dummies in safety research and testing.

31 Explain the difference in manufacture between a medium-bodied mass-produced vehicle and a high-quality coach-built limousine.

32 Describe the bodywork styling of a sports or GT vehicle.

33 What is the difference in design between a saloon and a hatchback vehicle?

34 With the aid of a sketch, explain the body styling of a coupé vehicle.

35 Explain ABS as an active safety feature on a vehicle.

36 How are vehicles made safe against side impact involvement?

37 Explain how the airbag system works in a vehicle.

38 Explain the VIN number and why it is used on a vehicle.

39 Name the two main types of seatbelt arrangement which are fitted to a standard saloon vehicle.

40 State the letters used in design to identify the body pillars on a four-door saloon.

41 State the main purpose of a vehicle subframe.

42 Explain why seatbelt anchorages must be reinforced on a vehicle body.

43 State why GRP bodywork is normally associated with separate body construction.

44 List the design features that characterize a vehicle body as a limousine.

45 Explain the necessity for a hydraulic damper in the suspension of a motor vehicle.

46 Why is GRP not used in the mass production of vehicle body shells on an assembly line?

47 Name one of the persons associated with the early development of the mass production of the motor vehicle and state his involvement.

48 State the purposes of the inner reinforcement members of a bonnet panel and say how they are held in place.

49 State the reasons for swaging certain areas of a vehicle floor pan.

50 Explain the importance of the use of scale models in vehicle design.

3

Hand and power tools

3.1 HAND TOOLS USED IN BODY REPAIR WORK

Mass production methods have made the present day motor car such that it requires special techniques, skills and tools for the rectification of body damage. Specialist tools have been designed to suit the varying contours and shapes of the present all-steel bodies and panels. These tools are made of high-carbon tool steel, which is forged and then heat treated to give long service in the hands of a skilled body repair worker. In a body repair toolkit the basic tools are the hammer and dolly. All other tools have been developed around these, giving us the specialist tools which are now currently available. A repair job cannot be successfully carried out before one has completely mastered the skill of using the planishing hammer and dolly in coordination with each other, as this skill is the basis of all body repair work involving the use of hand tools.

Sections 3.2 to 3.8 describe body repair hand tools.

3.2 HAMMERS

Planishing hammer
The planishing or panel hammer is used more than any other tool in the body repair trade, and for this reason the best hammer available should be obtained. The principal purpose of the panel hammer is for the smoothing and finalizing of a panel surface after it has been roughed out to the required shape. The planishing hammer should have a true and unmarked face, and it must be kept polished and free from road tar, underseal and paint, which readily adhere to its working faces during use. This tool is designed solely to be used in conjunction with a dolly block; it must never be used for chiselling or any other work which might mark or impair the faces of the hammer, for if the face of the hammer became marked the marks would be transferred to the surface of the panel.

These particular hammers are generally made with one face square. This face is usually flat, while the other, round end is slightly domed or crowned. However, hammers are available with the square end domed and the round end flat, or alternatively with both faces flat or both faces crowned. In practice, the square end, which is usually flat, is used for planishing on a curved surface of a panel, or in corners, or against swaged recessed sections, and the crowned end for reasonably flat panels. The difference in the faces stops the panel surface being marked with the edge of the hammer when used in conjunction with the dolly block. The weight of the planishing hammer for general and new work ranges from 12 oz (340 g) to 16 oz (450 g), and the handles, which are usually very thin at the neck of the shaft for balance purposes, are made of hickory or ash to give the hammer a good rebound action when used with a dolly block.

Standard bumping hammer
This hammer (Figure 3.1a, b) is used for initial roughing out of work on damaged panels. It is also used for finalizing and finishing. The round face is $1\frac{3}{8}$ in (35 mm) in diameter and the square face is $1\frac{1}{2}$ in (38 mm) square, and the total weight is 14 oz (395 g). The hammer is made with either flat or crowned faces.

Light bumping hammer
This tool (Figure 3.1c, d) is ideal for work on light-gauge materials. It is used in the same manner as the standard bumping hammer. The squared face is 1 in (25 mm) square and the round face is $1\frac{1}{4}$ in (32 mm) in diameter, and it has a weight of 12 oz (340 g). This hammer is also obtainable in flat or crowned faces.

Dinging hammer
This hammer (Figure 3.2a, b) is a long-reach planishing hammer and is designed for careful, controlled finishing work. It is extremely well balanced and gives a very good finish when used correctly. Hammers can be obtained for light or heavy work with weights from 12 oz (340 g) to 18 oz (510 g).

Shrinking hammers
Shrinking hammers (Figure 3.2c, d, e) are similar in design to a normal planishing hammer but have faces which, instead of being smooth, are serrated, giving a cross-milled effect like a file. The purpose of these serrations is to achieve a shrinking effect when the hammer is used in conjunction with a dolly block.

Figure 3.1 (a) Standard bumping hammer (crowned faces (b) standard bumping hammer (flat faces) (c) light bumping hammer (crowned faces) (d) light bumping hammer (flat faces) (*Sykes-Pickavant Ltd*)

Figure 3.2 (a) Heavy dinging hammer (flat faces) (b) light dinging hammer (crowned faces) (c) heavy shrinking hammer (serrated flat face) (d) light shrinking hammer (milled flat face) (e) light shrinking hammer (shallow milled flat faces) (*Sykes-Pickavant Ltd*)

This is caused by the fact that the contact area between hammer and metal is greatly reduced by the serrations on the face. This tool is used largely when beating the surface on overstretched panel areas which have to be hot-shrunk in order to return them to their normal contours. Hammers are available for light or heavy shrinking, according to the depth of the serrations.

Pick and finishing hammer
This tool (Figure 3.3a, b) is used in place of, or in conjunction with, the planishing hammer. Its main use is to pick up small, low areas on the surface of a panel which is in the process of being repaired by planishing. On panels that are reasonably flat, such as door panels, parts of roof panels and bonnets, this method of raising low areas is quick and, if carried out correctly, does not unduly stretch the metal. To lift a low area with a pick hammer, one or two taps with the pick end of the hammer are directed from underneath the panel under repair to the centre of the low area. The blows stretch the metal sufficiently to raise the surface surrounding the point of the low spots where the blows were struck. This slightly raised area is next tapped down lightly with a planishing hammer or the finishing end of the pick hammer on to a suitably shaped dolly block, and the panel is finished off by filing with a panel file. When one becomes proficient in using this tool it is possible to raise the surface with light blows and finish off by filing only. However, without sufficient experience there is a danger of overstretching the metal owing to the inability to direct the blow accurately on to the low area under repair.

The pick and finishing hammer has a pointed end which is suitable for removing low spots and is also a useful finishing hammer, having a crowned surface on a round face of $1\frac{1}{2}$ in (38 mm) diameter; it is well balanced and weighs 14 oz (395 g).

Straight pein and finishing hammers
These hammers (Figure 3.3c, d) are used in a similar manner to the pick and finishing hammer, but are designed with either a straight or a curved peined end which acts like a chisel, and a domed round end which is used for planishing. They are suitable for roughing out prior to planishing, or in the finishing stages of planishing for stretching small low areas. These hammers can be used to dress out sections which are difficult to work on owing to their awkward shape or position, such as around lamp openings and in recessed and moulded sections on panels.

Curved pein and finishing hammer
This tool (Figure 3.3e) is identical in use to the straight pein and finishing hammer except that its curved pein end allows for greater flexibility in dressing out sections which are difficult to work on owing to their awkward shape or position.

Figure 3.3 (a) Pick and finishing hammer (crowned face) (b) pick and finishing hammer (flat face) (c) straight pein and finishing hammer (crowned face) (d) straight pein and finishing hammer (flat face) (e) curved pein and finishing hammer (crowned face) (f) fender bumping hammer (*Sykes-Pickavant Ltd*)

Figure 3.4 Beating files (*Sykes-Pickavant Ltd*)

Fender bumping hammer

This tool (Figure 3.3f) has a long curved head with one face which is circular to reduce the effect of stretching the metal when in use. This hammer is used for roughing out and dressing out damaged sections on panels to restore them to their correct shape and curvature before planishing begins. The heavy weight of this hammer, together with the curve, makes it very effective for hammering out difficult and inaccessible sections.

File hammer or beating file

This tool (Figure 3.4) is designed to be used like a hammer in conjunction with a dolly block, although it is actually a file with a serrated face and is suitably shaped for holding in the hand. The milling on the file blade tends to shrink the panel as well as leaving a regular rough patterned surface ideal for locating low spots on the panel under repair and for finishing with a body file. The tool is used in conjunction with a hand dolly, and with a glancing blow. It is most effective on large flat sections, where it will be found ideal for smoothing and levelling out wavy panels. Two types of beating file are available; one is flat for use on low- and high-crowned surfaces, while the other is half-round in shape and is used on convex or reverse-curved panel sections.

Mallets

Mallets can be of the round or pear-shaped type made from boxwood or lignum vitae, or can be rubber, aluminium or plastic faced (Figure 3.5). Some mallets have interchangeable heads so that the correct head can be used for the material being worked. A mallet is greatly used in the initial stages of smoothing and roughing out of a panel prior to planishing. When hot shrinking, the mallet is the tool to achieve a most successful shrink because a normal planishing hammer would tend to stretch the metal rather than shrink it. Without a mallet, aluminium work would be most difficult as this metal is so easily marked and stretched. The working faces of the mallet must be kept in first-class order, or marks on the surface of the metal will result.

3.3 HAND DOLLIES

These are either cast or drop forged steel blocks, heat treated to provide the correct degree of hardness. The shapes of the dolly blocks have been designed to provide a working surface that is highly polished and suitable for use on the many contours found on motor vehicle bodies. They are used in conjunction with the

Figure 3.6 (a) Shrinking dolly (b) lightweight curved dolly or comma block (c) regular dolly (d) toe dolly (e) round dolly (f) heel dolly (*Sykes-Pickavant Ltd*)

Figure 3.5 Mallets (*Sykes-Pickavant Ltd*)

planishing hammer or beating file and act as a support or anvil to smooth out the surface area of panels that have been damaged. These dollies, together with the planishing hammers, are the most essential tools for the panel beating trade. Obviously one dolly block will not be suitable for all shapes requiring planishing; therefore it is advisable to have a set of these dollies which would be suitable for a wide range of the shapes and contours encountered on the ever-changing body styles of the modern motor vehicle.

When selecting a dolly block for a particular job, it should always be remembered that a dolly block should be used which is as flat as possible for the job in hand; then the dolly will not only cover the panel area quicker because of its bigger face area, but will smooth out the metal without excessive stretching. When working on panel contours it must be borne in mind that a dolly block having a high-crowned surface will tend to stretch the metal much quicker than one having a low-crowned surface; hence the choice of block depends on whether the particular section under repair needs to be stretched quickly or just smoothed and planished without stretching.

It is very common for the faces of the dolly blocks to become coated with paint, road tar, or anti-drum

compounds which it picks up from the underside of panels under repair. This coating must be removed from the surface of the dolly block so that when it is used with the hammer there is a metallic contact (metal to metal) between dolly block and work and hammer. This contact should be heard as a ringing noise if successful planishing is to be achieved.

Various dollies are shown in Figures 3.6 and 3.7. Some details are as follows.

Double-ended hand dolly is conveniently designed for a good grip with two useful surfaces, one high crowned and one low crowned. It is ideal for general planishing and roughing out. Its weight is 3 lb 4 oz (1473 g).

Utility dolly forms the basis of every body kit. It offers a variety of useful faces, and is found ideal for working in confined spaces.

General-purpose dolly is very well shaped and easy to hold and offers wide, low-crowned faces which are essential when working on the new body styles. Its weight is 2 lb 12 oz (1247 g).

Heel dolly has a low flat face with radiused corners. It is suitable for corner and angle work and is easy to handle because of its fairly small weight of 2 lb 14 oz (1020 g).

Toe dolly combines a large flat face with a low crown on other faces and is long and thin for easy handling in narrow sections. The bottom face is ground flat which adds to the versatility of this block. Its weight is 3 1b (1360 g).

Figure 3.7 (a) Thin toe dolly (b) angle dolly (c) utility dolly (d) general-purpose dolly (e) grid dolly (f) double-ended dolly (g) curved dolly or comma block (*Sykes-Pickavant Ltd*)

Figure 3.8 (a) Surface spoon (b) general-purpose spoon (c) high-crowned spoon (d) drip moulding spoon (*Sykes-Pickavant Ltd*)

Thin toe dolly has similar surfaces to the toe dolly but is thinner and is ideal for working in awkward places where other dollies cannot be used. Its weight is 2 lb 4 oz (1020 g).

Shrinking dolly block is designed for shrinking welded seams and reducing stretched areas prior to filling. It has a groove down the centre of the block into which the stretched or welded seams can be dressed. Its weight is 3 lb (1360 g).

Grid dolly is similar in shape to the toe dolly but has a large crowned grid face on the upper surface. The base has a plain flat face for normal finishing work. It has been designed to act as a shrinking dolly when used in combination with a shrinking hammer and the application of heat. The weight is 2 lb 4 oz (1130 g).

Curved dolly or comma block has a long curved face, combined with the high- and low-crowned areas and the tapering face; it is extremely well suited to the modern body design, and is comfortable to hold in difficult areas and narrow corners. The weight is 3 lb 6 oz (1530 g).

Round dolly is light and small and very easy to hold. It offers high- and low-crowned faces for work on small areas of damage. The weight is 1 lb 10 oz (736 g).

3.4 BODY SPOONS

These tools are made from a high-grade steel which has been drop forged and heat treated. They are sometimes called prying spoons because the spoon end is used in the same manner as a dolly in conjunction with a hammer. The body spoon really does the same job as a dolly block but is designed for use in confined spaces where a normal dolly block cannot be held in the hand, e.g. between door frames and outer door panels. The spoon end, which acts as the dolly, must be kept in good condition and free from anti-drum compound so that it gives a metal-to-metal contact when used in conjunction with a hammer. The spoon can also be used for roughing or easing out by wedging the spoon in between panels.

Surface spoon (Figure 3.8a) has an extra large working area which is very slightly crowned, and it is ideal for working in between and round struts and brackets without much dismantling.

General-purpose spoon (Figure 3.8b) is a double-ended body spoon and is also a basic item in most panel beaters' toolkits. The applications for a spoon offering such different curves are many and varied and meet the needs of modern body shapes. High-crowned spoon (Figure 3.8c) has been designed to

Figure 3.9 (a) Spring hammering spoon (b) heavy-duty pry spoon (c) pry and surfacing spoon (d) long-reach dolly spoon (e) thin spoon (*Sykes-Pickavant Ltd*)

offer a broad working blade with a high crown to work in positions where other dollies and spoons cannot be used.

Drip moulding spoon (Figure 3.8d) has a special lip which can be hooked under the drip moulding of the roof section and hence simplifies the repair. The curved surface is fully finished to enable the tool to be used as a short standard spoon.

Spring hammering spoon (Figure 3.9a) is a light pressed steel spoon which is designed for spring hammering on panels which have minor blemishes in their finishing stages. The broad blade spreads the blow evenly over a larger contact area, thereby reducing the possibility of sinking the metal. This spoon is not made for prying or levering.

Heavy-duty pry spoon (Figure 3.9b) is ideal for heavy prying and roughing-out work. It has a long low curved blade which can be inserted into very thin sections.

Pry and surfacing spoon (Figure 3.9c) has a short handle which gives easy access in limited spaces and can be used efficiently for prying behind brackets and panel edges.

Long-reach dolly spoon (Figure 3.9d) is a special long-handled body spoon designed to be used in restricted spaces between double-skinned panels such as doors and quarter panels.

Thin spoon (Figure 3.9e) is a very special thin-bladed spoon, the blade having a very slow taper which permits entry into restricted spaces between double-skinned panels which would not be possible by using a normal spoon.

3.5 BODY FILES

Flexible panel file
This tool (Figure 3.10a) is designed with a two position handle, and has a 14 in (30 cm) spring steel backing plate to give adequate support over the whole blade. Positioned between the two hand grips is a turnscrew threaded left and right hand for adjusting the blade to concave or convex positions to suit the user's requirements. The main use of this tool is to assist in the final planishing of the work. First and most important, it locates areas which are low on the surface of the panel under repair; second, it files out small marks or defects on the panel surface. It can be adapted to file the surface of almost any shaped panel by setting the blade either straight, concave or convex. The file blades are specially designed so that they do not remove too much metal, and the milled serrations are wide apart and curved to prevent clogging when filing metal which has been painted, soldered or plastic filled. It is important to release the tension on the file blade after use in order to reduce the risk of breakage if it is dropped or struck by accident.

Flat file
This file (Figure 3.10b) has a solid wood holder designed to take a standard 14 in (30 cm) blade, which must be used in a rigid position.

Half-round bodyfile
This tool (Figure 3.10c) is similar in design to the flat file but the blade is half-round. It is very useful for curved surfaces.

Abrasive file
This file (Figure 3.10d) is not a normal file but an abrasive holder with a wood handle having spring clips at either end on to which can be attached abrasive grit paper. This tool is of greatest use when rubbing down plastic body fillers to their final finish.

Body file blades
These flexible, double-sided blades are produced from a special alloy steel and heat treated. The milled teeth allow a smooth filing operation and are specially shaped to reduce clogging. The blades are either flat or radiused according to the surface to be filed.

(a)

(b)

(c)

(d)

Figure 3.10 (a) Flexible panel file (b) flat file (c) half-round body file (d) abrasive file (*Sykes-Pickavant Ltd*)

Supercut blades are 8 tpi (teeth per inch) general-purpose standard blades.

Standard cut blades are 9 tpi and used for soft metals such as lead and solder fillers.

Fine cut blades are 13 tpi and used for aluminium, copper and brass.

Extra fine cut blades are 17 tpi and suitable for cast iron, steel or any narrow section of metal.

Plasticut blades are 6.5 tpi and used for plastic body fillers only.

3.6 HAND SNIPS

The offset combination of universal snips is preferred by the panel beater when cutting thin gauge metal. Universal snips (Figure 3.11a, b) are suitable for cutting straight lines, outside and inside curves. A right- and left-hand pair of combination snips will be suitable for most of the sheet metal cutting that will be encountered by the panel beater, and there is no need for any curved-blade snips. When the more popular right-hand snips are used, the waste metal forms a coil to the left of the cutting blades, thus causing little distortion to the surface of the sheet or panel being cut; similarly, with the left-hand pair of snips the waste metal passes to the right of the cutting blades, leaving the undistorted sheet or panel on the left. Snips can be obtained in varying sizes with either straight or crank handles. A straight pair of snips is often necessary for long straight cuts (Figure 3.11c). Section 3.15.1 gives further information on hand snips.

3.7 SPECIALIST PANEL BEATING TOOLS

Panel puller
This tool (Figure 3.12) comprises a long steel rod with a cross T-piece at the top which acts as a hand grip. At the other end a fixed hexagonal nut holds a strong self-tapping screw, while a heavy cylindrical weight can slide up and down the shaft against a stop which is near the handle. This tool has been designed to pull out dents and creases from the face side of the panel without the necessity of removing the trim and lining materials to gain access behind the dents. It can also be used on double-skinned panels where access is impossible with conventional tools.

The panel puller is used by drilling a $\frac{1}{8}$ in (3.175 mm) diameter hole at the deepest part of the dent, then inserting the self-tapping screw in the hole and screwing it until a firm grip is obtained. One hand holds the T-bar while the other pulls the sliding weight towards the stop; there the weight rebounds, forcing the dented panel out under the impact of the blow.

Zipcut spot-weld remover
The Zipcut spot-weld remover (Figure 3.13) is used with an electric or air drill, and is ideal for removing spot welds on all areas of bodywork and subframes. The cutter blade A is reversible with two cutting edges.

| (a) | (b) | (c) |

Figure 3.11 (a) Universal combination snips RH (b) universal combinations snips LH (c) standard pattern straight snips (*Sykes-Pickavant Ltd*)

Figure 3.12 Panel pullers (*Sykes-Pickavant Ltd*)

Adjustment B provides for varying depth of cut so that only the upper panel C is released, leaving the original spot weld behind on the lower panel.

Cone drills or variable hole cutters
These are special alloy steel drill bits which have been hardened to give a fine cutting edge (Figure 3.14a). They are shaped like a cone and fit in the chuck of a standard power drill. The hole diameter can vary from 6 to 40 mm depending on the hole cutter in use. These cutters are used for fitting wing mirrors, aerials and rubber grommets into body structures.

Cobalt drills or spot drills
These are special alloy steel drills to which cobalt has been added to give a very hard sharp cutting edge (Figure 3.14b). The design of the cutting edge allows spot welds to be drilled out of panel assemblies without creating any panel distortion.

Impact driver
The impact driver (Figure 3.15) will loosen or tighten the most stubborn screws, nuts and bolts. The tool is

Figure 3.13 Zipcut spot-weld remover (*Sykes-Pickavant Ltd*)

(a)   (b)

Figure 3.14 (a) Cone drills or variable hold cutters (b) cobalt drills or spot drills (*Sykes-Pickavant Ltd*)

Figure 3.15 Impact driver (*Sykes-Pickavant Ltd*)

supplied with a complete range of interchangeable bits.

Body trim tool
This is a universal spring steel tool for removing body trims and clips, and also weather strips, door trims, headlamp fittings, windscreen clips, plastic mouldings, motifs and badges (Figure 3.16a).

Door handle spring clip removers
These are specially designed pliers for fitting or removing the spring clips used on many modern door

handles. One jaw sets in the neck of the spring while the other grips the other end, and the whole spring is then levered out (Figure 3.16b).

Trim panel remover

This tool is designed to remove vehicle trim panels, upholstery and roof liners without damage (Figure 3.16c). It also fits a wide variety of button-type fasteners used on vehicle trim.

Door hinge pin remover and replacer

This is designed for the removal and replacement of hollow hinge pins used on vehicle door hinges (Figure 3.16d).

Corrosion assessment tool

This tool has been designed for vehicle inspection (Figure 3.16e). It acts as a combined tapping hammer, blunt scraper and short lever. It has been introduced to standardize the methods of corrosion assessment employed by MOT testers, and is ideal for bodyshops conducting pre-MOT checks and assessment for corrosion.

Bendable file

This tool is a standard round file but it can be bent to the desired shape, which allows it to be used in difficult locations where a normal straight file would not have easy access (Figure 3.16f).

Clamps

Sheet metal clamp (Figure 3.17a) is a general purpose clamp which can be locked on to sheet metal with a powerful quick-release grip, making panel assembly and tack welding procedures much easier operations.

Welding clamp (Figure 3.17b) has a powerful grip which holds parts in alignment while leaving both hands free for the welding operation. The deep-throated jaws and centre opening provide the operator with maximum visibility and full access to the welding area.

C clamp (Figure 3.17c, d) has a wide jaw opening with a relatively small gripping area, which produces pressure without permanent jaw damage to panel surfaces. It allows accurate close-up working in restricted areas and on awkward shapes, e.g. still panels.

Figure 3.16 (a) Body trim tool (b) door handle spring clip remover (c) trim panel remover (d) door hinge pin remover and replacer (e) corrosion assessment tool (f) bendable files (*Sykes-Pickavant Ltd*)

81

Figure 3.17 (a) Sheet metal clamp (b) welding clamp (c) extra large C clamp (d) C clamp (*Sykes-Pickavant Ltd*)

(a)   (b)

Figure 3.18 (a) Hole punch (b) wing punch (*Sykes-Pickavant Ltd*)

Punches
Hole punches (Figure 3.18a) have interchangeable heads to punch holes of either $\frac{3}{16}$ in (5 mm) or $\frac{1}{4}$ in (6 mm) diameter, and enable joining panels to be accurately aligned for welding. The $\frac{3}{16}$ in (5 mm) diameter hole is for gas welding or brazing and the $\frac{1}{4}$ in (6 mm) hole is for MIG welding.

Wing punch (Figure 3.18b) is a hole punch with a specially designed head which allows it to be used on wing panels and channel sections and also fits over roof gutters and wheel arches.

Edge setters
The edge setter (Figure 3.19a) is a portable, hand-operated tool designed to provide a 'joggled' joint or stepped edge on a repaired or new panel, thus creating a flush-fitting lap joint. The joggled panel edge provides a stiff joint and helps prevent distortion when welding. It can be used on mild steel up to 1.2 mm (18 gauge) and applied in many situations which require this type of joint.

The Rolastep edge setter (Figure 3.19b) is a portable tool used on the vehicle or a panel assembly. Its rollers produce a smooth, uniform stepped panel edge to create a flush-fitting lap joint, allowing a panel replacement to be inserted.

Door skinner
This is a special tool (Figure 3.20) for crimping flanges tightly on replacement door skins. It is used by first bending the flange to an acute angle and then tightening or crimping the flange to the door frame. During this operation, interchangeable tough nylon pads prevent damage to the surface of the door skin.

Inter-grip welding clamp
The inter-grip clamp is approximately 25 mm cube shaped, and uses a wing nut and toggle bar to firmly clamp pieces of metal together edge to edge and perfectly level, leaving only a small gap which will allow full penetration of the weld and filler rod (Figure 3.21). Once the two sections are tack welded together the wing nut is slackened, the toggle bar removed and the clamp lifted from the job, prior to final welding. The end result is a first-class butt weld requiring very little dressing. The clamps are ideal when welding patch repairs in floors, wings and door skinning, or when assembling fabricated or new panels.

Temporary sheet metal fastener system
This sheet metal holding system is a set of pins, installed with special pliers, which quickly and easily clamps panels together before final welding, bonding or riveting (Figure 3.22). The clamps will securely hold together body panels and sections where no other clamp will reach because there is no rear access. The 3 mm blind fasteners have an expanding pin which,

(a)

(b)

Figure 3.19 (a) Edge setter (b) Rolastep edge setter (*Sykes-Pickavant Ltd*)

Figure 3.20 Door skinner (*Sykes-Pickavant Ltd*)

Figure 3.21 Inter-grip welding clamps (*Frost Auto Restoration Techniques Ltd*)

when inserted through the panel and released, exerts over 8 kg (18 lb) holding pressure. The edge grips have 12 mm deep jaws to clamp flanges and other edge work. To install or remove either, the pliers are needed to overcome the powerful spring pressure.

3.8 RECOMMENDED BASIC TOOLKITS FOR PANEL BEATERS

The pride of the craftsman is the set of tools he possesses. Care of tools throughout their working life is important. All bright surfaces should be kept clean and free from scours and blemishes that could be transferred to the body panels. Stowage of tools when not in use is also important, but this will depend on the working conditions in the bodyshop. Wall boards with the necessary clips and tool silhouettes can be used with a specified set of tools. This is ideal for general usage from a central store, as missing tools can be quickly identified. Metal toolboxes are most useful when each worker maintains his own toolkit.

The apprentice, improver and tradesman will each collect his or her own basic toolkit: suggested sets are shown in Figures 3.23, 3.24 and 3.25 respectively.

3.9 HAND TOOLS USED IN THE FABRICATION OF SHEET METAL

The panel beater often finds the need to fabricate articles or components in mild steel, using specialist hand tools. This need usually arises when replacement panels and sections are not readily available. These specialist tools are also frequently used in the coach-building industry during the construction of new vehicles.

Sections 3.10 to 3.16 cover fabrication tools.

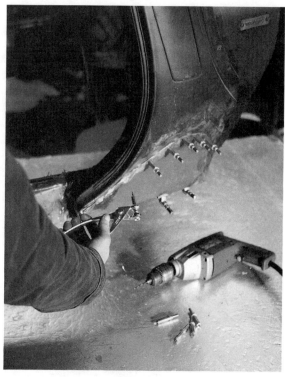

(a)

(b)

Figure 3.22 Temporary sheet metal fastener: (a) system (b) in use (*Frost Auto Restoration Techniques Ltd*)

Figure 3.23 Apprentice basic toolkit (*Sykes-Pickavant Ltd*)

3.10 HAMMERS AND MALLETS

3.10.1 Hammers

Hammers (Figure 3.26) are still the most important forming tools as far as the body worker is concerned, and from the commencement of his career he should attempt to acquire a skilful hammering technique. The essential points to look for when hammering are first, to hold the hammer correctly, gripping the shaft firmly but not tightly and towards the shank end in order to take full advantage of its length. Second, the action should be produced by the wrist rather than the forearm, and as strength is developed in the wrist it will be found that it is possible to control the hammer under all circumstances. The hammer head should only be swung sufficiently to ensure that the metal is struck where required using the correct amount of force.

Engineer's ball-pein hammer
This is a general purpose hammer. Its main uses are for riveting, chiselling, forming angles and brackets, planishing heavy welds to refine their structure and flattening heavy-gauge plate. The hammer has one end round and flat and the other a rounded ball-pein,

84

Figure 3.24 Improver basic toolkit (*Sykes-Pickavant Ltd*)

Figure 3.25 Tradesman basic toolkit (*Sykes-Pickavant Ltd*)

and it usually has an ash handle fitted into the head. It is made in a variety of weights to suit individual needs.

Stretching and flanging hammer
This is used to form external and internal flanges on curved surfaces by hand. The hammer is curved with two rounded cross-peins which allow blows to be struck at right angles in the direction of stretching. By tilting the hammer very slightly it is possible to gain maximum stretching on the outside of curved work. This hammer is designed for turning small flanges on highly curved work and is normally used in conjunction with a stake.

Wiring hammer
This is designed for closing thin-gauge metal over wire to form wired edges. The head of the hammer is curved and has two very sharp chisel-like cross-peins which allow it access to tuck down the metal around the wired edge. It can be used for either straight or curved wiring, and is used extensively in the manufacture of wings made for heavy transport.

Hollowing or blocking hammer
This is a shaping hammer which has two ball-pein ends and is rather heavy. It is designed to be used on mild steel in conjunction with a sandbag or wood hollowing block, and to create a double-curved shape by hand. The hammer is used on the initial stages of shaping metal, the component normally being planished or wheeled to its final shape.

3.10.2 Mallets

Mallets (Figure 3.27) come in two shapes.

Round-faced mallets
These are used in conjunction with steel stakes for forming and shaping. There are two types of mallet – boxwood and rawhide. The latter is made in strips which are rolled and pinned in position. Usually rawhide is used on aluminium and the lighter metals as it gives a softer blow than boxwood and is less liable to mark the metal. The boxwood type is an all-purpose mallet and can be used on either mild steel or aluminium with equal success.

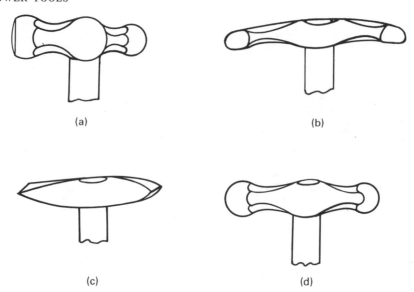

(a)

(b)

(c)

(d)

Figure 3.26 (a) Engineer's ball-pein hammer (b) stretching and flanging hammer (c) wiring hammer (d) hollowing or blocking hammer

Figure 3.27 Round-faced mallet, pear-shaped mallet and sandbags (*F. J. Edwards Ltd*)

When using a round-faced mallet the metal should be struck as squarely as possible to avoid wear on one side of the face. Care should also be taken to avoid striking the raw edges of sheet metal, as these could split the mallet head or damage the faces. At all times the faces of these mallets must be kept smooth, true and free from marks as these could be automatically transferred on to the workpiece.

Pear-shaped mallets
These are usually made in boxwood or lignum vitae which is a very hard wood and hence is ideally suitable for this type of work. The mallet is used in conjunction with a sandbag or wood block for either hollowing or raising when shaping metal by hand to a double curvature shape. The high-crowned end of the mallet is used for hollowing into a sandbag and the small-radiused end of the pear shape is used for

glancing blows as used in raising. The mallet is normally used on aluminium and thin-gauge mild steel. Care should be taken not to allow the faces of the mallet to become damaged when in use.

3.11 SANDBAGS AND HARDWOOD BLOCKS

Sandbags are leather bags made from two pieces of the finest quality leather, filled with very fine sand and stitched together. They are available in a variety of weights and sizes but are usually round or square in shape (Figure 3.27). The sandbag is used with the pear-shaped mallet or the blocking hammer to create panels by hand to a double curvature shape. The sandbag is resilient and at each blow of the mallet allows the metal to shape into the sandbag.

In some instances hardwood blocks are hollowed out to different depths and diameters. These blocks are used in the same manner as the sandbag for shaping metal, although the blocks are more solid and do not 'give' as much as the resilient sandbags.

3.12 SHEET METAL BENCH STAKES

Quite often when making panels and parts of panels in sheet metal, it is necessary to perform some operation such as bending, flanging, seaming, shaping and planishing which cannot be done by machine. In such cases these operations will have to be carried out by hand using bench stakes. There are many different types of stake in use; the smaller types are usually made from cast steel, the heavier are of cast iron, and for special work stainless-steel stakes may be used.

All these stakes must have highly polished working surfaces and should be kept in a dry atmosphere to reduce the possibility of corrosion on the working surface. Certain stakes are used only occasionally, and to maintain a bright, smooth surface they must be given a coating of light oil from time to time. The condition of the stakes has much to do with the workmanship of the finished job, for if a stake has been roughened by hammer or chisel marks the completed job will look rough and lack finish. For this reason stakes should not be used to 'back up' a sheet of metal or a panel directly when cutting it with a chisel; hammer blows should be aimed with care, and a mallet should be used whenever possible when forming sheet metal over the stakes.

Special reinforced square holes of various sizes are made at intervals in the bench for insertion of the bases of the stakes, which are usually square in cross-section and taper in shape to facilitate a good grip in the bench. There are many different types of stake available, and those most commonly used are as follows (Figure 3.28):

Pipe stake consists of one or two cylindrical arms having different diameters. This stake is used for forming pipes and cylindrical workpieces.

Grooving stake has a grooved slot cut along the top face. The slots are used for wiring and swaging.

Funnel stake has a thick tapered head and is used in forming, riveting and seaming tapered articles such as funnels.

Anvil stake has a flat, square-shaped head with a short shank and is used for general working operations.

Side stake consists of one long elliptical-shaped head. It is used for bending, seaming and forming curved radii.

Beck iron stake has a square tapering flat head on one side and a round tapered head on the other side. It serves as a general purpose anvil for riveting and shaping round and flat surfaces, straight bending and corner seams.

Horse stake with heads has holders (the horse part of the stake) which can take various shaped small heads. This stake is useful in many operations for which other stakes are not suitable.

Round-bottom stake consists of a single vertical piece with a flat round head on top. It is used for flanging circular and curved work.

Tinman's mandrel is a single horizontal metal bar, one section of which has a flat surface and the other section of which is rounded. The flat length has a slot cut in it which permits the stake to be fastened directly to the bench. The stake is used for riveting, seaming and forming.

Half-moon stake consists of a single vertical shank with a half-rounded head on top. The stake is used for forming or shaping curved flanges.

Hatchet stake consists of a horizontal, sharp, straight edge, and is used for making straight sharp bends.

Panel head stake is shaped like a mushroom and is made in various sizes. It is used for raising, tucking and planishing.

Ball stake is shaped like a ball and is used for the planishing of hollowed or raised articles. It is also used for raising domes or hemispherical shapes by mallet or raising hammer.

3.13 HAND GROOVING TOOLS

The hand groover is used when making a seam joint by hand between two pieces of sheet metal. The end of the tool is recessed to fit over the joint formed when the edges of the two pieces of metal are prebent into a U-shape and interlocked. The grooving tool is then placed over the interlocked edges and hammered. One edge of the tool acts as a guide while the other forces the metal down into a crease, thus forming a groove. This crease or set in the metal should be made gradually, the tool being hammered while tilted very slightly in the direction in which the crease is to be made. This will avoid marking the metal on the opposite side of the joint to the crease. A tool a size larger than that of the grooved joint should be chosen to give clearance in use. The tools are manufactured in various sizes from $\frac{1}{8}$ in to $\frac{3}{4}$ in (3 to 19 mm). These grooved joints can be used to advantage when fastening large flat panels together as used on commercial vehicles.

3.14 RIVET SETS

A rivet set is made of tool steel. A deep hole in the bottom of the set is used to draw the rivet through the metal sheet before riveting, and a cup-shaped hole is used to form the finished head on the rivet. The drawing-up hole and the cup hole are offset slightly to the direction of the vertical hammer blows, and therefore great care should be taken to hold the set in an upright position when riveting. If the tool is allowed to

Figure 3.28 Sheet metal bench stakes
1 Beck iron take
2 Horse stake with heads
3 Round-bottom stake
4 Half-moon stake
5 Tinman's mandrel
6 Hatchet stake
7 Pipe stake
8 Anvil stake
9 Side stake
10 Funnel stake
11 Grooving stake

Figure 3.29 Aviation snips (*Frost Auto Restoration Techniques Ltd*)

tilt it is liable to make indentations on the area of the metal which has been riveted. Hand rivet sets are made in various sizes ranging from $\frac{1}{8}$ in to $\frac{3}{4}$ in (3.1 to 19 mm).

3.15 CUTTING TOOLS

3.15.1 Hand snips

These are used to a great extent in the fabrication or repair side of the panel beating trade, for cutting thin-gauge mild steels and aluminium alloys. The limits to which these snips can cut satisfactorily, leaving a good edge, is a thickness of 20 SWG (1 mm) in mild steel and slightly greater thicknesses in aluminium. Snips are available in a variety of types and sizes and are made from the finest tool steel forgings. The blades are ground and set for the accurate cutting of all sheet material. The most popular hand snips are the universal combination snips, which are made in sizes 10 in to 13 in (254 to 280 mm) with narrow or broad blades, with straight or cranked handles, and left or right handed. The handles are offset on the cranked variety so that straight and curved cuts can be made in any direction in one operation with the sheet kept flat and the operator's hand clear of the metal, the cut being followed from above. The word 'universal' means that this single pair of snips can be used for cutting straight lines and both external and internal curved edges.

Standard pattern straight snips are also very popular, although limited in their use to straight line cutting or large external curves. Sizes vary from 6 in to 12 in (152 to 305 mm).

Standard pattern curved or bent snips are designed for cutting circular outlines and inside circles or curved shapes, as the actual cutting blades themselves are curved. (see Figure 3.11).

The cutting tools known as aviation snips were originally developed for the aircraft industry (Figure 3.29). In contrast to the single pivot of ordinary tin snips, aviation snips feature compound leverage for greater shearing power, being able to cut up to 18 gauge (1.2 mm) steel and 16 gauge (1.6 mm) aluminium. The blades are made from heat-treated forged chrome steel and are radiused in order to maintain a constant cutting angle from the back of the jaw to the front, allowing good cutting pressure for the user.

The terms 'left hand' and 'right hand' used for snips in this country have the continental meaning. Left hand means that the lower blade, which should be on the underside of the sheet of metal being cut, is on the left-hand side. Right hand means that the lower blade is on the right-hand side of the metal being cut. The US reference is exactly opposite to that used in this country.

3.15.2 Monodex cutters

This tool is designed for cutting thin sheet metal. Unlike snips, it has a flat face with one central serrated blade which cuts a slot equal in width to the thickness of the blade, about $\frac{1}{8}$ in (3.1 mm). As the material is cut, it coils up in front of the cutters. The advantage of this tool is that it can cut sheet metal internally, and work along either a straight or curved line by drilling a small access hole in the metal to allow the blade to penetrate through the metal to commence cutting. Allowance must be made for the wastage of a $\frac{1}{8}$ in (3.1 mm) strip when cutting to a final size.

3.15.3 Cold chisels

These are often used by the body repair worker for cutting out components which have been damaged, chipping off rusted bolts which cannot be removed by normal methods, and chiselling sections which cannot be cut by snips or hacksaws. Chisels are made from high-quality steel. The cutting edge is specially hardened and tempered, while the remainder of the chisel is left soft to enable it to withstand hammer blows.

The chisel is subdivided into cutting edge, shank and head. The cutting end has a wide, flat taper and is ground on both sides to form the cutting edge. Metal working chisels should have sufficient length to allow the shank to be gripped properly, as short chisels are difficult to handle and may lead to accidents through hammer blows if the head projects insufficiently beyond the gripping hand. On the other hand, excessively long chisels cannot be guided so well and consequently may vibrate and break easily. Only the cutting edge of the chisel is hardened. When the chisel has been in use for some time a ridge forms on its head which is called a burr; this needs to be removed because it may lead to accidents during use. Chisel joint angles vary between about 30 degrees and 60 degrees, the sharper angles being used for cutting softer metals. The metal worker's chisel is flat, and is used for working on flat or curved surfaces of thin sheet. It is also used for cutting solid bolts and rivets.

3.15.4 Hacksaws

The hacksaw is used by the body repair worker to advantage where a clean, neat cut is required, usually where two pieces have to be cut to form a welded joint, and is ideal for cutting irregular-shaped panels which could not be cut with snips or chisel. There are many different types of hacksaw, but in general they consist of a fixed or adjustable frame fitted with a renewable blade of hardened and tempered high-carbon or alloy steel. The hacksaw blades are classified by length and the number of teeth to the inch. Coarse blades have 14–16 teeth to 1 in (25.4 mm) and are used to cut soft metals; finer blades have 18–24 teeth to 1 in (25.4 mm) and are used to cut harder metals. The blades must be fitted with the teeth pointing away from the operator to the front of the frame, and the blade should be slightly tensioned in the frame.

3.15.5 Mini sheet metal cutter

This is a lightweight metal shear (Figure 3.30) which will produce curved and straight cuts in mild steel up to 1.6 mm (16 gauge). A lever and ratchet action operates the roller cutters, which are adjustable for metal thickness, and the cutting action can be reversed for cutting internal angles. The cutter can be bench mounted or used in a vice. This tool is ideally suited for the small bodyshop where limited cutting is required.

3.15.6 Drill cutting attachment

This is a drill attachment for cutting sheet metal up to 18 gauge (1.2 mm) mild steel and 16 gauge (1.6 mm) aluminium (Figure 3.31). This tool provides the user with clear visibility of the cutting line, allowing an accurate cut. When cutting it removes a continuous 3 mm strip from a panel without distortion. It will fit any drill chuck, air or electric.

Figure 3.30 Mini sheet metal cutter (*Sykes-Pickavant Ltd*)

Figure 3.31 Drill cutting attachment (*Frost Auto Restoration Techniques Ltd*)

Figure 3.32 Sheet metal folder (*Sykes-Pickavant Ltd*)

3.16 BENDING AND SWAGING TOOLS

3.16.1 Sheet metal folder

This is a small, compact folder constructed and designed for mounting in a vice (Figure 3.32). It can be used to fold mild steel sheet up to 1.2 mm (18 gauge) with a bend length of 24 in (610 mm). The tool is capable of producing bends of up to 100° and will produce both channel and box sections. It is a useful tool for the fabrication of small metal sections needed in vehicle repair.

3.16.2 Swaging tool or edge setter

This tool is designed for bench mounting or to be used in a vice (Figure 3.33). The fixed rollers produce a smooth, uniform stepped panel edge on a straight or curved panel. The bottom roller is adjustable to accept varying gauges of material up to 1.2 mm (18 gauge) mild steel. The swaged or joggled edge can be used to strengthen panel edges or to create a flush-fitted lap joint when working on panel replacement.

Figure 3.33 Swaging tool or edge setter (*Sykes-Pickavant Ltd*)

Figure 3.34 Shrinker and stretcher machine (*Frost Auto Restoration Techniques Ltd*)

3.16.3 Shrinker and stretcher machine

This is a versatile sheet metal working tool, and will quickly and easily pull curved shapes into steel up to 18 gauge (1.2 mm) or aluminium up to 14 gauge (2.0 mm) (Figure 3.34). It shrinks or stretches the metal into smooth even curvature with a radius as small as

91

3 in (75 mm). It is used to fabricate and repair panels where curves are needed in angle sections, especially around headlights, edges of window frames, door edges and wheel arches.

3.17 GENERAL-PURPOSE ASSEMBLY AND DISMANTLING TOOLS

Having the right tool for the job is a sign of a prepared body repair worker. Knowing how to use the tool is a mark of an experienced repair worker. Knowledge and experience come with study and time, but without the right tools, even the best body worker cannot carry out quality repair work.

3.17.1 Spanners or wrenches

A complete collection of spanners or wrenches is indispensable for the body repair worker. A variety of vehicle body parts, accessories and related parts all utilize common bolt and nut fasteners as well as a range of special fasteners.

The word 'wrench' means 'twist'. A wrench is a tool for twisting or holding bolt heads and nuts. The width of the jaw opening determines the size of the spanner, so that it fits around a nut and a bolt head of equal size. The larger the spanner size, the longer the spanner: the extra length provides the user with more leverage to turn the larger nut or bolt. Spanners are drop forged and made from chrome-vanadium steels.

Open-ended spanner
This is the most commonly used spanner. However, it has the disadvantage that it fits the nut or bolt on two sides only: consequently there is a greater tendency for the open-ended spanner to slip off the bolt or nut, resulting in rounded nuts and injured hands. Open-ended spanners can be single-ended, or double-ended to fit nuts of consecutive sizes. The head of the spanner is usually set at an angle for use in constricted spaces: when the spanner is turned over, the nut can be approached from a different angle. The open-ended spanner fits both square head (four-cornered) or hexagonal (hex) head (six-cornered) nuts. These spanners come in sets ranging in AF from $\frac{1}{4}$ in to $1\frac{5}{8}$ in and in metric from 3.2 mm to 42 mm (Figure 3.35).

Ring spanner
The ring spanner is made in a variety of sizes, points and offsets, and may be flat or cranked. It fits the nut all round by means of teeth cut in the inner surface of the ring. This is a very popular type of spanner as it enables the nut to be tightened quickly and can be

Figure 3.35 A set of open-ended metric spanners (*Facom Tools Ltd*)

Figure 3.36 Straight and offset ring spanners (*Facom Tools Ltd*)

used where movement is restricted. The ring spanner is much safer to use as more force can be applied without slipping and rounding the corners of the nut. The handle of the ring spanner can be straight or offset to provide hand clearance. Each end is usually a different size. The ring spanner does have limitations, for there must be sufficient clearance for the jaws to fit over and around the head of the nut or bolt. Ring spanners are available in 6, 8 or 12 points. The advantage of the 12-point ring spanner is that it can hold the nut in 12 different positions, which is ideal for working in confined spaces. Ring spanner sets are available in AF $\frac{1}{4}$ in to $1\frac{1}{4}$ in and metric 6 mm to 50 mm (Figure 3.36).

Combination spanner
The combination spanner has an open-ended jaw at one end and a ring on the other end. Both ends are the same size. The combination is probably the best choice of second set, for it complements either open-ended spanner or ring spanner sets. Combination spanner sets are available in AF $\frac{1}{4}$ in to $1\frac{1}{4}$ in and metric 3.2 mm to 32 mm (Figure 3.37).

Figure 3.37 Combination and offset combination spanners (*Facom Tools Ltd*)

Figure 3.38 A range of adjustable wrenches (*Facom Tools Ltd*)

Adjustable wrench
An adjustable wrench has one fixed jaw and one movable jaw. The movable jaw is adjusted by means of a worm wheel fitted in the handle, which is meshed with teeth in the jaw. These wrenches are useful because they are manufactured in a range of sizes and each one can be adjusted to fit many sizes of nuts (Figure 3.38).

3.17.2 Socket sets

In many situations a socket ratchet is much faster and easier to use than an open-ended or ring spanner because of its versatility in use, and in some body repair applications it is absolutely essential. A basic socket ratchet set consists of a ratchet, bar extensions, a universal joint and a set of sockets (Figure 3.39).

The barrel-shaped socket fits over and around a given size of nut; inside it is shaped liked the ring spanner, having a set of teeth to grip the points of the nut. Sockets are available with 6 pointed teeth and 12 pointed teeth. A 6-point socket gives a tight hold on a hex nut, minimizing slippage and rounding of the nut's points. The 12-point socket does not have the holding power of the 6-point socket, but its numerous positions maximize the possible turning radius (Figure 3.40a).

The closed end of the socket has a square hole into which the drive shaft of the ratchet fits (Figure 3.40b). Socket sets can be purchased in $\frac{1}{4}$, $\frac{3}{8}$, $\frac{1}{2}$ and $\frac{3}{4}$ in drive sizes. The smaller drive sizes are used for turning small fasteners, badges and trim where little torque is required. The larger drive sizes with the corresponding longer handles are used where greater torque is needed. A body repairer will need sets of $\frac{1}{4}$, $\frac{3}{8}$ and $\frac{1}{2}$ in drive sockets.

The size of the individual sockets in a set depends on the drive size of the set as well as the number of sockets in the set. The socket size is the same as the face-to-face dimension of the bolt it fits. A $\frac{1}{4}$ in set has sockets ranging from $\frac{3}{16}$ to $\frac{1}{2}$ in (5 to 18 mm), whereas a $\frac{1}{2}$ in socket set has sockets ranging from $\frac{7}{16}$ to $1\frac{1}{4}$ in (13 to 40 mm).

Sockets are available not only in standard face-to-face diameters, but also in various lengths or bore depths. Normally the larger the socket size, the deeper the well. Deep well sockets are made extra long for reaching nuts or bolts in limited access areas (Figure 3.40c).

Socket set accessories
Socket set accessories multiply the usefulness of the socket set. A good socket set has a variety of accessories such as:

Ratchet
Ratchet attachment
Extension bars
Speed brace
Long-hinged handle with universal joint
Sliding T-bar
Universal joint
Flexible spinner

Figure 3.39 Socket set (*Facom Tools Ltd*)

Flexible extension
Coupler

Screwdriver attachments
Screwdriver attachments are also available for use with socket ratchets. These attachments are very useful when a fastener cannot be loosened with a regular screwdriver owing to lack of access and space. The leverage that the ratchet handle provides is often all it takes to move a stubborn screw.

3.17.3 Screwdrivers

A variety of threaded fasteners used in the automotive industries are assembled by the use of a screwdriver. Each fastener requires a specific kind of screwdriver, and a body repairer should have several sizes of each type.

All screwdrivers, regardless of type, are designed to have several things in common. The size of the screwdriver is determined by the width or diameter of the blade and the length of the shank. It is important to select the blade tip accurately by matching it to the size of the slot or the type of fastener being used. The larger the handle, the better the grip and the more torque it will generate when turned.

Standard screwdriver (for slotted heads)
A slotted screw accepts a screwdriver with a standard tip. The standard tip screwdriver is probably the most common type used. The blade should match the slot: an oversize screwdriver will not reach the bottom of the slot and an undersize screwdriver will float in the slot, and either condition could result in damage to the tool and the fastener.

Phillips screwdriver (for cross-heads)
Phillips screws have a four-pronged funnel-shaped depression in the screw head, and are known as cross-heads. The tip of the Phillips screwdriver has four prongs that fit the four slots in the screw head. The four surfaces enclose the screwdriver tip so that there is less likelihood that the screwdriver will slip off the fastener. The most useful set of Phillips screwdrivers ranges from number 0 to number 4.

Pozidriv screwdriver
This screwdriver is like a Phillips in that the head is in the form of a cross, but the tip is flatter and blunter. The square tip grips the screw head and slips less than a Phillips screwdriver. Although Pozidriv and Phillips look alike, they are not interchangeable. The most useful set of Pozidriv screwdrivers ranges from number 1 to number 4.

Torx screwdriver
The Torx fastener is used quite a lot on vehicle bodies. The screwdriver has a six-pronged star profile which provides greater turning power and less slippage, and also ensures optimum pressure to prevent the tool from slipping out of the fastener's head.

Speciality screwdriver
These are normally in sets of screwdriver tips and assorted drivers which are all interchangeable and prove most useful in vehicle body repair work.

working area of the body shop. Figure 3.42 shows a complete set of all assembly tools.

3.18 POWER TOOLS USED IN BODY REPAIR WORK

Choosing between pneumatic or electric power tools has always been difficult because, while they are designed to perform basically the same function, the particular advantages and disadvantages of each are so different.

Electric tools are simple to set up. They require only a source of electric current, and so are suitable for immediate use anywhere in the workshop. The disadvantage is that because they have their own power supply (the motor) incorporated, they tend to be heavy and awkward for some jobs. Not only that, but over-heavy use can wear the motor, causing it to burn out.

Pneumatic tools, by contrast, are more complex. Among the advantages they offer are the regulation of air flow to suit the job, and the fact that they are usually lighter, smaller and easier to handle. They also require less maintenance than a comparable electric tool. These factors can only be achieved, however, if a high-performance air compressor system is available. Moreover, it has long been a disadvantage that, despite filters and regulators, pneumatic tools can still blow oil, rust, dust and other impurities into the atmosphere and on to the work being treated.

Power tools play an important part in the modern techniques used by the panel beater in the repairing of crash damage to motor vehicles. Their use reduces man hours to a minimum and they also enable the operators to achieve better results than those possible using hand tools. A wide range of equipment is available to suit all types of crash damage.

Sections 3.19 to 3.25 describe the typical range of power tools.

3.19 AIR POWER CHISEL

This tool (Figure 3.43) is designed for the removal of damaged panels so that essential stripping can be carried out easily and quickly. It consists of a chisel bit which is retained by a spring through one end of a barrel, and a piston which moves to and fro within the barrel, striking the end of the chisel bit as it does so. The barrel must be kept dirt free to eliminate the possibility of undue wear by the reciprocating movement of the chisel. A feather-action trigger in the handle allows for variation in the strength of the blow

(a)

(b)

(c)

Figure 3.40 (a) Standard sockets (b) ratchet with $\frac{1}{2}$ in drive (c) standard and deep well sockets (*Facom Tools Ltd*)

3.17.4 Toolchests

A cabinet-type toolchest as shown in Figure 3.41 is standard equipment in most body shops. A portable toolbox on top of the chest holds large hand and power tools. A chest of drawers holds spanners, sockets and all the necessary assembly tools. The toolchest is on castors so that it can be conveniently located in any

Figure 3.41 Portable toolchest (*Facom Tools Ltd*)

according to the amount of pressure applied. To provide additional safety a beehive or volute spring is fitted over the end of the barrel to prevent the chisel leaving the tool accidentally.

A wide range of special chisel bits is produced for the power tool. Most of these are cutting chisels of various sizes, used for general dismantling, cutting rivets, nuts, bolts and the removal of spot-welded sections. There is also a special thin-gauge metal cutting chisel for use on panel work, and a recessing tool which can be fitted on the end of the chisel. The recessing tool can be used on the edges of panels to form a lip or joggled section so that one panel passes over the face of the other, forming a flush finish which is ideal for spot-weld connections and joints in panels.

3.20 METAL CUTTING SHEARS AND NIBBLERS

3.20.1 Metal shears

These are usually electrically operated (Figure 3.44), but in some cases can be driven by compressed air (Figure 3.45). They are designed to be used in the hand with an on/off trigger control built in the handle. The blade holding shoe is designed in a spiral so that it parts the metal as it cuts it. The machine is based on the principle of shearing metal, and this is done by a pair of very narrow blades, one of which is usually fixed while the other moves to and fro from the fixed blade at high speed. The blades have a very

Figure 3.42 A full set of general and assembly tools (*Facom Tools Ltd*)

pronounced angle or set to permit the blade to pierce the sheet for internal cutting. The tool can be easily turned when cutting owing to the narrow width of the blades, and so can cut curved as well as straight shapes. The shears are capable of cutting sheet metal up to a maximum of 2 mm (14 SWG) or 3 mm (10 SWG) aluminium, which more than covers the automobile requirements. The shear is used extensively in the cutting of light materials for the construction of new vehicles, but also plays an important role in the removal of damaged sections in crash repairs, as it leaves a nice neat cut and there is no risk of flame damage as with the more traditional methods of oxy-acetylene cutting.

3.20.2 Pneumatic metal shear

This tool uses the same action as snips, having two fixed blades and one blade moving vertically between them (Figure 3.46). This central movable blade cuts out a thin ribbon of metal which coils and is discarded. Cutting can be started from the edge of the

panel, or from any point on the panel surface using a predrilled hole large enough to insert the central cutting blade. Radiuses up to $7\frac{3}{4}$ in (200 mm) can be cut on material up to 1.2 mm (18 gauge). Care must be taken not to damage the panel surface by causing buckling during the cutting action.

3.20.3 Metal cutting nibbler

This is a portable nibbler which uses a punch and die (Figure 3.47). The actual cutting is done by the edge of the punch which is reciprocated at high speed, leaving a slot or channel in the metal. Cutting can be commenced from the panel edge, or from a hole predrilled in the panel surface to allow entry of the punch. Allowances must be made for the width of the cut and, when accurate positioning of the cut is essential, templates can be used as a guide.

3.21 POWER SAW

This is a high-speed pneumatic tool using interchangeable, reciprocating hacksaw blades (Figure 3.48). It is able to cut from straight lines to tight curves. Cutting can be started anywhere on a panel without the need for pilot holes. Single- or double-skinned panel assemblies can be easily cut owing to the short blade stroke. The tool can be used to cut a wide variety of materials including light-gauge steel, aluminium, reinforced glass fibre, wood and hardboard. Its fine cut is ideally suited for panel replacement where joints have to be cut and welded.

Another power saw is the rotary or circular saw (Figure 3.49).

3.22 POWER DRILLS

3.22.1 Standard drills

There are two types of power drill used in the bodyshop: the majority are usually electrically driven and require a 13A electrical power point (Figure 3.50), while the others are air powered and require a compressor and air points (Figure 3.51). The most popular sizes in common use are the $\frac{1}{4}$ in (6.3 mm) pistol drill, and the $\frac{3}{8}$ in and $\frac{1}{2}$ in (9.5 mm and 12.6 mm) heavy-duty machines. Drills are used mostly for drilling out spot welds along damaged panels which need removing, and also for drilling out broken rivets and bolts. As well as the standard size drills there is a special drill called an angle drill, which is extremely useful in bodywork as it can be used in confined spaces

97

1 Silencer cutting tool
2 Sheet metal tool
3 Panel cutting tool
4 Bush removing tool
5 Rivet cutting tool

6 Undercoat scraper
7 Tapered punch
8 Bush remover chisel
9 Spot weld breaker
10 175 mm nut and bolt cutting tool

11 Shock absorber chisel
12 Bush installing tool
13 Fork chisel
14 Universal joint and track rod tool
15 Exhaust pipe cutting tool

Figure 3.43 Air power chisel and accessories (*Black and Decker Ltd*)

Figure 3.44 Metal cutting shears (*Black and Decker Ltd*)

Figure 3.45 Air shears (*Desoutter Automotive Ltd*)

Figure 3.46 Pneumatic metal shear (*Desoutter Automotive Ltd*)

Figure 3.47 Metal cutting nibbler (*Desoutter Automotive Ltd*)

and enables many otherwise impossible drilling tasks to be carried out (Figure 3.52).

3.22.2 Cordless drill

This uses an energy pack to supply the power, with a fast charge facility for recharging from a mains supply (Figure 3.53). It can be single speed or two speed, and can drill up to 3 mm steel. When fitted with a reversible adjustable clutch this tool can be used as a power screwdriver, thus making it a tremendously

Figure 3.48 Power saw (*Desoutter Automotive Ltd*)

Figure 3.51 Air drill (*Desoutter Automotive Ltd*)

Figure 3.49 Circular metal cutting saw (*Desoutter Automotive Ltd*)

Figure 3.52 Angle drill (*Desoutter Automotive Ltd*)

Figure 3.50 General duty drill (*Black and Decker Ltd*)

Figure 3.53 Cordless screwdriver/drill (*Black and Decker Ltd*)

Figure 3.54 Selection of air tools (*Consolidated Pneumatic Tool Co. Ltd*). From top:
Spotle specialized air drill for removing spot welds
Supa-Saw (air power saw)
Supa-Sander (miniature belt sander)
Metal nibbler
Dual-action orbital sander

Figure 3.55 Disc sander (*Black and Decker Ltd*)

versatile piece of equipment, especially in the body building industry.

3.22.3 Specialized air drill (spot-weld remover)

This is a hand-held clamp-type drilling tool designed for cutting out spot welds (Figure 3.54). It is powered by compressed air with controllable speeds, and has a removable cutting drill supplied in two sizes, 6 mm and 8 mm; the depth of cut is also adjustable. When there is a flange at the rear of the spot weld it is supported by the clamping action of the C-shaped arm, while the drill is cutting out the spot weld to a preset depth, allowing the panels to separate. Owing to the shape and clamping action of the tool it is restricted to removing spot welds from an open panel edge only. Welds on panel edges which have no access from the rear would entail the cutting of the panel to be replaced, to obtain access for the tool clamp. This tool could be a worthy addition to any bodyshop because of its time saving over conventional methods and its neatness of finish.

3.23 SANDING MACHINES

Whether they are disc, belt, orbital, flat or finishing, sanders are the most frequently used power tools in the body repair shop.

3.23.1 Disc sander

This is the most popular sander. It is a powerful machine with a hard rubber flexible pad on to which the actual sanding disc is fastened by means of a centre nut. This nut is threaded in such a way that it tightens as the machine rotates, thus avoiding the risk of a disc coming loose. Disc sanders are driven either electrically (Figure 3.55) or by compressed air (Figure 3.56).

The main uses of the disc sander in the repair shop are sanding sections on panels which are either rusted or have been repaired by planishing and require sanding to a smooth finish in readiness for painting; cleaning sections that need to be filled with solder prior to tinning; stripping paint prior to planishing or dressing out; dressing off surplus weld metal after welding new sections; feather edging minor paint blemishes; and blending in body solder or plastic filler in sections that have been filled.

3.23.2 Belt sander

This can be used for repair to bodywork, and is extremely good on convex or concave surfaces where

Figure 3.56 Air driven sander (*Desoutter Automotive Ltd*)

Figure 3.58 Geared orbital sander/polisher (*Desoutter Automotive Ltd*)

action which speeds up feather edging or filing materials and results in a smooth surface finish. A standard file blade can be fitted to the tool's base to convert it into a power-operated body file with a speed of up to 3000 strokes per minute.

3.23.4 Dual-action sander

The dual action (DA) on this sander makes the pad oscillate counterclockwise while the head revolves clockwise, resulting in a non-repeating surface pattern that eliminates scratches on the surface of the panel (Figure 3.54).

3.23.5 Geared orbital sander/polisher

This is a multi-orbital action machine which eliminates swirl marks and allows coarse grit paper to be used for high stock removal rates (Figure 3.58). On paint and fibreglass it leaves a perfect key for primers. The multi-orbital action reduces work surface heat generation, which is particularly important when sanding fillers and paint. The tool can also be used for polishing because of its rotary gearing. It can also be connected to a centralized or free-standing dust collection system.

Figure 3.57 Straight line sander (*Desoutter Automotive Ltd*)

access with a disc sander would be difficult. This type of machine uses an endless sanding belt, which is 3 in (16.1 mm) wide, instead of the normal round disc. Some models are fitted with a vacuum unit so that the dust is kept to an absolute minimum in the workshop.

3.23.3 Pneumatic sander/filer

This is a dual-purpose tool either for sanding or filing (Figure 3.57). For sanding, an abrasive paper sheet is clipped to the tool. It has a reciprocating straight-line

3.23.6 Small angle grinder

The small angle grinder (Figure 3.59) is sometimes known as a mini-grinder or a grinderette. It is a versatile one-handed machine, and will cut away damaged metal, remove rust, grind down spot, MIG and

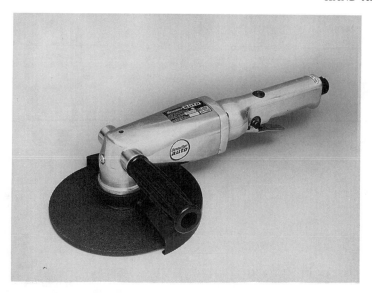

Figure 3.59 Small (178 mm) angle grinder (*Desoutter Automotive Ltd*)

Figure 3.60 Oscillating sander (*Fein/George Marshall Ltd*)

Figure 3.61 Rotex sander with full dust extraction (*Minden Industrial Ltd*)

3.23.7 Oscillating sander

This special sander (Figure 3.60) is an oscillating power tool, only available in this form from the company Fein. Oscillating means that the grinding plate – here a triangle rather than a disc shape – does not rotate, but moves to and fro through only 2 minutes of angle at a frequency of 20 000 oscillations per minute. This ensures high grinding performance, with multiple contact between the grinding particles and virtually all materials: wood, paint, plastic, filler, metal, non-ferrous metals and so on. With the aid of the triangular grinding plate you can reach into any corner or inside the narrowest of openings, for ideal sanding of edges and profiles. Good-quality transitions can even be obtained when spot grinding. This sander is the ideal complement to orbital sanders, eccentric sanders and other portable grinding equipment used in a body repair workshop.

3.23.8 Rotex sander

This tool (Figure 3.61) can be used as a fine sanding random orbital machine or as a rough sanding machine; in the latter mode it can also be used as a polisher. As part of the process of repairing vehicle bodywork, old layers of paint can be removed with this sander. Because of the efficient dust extraction the sandpaper does not become loaded, and so the transition to undamaged paintwork remains smooth and free of scratches, thus considerably reducing repair work.

gas welds, smooth infills and generally grind down prepared surfaces. Owing to its small size and light weight it is ideal for grinding in confined spaces and tight corners. These machines normally use a hard disc for grinding.

Figure 3.62 Miniature belt sander (*Desoutter Automotive Ltd*)

3.23.9 Supa-sander (miniature belt sander)

This machine (Figures 3.54, 3.62) has a 20 mm wide belt and is designed to handle small and accurate convex and concave contours. It has an adjustable head feature for flexibility of operation. It can be efficiently operated in one hand owing to its small size and light weight, and thus may be used to complement conventional angle grinders or disc sanders. It can be used for the removal of paint to reveal production spot welds, and for dressing small plug welds or tack welds in awkward locations such as wing and inner valances, floor pans and inner sills.

3.24   OTHER POWER TOOLS

3.24.1   Impact air screwdriver

The impact air screwdriver has a quick-change bit holder for inserting different screwdriver bit heads: slot, Phillips and Pozidriv (Figure 3.63). It is ideal for the removal of rusted-in screws and other fasteners in locations such as door locks and door hinges.

3.24.2   Ratchet wrench

Ratchet wrenches can have $\frac{3}{8}$ in or $\frac{1}{2}$ in drives (Figure 3.64). They are ideally suited to a wide variety of nut turning operations, either fastening or unfastening. Initial hand ratcheting enables a tight or seized fastener to be slackened off prior to rapid runoff using the air power. Also final tightening can be controlled by hand ratcheting after fast rundown using the air drive.

Figure 3.63 Impact air screwdriver (*Desoutter Automotive Ltd*)

Figure 3.65 Bonded windscreen electric cutter (*Fein/George Marshall Ltd*)

3.24.3 Bonded windscreen electric cutter

This cutter (Figure 3.65) greatly simplifies what was formerly a time-consuming task for two people. With this tool, windows bonded in with polyurethane adhesive can be taken out without difficulty. There is no environmental hazard, and no fumes which might constitute a health risk. Residual adhesive can be removed without damaging the body.

The special cutter uses an AC/DC motor. An electric circuit permits the blade oscillating frequency to be varied to suit the required cutting speed. A wide selection of special-purpose steel cutting blades is now available for all current car models. To simplify operation at various points on the body, the cutter blade has a 12-sided mount to vary its position in relation to the tool.

This precision tool is used to cut through seals, joints and hard-bonded connections with exceptional speed and ease. Bonded-in car windscreens, for example, can be removed without damaging either the glass or the frame.

3.25 DUST EXTRACTION FOR POWER TOOLS

Built-in dust extraction should be a must in any new equipment programme, for it is essential that airborne dust levels in bodyshops are reduced to a minimum for the safety of bodyshop employees. Sanding, grinding and cutting operations in the bodyshop usually generate quantities of airborne dust; this is a major hazard not only to health but also for refinishers wanting a quality paint finish. Systems therefore have been specifically designed to overcome problems of dust, noise and oil pollution.

The equipment consists of a high-performance dust extractor unit and a range of plug-in air tools which includes random orbital sanders, orbital sanders, saws and grinders (Figures 3.66, 3.67). Dust created during the sanding or sawing process is immediately extracted into a handy, easily emptied vacuum pump. In the case of the sanders, a series of holes in the pad itself

Figure 3.64 Ratchet wrench (*Desoutter Automotive Ltd*)

Figure 3.66 Centralized dust extraction system for use with FESTO tools (*Minden Industrial Ltd*)

Figure 3.67 Dust extraction system in a workshop (*Minden Industrial Ltd*)

Figure 3.68 Two extraction points with self-closing flaps (*Minden Industrial Ltd*)

is used to remove the dust and debris which, with conventional systems, form a cloud and obscure the surface to be worked on as well as necessitating breathing apparatus for safety's sake. A single quick-fix hose connects the hand tool to the power source. The hose has three separate compartments for compressed air supply, exhaust and dust extraction (Figures 3.68, 3.69, 3.70). Most sanding and flatting tools have adjustable speed control. They have housings made of high-impact GRP, which makes them light in weight and suitable for prolonged usage without operator fatigue.

QUESTIONS

1 Sketch and describe each of the following hand tools, giving an example of the type of work it would be used for: (a) cross-pein and finishing hammer (b) body spoon (c) planishing hammer.
2 List the hand tools which you would expect to find in a body repairer's toolkit.
3 Describe a suitable application for the use of a flexible body file.
4 Describe a suitable application for (a) a toe dolly (b) an anvil dolly.

Figure 3.69 Air tool with hose attachment for centralized system (*Minden Industrial Ltd*)

Figure 3.70 Dust-free hand sanding tools: Vacbloc and Vacfile (*Minden Industrial Ltd*)

Q15 Explain a repair situation where a body spoon may be used instead of a panel dolly.

16 Sketch and describe four essential hand tools used by the body repairer.

7 Name and explain the use of a hand tool which would have the effect of spreading a blow, thus reducing the stretching of the metal.

8 For what purpose would a sandbag and a wooden hollowing block be used?

9 State a typical use for a pear-shaped mallet.

10 Describe a typical repair application in which a pick hammer would be used.

11 Describe a repair situation in which each of the following special hand tools would be used: (a) impact driver (b) panel puller (c) edge setting tool (d) door skinner.

12 Describe how the following four power tools could be used by the body repair worker: (a) power saw (b) spot-weld remover (c) bonded windscreen cutter (d) miniature belt sander.

13 Describe the movement of a dual-action (DA) sander.

14 In what circumstances would a grid dolly be used?

15 Compare the advantages of a beating file with those of a planishing hammer.

16 When referring to sheet metal snips, what do the terms 'right hand' and 'left hand' mean?

17 Describe three types of sheet metal bench stakes, and sketch one of them.

18 Explain two safety precautions which must be observed when using a cold chisel.

19 What safety precautions must be observed before using an electric drilling machine?

20 Describe the safety measures which would be necessary when using hand and small power tools in a workshop.

21 What action should be taken to render a panel hammer safe for further use after its head has become loose?

22 Why are the teeth on a body file milled in a curved formation?

23 Some beating files and panel hammers have serrated faces. Explain the reasons for this.

24 Name a pneumatic tool which can be used for the removal of a damaged panel section.

25 Name three types of spanner that could be used by a body repair worker.

26 Describe the advantages of socket sets in removing and replacing damaged panels.

27 Sketch a Torx screwdriver bit that could be used with an impact screwdriver.

28 State the function of an air transformer and its importance when used with power tools.

29 Explain the two different types of air hose couplings used with pneumatic tools.

30 Explain the reason why the face of a planishing hammer should be maintained in perfect condition.

31 State the dangers of carrying sharp or pointed tools in pockets or protective clothing.

32 When a fault develops on an electrical power tool, what action must be taken?

33 Explain the reasons why some tools have a built-in dust extraction system while others are connected to a centralized dust extraction system.

34 Identify and sketch two types of mole grips used in body repair applications.

35 With the aid of a sketch, identify the BS symbol used on power tools to indicate double insulation.

4

Materials used in vehicle bodies

4.1 MANUFACTURE OF STEEL COIL AND SHEET FOR THE AUTOMOBILE INDUSTRY

In the manufacture of steel coils, the raw material iron ore is fed into a blast furnace, together with limestone and coke; the coke is used as a source of heat, while the limestone acts as a flux and separates impurities from the ore. The ore is quickly reduced to molten iron, known as pig iron, which contains approximately 3–4 per cent carbon. In the next stage of manufacture, the iron is changed into steel by reheating it in a steelmaking furnace and blowing oxygen either into the surface of the iron or through the liquid iron, which causes oxidation of the molten metal. This process burns out impurities and reduces the carbon content from 4 per cent to between 0.08 and 0.20 per cent.

4.1.1 Casting

The steel is cast into ingots; these are either heated in a furnace and rolled down to a slab, or more commonly continuously cast into a slab. Slabs by either casting process are typically 8–10 in (200–250 mm) thick, ready for further rolling. These slabs are reheated prior to rolling in a computer-controlled continuous hot strip mill to a strip around twice the thickness required for body panels. The strip is closely wound into coil ready for further processing.

4.1.2 Pickling

Before cold rolling, the surfaces of the coils must be cleaned of oxide or black scale formed during the hot rolling process and which would otherwise ruin the surface texture. This is done by pickling the coils in either dilute hydrochloric acid or dilute sulphuric acid and then washing them in hot water to remove the acid. The acid removes both the oxide scale and any dirt or grit which might also be sticking to the surface of the coil.

4.1.3 Cold rolling

In the cold rolling process the coil is rolled either in a single-stand reversing mill (narrow mills using either narrow hot mill product or slit wide mill product) or in a multiple-stand tandem mill to the required thickness. Most mills are computer controlled to ensure close thickness control, and employ specially prepared work rolls to ensure that the right surface standard is achieved on the rolled strip. The cold rolling process hardens the metal, because mild steel quickly work hardens. The cold rolled coils are suitable for applications such as panelling where no bending or very little deformation is needed. At this stage the coil is still not suitable for the manufacture of the all-steel body shell and it must undergo a further process to soften it; this is known as annealing.

4.1.4 Annealing

Coils used for the manufacture of a car body must not only have a bright smooth surface but must also be soft enough for bending, rolling, shaping and pressing operations, and so the hardness of cold rolled coils to be used for car bodies must be reduced by annealing. If annealing were carried out in an open furnace this would destroy the bright surface of the coil and therefore oxygen must be excluded or prevented from attacking the metal during the period of heating the coils.

The normal method of annealing the coils is box annealing. The coils are stacked on a furnace base, covered by an inner hood and sealed. The atmosphere is purged with nitrogen and hydrogen to eliminate oxygen. A furnace is then placed over the stack and fired to heat the steel coils to a temperature of about 650°C for around 24 hours, depending upon charge size and steel grade.

4.1.5 Temper rolling

During the process of annealing the heat causes a certain amount of buckling and distortion, and a further operation is necessary to produce flat coils. The annealed coil is decoiled and passed through a single-stand temper mill using a specially textured work roll surface, where it is given a light skin pass, typically of 0.75–1.25 per cent extension. This is necessary to remove buckles formed during annealing, to impart the appropriate surface texture to the strip, and to control the metallurgical properties of the strip. The strip is then rewound ready for despatch or finishing as appropriate.

4.1.6 Finishing

The temper rolled coils can be slit to narrow coil, cut to sheet, reinspected for surface critical applications, or flattened for flatness critical applications as appropriate. Material can be supplied with a protective coating oil, and packed to prevent damage or rusting during transit and storage.

4.2 SPECIFICATIONS OF STEELS USED IN THE AUTOMOBILE INDUSTRY

The motor body industry uses many different types of steel. Low-carbon steel is used for general constructional members. High-tensile steels are used for bolts and nuts which will be subjected to a heavy load. Specially produced deep-drawn steel including micro-alloyed steel is used for large body panels which require complex forming. Zinc-coated steel sheets are increasingly being specified for automobile production, both for body and chassis parts, as improved corrosion protection is sought. Stainless steel is used for its non-rusting, hard wearing and decorative qualities. The many different types of springs used in the various body fittings are produced from spring steel, while specially hardened steels make the tools of production. Drills, chisels, saws, hack-saws and guillotine blades are all produced from special alloy steels, which are made from an appropriate mixture of metals and elements.

Steel varies from iron chiefly in carbon content; iron contains 3–4 per cent carbon while carbon steels may contain from 0.08 to 1.00 per cent carbon. The chemical composition and mechanical properties of these carbon steels, especially when alloyed with other elements such as nickel, chromium and tungsten, have been gradually standardized over the years, and now the different types of steels used are produced to specifications laid down by the British Standards Institution. A British Standard specification defines the chemical composition and mechanical properties of the steel, and also the method and apparatus to be used when testing samples to prove that the mechanical properties are correct. The tensile strength and, in the case of sheet and strip steel, the bend test are the properties of most interest, but the British Standard specification also defines the elongation, the yield point and the hardness of the steel.

The steels used in the motor trade may be grouped as follows:

1 Cold forming steels.
2 Carbon steels.
3 Alloy steels.
4 Free cutting steels.
5 Spring steels.
6 Rust-resisting and stainless steels.

As each group may contain many different specifications, some idea of the variety of steels may be gained. However, in the motor body industry the specifications which apply are those pertaining to cold forming steels, namely BS 1449: Part 1: 1983.

The greatest percentage of steel used in motor bodies is in the form of coil, strip, sheet or plate. Sheet steel is a rolled product produced from a wide rolling mill (600 mm or wider); to come under the heading of sheet steel, the steel must be less than 3 mm thick. Steel 3–16 mm thick comes under the heading of plate.

Tables 4.1, 4.2 and 4.3 are the specifications for steel sheet strip and coil for the manufacture of motor body shells in the automobile industry.

4.3 CARBON STEEL

Carbon steels can be classified as follows (Table 4.3):

Low-carbon steel
Carbon-manganese steel
Micro-alloyed steel
Medium-carbon steel
High-carbon steel

The properties of plain carbon steel are determined principally by carbon content and micro-structure, but it may be modified by residual elements other than carbon, silicon, manganese, sulphur and phosphorus, which are already present. As the carbon content increases so does the strength and hardness, but at the expense of ductility and malleability.

4.3.1 Low-carbon steel   MILD STEEL.

For many years low-carbon steel (sometimes referred to as mild steel) has been the predominant autobody material. Low-carbon coil, strip and sheet steel have

Table 4.1 Symbols for material conditions: BS 1449: Part 1: 1983

Condition	Symbol	Description
Rimmed steel	R	Low-carbon steel in which deoxidation has been controlled to produce an ingot having a rim or skin almost free from carbon and impurities, within which is a core where the impurities are concentrated
Balanced steel	B	A steel in which processing has been controlled to produce an ingot with a structure between that of a rimmed and a killed steel. It is sometimes referred to as semi-killed steel
Killed steel	K	Steel that has been fully deoxidized
Hot rolled on wide mills narrow mills	HR HS	Material produced by hot rolling. This will have an oxide scale coating, unless an alternative finish is specified (see Table 4.2)
Cold rolled on wide mills narrow mills	CR CS	Material produced by cold rolling to the final thickness
Normalized	N	Material that has been normalized as a separate operation
Annealed	A	Material in the annealed last condition (i.e. which has not been subjected to final light cold rolling)
Skin passed	SP	Material that has been subjected to a final light cold rolling
Temper rolled		Material rolled to the specified temper and qualified as follows:
	H1	Eighth hard
	H2	Quarter hard
	H3	Half hard
	H4	Three-quarters hard
	H5	Hard
	H6	Extra hard
Hardened and tempered	HT	Material that has been continuously hardened and tempered in order to give the specified mechanical properties

been used in the manufacture of car bodies and chassis members. This material has proved an excellent general-purpose steel offering an acceptable combination of strength with good forming and welding properties. It is ideally suited for cold pressings of thin steel sheet and is used for wire drawing and tube manufacture because of its ductile properties.

Low-carbon steel is soft and ductile and cannot be hardened by heating and quenching, but can be case hardened and work hardened. It is used extensively for body panels, where its high ductility and malleability allow easy forming without the danger of cracking. In general, low-carbon steel is used for all parts not requiring great strength or resistance to wear and not subject to high temperature or exposed to corrosion.

However, factors such as a worldwide requirement for fuel conservation for lighter-weight body structures, and safety legislation requiring greater protection of occupants through improved impact resistance have brought about a change in materials and production technology. This has resulted in the range of micro-

alloyed steels known as high-strength steels (HSSs) or high-strength low-alloy steels (HSLAs).

4.3.2 Micro-alloyed steel = HSS

This steel is basically a carbon-manganese steel having a low carbon content, but with the addition of micro-alloying elements such as niobium and titanium. Therefore it is classed as a low-alloy high-strength steel within the carbon range. As a result of its strength, toughness, formability and weldability, car body manufacturers are using this material to produce stronger, lighter-weight body structures.

A typical composition utilized for a micro-alloyed high-strength steel (HSS) is as follows:

	Percentage
Carbon (C)	0.05–0.08
Manganese (Mn)	0.80–1.00
Niobium (Nb)	0.015–0.065

include.

The percentage of niobium used depends on the minimum strength required.

111

Table 4.2 Symbols for surface finishes and surface inspection: BS 1449: Part 1: 1983

Finish	Symbol	Description
Pickled	P	A hot rolled surface from which the oxide has been removed by chemical means
Mechanically descaled	D	A hot rolled surface from which the oxide has been removed by mechanical means
Fully finish	FF	A cold rolled skin passed material having one surface free from blemishes liable to impair the appearance of a high-class paint finish
General-purpose finish	GP	A cold rolled material free from gross defects, but of a lower standard than FF
Matt finish	M	A surface finish obtained when material is cold rolled on specially prepared rolls as a last operation
Bright finish	BR	A surface finish obtained when material is cold rolled on rolls having a moderately high finish. It is suitable for most requirements, but is not recommended for decorative electroplating
Plating finish	PL	A surface finish obtained when material is cold rolled on specially prepared rolls to give one surface which is superior to a BR finish and is particularly suitable for decorative electroplating
Mirror finish	MF	A surface finish having a high lustre and reflectivity. Usually available only in narrow widths in cold rolled material
Unpolished finish	UP	A blue/black oxide finish; applicable to hardened and tempered strip
Polished finish	PF	A bright finish having the appearance of a surface obtained by fine grinding or abrasive brushing; applicable to hardened and tempered strip
Polished and coloured blue	PB	A polished finish oxidized to a controlled blue colour by further heat treatment; applicable to hardened and tempered strip
Polished and coloured yellow	PY	A polished finish oxidized to a controlled yellow colour by further heat treatment; applicable to hardened and tempered strip
Vitreous enamel	VE	A surface finish for vitreous enamelling of material of specially selected chemical composition
Special finish	SF	Other finishes by agreement between the manufacturer and the purchaser

Formable HSSs were developed to allow the automotive industry to design weight out of the car in support of fuel economy targets. A range of high-strength formable steels with good welding and painting characteristics has been developed. The steels are hot rolled for chassis and structural components, and cold reduced for body panels. Through carefully controlled composition and processing conditions, these steels achieve high strength in combination with good ductility to allow thinner gauges to be used: a reduction from 0.90 mm down to 0.70 mm is a general requirement.

There was a danger that the new HSS, thinner but just as strong, would lack the ductility which allows it to be press formed into shape. This problem was overcome by the use of micro-alloying. In a metal crystal the atoms are in layers; when the crystals are stretched (as in forming), one layer of atoms slides over another. The layers of atoms slide like playing cards in a pack, and in doing so are changing shape in a ductile way. The sliding can be controlled by adding elements to the steel such as niobium or titanium. The element reacts with the carbon to produce fine particles which spread through the steel. The element controls the ductility and strengthens the steel, thereby improving the properties of the material.

These steels are low carbon, employing solution strengthening (cold reduced rephosphorized) or precipitation hardening (hot rolled and cold reduced micro-alloyed) elements to produce fine-grained steels which are suitable for welding by spot and MIG processes only.

4.3.3 Medium-carbon steel

This can be hardened by quenching, and the amount it can be hardened by increases with its carbon content.

Table 4.3 Summary of material grades, chemical compositions and types of steel available: BS 1449: Part 1: 1983

Material grade	Rolled condition (see Table 4.1)	C min.	C max.	Si min.	Si max.	Mn min.	Mn max.	S max.	P max.	
		%	%	%	%	%	%	%	%	

Materials having specific requirements based on formability

Material grade	Rolled condition	C min.	C max.	Si min.	Si max.	Mn min.	Mn max.	S max.	P max.	
1	HR, HS, –, –,	–	0.08	–	–	–	0.45	0.030	0.025	Extra deep drawing luminium-killed steel
1	–, –, CR, CS,	–	0.08	–	–	–	0.45	0.030	0.025	Extra deep drawing aluminium-killed stabilized steel
2	HR, HS, CR, CS	–	0.08	–	–	–	0.45	0.035	0.030	Extra deep drawing
3	HR, HS, CR, CS	–	0.10	–	–	–	0.50	0.040	0.040	Deep drawing
4	HR, HS, CR, CS	–	0.12	–	–	–	0.60	0.050	0.050	Drawing or forming
14	HR, HS, –, –,	–	0.15	–	–	–	0.60	0.050	0.050	Flanging
15	HR, HS, –, –,	–	0.20	–	–	–	0.90	0.050	0.060	Commercial

Materials having specific requirements based on minimum strengths

Carbon-manganese steels

Material grade	Rolled condition	C min.	C max.	Si min.	Si max.	Mn min.	Mn max.	S max.	P max.	
34/20	HR, HS, CR, CS	–	0.15	–	–	–	1.20	0.050	0.050	Available as rimmed (R), balanced (B) or killed (K) steels
37/23	HR, HS, CR, CS	–	0.20	–	–	–	1.20	0.050	0.050	
43/25	HR, HS, –, –,	–	0.25	–	–	–	1.20	0.050	0.050	
50/35	HR, HS, –, –,	–	0.20	–	–	–	1.50	0.050	0.050	Grain-refined balanced (B) or killed (K) steel

Micro-alloyed steels

Material grade	Rolled condition	C min.	C max.	Si min.	Si max.	Mn min.	Mn max.	S max.	P max.	
40/30	HR, HS, –, CS	–	0.15	–	–	–	1.20	0.040	0.040	Grain-refined niobium- or titanium-treated
43/35	HR, HS, –, CS	–	0.15	–	–	–	1.20	0.040	0.040	fully killed steels having high yield
46/40	HR, HS, –, CS	–	0.15	–	–	–	1.50	0.040	0.040	strength and good formability
50/45	HR, HS, –, CS	–	0.20	–	–	–	1.50	0.040	0.040	
60/55	–, HS, –, CS	–	0.20	–	–	–	1.50	0.040	0.040	
40F30	HR, HS, –, CS	–	0.12	–	–	–	1.20	0.035	0.030	The steels including F in their designations
43F35	HR, HS, –, CS	–	0.12	–	–	–	1.20	0.035	0.030	in place of the oblique line offer superior
46F40	HR, HS, –, CS	–	0.12	–	–	–	1.20	0.035	0.030	formability for the same strength levels
50F45	HR, HS, –, CS	–	0.12	–	–	–	1.20	0.035	0.030	
60F55	–, HS, –, CS	–	0.12	–	–	–	1.20	0.035	0.030	
68F62	–, HS, –, –	–	0.12	–	–	–	1.50	0.035	0.030	
75F70	–, HS, –, –	–	0.12	–	–	–	1.50	0.035	0.030	

Narrow strip supplied in a range of conditions for heat treatment and general engineering purposes

Material grade	Rolled condition	C min.	C max.	Si min.	Si max.	Mn min.	Mn max.	S max.	P max.	
4	–, HS, –, CS	–	0.12	–	–	–	0.60	0.050	0.050	Low-carbon steel available hot rolled, annealed, skin passed or cold rolled to controlled hardness ranges H1 to H6 inclusive
10	–, HS, –, CS	0.08	0.15	0.10	0.35	0.60	0.90	0.045	0,045	For case hardening
12	–, HS, –, CS	0.10	0.15	–	–	0.40	0.60	0.050	0.050	A range of carbon steels available in the
17	–, HS, –, CS	0.15	0.20	–	–	0.40	0.60	0.050	0.050	hot rolled or annealed condition
20	–, HS, –, CS	0.15	0.25	0.05	0.35	1.30	1.70	0.045	0.045	
22	–, HS, –, CS	0.20	0.25	–	–	0.40	0.60	0.050	0.050	
30	–, HS, –, CS	0.25	0.35	0.05	0.35	0.50	0.90	0.045	0.045	
40	–, HS, –, CS	0.35	0.45	0.05	0.35	0.50	0.90	0.045	0.045	A range of carbon steels for use in the hot
50	–, HS, –, CS	0.45	0.55	0.05	0.35	0.50	0.90	0.045	0.045	rolled, normalized, annealed and (except
60	–, HS, –, CS	0.55	0.65	0.05	0.35	0.50	0.90	0.045	0.045	for grade 95) in the temper rolled (half
70	–, HS, –, CS	0.65	0.75	0.05	0.35	0.50	0.90	0.045	0.045	hard) conditions. Grades 40 and 50 may be
80	–, HS, –, CS	0.75	0.85	0.05	0.35	0.50	0.90	0.045	0.045	induction or flame hardened and grades 60,
95	–, HS, –, CS	0.90	1.00	0.05	0.35	0.30	0.60	0.040	0.040	70, 80 and 95 may be supplied in the hardened and tempered condition

This type of steel can be used for moving parts such as connecting rods, gear shafts and transmission shafts, which require a combination of toughness and strength, but it is being replaced in the car industry by high-alloy steels.

4.3.4 High-carbon steel

This can be hardened to give a very fine cutting edge, but with some loss of its ductile and malleable properties. It is used for metal and wood cutting tools, turning tools, taps and dies, and forging and press dies because of its hardness and toughness, but is seldom used now for motor vehicle parts because of the introduction of high-alloy steels.

4.3.5 Zinc coated steels

The automotive industry, in seeking to provide extended warranties, is turning increasingly to the use of zinc coated steels. Modern automobiles must be not only of high quality but also durable and economical, as perceived by their purchasers. These vehicles are expected to exceed an average of seven years without structural or cosmetic deterioration due to corrosion. Increasingly aggressive environmental influences tend to shorten the life of the car, whereas ever more specialized steel sheets are being incorporated into vehicle construction in the battle against corrosion.

The use of zinc coated steels has dramatically increased to meet these challenges. Different areas of a vehicle require different zinc coatings and coating weights to meet appearance and performance criteria. These are available in both hot dipped (BS 2989: 1982) and electrolytically deposited (BS 6687: 1986) versions in a range of coating weights or thickness. Both types offer barrier and sacrificial corrosion protection, and the choice of product depends on the particular application and requirements. The hot dip product (available as plain zinc, or iron-zinc alloy) is generally used for underbody parts. The electrolytic product is used for exposed body panels, where a full-finish surface quality is available to ensure that a showroom paint finish is achieved. The electrolytic product is available in single-sided and double-sided coating (see Figure 4.1).

Single-sided zinc coated steel Free zinc is applied to one side of a steel sheet either by the hot dip or the electrolytic process for this material. Its uncoated side provides a good surface for paint appearance, so it is used mainly for outer body panels. Since free zinc is towards the inside of the car, it protects against perforation corrosion.

One-and-a-half-sided zinc coated steel In this case, one side of the sheet is coated with free zinc, and a thin layer of zinc-iron alloy is formed on the other side. This product is produced mainly by the hot dip process. It is primarily used for exposed panels, where the zinc-iron layer is on the outside for cosmetic protection and the free zinc side provides perforation protection.

Double-sided zinc coated steel This product is manufactured by applying free zinc to both sides of the sheet with equal or differential coating weight.

All types are readily paintable and weldable. However, care should be taken to ensure that welding conditions are comparable with the material used: for example, higher weld current ratings may be necessary on the heavier coatings.

4.4 ALLOY STEELS

Alloy steel is a general name for steels that owe their distinctive properties to elements other than carbon. They are generally classified into two major categories:

1 Low-alloy steel possesses similar microstructures and requires similar heat treatments to plain carbon steels (see Section 4.3.2 on micro-alloyed steel).
2 High-alloy steel may be defined as a steel having enhanced properties owing to the presence of one or more special elements or a larger proportion of elements than are normally present in carbon steel.

This section is concerned primarily with high-alloy steels.

Alloy steels usually take the name of the element or elements, in varying percentages, having the characteristics the alloy.

Chromium	Increased hardness and resistance to corrosion.
Cobalt	Increased hardness, especially at high temperatures.
Manganese	High tensile strength, toughness and resistance to wear.
Molybdenum	Increased hardness and strength, at high temperatures.
Nickel	Increased tensile strength, toughness, hardness and resistance to fatigue.
Niobium	Strong carbide forming effect; increases tensile strength and improves ductility.

Figure 4.1 Body shell panels showing galvanized protection (*Motor Insurance Repair Research Centre*)

1	Front grille panel	B		28	Rear door frame RH and LH	B
2	Reinforcement	B		29	Rear door frame stiffener RH and LH	A
3	Front bumper mounting reinforcement RH and LH	B		30	Rear door frame gusset RH and LH	B
4	Bonnet lock reinforcement RH and LH	B		31	Rear door skin stiffener RH and LH	A
5	Front wing RH and LH	B		32	Rear door lock stiffener RH and LH	A
6	Bonnet lock panel	B		33	Front window frame stiffener RH and LH	A
7	Front suspension turret stiffener RH and LH	A		34	Front door frame RH and LH	B
8a/8b	Front wheel arch gussets RH and LH	B(a)/C(b)		35	Front door skin stiffener RH and LH	A
9	Front bulkhead stiffener RH and LH	A		36	Front door lock stiffener RH and LH	A
10	Front inner wing RH and LH	B		37	Sill rear gusset RH and LH	A
11	Front suspension turret RH and LH	A		38	Rear chassis leg RH and LH	A
12	A-post reinforcement RH and LH	B		39	Floor/heelboard gussets	A
13	Body side gussets RH and LH	B		40	Rear chassis leg gusset RH and LH	B
14	Body side RH and LH	A		41	Boot floor cross members	A
15	Inner sill RH and LH	A		42	RH boot floor brace closing panel	A
16	Inner sill reinforcement RH and LH	A		43	Boot floor brace RH and LH	A
17	B-post gusset RH and LH	A		44	Boot floor bracket RH and LH	A
18	Upper dash panel	B		45	Rear bumper mounting gusset RH and LH	B
19	Bonnet skin	B		46	Boot lid frame	B
20	Bonnet frame	B		47	Exhaust rear hanger stiffener	B
21	Dash stiffener RH and LH	B		48	Boot lid skin	A
22	Front chassis leg closing panel RH and LH	A		49	Boot lid lock mounting stiffener	B
23	Front chassis leg gusset RH and LH	B		50	Rear wing RH and LH	A
24	Front chassis leg RH and LH	A		51	Rear suspension turret RH and LH	A
25	Front door frame stiffener RH and LH	A		52	Suspension turret capping RH and LH	B
26	Front door skin RH and LH	A		53	Boot floor side extension RH and LH	A
27	Rear door skin RH and LH	A		54	Outer rear wheel arch RH and LH	A

A = Galvanized one side only
B = Galvanized both sides
C = Galvanized layer applied individually

Silicon   Used as a deoxidizing agent, and has the slight effect of improving hardness.

Titanium   Strong carbide forming element.

Tungsten   Greater hardness, especially at high temperatures; improved tensile strength and resistance to wear.

Vanadium   Increased toughness and resistance to fatigue.

Correct heat treatment is essential to develop the properties provided by alloying elements.

There are many alloy steels containing different combinations and percentages of alloying elements, of which some of the most popular are as follows:

High-tensile steel Used whenever there is an essential need for an exceptionally strong and tough steel capable of withstanding high stresses. The main alloying metals used in its manufacture are nickel, chromium and molybdenum and such steels are often referred to as nickel-chrome steels. The exact percentage of these metals used varies according to the hardening processes to be used and the properties desired. Such steels are used for gear shafts, engine parts and all other parts subject to high stress.

High speed steels These are mostly used for cutting tools because they will withstand intense heat generated by friction and still retain their hardness at high temperatures. It has been found that by adding tungsten to carbon steel, an alloy steel is formed which will retain a hard cutting edge at high temperatures. High-speed steels are based on tungsten or molybdenum or both as the primary heat-resisting alloying element; chromium gives deep hardening and strength, and vanadium adds hardness and improves the cutting edge.

Manganese steel An addition of manganese to steel produces an alloy steel which is extremely tough and resistant to wear. It is used extensively in the manufacture of chains, couplings and hooks.

Chrome-vanadium steel This contains a small amount of vanadium which has the effect of intensifying the action of the chromium and the manganese in the steel. It also aids in the formation of carbides, hardening the alloy and increasing its ductility. These steels are valuable where a combination of strength and ductility are desired. They are often used for axle half-shafts, connecting rods, springs, torsion bars, and in some cases hand tools.

Silicon-manganese steel This is a spring steel using the two elements of manganese and silicon. These steels have a high strength and impact resistance and are used for road springs and valve springs.

4.5 STAINLESS STEEL

The discovery of stainless steel was made in 1913 by Harry Brearley of Sheffield, while experimenting with alloy steels. Among the samples which he threw aside as unsuitable was one containing about 14 per cent chromium. Some months later he saw the pile of scrap test pieces and noticed that most of the steels had rusted but the chromium steel was still bright. This led to the development of stainless steels. The classic Rolls-Royce radiator was one of the first examples of the use of stainless steel.

The designer, engineer or fabricator of a particular component may think that stainless steel is going to be both difficult to work and expensive. This is quite wrong, and perhaps stems from the fact that many people tend to fall into the trap of the generic term 'stainless steels'. In fact, this is the title for a wide range of alloys. Therefore if such materials are to be used effectively and maximum advantage is to be taken of the many benefits they have to offer, there should be very close collaboration and consultation over which grade of stainless steel is best for the particular job in hand.

There are over 25 standard grades of stainless steel specified by BS 1449: Part 2. Each provides a particular combination of properties, some being designed for corrosion resistance, some for heat resistance and others for high-temperature creep resistance. Many, of course, are multipurpose alloys and can be considered for more than one of these functions. In terms of composition, there is one element common to all the different grades of stainless steel. This is chromium, which is present to at least 10 per cent. It is this element which provides the basis of the resistance to corrosion by forming what is known as a 'passive film' on the surface of the metal. This film is thin, tenacious and invisible and is essentially a layer of chromium oxide formed by the chromium in the steel combining with the oxygen in the atmosphere. The strength of the passive film, in terms of resistance to corrosion, increases within limits with the chromium content and with the addition of other elements such as nitrogen and molybdenum. The formation of the passive film, therefore, is a natural characteristic of this family of steels and requires no artificial aid. Consequently, if stainless steels are scratched or cut or drilled, the passive film is automatically and instantaneously repaired by the oxygen in the atmosphere.

Stainless steels can be conveniently divided into the following four main groups:

Austenitic Generally containing 16.5–26 per cent chromium and 4–22 per cent nickel.

Table 4.4 Typical stainless steels used in vehicle: BS 1449: Part 2

Steel grade	Typical alloying elements (%)	Characteristics	Typical applications
Austenitic			
301 S21	17Cr 7Ni	Good corrosion resistance	Riveted body panels, wheel covers, hubcaps, rocker panel mouldings
304 S16	18Cr 10Ni 0.06C	Good corrosion resistance	Mild corrosive tankers
305 S19	18Cr 11Ni 0.10C	Low work hardening rate	Rivets
316 S31	17Cr 11Ni 2.25Mo 0.07C	Highest corrosion resistance of the commercial grades	Road tankers for widest cargo flexibility
Ferritic			
409 S19	11Cr 0.08C + Ti	Reasonable combination of weldability, formability and corrosion resistance	Exhaust systems and catalytic converter components and freight container cladding
430 S17	17Cr	Good corrosion resistance. Can be drawn and formed	Tanker jackets, interior trim, body mouldings, windshield wiper arms
Martensitic			
410 S21	13Cr 0.12C	Corrosion resistant. Heat-treatable composition capable of high hardness	Titanium modified for silencer components

Ferritic Usually containing 12–18 per cent chromium.

Austenitic/ferritic duplex Usually containing 22 per cent chromium, 5.5 per cent nickel, 3 per cent molybdenum, and 0.15 per cent nitrogen.

Martensitic Based on a chromium content of 11–14 per cent, although some grades may have a small amount of nickel.

Of the above groups, the austenitic steels, are by far the most widely used because of the excellent combination of forming, welding and corrosion resisting properties that they offer. Providing that the correct grade is selected as appropriate to the service environment, and that the design and production engineering aspects are understood and intelligently applied, long lives with low maintenance costs can be achieved with these steels.

HyResist 22/5 duplex is a highly alloyed austenitic/ferritic stainless steel. It has more than twice the proof strength of normal austenitic stainless steels while providing improved resistance to stress corrosion cracking and to pitting attacks. It possesses good weldability and can be welded by conventional methods for stainless steel. The high joint integrity achievable combined with good strength and toughness permit fabrications to be made to a high standard. It is being increasingly used in offshore and energy applications.

Table 4.4 shows typical stainless steels used in motor vehicles.

4.6 ALUMINIUM

In the present-day search for greater economy in the running of motor vehicles, whether private, public or commercial, the tendency is for manufacturers to produce bodies which, while still maintaining their size and strength, are lighter in weight. Aluminium is approximately one-third of the weight of steel, and aluminium alloys can be produced which have an ultimate tensile strength of 340–620 MN/m^2. In the early 1920s the pioneers of aluminium construction were developing its use for both private and commercial bodies; indeed, the 1922 40 hp Lanchester limousine body had an aluminium alloy construction for the bulkhead and bottom frame, and aluminium was used for all the body panels. Before the Second World War aluminium was used mainly for body panels, but since the war aluminium alloys have been and are now being used for body structures. Although aluminium is more expensive than steel, it is easy to work and manipulate and cleaner to handle. It also has the advantage of not rusting, and, provided that the right treatment is adopted for welding, corrosion is almost non-existent. In recent years the use of aluminium and aluminium alloys for motor bodies, especially in the commercial field, has developed enormously.

In the modern motor body the saving of weight is its most important advantage, and although on average the panel thickness used is approximately double that of steel, a considerable weight saving can be achieved. One square metre of 1.6 mm thick aluminium weighs 4.63 kg while one square metre of 1.00 mm thick steel weighs 7.35 kg; the use of aluminium results in a saving in weight of just under 40 per cent.

The non-rusting qualities of the aluminium group are well known and are another reason for their use in bodywork. An extremely thin film of oxide forms on all surfaces exposed to the atmosphere, and even if this film is broken by a scratch or chip it will reform, providing complete protection for the metal. The oxide film, which is only 0.0002 cm thick, is transparent, but certain impurities in the atmosphere will turn it to various shades of grey.

4.6.1 Production

The metal itself has only been known about 130 years, and the industrial history of aluminium did not begin until 1886 when Paul Heroult in France discovered the basis of the present-day method of producing aluminium. Aluminium is now produced in such quantities that in terms of volume it ranks second to steel among the industrial metals. Aluminium of commercial purity contains at least 99 per cent aluminium, while higher grades contain 99.5–99.8 per cent of pure metal.

In the production of aluminium, the ore bauxite is crushed and screened, then washed and pumped under pressure into tanks and filtered into rotating drums, which are then heated. This separates the aluminium oxide from the ore. In the next stage the aluminium oxide is reduced to the metal aluminium by means of an electrolytic reduction cell. This cell uses powdered cryolite and a very heavy current of electricity to reduce the aluminium oxide to liquid metal, which passes to the bottom of the cell and is tapped off into pigs of aluminium of about 225 kg each.

4.6.2 Types of sheet

Sheet, strip and circle blanks are sold in hard and soft tempers possessing different degrees of ductility and tensile strength. Sheet is supplied in gauges down to 0.3 mm, but it is generally more economical to order strip for gauges less than 1.6 mm.

4.6.3 Manufacturing process

Sheet products are first cast by the semicontinuous casting process, then scalped to remove surface roughness and preheated in readiness for hot rolling. They are first reduced to the thickness of plate, and then to sheet if this is required. Hot rolling is followed by cold rolling, which imparts finish and temper in bringing the metal to the gauge required. Material is supplied in the annealed (soft) condition and in at least three degrees of hardness, H1, H2 and H3 (in ascending order of hardness).

4.7 ALUMINIUM ALLOYS

From the reduction centre the pigs of aluminium are remelted and cast into ingots of commercial purity. Aluminium alloys are made by adding specified amounts of alloying elements to molten aluminium. Some alloys, such as magnesium and zinc, can be added directly to the melt, but higher-melting-point elements such as copper and manganese have to be introduced in stages. Aluminium and aluminium alloys are produced for industry in two broad groups:

1 Materials suitable for casting.
2 Materials for the further mechanical production of plate sheet and strip, bars, tubes and extruded sections.

In addition both cast and wrought materials can be subdivided according to the method by which their mechanical properties are improved.

Non-heat-treatable alloys Wrought alloys, including pure aluminium, gain in strength by cold working such as rolling, pressing, beating and any similar type of process.

Heat-treatable alloys These are strengthened by controlled heating and cooling followed by ageing at either room temperature or at 100–200°C.

The most commonly used elements in aluminium alloys are copper, manganese, silicon, magnesium and zinc. The manufacturers can supply these materials in a variety of conditions. The non-heat-treatable alloys can be supplied either as fabricated (F), annealed (O) or strain hardened (H1, H2, H3). The heat-treatable alloys can be supplied as fabricated (F) or annealed (O), or, depending on the alloy, in variations of the heat treatment processes (T3, T4, T5, T6, T8).

4.7.1 Wrought light aluminium alloys: BS specifications 1470–75

Material designations
Unalloyed aluminium plate, sheet and strip:

1080A commercial pure aluminium 99.8 per cent
1050A commercial pure aluminium 99.5 per cent
1200 commercial pure aluminium 99.0 per cent

Non-heat-treatable aluminium alloy plate, sheet and strip:

3103   AlMn
3105   AlMnMg
5005   AlMg
5083   AlMgMn
5154A   AlMg
5251   AlMg
5454   AlMgMn

Heat-treatable aluminium alloy plate, sheet and strip:

2014A   AlCuSiMg
Clad 2014A AlCuSiMg clad with pure aluminium
2024   AlCuMg
Clad 2024   AlCuMg clad with pure aluminium
6082   AlSiMgMn

Abbreviations for basic temper
As fabricated: F The temper designation F applies to the products of shaping processes in which no special control over thermal conditions or strain hardening is employed. For wrought products there are no specified requirements for mechanical properties.

Annealed: O The temper designation O applies to wrought products which are annealed to obtain the lowest strength condition.

Abbreviations for strain hardened materials
The temper designation H for strain hardened products (wrought products only) applies to products subjected to the application of cold work after annealing (hot forming) and partial annealing or stabilizing, in order to achieve the specified mechanical properties. The H is always followed by two or more digits, indicating the final degree of strain hardening. The first digit (1, 2 or 3) indicates the following:

H1 strain hardened only
H2 strain hardened and partially annealed
H3 strain hardened and stabilized

The second digit (2, 4, 6 or 8) indicates the degree of strain hardening, as follows:

HX2 tensile strength approximately midway between O temper and HX4 temper

HX4 tensile strength approximately midway between O temper and HX8 temper

HX6 tensile strength approximately midway between HX4 temper and HX8 temper

HX8 full hard temper

Abbreviations for heat-treated materials
The temper designation T applies to products which are thermally treated, with or without supplementary strain hardening, to produce stable tempers. The T is always followed by one or more digits, indicating the specific sequence of treatments as follows:

T3 solution heat treated, cold worked, and naturally aged to a substantially stable condition

T4 solution heat treated and naturally aged to a substantially stable condition

T5 cooled from an elevated temperature shaping process and then artificially aged

T6 solution heat treated and then artificially aged

T8 solution heat treated, cold worked and then artificially aged

The additional digits for the T tempers TX51 indicate that the products have been stress relieved by controlled stretching.

Tables 4.5, 4.6, 4.7 and 4.8 show the characteristics and properties of aluminium alloys.

4.7.2 Aluminium alloys used in bodywork

The choice of material and the condition in which it is required must depend largely upon design requirements and the manufacturing processes within the factory. The alloys most commonly used in vehicle bodywork are as shown in Table 4.9.

Alloy 5154A is suitable for use in car panels which are to be pressed into shape; it is supplied in either annealed condition or H2 condition, which are the most suitable for press work on vehicle bodies. Of the other materials, 1200 is a commercial purity sheet, and is widely used for exterior and interior panelling where no great strength is required. Types 3103, 5251, 5154A and 5056A are non-heat-treatable alloys of the aluminium-magnesium range with a strength of 90–325 N/mm^2. They come in sheet form, and provide a range of mechanical properties to suit different applications. They are used extensively in panel work, and also for forming, pressing and machining, and can be welded without much difficulty. The plate material 5083 is a medium-strength, non-heat-treatable alloy particularly suitable for welding. It can be used for parts carrying fairly high stress loads and is often used in the form of patterned tread plate for floor sections.

For internal structure members which need to be stronger than the outer panels, the heat-treatable alloys usually used are 6063 and 6082, and in odd cases 2014A. Type 6082 is a heat-treatable, medium-strength alloy which combines good mechanical properties with high corrosion resistance. Permissible stresses in this alloy can be as high as 200 N/mm^2 under static loading conditions, although some reduction below this

119

Table 4.5 General characteristics of all wrought forms of aluminium alloys

Purity or alloy	Temper or condition	General characteristics[a]						
		Cold forming	Machining	Durability	Inert-gas shielded arc (MIG or TIG)	Welding resistance (spot, seam, flash butt or stub)[b,c]	Oxy-acetylene[d]	Metal arc
5251	F	V	G	V	V[e]	E	G[e]	F[e]
	O	V	G					
	H22	G	G					
	H24	G	V					
	H28	G	V					
	H39X	F	V	F	V[e]	E	G[e]	G[e]
5454	F	V	V	V	V[e]	E	F[e]	N
	O	V		V				
	H22	G		G				
	H24	G		G				
5154	F	V	V	V[f]	E	E	F	N
	O	V		V[f]				
	H22	G		G[f]				
	H24	F		G[f]				
	H28							
5083	F	G	E	V[f]	E	E	F	N
	O	G		V[f]				
	H22	F		F[f]				
	H24	G		F[f]				
6082	F	V	G	G	V[e]	V	F[e]	G[e]
	O	E	G	G				
	T4	G	V	V				
	T6	F	E	G				
	T451							
	T651							
1200	F	E	F	V	E	V	V	G
	O	E	F					
	H12	V	F					
	H14	V	F					
	H16	G	G					
	H18	F	G					
3103	F	E	F	V	E	E	V	G
	O	E	F					
	H12	V	F					
	H14	V	F					
	H16	G	G					
	H18	F	G					

(a) Materials are graded thus: E excellent; V very good; F fair; P poor; N not recommended.
(b) The mechanical properties of work hardened or heat-treated materials will be reduced in the vicinity of the weld.
(c) The weld zone is generally discernible after anodic treatment, the degree depending on the material and welding process.
(d) The oxy-acetylene process is normally recommended only for material thinner than 6–4 mm.
(e) Filler or electrode of other than parent metal composition is recommended.
(f) Applicable at temperature of 70°C and less.

Table 4.6 Chemical composition limits[1] and mechanical properties of unalloyed aluminium plate, sheet and strip (BS 1470)

Material designation	Tolerance category	Silicon (%)	Iron (%)	Copper (%)	Manganese (%)	Magnesium (%)	Chromium (%)	Nickel (%)	Zinc (%)	Gallium (%)	Titanium (%)	Others[2] Each (%)	Others[2] Total (%)	Aluminium min. (%)	Temper[4]	Thickness > (mm)	Thickness ≤ (mm)	Tensile strength Min. (N/mm²)	Tensile strength Max. (N/mm²)	Elong. 0.5 mm min (%)	Elong. 0.8 mm min (%)	Elong. 1.3 mm min (%)	Elong. 2.6 mm min (%)	Elong. 3.0 mm min (%)	Elongation on 5.65 √S, over 12.5 mm thick (min.) (%)
1080A	A	0.15	0.15	0.03	0.02	0.02	-	-	0.06	0.03	0.02	0.02	-	99.80[3]	F	3.0	25.0	-	-	-	-	-	-	-	-
															O	0.2	6.0	-	90	29	29	29	35	35	-
															H14	0.2	12.5	90	125	5	6	7	8	8	-
															H18	0.2	3.0	125	-	3	4	4	5	-	-
1050A	A	0.25	0.40	0.05	0.05	0.05	-	-	0.07	-	0.05	0.03	-	99.50[3]	F	3.0	25.0	-	-	-	-	-	-	-	-
															O	0.2	6.0	55	95	22	25	30	32	32	-
															H12	0.2	6.0	80	115	4	6	8	9	9	-
															H14	0.2	12.5	100	135	4	5	6	6	8	-
															H18	0.2	3.0	135	-	3	3	4	4	-	-
1200	A	1.0 Si + Fe		0.05	0.05	-	-	-	0.10	-	0.05	0.05	0.15	99.00[3]	F	3.0	25.0	-	-	-	-	-	-	-	-
															O	0.2	6.0	70	105	20	25	30	30	30	-
															H12	0.2	6.0	90	125	4	6	8	9	9	-
															H14	0.2	12.5	105	140	3	4	5	5	6	-
															H16	0.2	6.0	125	160	2	3	4	4	4	-
															H18	0.2	3.0	140	-	2	3	4	4	-	-

1 Composition in per cent (m/m) maximum unless shown as a range or a minimum.
2 Analysis is regularly made only for the elements for which specific limits are shown. If, however, the presence of other elements is suspected to be, or in the case of routine analysis is indicated to be, in excess of the specified limits, further analysis should be made to determine that these other elements are not in excess of the amount specified.
3 The aluminium content for unalloyed aluminium not made by a refining process is the difference between 100.00% and the sum of all other metallic elements in amounts of 0.010% or more each, expressed to the second decimal before determining the sum.
4 An alternative method of production, designated H2, may be used instead of the H1 routes, subject to agreement between supplier and purchaser and providing that the same specified properties are achieved.

Table 4.7 Chemical composition limits[1] and mechanical properties of aluminium alloy plate, sheet and strip (non-heat-treatable) (BS 1470)

Material designation	Tolerance category	Silicon (%)	Iron (%)	Copper (%)	Manganese (%)	Magnesium (%)	Chromium (%)	Nickel (%)	Zinc (%)	Other restrictions (%)	Titanium (%)	Others[2] Each (%)	Others[2] Total (%)	Aluminium (%)	Temper[3]	Thickness > (mm)	Thickness ≤ (mm)	0.2% proof stress min. (N/mm²)	Tensile Min. (N/mm²)	Tensile Max. (N/mm²)	Elong. 50mm 0.5mm min. (%)	0.8mm min. (%)	1.3mm min. (%)	2.6mm min. (%)	3.0mm min. (%)	Elong. 5.65√S over 12.5mm thick (min.) (%)
3103	A	0.50	0.7	0.10	0.9–1.5	0.30	0.10	–	0.20	0.10 Zr + Ti	–	0.05	0.15	Rem.*	F	0.2	25.0	–	–	–	–	–	–	–	–	–
															O	0.2	6.0	–	90	130	20	23	24	24	25	–
															H12	0.2	6.0	–	120	155	5	6	7	9	9	–
															H14	0.2	12.5	–	140	175	3	4	5	6	7	–
															H16	0.2	6.0	–	160	195	2	3	4	4	4	–
															H18	0.2	3.0	–	175	–	2	3	4	4	–	–
3105	A	0.6	0.7	0.30	0.30–0.8	0.20–0.8	0.20	–	0.40	–	0.10	0.05	0.15	Rem.	O	0.2	3.0	–	110	155	16	18	20	20	–	–
															H12	0.2	3.0	115	130	175	2	3	4	5	–	–
															H14	0.2	3.0	145	160	205	2	2	3	4	–	–
															H16	0.2	3.0	170	185	230	1	1	2	3	–	–
															H18	0.2	3.0	190	215	–	1	1	1	2	–	–
5005	A	0.30	0.7	0.20	0.20	0.50–1.1	0.10	–	0.25	–	–	0.05	0.15	Rem.	O	0.2	3.0	–	95	145	18	20	21	22	–	–
															H12	0.2	3.0	80	125	170	4	5	6	8	–	–
															H14	0.2	3.0	100	145	185	3	3	5	6	–	–
															H18	0.2	3.0	165	185	–	1	2	3	3	–	–
5083	B	0.40	0.40	0.10	0.40–1.0	4.0–4.9	0.05–0.25	–	0.25	–	0.15	0.05	0.15	Rem.	F	3.0	25.0	–	–	–	–	–	–	–	–	–
															O	0.2	80.0	125	275	350	12	14	16	16	16	14
															H22	0.2	6.0	235	310	375	5	6	8	10	8	–
															H24	0.2	6.0	270	345	405	4	5	6	8	6	–
5154A	B	0.50	0.50	0.10	0.50	3.1–3.9	0.25	–	0.20	0.10–0.50 Mn + Cr	0.20	0.05	0.15	Rem.	O	0.2	6.0	85	215	275	12	14	16	18	18	–
															H22	0.2	6.0	165	245	295	5	6	7	8	8	–
															H24	0.2	6.0	225	275	325	4	4	4	6	6	–
5251	A	0.40	0.50	0.15	0.10–0.50	1.7–2.4	0.15	–	0.15	–	0.15	0.05	0.15	Rem.	F	3.0	25.0	–	–	–	–	–	–	–	–	–
															O	0.2	6.0	60	160	200	18	18	18	20	20	–
															H22	0.2	6.0	130	200	240	4	5	6	8	8	–
															H24	0.2	6.0	175	225	275	3	4	5	5	5	–
															H28	0.2	3.0	215	255	285	2	3	3	4	4	–
5454	B	0.25	0.40	0.10	0.50–1.0	2.4–3.0	0.05–0.20	–	0.25	–	0.20	0.05	0.15	Rem.	F	3.0	25.0	–	–	–	–	–	–	–	–	–
															O	0.2	6.0	80	215	285	12	14	16	18	18	–
															H22	0.2	3.0	180	250	305	4	5	7	8	8	–
															H24	0.2	3.0	200	270	325	3	4	5	6	6	–

* Remainder

1 Composition in per cent (m/m) maximum unless shown as a range or a minimum.

2 Analysis is regularly made only for the elements for which specific limits are shown. If, however, the presence of other elements is suspected to be, or in the case of routine analysis is indicated to be in excess of the specified limits, further analysis should be made to determine that these other elements are not in excess of the amount specified.

3 An alternative method of production, designated H2, may be used instead of the H1 routes, subject to agreement between supplier and purchaser and providing that the same specified properties are achieved.

Table 4.8 Chemical composition limits and mechanical properties of aluminium alloy plate, sheet and strip (heat-treatable) (BS 1470)

Material designation	Tolerance category	Silicon (%)	Iron (%)	Copper (%)	Manganese (%)	Magnesium (%)	Chromium (%)	Nickel (%)	Zinc (%)	Other Restrictions (%)	Titanium (%)	Others² Each (%)	Others² Total (%)	Aluminium (%)	Temper	Thickness > (mm)	Thickness ≤ (mm)	0.2% proof stress min. (N/mm²)	Tensile strength Min. (N/mm²)	Tensile strength Max. (N/mm²)	Elong. 0.5 mm min. (%)	0.8 mm min. (%)	1.3 mm min. (%)	2.6 mm min. (%)	3.0 mm min. (%)	Elong. on 5.65√S, over 12.5 mm thick (min.) (%)
2014A	B	0.50–0.9	0.50	3.9–5.0	0.40–1.2	0.20–0.8	0.10	0.10	0.25	0.20 Zr + Ti	0.15	0.05	0.15	Rem.*	O	0.2	6.0	110	–	235	14	14	16	16	16	–
															T4	0.2	6.0	225	400	–	13	14	14	14	14	–
															T6	0.2	6.0	380	440	–	6	6	7	7	8	–
															T451	6.0	25.0	250	400	–	–	–	–	–	–	12
																25.0	40.0	250	400	–	–	–	–	–	–	10
																40.0	80.0	250	395	–	–	–	–	–	–	7
Clad 2014A	B	0.50–0.9	0.50	3.9–5.0	0.40–1.2	0.20–0.8	0.10	0.10	0.25	0.20 Zr + Ti	0.15	0.05	0.15	Rem.	T651	6.0	25.0	410	460	–	–	–	–	–	–	6
																25.0	40.0	400	450	–	–	–	–	–	–	5
																40.0	60.0	390	430	–	–	–	–	–	–	5
																60.0	90.0	390	430	–	–	–	–	–	–	4
																90.0	115.0	370	420	–	–	–	–	–	–	4
																115.0	140.0	350	410	–	–	–	–	–	–	4
2024	B	0.50	0.50	3.8–4.9	0.30–0.9	1.2–1.8	0.10	–	0.25	–	0.15	0.05	0.15	Rem.	O	0.2	6.0	100	–	220	14	14	16	16	16	–
															T4	0.2	1.6	240	385	–	13	14	14	–	–	–
																1.6	6.0	245	395	–	–	–	–	14	14	–
															T6	0.2	1.6	345	420	–	7	7	8	–	–	–
																1.6	6.0	355	420	–	–	–	–	9	9	–
															O	0.2	6.0	110	–	235	12	12	14	14	14	–
															T3	0.2	1.6	290	440	–	11	11	11	–	–	–
																1.6	6.0	290	440	–	–	–	–	12	12	–
															T351	6.0	25.0	280	430	–	–	–	–	–	–	10
																25.0	40.0	280	420	–	–	–	–	–	–	9
																40.0	60.0	270	410	–	–	–	–	–	–	9
																60.0	90.0	270	410	–	–	–	–	–	–	8
																90.0	115.0	270	400	–	–	–	–	–	–	8
																115.0	140.0	260	390	–	–	–	–	–	–	7

* Remainder

Table 4.9 Standard aluminium alloys: availability, physical properties, and applications

Purity or alloy (new nomenclature)	Related BS/GE specification (BS 1470–1475) (old BS alloy designation)	Nominal composition: % alloying elements (remainder aluminium and normal impurities)			Standard forms[a]					Physical properties				Typical road transport applications
		Mg	Si	Mn	Sheet	Plate	Extrusions	Hollow extrusions	Tube	Density g/cm³	lb/in³	Melting range °C (approx.)	Coefficient of linear expansion per °C (20–100°C)	
Non-heat-treatable alloys														
1200	IC	–	–	–	×	×	×	×	×	2.71	0.098	660	0.0000235	Vehicle panelling where panel beating is required; mouldings and trim. Tank cladding
3103	N3	–	–	1.2	×	×	×ᵇ	×ᵇ	×ᵇ	2.73	0.099	645–655	0.0000235	Flat panelling of vehicles and general sheet metal work. Tank cladding.
5251	N4	2.25	–	0.4	×	×	×	–	×	2.69	0.097	595–650	0.000024	Body panelling. Head boards and drop sides. Truss panels in buses. Cab panelling. Tanker shells and divisions
5154A	N5	3.5	–.	0.4	×	–	×	–	×	2.67	0.096	600–640	0.0000245	Welded body construction. Tipper body panelling. Truss panels in buses.
5454	N51	2.7	–	0.8	×									Tanker shells and divisions
5083	N8	4.5	–	0.5	×	×	×	–	×	2.65	0.096	580–635	0.0000245	Pressurized bulk transport at ambient or low temperature
Heat-treatable alloys														
6082	N30	0.7	1.0	0.5	×	×	×	×	×	2.70	0.098	570–660	0.0000235–0.000024ᶜ	All structural sections in riveted vehicle bodies. Tipper body panelling. Highly stressed underframe gussets, truss panels

(a) Other forms may be available by special arrangement.

(b) Not covered by British Standard (general engineering) specification.

(c) Depending on condition.

would normally be made for transport applications where there is a considerable element of dynamic loading. The alloy is weldable by the inert gas arc process, but there is a considerable loss of strength near the weld owing to the annealing effect of the welding process. Type 6063 is also a heat-treatable alloy but of somewhat lower strength, and is used mainly in applications requiring good surface finish or where the parts are required to be anodized. Alloy 2014A contains a greater percentage of copper than the others, is more expensive, is more difficult to form and is less resistant to corrosion, but has the advantage of a greater tensile strength.

Fastenings and solid rivets can be of commercial purity material or of aluminium alloy 5154A, and for smaller sizes 6082 is sometimes used. Rivets are also available in 5056A material, but should not be used in cases where high temperatures occur in service. Bolts used in bodywork are normally of the 6082 alloy.

The condition in which heat-treatable alloys are supplied should be related to their application or use in bodywork. For example, if a section is to remain straight and is part of a framework which is to be bolted, riveted or welded in place, it is obvious that the material used should already be fully heat treated so that maximum strength is provided to support the framework or structure of the body. On the other hand, if the section has to be shaped, bent or formed in any way the material should be used in the annealed condition and then heat treated after the shaping operations have all been carried out.

Aluminium alloys are now being accepted by the automobile manufacturers as a standard material for exterior and interior trim, and are used for all normal bright trim applications such as radiator grilles, headlamp bezels, wheel trims, instrument panels, body mouldings and window and windscreen surrounds. Alloys used for trimming can be divided into two groups: high-purity alloys bright finished on one side only, in which the majority of the trim components are made; and super-purity alloys for use when maximum specular reflectivity is an advantage, such as would be required by light units.

4.8 RUBBER

The value of rubber lies in the fact that it can be readily moulded or extruded to any desired shape, and its elastic quality makes it capable of filling unavoidable and irregular gaps and clearances. It is an ideal material in door shuts and as the gasket for window glass, and in both instances it provides the means for excluding dust and water, although with windscreens and backlights additional use has generally to be made of a sealing material. Rubber specifications have been built on the basis of the properties of material which has given satisfaction. One major difficulty has been to ensure and measure resistance to weathering; rubber is subject to oxidation by ozone in the atmosphere, and this results in cracking. In addition to natural rubber, a variety of types of synthetic rubbers are used by the motor industry; these vary in price and characteristics, and all are more expensive than natural rubber. For complete ozone resistance it is necessary to use either butyl or neoprene rubber: both satisfy atmospheric and ozone ageing tests. Butyl rubber, however, is 'dead' to handle and contains no wax, and so while neoprene is costly its use is essential for some parts.

Sponge sealing rubbers can be provided with built-in ozone resistance by giving them a live skin of neoprene, and a further way of providing ozone resistance is to coat the rubber components with Hypalon. More recently, continuously extruded neoprene sponge has been adopted. Apart from weather resistance, the important requirement of door and boot lid seals is that their compression characteristics should ensure that they are capable of accommodating wide variations in clearance, without giving undue resistance to door closing.

Various types of foam rubber have been evolved to suit the different parts of the car seating, and the designer's choice of material is governed by cost, comfort, durability, the type of base, the type of car, and whether it is a cushion or a squab, a rear or front seat. When considering the foams available, it is apparent that the number of permutations is large. The types of foam available today fall into seven broad categories. These are:

Moulded latex foam
Low-grade fabricated polyether
Fabricated polyether
Moulded polyether
Fabricated polyester
Polyvinyl chloride foam
Reconstituted polyether

Latex foam today utilizes a mixture of natural and synthetic latexes to obtain the best qualities of both. After being stabilized with ammonia, natural latex is shipped in liquid form to this country from Malaysia, Indonesia and other rubber producing countries. Synthetic latex, styrene butadiene rubber, is made as a by-product of the oil cracker plants. Polyether foam can now be made in different grades, and the physical properties of the best grades approach those of latex foam.

As a general guide, service life and physical properties improve as the density increases for any given hardness. As the cost is proportional to weight, it follows that the higher-performance foams are more costly.

Flexible polyurethane foam seats are replacing heavy and complicated padded metal spring structures. Moulded seats simplify assembly, reduce weight and give good long-term performance. A major innovation here has been the cold cure systems. These produce foams of superb quality, particularly in terms of strength, comfort and long-term ageing. The systems are particularly suitable for the newer seat technologies such as dual hardness, where the wings are firm to give lateral support, leaving the seat pad softer and more comfortable.

4.9 SEALERS

The history of sealers is longer than that of the motor car. Mastic, bitumen compounds and putties of various kinds have been used since the invention of the horseless carriage. It is likely that early coach builders used putties of some kind – possibly paint fillers – to bridge joints in various applications on motor bodies, but it is generally conceded that the first use of specialized sealers on a large scale was in the early 1920s when, in America, the pressed steel body became popular. In this country it was 1927 before one of the first truly effective sealers was introduced. It was known as Dum Dum and is still in use. It was a modified roof sealer, and proved to have many applications in body production. It was not until the late 1930s, when all-steel bodies and unitary construction became a common feature of mass-produced cars, that more thought was given to the points that required the use of sealing compounds, and to the nature of these products. Among the first developed was interweld sealing compound, primarily to prevent corrosion. Since then, particularly in the post-war years, there have been remarkable developments, probably accelerated by criticisms from overseas markets that British cars were susceptible to dust and water entry. Companies specializing in the manufacture of mastic compounds have developed a range of materials which is now used not only for welding and for general putty application but also for floor pans, drip rails, body joints, exterior trim and many other points, leading to well-sealed car bodies equal to any produced elsewhere in the world (Figure 4.2, Table 4.10).

The term 'sealer' covers a wide variety of materials used in the motor industry for sealing against water and dust, from products which remain virtually mastic throughout their life to others which harden up but still retain some measure of elasticity. They range from mixtures of inert fillers and semi-drying oils to heat curing plastisols which may be applied in a thin paste form as an interweld sealer or as extruded beads. Sealing compounds can be categorized into the following general groups: oil-based compositions, rubber-based compositions and synthetic-resin-based compositions. The choice of each of the types will be dependent on the site for application, on the eventual conditions of exposure and often on price. These categories can be subdivided further into the various physical forms in which they can be made available, which include mastic putties for hand application, extruded sections for placing in precise locations, gun grade compositions which have the advantage of speed and economy of application, and pouring and spraying grades.

The properties of sealers will obviously vary according to their type and to their application. Thus preformed strip or putty sealers must adhere to the surfaces to which they are applied, and must not harden or crumble in service. Glazing sealers must be capable of being readily applied from a gun, with the ability to harden off on the surface, but must remain mastic in the assembly so that they are capable of maintaining a leaktight joint whatever deflection the body undergoes. Heat gelling sealers must be capable of being readily applied by extrusion or possibly by spraying, and then must set up when cured but still retain a degree of flexibility.

As a result of soaring energy costs together with the need for car aerodynamic design, direct glazing of windscreens and fixed body glass were introduced and an adhesive was required to bond glass windscreens to the metal aperture. The material used is polyurethane adhesive sealant. It possesses a combination of adhesion, sealant and gap filling qualities; it is a one-component adhesive and sealing compound of permanent elasticity. This dual-purpose material is based on a special moisture cured polyurethane with an accelerated setting time. The curing time is dependent upon the humidity levels prevailing, as well as the temperature. For example, at 20°C with a relative humidity level of 65 per cent, a 6 mm diameter bead will be tack free within 1 hour and fully cured in 24 hours.

Table 4.11 indicates the uses of various sealant materials.

4.10 SOUND DEADENING, THERMAL INSULATING AND UNDERSEALING MATERIALS

The type of material used for sound damping or deadening depends on whether or not it is also required to provide undersealing. A material required for sound

WATER FOUND	PROBLEM AREA	ACTION REQUIRED
Front Footwell	1 'A' Post grommets	Ensure grommets are correctly fitted, seal if necessary
	2 Windscreen aperture	Apply sealer if necessary, pay attention to top corners
	3 Sunroof aperture flanges	Apply sealer into corner joints
	4 Lower 'A' post to inner wing join	Apply sealer into join
	5 Drip rail flanges	Apply sealer into joints
	6 Front door chrome finisher	Remove finisher, seal hung holes and fit new finisher
Front & Rear Footwell	7 Door shedders	Check integrity of seal to door, renew if damaged
	8 Door trim clips	Apply waterproof tape around fixing holes, renew if damaged
	9 Door seals	Ensure correct fitted position of seal, especially at top corners and base of 'C' channel
	10 Door harness leads	Apply lead loops on inside door to prevent water ingress through shedders
	11 Floor grommets	Ensure grommets are correctly fitted, seal if necessary
Rear Footwell	12 Rear seal slide weld nuts	Ensure nuts are completely sealed, apply sealer if necessary
	13 Petrol filler aperture	Remove filler flap and apply sealer into joints
	14 'D' : 'E' post seams	Apply sealer into joints
	15 Boot area seams	Apply sealer into joints
	16 Tooling hole grommets	Ensure grommets are correctly fitted, seal if necessary
Boot Area	17 Rear bumper formgs	Ensure flangs are completely sealed, apply sealer if necessary
	18 Rear lower panel seam	Remove bumper and apply sealer into joint
	19 Rear screen aperture	Apply sealer if necessary, pay attention to top corners
	20 Tail lamps	Check security of tail lamp fixings and integrity of seal
	21 Boot aperture seams	Apply sealer into joints
	22 Boot lid grommets	Check grommets are correctly fitted
	23 Boot lid flanges	Apply sealer into joints

3M DRIP CHECK 1, 5, 11, 14, 16, 23	3M SUPER SEAM SEALER 15, 18	URETHANE SEALER KIT 2, 19
3M CAULKING 3, 4, 6, 12, 13, 17, 21		CHECK AND RECTIFY SEAL 9
		CHECK AND RECTIFY 7, 8, 10, 20, 22

Figure 4.2 Problem areas requiring body sealing (*Rover Group Ltd*)

Table 4.10 Types of sealed joints used in vehicle bodywork (*Rover Group Ltd*)

Application		Material description	Application equipment
Bolted joints	Between panels	Preformed strip	Hand or palette/putty knife
		Zinc-rich primer	Brush or spray
	Panel edges	Seam sealer light	Applicator gun (hand)
Spot-welded joints	Between panels	Zinc-rich primer	Brush or spray
		Structural adhesive or seam sealer	
	Panel edges	Seam sealer light	Applicator gun (hand)
Bonded joints	Between panels	Metal-to-metal adhesive semi-structural	Caulking gun

deadening only will normally be applied to the interior of a vehicle, whereas one required to provide sound deadening and undersealing properties will be applied to the underside of the vehicle. Thus the former need not be fully water resistant, whereas the latter must be water resistant in addition to many other necessary requirements.

The sound deadening properties of a material are related to its ability to damp out panel vibrations, and this in turn is related to some extent (but not solely) to its weight per unit volume. Thus the cheapest sound deadening materials are based on mixtures of sand and bitumen, although these tend to be brittle. A better material is bitumen filled with asbestos; although this is probably less effective as a panel damper than sand-filled bitumen, it is nevertheless more suitable owing to its better ductility. In general, those sound deadeners applied to the interior of the vehicle are water-based bitumen emulsions with fillers, whereas sound deadener/sealers applied externally should be solvent-based materials. A more effective sound deadener than asbestos-filled bitumen now being phased out, is a clay-filled water dispersed polyvinyl acetate (PVA) resin emulsion; this has damping characteristics approximately three times better than the bitumen-based material, but naturally it is more expensive.

Other sound absorbing materials are now used for insulation in the automotive industry. Needle felts are blends of natural and manmade fibres locked together by needle punching. These are used in die-cut flat sheet forms for attachment to moulded carpets, floor boot mats and as anti-rattle pads. Bonded, fully cured felts are similar blends of fibres bonded together with synthetic resins. All the binder is cured during the felt making process. As with needled materials, these are mainly used for flat products, especially where low density is required such as in sound absorption pads and floor mats. In moulded felts and moulded glass wool the binder is only partially cured during the felt making process. The curing sequence is completed under the action of temperature and pressure in matched die compression moulded tools to produce components which have three dimensional form and a controllable degree of rigidity. Fully cured and needled products can be given various surface treatments including abrasion-resistant and waterproof coatings such as latex, PVC or rubber, or they can be combined with bitumen to improve the sound insulation properties. Moulded felt can be supplied covered with a range of woven textile covers or with various grades of PVC and heavy-layer bitumen EVA products.

Polyurethane flexible moulded foam can be modified or filled to meet different insulating requirements in the vehicle. The foam can also be moulded directly on to the hard layer, allowing simple tailoring of insulation thickness.

Table 4.12 indicates the use of various undersealing materials.

Table 4.11   Sealers used in vehicle body repair work

Type	Base material	Application
Visible seams	Polyurethane	Extremely adherent sealant used on front and rear aprons, rear panel, engine compartment, bottom of boot, passenger compartment, side panels, wheel arches, vehicle underbody, tank filler caps and wings. Can be painted over with primer and fillers after curing, is non-shrinking, can be brushed and smoothed with a spatula. Cures by means of air moisture
	Synthetic rubber	Particularly suitable for all automotive problem areas where cleaning is difficult. Extremely adherent to raw, degreased, bonded, primed and painted sheet steel. Can be painted over with lacquers after thoroughly drying. Following application, can be passed through drying ovens at a maximum temperature of 90°C
	Acrylic dispersion (water based)	Particularly suitable for sealing joints, welded seams and butt joints on vehicle bodies. Substrate must be primed and can be readily painted over. When cured, is resistant to water
Structural seams	MS polymer	Applied by means of an air pressure pistol. All structural seams sprayed by the manufacturer can be re-created with this sealant, so that the original finish can be restored after repair. Also can be painted over immediately wet-on-wet.
	Nitrile-butadiene rubber	Special brushable sealant used for front and rear aprons, bottom of boot, inside floor, side walls, wheel arches. Has excellent adhesion to raw, primed and painted sheet metal, and can be painted over after drying
Underbody seams	Bitumen rubber	Specially used for the underbody area of the vehicle. Resistant to water, salt spray, alcohol and dilute sulphuric acid
Overlapping joints	Synthetic rubber	Used for sealing bolted wings, headlight units, rear light housings and cable inlet holes
Sealing tape	Synthetic rubber	Suitable for all overlapping and screwable joints on vehicle bodies, metal to metal, metal to wood, metal to plastic, wood to wood or plastic to plastic
Rubber profiled windows	Synthetic resin, synthetic rubber	Particularly suitable for sealing rubber profiled front, rear and side window units between rubber and glass or rubber and the vehicle body

4.11   INTERIOR FURNISHINGS

4.11.1   Carpets and floor coverings

The body engineer has a choice of materials, ranging from carpeting of the Wilton type for prestige vehicles, through polyamide and polypropylene moulded needle felts, to rubber flooring for economy versions. The main requirements of flooring are wear resistance, colour fastness to light and water, and adequate strength to enable the customer to remove the flooring from the car without it suffering damage. The method of manufacture of pile carpets varies: in some cases the pile is bonded to hessian backing; in other cases it is woven simultaneously into the backing and then anchored in position with either a rubber coating on the back surface or a vinyl coating. Quality is normally controlled by characteristics such as number of rows of tufts of pile per unit length, height and weight of the free pile, overall weight of the carpet, strength as determined by a tensile test in both the warp and weft directions, together with adhesion of pile if applicable. Rubber flooring generally has a vinyl coating to provide colour.

4.11.2   Leather (hide)

Large numbers of motor vehicle users all over the world continue to specify hide upholstery when the option is available, and will gladly pay the extra cost involved for a material which defies complete simulation. Great advances have been made in the development of suitable substitutes, and the best of the plasticized materials are to many people quite

Table 4.12 Undersealing and protection materials used in vehicle body repair work

Type	Base material	Application
Coatings for underbodies, spray type	Bitumen/rubber	Coating for underbodies, wheel arches, new and repaired parts. Also a corrosion protection for vehicle underbodies against elements such as moisture, road salt, road stone chippings. Good adhesion, and durable at extreme temperatures. Applied with a spray pistol
	Rubber/resin	Suitable for underbodies, wheel arches, front and rear aprons, sills, new parts, repair sheets. Can be painted over and has high abrasion resistance. Applied with a spray pistol
	Wax	Suitable for underbodies, touching up and subsequent treatment of all protective coatings
	Polymer wax	Long-term corrosion protection even when thinly applied. Has good flowing properties
Small-scale repair application (brushable)	Rubber/bitumen	Brushable coating, suitable for underbody and wheel arches. High abrasion resistance and good sound deadening properties
Road stone chip repair material	Synthetic/dispersion	Good protection against stone chips and corrosion. Particularly suitable for front and rear aprons, sills, spoilers, wheel arches

indistinguishable by eye from leather. The unique character of leather lies in its micro-structure, the like of which is not obtained in any manmade material. Under a microscope leather can be seen to consist of the hairy epidermis and under that the corium, or bulk of the hide, this being the basis of the leather as we know it. By virtue of the millions of minute air spaces between the fibres and bundles of fibres, leather is able to 'breathe'. To the motorist this means that leather does not get hot and uncomfortable in warm weather or cold and inflexible in winter, and although permeable to water vapour it offers sufficient resistance if it is exposed to normal liquids. It is also strongly resistant to soiling, and when it does get dirty the dirt can usually be removed fairly easily without special materials. Unlike some plasticized materials, leather does not appear to attract dirt and dust as a result of static electricity. Many people, moreover, regard the distinctive smell of leather as an asset, and this defies imitation by manufacturers of substitute materials. However, natural hide has to go through many complex processes before it attains the form familiar to the upholsterer trimmer or motorist.

4.11.3 Fabrics for interior trim

Vinyl coated fabrics are now well established as trim material. Their vast superiority over the linseed oil coatings of yesteryear, and later the nitrocellulose coatings, are almost forgotten in the march of progress. Vinyl coatings are now sufficiently familiar for their merits to be taken for granted; nevertheless they continue to provide a material which for durability,

uniformity and appearance at a reasonable cost so far remains unsurpassed. The resin polyvinyl chloride, the main ingredient of the coating, became available in commercial quantities in the early 1930s, and now a coating based on polyvinyl chloride (PVC) is used for seating material in this country. Although by tradition PVC is produced with a simulated leather appearance, on the Continent and particularly in the USA it is widely used with fancy embosses and patterns. An extremely wide range of qualities is available, and in recent years there has been an effort to achieve some degree of rationalization. Additional qualities are necessary for tilt covers, headlinings and hoods for convertibles; the material for hooding convertibles must be resistant to mildew, to shrinkage and to wicking, this last term relating to the absorption of water on the inside surface of the cloth from the bottom edge of the hood. The characteristics necessary to provide serviceability over the life of the vehicle are the strength of the material under tension and under tearing conditions; adhesion of the coating to the backing cloth; resistance to flexing and resistance to cracking at low temperatures; low friction, to enable the owner to slide on the seat; colour fastness, soiling resistance and, of course, wear resistance. In the case of the breathable leathercloth, the air permeability of the fabric has to be controlled.

4.11.4 Modern trends

The interior furnishing of a car is gaining in importance within the automotive trade. In response stylists are endeavouring to upgrade and soften the interior, using fabrics with the appearance and feel of textiles to appeal visually and functionally. This has manifested itself in all areas of the car, including the boot, seating, carpets, door trims and headliner cover fabrics. In all four areas of fabric use in car interiors (seating, door and side panels, bolsters and headliners) fabrics are gaining ground against exposed plastics. Both polyamide and polyester are giving designers new scope for attractive colours and variation in seating upholstery and in panels, while fully meeting light fastness and other performance standards.

4.12 PLASTICS

4.12.1 Development

Celluloid might well qualify for the honour of being the first plastic, though its inventor, Alexander Parkes, was certainly not aware of that fact. He made it around 1860 and patented his method for making it in 1865. An American, John Hyatt, found a way of solving the technical problems which plagued Parkes, and he set up business in 1870 to sell the same sort of material. He called it celluloid to indicate its raw material, cellulose.

In 1920 a German chemist, Hermann Staudinger, put forward a theory about the chemical nature of a whole group of substances, natural and synthetic. He called them macromolecules; today we call them polymers. His theory not only explained the nature of plastics, but also indicated the ways in which they could be made. It provided the foundation for the world of plastics as we know it.

4.12.2 Polymerization

The raw materials for plastics production are natural products such as cellulose, coal, oil, natural gas and salt. In every case they are compounds of carbon (C) and hydrogen (H). Oxygen (O), nitrogen (N), chlorine (Cl) and sulphur (S) may also be present. Oil, together with natural gas, is the most important raw material for plastics production.

The term plastics in the broadest sense encompasses (a) organic materials which are based on (b) polymers which are produced by (c) the conversion of natural products or by synthesis from primary chemicals coming from oil, natural gas or coal.

The basic building blocks of plastics are monomers. These are simple chemicals that can link together to form long chains or polymers. The type of monomer used and the way it polymerizes, or links together, gives a plastic its individual characteristics. Some monomers form simple linear chains. In polyethylene, for example, a typical chain of 50 000 ethylene links is only about 0.02 mm long. Other monomers form chains with side branches. Under certain circumstances, the individual chains can link up with each other to form a three-dimensional or cross-linked structure with even greater strength and stability. Cross-linking can be caused either chemically or by irradiating the polymer.

To get the advantages of two different plastics, two different monomers can be combined in a copolymer. By combining the monomers in different proportions and by different methods, a vast range of different properties can be achieved (see Tables 4.13 and 4.14). The properties of plastics can also be enhanced by mixing in other materials, such as graphite or molybdenum disulphide (for lubrication), glass fibre or carbon fibre (for stiffness), plasticizers (to increase flexibility) and a range of other additives (to make them resistant to heat and light).

4.12.3 Thermoplastics and thermosetting plastics

The simplest way of classifying plastics is by their reaction to heat. This gives a ready subdivision into two basic groups: thermoplastics and thermosetting plastics. *Thermoplastic* materials soften to become plastic when heated, no chemical change taking place during this process. When cooled they again become hard and will assume any shape into which they were moulded when soft. *Thermosetting* materials, as the name implies, will soften only once. During heating a chemical change takes place and the material cures; thereafter the only effect of heating is to char or burn the material.

As far as performance is concerned, these plastics can be divided into three groups:

General-purpose thermoplastics
Polyethylene
Polypropylene
Polystyrene
SAN (styrene/acrylonitrile copolymer)
Impact polystyrene
ABS (acrylonitrile butadiene styrene)
Polyvinyl chloride
Poly(vinylidene chloride)
Poly(methyl methacrylate)
Poly(ethylene terephthalate)

Engineering thermoplastics
Polyesters (thermoplastic)
Polyamides
Polyacetals

Table 4.13 Physical properties of polymers

Material	P or S	Density (kg/m³)	Melting (softening) range (°C)	Specific-heat capacity (J/kg/K × 10³)	Thermal conductivity (W/m/K)	Coefficient of linear expansion (K × 10⁻⁶)
LD polyethylene	P	0.01–0.93	80	2.3	0.13	120–140
HD polyethylene	P	0.04–0.97	90–100	2.1–2.3	0.42–0.5	120
Polypropylene	P	0.90	100–120	1.9	0.09	120
GFR polypropylene	P	1.00–1.16	110–120	3.5	–	55–85
Polyvinylchloride	P	1.16–1.35	56–85	0.8–2.5	0.16–0.27	50–60
Polystyrene	P	1.04–1.11	82–102	1.3–1.45	0.09–0.21	60–80
Polystyrene copolymer (ABS)	P	0.99–1.10	85	1.4–1.5	0.04–0.30	60–130
Nylon 66	P	1.14	250–265	1.67	0.24	80
Nylon 11	P	1.04	185	2.42	0.23	150
PTFE (Teflon)	P	2.14–2.20	260–270	1.05	0.25	100
Acrylic (Perspex)	P	1.10–1.20	70–90	1.45	0.17–0.25	50–90
Polyacetals	P	1.40–1.42	175	1.45	0.81	80
Polycarbonates	P	1.20	215–225	1.25	0.19	65
Phenol formaldehyde	S	1.25–1.30	–	1.5–1.75	0.12–0.25	25–60
Urea formaldehyde	S	1.40–1.50	–	1.65	0.25–0.38	35–45
Melamine formaldehyde	S	1.50	–	1.65	0.25–0.40	35–45
Epoxies	S	1.20	–	1.65	0.17–0.21	50–90
Polyurethanes R	S	3.2–6.0	150–185	1.25	0.02–0.025	20–70
Polyurethanes F	S	4–8	150–185	1.25	0.035	50–70
Polyesters	S	1.10–1.40	–	1.26	0.17–0.19	100–150
Silicones	S	1.15–1.8	200–250	–	0.17	24–30

GFR glass fibre reinforced; P thermoplastic; S thermosetting; R rigid; F flexible; LD low density; HD high density

Polyphenylene sulphide
Polycarbonates
Polysulphone
Modified polyphenylene ether
Polyimides
Cellulosics
RIM/polyurethane
Polyurethane foam

Thermosetting plastics
Phenolic
Epoxy resins
Unsaturated polyesters
Alkyd resins
Diallyl phthalate
Amino resins

4.12.4 Amorphous and crystalline plastics

An alternative classification of plastics is by their shape. They may be crystalline (with shape) or amorphous (shapeless).

Amorphous plastics
Amorphous plastics basically are of three major types:

ABS: acrylonitrile butadiene styrene
ABS/PC blend
PC: polycarbonate

Amorphous engineering plastics have the following properties:

High stiffness
Good impact strength
Temperature resistance
Excellent dimensional stability
Good surface finish
Electrical properties
Flame retardance (when required)
Excellent transparency (polycarbonate only)

In the automotive industry use is made of the good mechanical properties (even at low temperatures), the thermal resistance and the surface finish. The applications are:

1 Body embellishment.
2 Interior cladding.
3 Lighting where, apart from existing applications of back lamp clusters, polycarbonate has replaced glass for headlamp lenses.

Table 4.14 Typical mechanical properties of representative plastics

Material	Modulus of elasticity E (MN/m^2)	Tensile strength (MN/m^2)	Compressive strength	Elongation (%)
LD polythylene	120–240	7–13	9–10	300–700
HD polyethylene	550–1050	20–30	20–25	300–800
Polypropylene	900–140	32–35	35	20–300
GFR polypropylene	1500+	34–54	40–60	5–20
Flexible PVC	3500–4800	10–25	7–12	200–450
Rigid PVC	2000–2800	40	90	60
Polystyrene	2400–4200	35–62	90–110	1–3
ABS copolymer	1380–3400	17–58	17–85	10–140
Perspex	2700–3500	55–75	80–130	2–3
PTFE	350–620	15–35	10–15	200–400
Nylon 11	1250–1300	52–54	55–56	180–400
GFR nylon 6	7800–800	170–172	200–210	3–4

Semi-crystalline plastics

Semi-crystalline plastics are in two basic types:

Polyamide 6 and 66 types
Polybutylene terephthalate (PBT)

Semi-crystalline plastics have the following properties:

High rigidity
Hardness
High heat resistance
Impact resistance
Abrasion, chemical and stress crack resistance

The semi-crystalline products find major application in the automotive sector, where full use is made of their mechanical and thermal properties, together with abrasion and chemical resistance. Examples include:

1 Underbonnet components
2 Mechanical applications
3 Bumpers, using elastomeric PBT for paint on-line
4 Body embellishment (wheel trims, handles, mirrors)
5 Lighting, headlamp reflectors

Blended plastics

Blended plastics have been developed to overcome inherent specific disadvantages of individual plastics. For large-area body panels, the automotive industry demands the following properties:

Temperature resistance
Low-temperature impact resistance
Toughness (no splintering)
Petrol resistance
Stiffness

Neither polycarbonate nor polyester could fulfil these requirements totally. This led to the combination of

PC and PBT to form Macroblend PC/PBT, which is used for injection moulded bumpers.

4.12.5 Plastics applications

Plastic products can be decorated by vacuum metallizing and electroplating. They have replaced metals in a lot of automotive applications, such as mirror housings, control knobs and winder handles as well as decorative metallic trim. It is a field which uses their advantages to the full without relying on properties they lack.

Thin parts must be tough and resistant to the occasional impact. They must be impervious to attack by weather, road salts, extremes of temperatures and all the other hazards that reduce older forms of body embellishments to pitted, rusted, dull, crumbling metal. They do not need high tensile strength or flexural strength as they do not have to carry heavy stresses. They must be cheap and capable of being formed into highly individual and complex shapes. All these requirements are satisfied by thermoplastics and thermosetting resins. They can be pressed, stamped, blow moulded, vacuum formed and injection moulded into any decorative shape required.

Apart from their decorative properties, the mechanical properties of acrylic resins are among the highest of the thermoplastics. Typical values are a tensile strength of 35–75 MN/m^2 and a modulus of elasticity of 1550–3250 MN/m^2. These properties apply to relatively short-term loadings, and when long-term service is envisaged tensile stresses in acrylics must be limited to 10 MN/m^2 to avoid surface cracking or crazing. Chemical properties are also good, the acrylics being inert to most common chemicals. A particular advantage to the automotive industry is their complete stability against petroleum products and salts.

Acetal resins are mostly used for mechanical parts such as cams, sprockets and small leaf springs, but also find application for housings, cover plates, knobs and levers. They have the highest fatigue endurance limits of any of the commercial thermoplastics, and these properties, coupled with those of reduced friction and noise, admirably qualify the acetal resins for small gearing applications within the vehicle.

Plastics can be self-coloured so that painting costs are eliminated and accidental scratching remains inconspicuous, and they can be given a simulated metal finish. For large-scale assemblies, such as automobile bodies, painting is necessary to obtain uniformity of colour, especially when different types of plastics are used for different components. Plastics can also be chrome plated, either over a special undercoating which helps to protect and fix the finish, or by metal spraying or by vacuum deposition in which the plastic part is made to attract metal particles in a high-vacuum chamber. The use of a plastic instead of a metal base for chrome plating eliminates the possibility of the base corroding and damaging the finish before the chromium plating itself would have deteriorated. The chrome coating can be made much thinner and yet have a longer effective life, with a consequent saving in cost.

Originally polymer materials were joined only by means of adhesives. Now the thermoplastic types can be welded by using various forms of equipment, in particular by hot gas welding, hot plate machines which include pipe welding plant, ultrasonic and vibration methods, spin or friction welding machines, and induction, resistance and microwave processes. Lasers have been used experimentally for cutting and welding. The joining of metals to both thermoplastic and thermosetting materials is possible by some welding operations and by using adhesives.

4.12.6 Future of plastics in the automotive industry

The automotive industry has grown to appreciate the potential of plastics as replacements for metal components within their products. The realization that plastics are, in their own right, engineering materials of high merit has led to rapid advancement of material and application technology, with the end result that plastics have gained a firm and increasing footing in the motor vehicle. Many factors have aided the adoption of plastics by the automotive industry, which uses them in the following areas: body, chassis, engine, electrical system, interior and vehicle accessories.

Lower costs of plastics parts must, of course, be the major contributing factor in the replacement of existing parts, and this is closely followed by the ease with which modern plastics can be formed by comparatively inexpensive tooling. The inert properties of synthetic materials also contribute greatly; properties like corrosion resistance, low friction coefficients and light weight are of prime importance.

The use of plastics in the automotive industry continues to accelerate at a phenomenal rate as research into plastics technology results in new developments and applications. The future growth of plastics in the automotive industry will be controlled by two factors: the growth of the industry itself, and the greater penetration of plastic per car (see Figure 4.3). A key constituent in world growth, therefore, is the developing nations which are involved in the assembly and production of motor vehicles. They will consequently favour the use of plastics as a first choice, rather than as a replacement for metal.

Over the past years, the natural applications for plastics in automobiles (interior fittings, cushioning and upholstery, trim, tail lights, electrical components) have become saturated. The growth for the future can be expected to come from the use of plastic for bodywork and some mechanical components. There is a widespread use of plastics for front and rear bumpers. We now see bonnets, boot lids and front wings in plastics.

All the major volume producers of cars are engaged in long-term development work towards the all-plastic car. Whether or not such targets can be realized remains to be seen. Factors such as energy costs and availability of resources may play a greater part in the total picture than simple objects like vehicle weight reduction.

4.13 SAFETY GLASS

More and more glass is being used on modern cars. Pillars are becoming slimmer and glass areas are increasing as manufacturers approach the ideal of almost complete all-round vision and the virtual elimination of blind spots. Windscreens have become deeper and wider. They may be gently curved, semi-wrapped round, or fully wrapped. With few exceptions they are of one-piece construction, sometimes swept back as much as 65° from the vertical. Styling trends, together with a growing knowledge of stress design in metal structures, have resulted in a significant increase in the glazed areas of modern car body designs. As a result of this move towards a more open style, the massive increase in the cost of energy has brought growing pressure on vehicle designers to achieve more economic operations, principally in respect to lower fuel consumption through better power/weight ratios. An outcome of these two lines of development has been a situation in which although the area of glass has increased, the total weight of glass has remained constant or even decreased.

Broadly speaking, motor vehicle regulations specify that windscreens must be of safety glass. To quote one section: 'On passenger vehicles and dual-purpose vehicles first registered on or after 1 January 1959, the glass of all outside windows, including the windscreen, must be of safety glass.' The British Standards Institution defines safety glass indirectly as follows: 'All glass, including windscreen glass, shall be such that, in the event of shattering, the danger of personal injury is reduced to a minimum. The glass shall be sufficiently resistant to conditions to be expected in normal traffic, and to atmospheric and heat conditions, chemical action and abrasion. Windscreens shall, in addition, be sufficiently transparent, and not cause any confusion between the signalling colours normally used. In the event of the windscreen shattering, the driver shall still be able to see the road clearly so that he can brake and stop his vehicle safely.'

Two types of windscreen fulfil these requirements – those made from heat-treated (or toughened) glass, and those of laminated glass. In addition there are plastic coated laminated or annealed safety glasses. Most windscreens and some rear windows fitted in motor vehicles are of ordinary laminated glass. For the main part, toughened glass is confined to door glass, quarter lights and rear windows where the use of more expensive laminated products has yet to be justified. However, laminated glass is being increasingly used in areas other than windscreens for reasons of vehicle security and also for passenger safety (containment in an accident), especially in estates with seating in the rear. Note that the applicable EEC Directive (see later) has effectively banned the fitment of toughened windscreens from the end of 1992.

Ordinary laminated safety glass is the older of the two types and is the result of a basic process discovered in 1909. Some years earlier a French chemist, Edouard Benedictus, had accidentally knocked down a flask which held a solution of celluloid. Although the flask cracked it did not fall into pieces, and he found that it was held together by a film of celluloid adhering to its inner surface. This accident led to the invention of laminated safety glass, made from two pieces of glass with a celluloid interlayer. An adhesive, usually gelatine, was used to hold them together and the edges had to be sealed to prevent delaminating. However, despite the edge sealing, the celluloid (cellulose nitrate plastic) discoloured and blistered; hence celluloid was replaced by cellulose acetate plastic, but this, although a more stable product than celluloid, still needed edge sealing. Nowadays a polyvinyl butyral (PVB) self-bonding plastic interlayer is used; no adhesive is necessary and the edges do not need sealing, making it quite practical to cut to size after laminating. When producing glass to a particular size, however, the glass and vinyl interlayer are usually cut to size first. In the process the vinyl plastic interlayer is placed between two clean, dry pieces of glass and the assembly is heated and passed between rubber-covered rollers to obtain a preliminary adhesion. The sandwich of glass and interlayer is then heated under pressure for a specified period in an autoclave. This gives the necessary adhesion and clarity to the interlayer, which is not transparent until bonded to the glass. If a piece of laminated glass is broken, the interlayer will hold the splinters of glass in place and prevent them flying.

Plastic coated laminated safety glass is an ordinary laminated glass which has soft elastic polyurethane films bonded on to the inner surface to provide improved passenger protection if fragmentation occurs. There is some interest in the use of bilayer construction which uses 3 mm or 4 mm annealed glass bonded with a load bearing surface layer of self-healing polyurethane.

Uniformly toughened glass is produced by a completely different process, involving heating of the glass followed by rapid cooling. Although patents were taken out in 1874 covering a method of increasing the strength of flat glass sheet by heating and cooling it in oil, toughened glass was not in common use until the 1930s. Modern toughened glass is produced by heating the glass in a furnace to just below its softening point. At this temperature it is withdrawn from the furnace and chilled by blasts of cold air. The rapid cooling hardens and shrinks the outside of the glass; the inside cools more slowly. This produces compressional strain on the surfaces with a compensating state of tension inside, and has the effect of making the glass far stronger mechanically than ordinary glass. If, however, the glass does fracture in use, it disintegrates into a large number of small and harmless pieces with blunted edges. The size of these particles can be predetermined by an exact temperature control and time cycle in the toughening process, and manufacturers now produce a uniformly toughened safety glass which will, when broken, produce not less than 40 or more than 350 particles within a 50 mm square of glass. This conforms to the British Standard specification.

The main standards for the UK are:

BS 857

ECE R43 (UN regulation)

EEC Directive (AUE/178) (A common market regulation)

BS 857 glazing is still valid but is seldom used because ECE R43 is accepted throughout Europe, Japan and Australia.

There are other types of safety glass – mostly crossbreeds of the pure toughened glass screen which are designed to combine vision with safety. These are modified zone-toughened glasses, having three zones with varying fragmentation characteristics. The inner zone is a rectangular area directly in front of the driver,

not more than 200 mm high and 500 mm long. This is surrounded by two other zones, the outer one of which is 70 mm wide all round the edge of the windscreen. This type of windscreen has been fitted to various vehicles since 1962. As a result of ECE Regulation 43 this type of windscreen has been superseded by the fully zebra-zoned windscreen. Many countries, including the USA but with the exception of the UK, legislate against toughened windscreens.

Although sheet and plate glass are manufactured satisfactorily for use in doors, rear lights and windscreens, float glass has now largely superseded their use for reasons of economy and improved flatness.

Most laminated windscreens used in the motor

136

vehicle trade are 4.4 mm, 5 mm, 5.8 mm or 6.8 mm in overall thickness, with a 0.76 mm PVB interlayer. However, 4.4 mm is the thinnest laminated glass available, and as this has to be made from two pieces of glass it needs very careful handling during manufacture and is therefore expensive. Windscreens made from float glass should be a maximum of 6.8 mm thick, whether toughened or laminated. However, some large coaches and lorry windscreens are 7.8 mm thick (4 mm glass + 0.76 mm PVB interlayer + 3 mm glass). This gives immense strength and robustness against stone impact. Other body glasses, because they can be made from sheet glass and also can be toughened safety glass, are usually between 3 mm and 4 mm thick.

From our brief look at the history of glass manufacture it is obvious that the curving of glass presents no problems; in fact the problem has been to produce flat, optically perfect glass. However, to curve safety glass and still retain its optical and safety qualities requires careful control. Glass has no definite melting point, but when it is heated to approximately 600°C it will soften and can be curved. Curved glass should be specified as 6.8 mm thick, as it is more difficult to control the curving of 4.4 mm glass. Even 6.8 mm thick glass will have slight variations of curvature. To accommodate this tolerance, all curved glass should be glazed in a rubber glazing channel, of which there are many different sections available. Glazed edges of glasses should be finished with a small chamfer known as an arrissed edge, while edges of glasses that are visible or which run in a felt channel should be finished with a polished, rounded edge. Should a glass be required for glazing in a frame, a notch will usually be required to clear the plate used to join the two halves of the frame together. The line of this notch must not have sharp corners because of the possibilities of cracking. Although laminated safety glass can be cut or ground to size after laminating, toughened safety glass must be cut to size and edge finished before the heat treating process.

Nearly all fixed glazing is now glazed using adhesive systems. Shapes are becoming more complex, needing very good angles of entry control to meet bonding requirements. The trend is towards aerodynamic designs involving flush glazing and the removal of sudden changes in vehicle shape; therefore corners must be rounded rather than angular as in older vehicle designs. Glass is often supplied with moulded-on finisher (encapsulation). Consequently bending processes are becoming very sophisticated. Adhesive glazing (polyurethane is the adhesive normally used) has added considerably to the complexity of vehicle glazing in a scientific sense. It has many advantages, however, if carried out correctly: it will reduce water leaks, it suits modern car construction, it results in a load bearing glazing member, and it lends itself to robotic assembly in mass production. As a consequence of adhesive glazing, all the associated glazing is now printed with a ceramic fired-in black band to

---

(Facing page)

Figure 4.3 Applications of plastics in automobiles (*Motor Insurance Repair Research Centre*)

1 Front bumper (Pocan S7913)
2 Front spolier (Santoprene grade 123-50 and 121 with aluminium insert)
3 Fog lamp blanking plate (Xenoy EPX500)
4 Lower front grille (Xenoy CL100)
5 Front number plate plinth (Xenoy CL100)
6 Front bumper insert (PVC and EB-type Nylar)
7 Front grille (moulding, ABS; Bezel, MS Chrome)
8 Bonnet/boot lid/tailgate badges (ABS, aluminium and PU skin)
9 Underbonnet felt (moulded felt)
10 Door mirror casing RH and LH (polymide, 15% glass reinforced)
11 Door mirror mouning RH and LH (polymide, 15% glass reinforced)
12 Front/rear wheel trims RH and LH (*cap*, Noryl 731; *moulding*, Bayer Duretan BM30X, ICI Maranyl TB570)
13 Front/rear mudflaps RH and LH (front, rubber to BLS.22 RD.27 Ref. 421; rear, EPDM mix 4080)
14 Scuttle grille/mouldings (ABS)
15 Front/rear screen upper and side mouldings (PVC with stainless steel co-extrusion)
16 Front/rear wing splashguards RH and LH (PP)
17 Front wing waist moulding RH and LH (Noryl)
18 Front door waist moulding RH and LH (Noryl)
19 Rear door waist moulding RH and LH (Noryl)
20 Rear wing waist moulding RH and LH (Noryl)
21 Front/rear door outer handles RH and LH (*body*, Xenoy; *flap*, Glass-filled nylon)
22 Rear quarterlight moulding RH and LH (*4-door*, PVC/Stainless steel extrusion; *5-door and coupé*, PU with stainless steel moulding)
23 Boot lid moulding (ABS)
24 Rear spoiler (PU core and polyester skin)
25 Rear number plate plinth (ABS)
26 Rear bumper insert (PVC and EB-type Nylar)
27 Rear bumper (Pocan S7913)
28 Front/rear door upper mouldings RH and LH (PVC with stainless steel moulding)
29 Front/rear door outer weatherseals RH and LH (PVC with stainless steel co-extrusion)
30 Fog lamp bezel (PP)

Table 4.15   Physical properties of metals and alloys

Metal	Melting temperature range (°C)	Density (kg/m³)	Specific heat capacity/ (J/kg/K × 10³)	Thermal conductivity (W/m/K)	Electrical conductivity (% IACS)	Coefficient of linear expansion/ (K × 10⁻⁶)
Aluminium	660	2.69	0.22	218	63	23
Al-3.5 magnesium	550/620	2.66	0.22	125	25	23
Duralumin type	530/610	2.80	0.21	115–140	20–36	23
Copper	1085	8.92	0.39	393	101	17
70/30 brass	920/950	8.53	0.09	120	17	19
95/5 tin bronze	980/990	8.74	0.09	80	12	17
Lead	327	11.34	0.13	35	8	29
Magnesium	650	1.73	1.04	146	35	30
Nickel	1455	8.90	0.51	83	21	13
Monel	1330/1360	8.80	0.43	26	3	10
Tin	232	7.30	0.22	64	13	20
Titanium	1665	4.50	0.58	17	3	8.5
Zinc	419	7.13	0.39	113	26	37
Iron	1535	7.86	0.46	71	7	12
Mild steel	1400	7.86	0.12	45	31	11

protect the polyurethane adhesive from ultraviolet degradation, and also for cosmetic reasons so that the adhesive cannot be seen.

By a Ministry of Transport regulation, safety glass was made compulsory in 1937 for windscreens and other front windows. As already indicated, with effect from 1 January 1959 the Road Traffic and Vehicle Order 359 has demanded that for passenger vehicles and dual-purpose vehicles, all glass shall be safety glass. For goods vehicles, windscreens and all windows in front of, or at the side of, the driver's seat shall be safety glass.

4.14   PROPERTIES OF METALS

Metals and alloys possess certain properties which make them especially suitable for the processes involved in vehicle bodywork, particularly the forming and shaping of vehicle body parts either by press or by hand, and some of the jointing processes. These properties are described in the following sections, and some typical values of characteristics are shown in Tables 4.15 and 4.16.

4.14.1   Malleability

A malleable metal may be stretched in all directions without fracture occurring, and this property is essential in the processes of rolling, spinning, wheeling, raising, flanging, stretching and shrinking. In the operation of beating or hammering a metal on a steel block

(such as planishing) an action takes place at each blow wherein the metal is squeezed under the blow of the hammer and is forced outwards around the centre-point of the blow. The thinner the metal can be rolled or hammered into sheet without fracture the more malleable is the metal.

After cold working, metals tend to lose their malleable properties and are said to be in a work hardened condition. This condition may be desirable for certain purposes, but if further work is to be carried out the malleability may be restored by annealing. Annealing, or softening, of the metal is usually carried out before or during curvature work such as raising and hollowing, provided the metal is not coated with a low-melting-point material. However, the quality of modern sheet metal is such that many forming operations, such as deep drawing and pressing, may be carried out without the need for an application of heat.

The following are examples in which the properties of malleability are most evident:

Riveting   Here the metal will be seen to have spread to a marked degree. If splitting occurs the metal is insufficiently malleable or has been overworked (work hardened).

Shaping   The blank for a dome consists of a flat disc which has to be formed by stretching and shrinking into a double-curvature shape. The more malleable and ductile the material of the blank is, the more readily it can be formed; the less malleable and ductile, the more quickly does the metal work hardened thus needs more frequent annealing.

Table 4.16 Typical mechanical properties of metals and alloys

Material	Modulus of elasticity E (kN/mm^2)	Tensile and compressive strength (N/mm^2)	Elongation (%)	Hardness (HV)
Pure aluminium	68–70	62–102	45–7	15.30
Aluminium alloys	68–72	90–500	20–5	20–80
Magnesium	44	170–310	5–8	30–60
Cast irons (grey)	75–145	150–410	0.5–1.0	160–300
SG cast iron	170–172	370–730	17–2	150–450
Copper	122–132	155–345	60–5	40–100
Copper alloys	125–135	200–950	70–5	70–250
Mild steel	190	420–510	22–24	130
Structural steels	190	480–700	20–24	130
Stainless steel	190	420–950	40–20	300–170
Titanium	100–108	300–750+	5–35	55–90
Zinc	90	200–500	25–30	45–50

The degree of malleability possessed by a metal is measured by the thinness of leaves that can be produced by hammering or rolling. Gold is extremely malleable and may be beaten into a very thin leaf. Of the metals used for general work, aluminium and copper are outstanding for their properties. The property of malleability is used to advantage in the manufacture of mild steel sheets, which are rolled to a given size and gauge for the motor industry. It is also evident in the ability of mild steel and aluminium panels to be formed by mechanical presses into complicated contours for body shells. Malleability and ductility are the two essential properties needed in order to mass produce vehicle body shells by pressing.

The order of malleability of various metals by hammering is as follows: gold, silver, aluminium, copper, tin, lead, zinc, steel.

4.14.2 Ductility

Ductility depends on tenacity or strength in tension and the ease with which a metal is deformed, and is the property which enables a metal to be drawn out along its length, that is drawn into a wire. In wire drawing, metal rods are drawn through a hole in a steel die; the process is carried out with the metal cold, and the metal requires annealing when it becomes work hardened.

Ductile properties are also necessary in metals and alloys using the following processes:

Pressed components Special sheets which have extra deep drawing qualities are manufactured especially for press work such as that used in modern motor vehicle body production. These sheets undergo several deformations during the time they are being formed into components, yet because of their outstanding ductile properties they seldom fracture.

Welding electrodes and rods Ductility is an essential property in the production of electrodes, rods and wires. The wire drawing machines operate at exceptionally high speeds and the finished product conforms to close tolerances of measurement; frequent failure of the material during the various stages of drawing would be very costly.

The order of ductility of various metals is as follows: gold, aluminium, steel, copper, zinc, lead.

4.14.3 Tenacity

A very important property of metals is related to its strength in resistance to deformation; that property is tenacity, which may be defined as the property by which a metal resists the action of a pulling force. The ultimate tensile strength of a metal is a measure of the force which ultimately fractures or breaks the metal under a tensile pull. The ultimate tensile strength (UTS) of a material is normally expressed in tons per in^2 or MN/m^2 and may be calculated as follows:

$$\text{UTS} = \frac{\text{tensile force in N}}{\text{cross-sectional area in mm}}$$

In this case the load is the maximum required to fracture a specimen of the material under test, and the calculation is based on fracture taking place across the original cross-sectional area. In ductile materials a special allowance must be made for wasting or reduction of original cross-sectional area.

High-carbon steels possess a high degree of tenacity, evidence of which can be seen in the steel cables used to lift heavy loads. The mild steels used in general engineering possess a small amount of tenacity, yet a bar of metal of one inch square (6.5 cm^2) cross-section, made from low-carbon steel, is capable of supporting a load in excess of 20 tonnes.

Methods of increasing tensile strength
It is possible to increase the tensile strength of both sheet steel and pure aluminium sheets by cold rolling, but this has the added effect of reducing their workable qualities. In the manufacture of vessels to contain liquids or gases under pressure it is not always possible to use metals with a high tensile strength; for instance, copper is chosen to make domestic hot water storage cylinders because this metal has a high resistance to corrosion. In this case, the moderate strength of copper is increased by work hardening such as planishing, wheeling and cold rolling. Work hardening has the added effect of decreasing the malleability.

The order of tenacity of various metals in tons per in^2 (MN/m^2) is: steel 32 (494); copper 18 (278); aluminium 8 (124); zinc 3 (46); lead 1.5 (23).

4.14.4 Hardness

When referring to hardness, it should be carefully stated which kind of hardness is meant. For example, it may be correctly said that hardness is that property in a metal which imparts the ability to:

1 Indent, cut or scratch a metal of inferior hardness.
2 Resist abrasive wear.
3 Resist penetration.

A comparison of hardness can be made with the aid of material testing machines such as those used to carry out the Brinell or Vickers Diamond tests. Hardness may be increased by the following methods:

Planishing In addition to increasing the tensile strength of a metal, planishing also imparts hardness.
Heat treatment Medium- and high-carbon steels, such as those used in many body working tools, can be hardened by heating to a fixed temperature and then quenching.

The order of hardness of various metals is as follows: high-carbon steel, white cast iron, cast iron, mild steel, copper, aluminium, zinc, tin, lead.

4.14.5 Toughness

This property imparts to a metal the ability to resist fracture when subjected to impact, twisting or bending. A metal need not necessarily be hard to be tough; many hard metals are extremely brittle, a property which may be regarded as being opposite to toughness.

Toughness is an essential property in rivets. During the forming process the head of the rivet is subject to severe impact, and when in service rivets are frequently required to resist shear, twist and shock loads. Toughness is also a requisite for steel motor car bodies, which must be capable of withstanding heavy impacts and must often suffer severe denting or buckling without fracture occurring. Further, when repairs are to be made to damaged areas it is often necessary to apply force in the direction opposite to that of the original damaging force; and the metal must possess a high degree of toughness to undergo such treatment.

4.14.6 Compressibility

Compressibility may be defined as the property by which a metal resists the action of a compressing force. The *ultimate compressive strength* of a metal is a measure of the force which ultimately causes the metal to fail or yield under compression. Compressibility is related to malleability in so far as the latter refers to the degree to which a metal yields by spreading under the action of a compressing or pushing force, while the former represents the degree to which a metal opposes that action.

4.14.7 Elasticity

All metals possess some degree of elasticity; that is, a metal regains its original shape after a certain amount of distortion by an external force. The elastic limit of a metal is a measure of the maximum amount by which it may be distorted and yet return to its original form on removal of the force. Common metals vary considerably in elasticity. Lead is very soft yet possesses only a small amount of elasticity. Steel, on the other hand, may reveal a considerable degree of elasticity as, for example, in metal springs. The elasticity of mild steel is very useful in both the manufacture of highly curved articles by press work and in the repair of motor car bodies.

4.14.8 Fatigue

Most metals in service suffer from fatigue. Whether the metal ultimately fails by fracture or by breaking depends on a number of factors associated with the type and conditions of service. When metal structures in service are subjected to vibration over long periods, the rapid alterations of push and pull, i.e. compressive and tensile stresses, ultimately cause hardening of the metal with increased liability to fracture. Any weak points in the structure are most affected by the action and become the probable centres of failure, either by fracture or by breaking. Various methods have been devised for testing the capacity of metals to resist fatigue, all of which depend on subjecting the metal specimen to alternating vibratory stresses until failure occurs. The rate and extent of vibration over a specified time form the basis of most fatigue tests.

4.14.9 Weldability

This property is a measure of the ease with which a metal can be welded using one of the orthodox systems of welding. Certain metals are welded very easily by all recognized methods; some metals can only be welded by special welding processes; and other metals and alloys cannot be welded under any circumstances.

4.15 HEAT TREATMENT OF METALS AND METAL ALLOYS

Heat treatment can be defined as a process in which the metal in the solid state is subjected to one or more temperature cycles, to confer certain desired properties. The heat treatment of metals is of major importance in motor bodywork. All hand tools used by the body worker are made from a type of steel which is heat treatable so that the tools are strong, hard and have lasting qualities. The mechanical parts of a motor vehicle are also subject to some form of heat treatment, and in the constructional field heat-treatable aluminium alloys are being used extensively in commercial bodywork.

4.15.1 Work hardening and annealing

Most of the common metals cannot be hardened by heat treatment, but nearly all metals will harden to some extent as a result of hammering, rolling or bending. Annealing is a form of heat treatment for softening a metal which has become work hardened so that further cold working can be carried out. The common metals differ quite a lot in their degree and rate of work hardening. Copper hardens rather quickly under the hammer and, as this also reduces the malleability and ductility of the metal, it needs frequent annealing in order that it may be further processed without risk of fracture. Lead, on the other hand, may be beaten into almost any shape without annealing and without undue risk of fracture. It possesses a degree of softness which allows quite a lot of plastic deformation with very little work hardening. However, copper, though less soft than lead, is more malleable. Aluminium will withstand a fair amount of deformation by beating, rolling and wheeling before it becomes necessary to anneal it. The pure metal work hardens much less rapidly than copper, though some of the sheet aluminium alloys are too hard or brittle to allow very much cold working. Commercially pure iron may be cold worked to a fair extent before the metal becomes too hard for further working. Impurities in iron or steel impair the cold working properties to the extent that most steels cannot be worked cold (apart from very special low-carbon mild steel sheets used in the car industry), although nearly all steels may be worked at the red-heat condition.

The exact nature of the annealing process used depends to a large extent on the purpose for which the annealed metal is to be used. There is a vast difference in technique between annealing in a steel works where enormous quantities of sheet steel are produced, and annealing in a workshop where single articles may require treatment. Briefly, cold working causes deformation by crushing or distorting the grain structure within the metal. In annealing, a metal or alloy is heated to a temperature at which recrystallization occurs, and then allowed to cool at a predetermined rate. In other words, crystals or grains within the metal which have been displaced and deformed during cold working are allowed to rearrange themselves into their natural formation during the process of annealing. Iron and low-carbon steels should be heated to about 900°C and allowed to cool very slowly to ensure maximum softness, as far as possible out of contact with air to prevent oxidation of the surface; this can be done by cooling the metal in warm sand. High-carbon steels require similar treatment except that the temperature to which the steel needs to be heated is somewhat lower and is in the region of 800°C. Copper should be heated to a temperature of about 550°C or dull red, and either quenched in water or allowed to cool out slowly. The rate of cooling does not affect the resulting softness of this metal. The advantage of quenching is that the surface of the metal is cleaned of dirt and scale. Aluminium may be annealed by heating to a temperature of 350°C. This may be done in a suitable oven or salt bath. In the workshop aluminium is annealed by the use of a blowpipe, and a stick or splinter of dry wood is rubbed on the heated metal; when the wood leaves a charred black mark the metal is annealed. Sometimes a piece of soap is used instead of wood; when the soap leaves a brown mark the heating should be stopped. The metal may then be quenched in water or allowed to cool out slowly in air. Zinc becomes malleable between 100 and 150°C, and so may be annealed by immersing it in boiling water. Zinc should be worked while still hot, as it loses much of its malleability when cold.

4.15.2 Heat treatment of carbon steel

Steel is an important engineering material because, although cheap, it can be given a wide range of mechanical properties by heat treatment. Heat treatment can both change the size and shape of the grains and alter the microconstituents. The shape of the grains can be altered by heating the steel to a temperature above that of recrystallization. The size of the grains can be controlled by the temperature and the duration of the heating, and the speed at which the steel is cooled after the heating; the microconstituents can be altered by heating the steel to a temperature that is sufficiently high to produce the solid solution austenite so that the carbon is dispersed, and then cooling it at a rate which will produce the desired structure. The micrograin structure of carbon steel has the following constituents:

Ferrite Pure iron.

Cementite Carbon and iron mixed.

Pearlite A sandwich layer structure of ferrite and cementite.

All low-carbon steels of less than 0.83 per cent carbon content consist of a combination of ferrite and pearlite. Carbon steel containing 0.83 per cent carbon is called eutectoid and consists of pure pearlite structure. Steels over 0.83 per cent carbon up to 1.2 per cent carbon are a mixture of cementite and pearlite structures. If a piece of carbon steel is heated steadily its temperature will rise at a uniform rate until it reaches 700°C. At this point, even though the heating is continued, the temperature of the steel will first remain constant for a short period and then continue to rise at a slower rate until it reaches 775°C. The pause in the temperature rise and the slowing down of the rate indicate that energy is being absorbed to bring about a chemical and structural change in the steel. The carbon in the steel is changing into a solid solution with the iron and forming what is known as austenite. The temperature at which this change in the structure of the steel starts is 700°C, which is known as the lower critical point; the temperature at which the change ends is known as the upper critical point. The difference between these points is termed the critical range. The lower critical point is the same for all steels, but the upper critical point varies with the

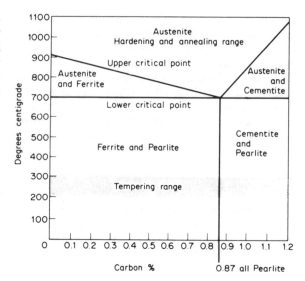

Figure 4.4 Changes in structure of carbon steel with temperature and carbon content

carbon content as shown in Figure 4.4. Briefly, steels undergo a chemical and structural change, forming austenite, when heated to a temperature above the upper critical point; if allowed to cool naturally they return to their normal composition.

Steel can be heat treated by normalizing, hardening, tempering and case hardening as well as by annealing, which has already been described in Section 4.15.1.

Normalizing

Normalizing is a process used to refine the grain structure of steel after it has been subjected to prolonged heating above the critical range (as in the case of forging) and to remove internal stresses caused by cold working. The process may appear to differ little from annealing, but as its name suggests the effect of normalizing is to bring the steel back to its normal condition and no attempt is made to soften the steel for further working. Normalizing is effected by slowly heating the steel to just above its upper critical range for just sufficient time to ensure that it is uniformly heated, and then allowing it to cool in still air.

Hardening

It has already been said that if a piece of steel is allowed to cool naturally after heating to above its upper critical point, it will change from austenite back to its original composition. If, however, the temperature of the heated steel is suddenly lowered by quenching it in clean cold water or oil, this change back from austenite does not take place, and instead of pearlite,

142

Table 4.17 Temperature colours for steel

Colour	Temperature (°C)
Black	450–550
Very dark red	600–650
Dark red	700–750
Cherry red	800–850
Full red	850–900
Bright red	950–1000
Dark orange	1050–1100
Light orange	1150–1200
Yellow white	1270–1300
White (welding heat)	1400–1550

a new, extremely hard and brittle constituent is formed, called martensite. This process makes steels containing 0.3 per cent or more carbon extremely hard, but steels having a carbon content of less than 0.3 per cent cannot be hardened in this way because the small amount of carbon produces too little martensite to have any noticeable hardening effect. The steel to be hardened should be quenched immediately it is uniformly heated to a temperature just above the upper critical point. It is also important not to overheat the steel and to allow it to cool to the quenching temperature. Whether water or oil is used for quenching depends on the use to which the steel is to be put. Water quenching produces an extremely hard steel but is liable to cause cracks and distortion. Oil quenching is less liable to cause these defects but produces a slightly softer steel. A more rapid and more even rate of cooling can be obtained if the steel is moved about in the cooling liquid, but only that part of the steel which is to be hardened should be moved up and down in the liquid in order to avoid a sharp boundary between the soft and hard portions.

A workshop method of hardening carbon tool steel is to heat the steel, using the forge or oxyacetylene blowtorch, to a dull red colour (see Table 4.17) and then quench it in water or oil. This would harden the article ready for tempering.

Tempering

Hardened steel is too brittle for most purposes, and the process of tempering is carried out to allow the steel to regain some of its normal toughness and ductility. This is done by heating the steel to a temperature below the lower critical point, usually between 200 and 300°C, thereby changing some of the martensite back to pearlite. The exact temperature will depend on the purpose for which the steel is intended; the higher the temperature, the softer and less brittle the tempered steel becomes. Methods used for controlling the tempering process depend on the size and class of the article to be tempered. One method is to heat the hardened steel in a bath of molten lead and tin, the melting points of various combinations of these two metals being used as an indication of the temperature. Another method of tempering small articles is to polish one face or edge and heat it with a flame. This polished surface will be seen to change colour as the heat is absorbed. The colour changes are caused by the formation at different temperatures of thin films of oxide, called tempering colours (Table 4.18). After tempering, the steel is either quenched or allowed to cool naturally.

Case hardening

Although mild steels having a carbon content of less than 0.3 per cent cannot be hardened, the surface of the mild steel can be changed to a high carbon steel. Case hardening of mild steel can be divided into three main processes:

1 Carburizing.
2 Refining and toughening the core.
3 Hardening and tempering the outer case.

A method called pack carburizing is often used in small workshops. After thoroughly cleaning them, the steel parts to be carburized are packed in an iron box so that each part is entirely surrounded by 2.5 cm of carburizing compound. The box is sealed with fireclay, heated in a furnace to 950°C and kept at that temperature for 2 to 12 hours, during which time the carbon

Table 4.18 Tempering colours for plain carbon steel

Colour	Temperature (°C)	Type of article
Pale straw	220–230	Metal turning tools, scrapers, scribers
Dark straw	240–245	Taps, dies, reamers, drills
Yellow-brown	250–255	Large drills, wood turning tools
Brown	260–265	Wood working tools, chisels, axes
Purple	270–280	Cold chisels, press tools, small springs, punches, knives
Blue	290–300	Springs, screwdrivers, hand saws

in the compound is absorbed by the surface of the steel parts. The steel parts are then allowed to cool slowly in the box. At this stage their cores will have a coarse grain structure due to prolonged heating, and the grain is refined by heating the steel parts to 900°C and quenching them in oil. Next the casing is hardened by reheating the steel to just under 800°C and then quenching it in water or oil. Tempering of the casing may then be carried out in the normal way.

Small mild steel parts can be given a very thin casing by heating them in a forge to a bright red heat and coating them with carburizing powder. The parts are then returned to the forge and kept at a bright red heat for a short period to allow the carbon in the compound to penetrate the surface of the metal. Finally the parts are quenched and ready for use.

4.15.3 Heat treatment of aluminium alloys

An aluminium alloy is heat treated by heating it for a prescribed period at a prescribed temperature, and then cooling it rapidly, usually by quenching. The particular form of heat treatment which results in the alloy attaining its full strength is known as solution treatment. The alloy is raised to a temperature of 490°C by immersing it in a bath of molten salt. The bath is usually composed of equal parts of sodium nitrate and potassium nitrate contained in an iron tank. This tank is heated by gas burners and, except for its open top, is enclosed with the burners in a firebrick structure which conserves the heat. The temperature of the bath must be carefully regulated, as any deviation either above or below prescribed limits may result in the failure of the metal to reach the required strength. The alloy is soaked at 490°C for 15 minutes and then quenched immediately in cold water.

At the moment of quenching the alloy is reasonably soft, but hardening takes place fairly rapidly over the first few hours. Some alloys, chiefly the wrought materials, harden more rapidly and to a greater extent than others. Their full strength is attained gradually over four or five days (longer in cold weather); this process is known as natural age hardening. As age hardening reduces ductility, any appreciable cold working must be done while the metal is still soft. Working of the natural ageing aluminium alloys must be completed within 2 hours of quenching, or for severe forming within 30 minutes. Age hardening may be delayed by storing solution-treated material at low temperatures. Refrigerated storage, usually at 6–10°C, is used for strip sheet and rivets, and work may be kept for periods up to 4 days after heat treatment. If refrigerated storage is not used to prevent age hardening

it may be necessary to repeat solution treatment of the metal before further work is possible.

Alloys of the hiduminium class may be artificially age hardened when the work is finished. Artificial ageing is often called precipitation treatment; this refers to the precipitation of the two intermetallic compounds responsible for the hardening, namely copper and manganese silicon. The process consists of heating the work in an automatically controlled oven to a temperature in the region of 170°C for a period of 10 to 20 hours. Artificial ageing at this temperature does not distort the work. The temperature of the oven must be maintained to within a few degrees, and a careful check on the temperature is kept by a recording instrument. In order to ensure uniform distribution of temperature a fan is fitted inside the oven to keep the air in circulation. At the end of a period of treatment the oven is opened to allow the work to cool down. One of the chief advantages of this process is that work of a complicated character may be made and completed before ageing takes place. Moreover, numerous parts may be assembled or riveted together and will not suffer as a result of the ageing treatment.

QUESTIONS

1 What would the following alloy steels be used for: (a) high-tensile steel (b) manganese steel (c) chrome-vanadium steel?
2 List the properties of commercially pure aluminium.
3 Explain why, in the construction of a motor vehicle, commercially pure aluminium has a very limited application.
4 Identify the grades of hardness in aluminium sheet and state how the hardness is achieved.
5 Explain how you would identify the following: (a) low-carbon steel (b) aluminium alloy (c) stainless steel.
6 Describe the difference between laminated safety glass and toughened safety glass.
7 Give three requirements of a body sealing compound, and describe one type of sealer used in vehicle repair.
8 Suggest reasons why stainless steel is sometimes used for trim and mouldings.
9 Explain the difference between hide and PVC materials.
10 Explain what is meant by micro-alloyed steel or HSS.
11 Give reasons why car manufacturers are using zinc-coated steels.
12 Name the three main groups of stainless steel.

13 Explain the following terms in relation to plastic: (a) monomer (b) polymer (c) copolymer.

14 Explain the difference between thermoplastics and thermosetting plastics.

15 Which safety glass, used for vehicle windscreens, shatters into small segments on impact?

16 Describe the basic properties required of a body joint sealing compound.

17 Identify the group of plastics that can be softened or remoulded by the application of heat.

18 Steel panels can be strengthened without adding weight. Name and explain the process.

19 Describe three different ways in which the surface of steel can be protected.

20 State the reasons why certain metals need to be protected from the effects of the atmosphere.

21 Describe how some metals can resist attack by the atmosphere.

22 What is the alloying effect when zinc and copper are added to aluminium?

23 Explain the different properties of heat-treatable and non-heat-treatable aluminium alloys.

24 State the reasons, other than weldability, why low-carbon steel is chosen in preference to aluminium as a vehicle body shell material.

25 Define the term 'HSLA steel'.

26 Define what is meant by the term 'non-ferrous metal'.

27 Explain the difference in properties between low-carbon steel and alloy steel.

28 Describe the two processes which can be used to join plastic.

29 Explain where plastic can be used on a vehicle.

30 State the applications where natural rubber has been replaced by synthetic materials in the automobile industry.

5

Electric resistance welding

5.1 RESISTANCE WELDING IN CAR BODY MANUFACTURE

Resistance welding is a joining process belonging to the pressure welding sector. With its locally applied heat and pressure it has an obvious relationship with the forge welding technique practised by blacksmiths when joining metal. The resistance welding process was invented in 1877 by Professor E. Thomson of Philadelphia, USA, when an accidental short circuit gave him the idea for what was originally termed short circuit welding. From the beginning of the twentieth century it was used on a small scale in industry, but it was only after the Second World War that resistance spot welding had its real beginning in the automobile industry. It has since grown to be the most important method of welding used in the construction and mass production of vehicle bodies.

Resistance welding is extensively used for the mass production assembly of the all-steel body and its component sheet metal parts (see Figure 5.1). Its wide adoption has been brought about by its technical advantages and the reductions in cost. Most mass-produced car bodies are assembled entirely by welding steel pressings together to produce an integral rigid chassis and body structure. Low-carbon steel thicknesses used in this unitary construction range from 0.8–1 mm for skin or floor panels to 3 mm for major structural pressings such as suspension brackets. Intermediate gauges such as 1.2 mm are used for hinge reinforcements, 1.6 mm for chassis structural members, and 1.8 mm to 2.5 mm for suspension and steering members. With the introduction of high-strength steels (HSLA steels), car manufacturers are producing body panels as thin as 0.55 mm, and structural members with gauges of between 1.2 and 2 mm. This reduction in thickness can be made without loss of strength.

There are a number of resistance welding processes. Resistance spot welding is the most widely used welding process in car body construction; there are approximately 4500 to 6000 spot welds per body, which accounts for approximately 80 per cent of the welding used. A further 10 per cent is composed of other resistance welding processes: seam, projection,

flash and butt welding. The remaining 10 per cent is divided between MIG/MAG welding and gas welding. Of the many welding techniques used in the mass production of car bodies, resistance welding dominates the field.

The fundamental principle upon which all resistance welding is based lies in the fact that the weld is produced by the heat obtained from the resistance to flow of electric current through two or more pieces of metal held together under pressure by electrodes which are made from copper or copper alloys. The engineering definition of heat (heat being the essence of all welding) is (energy) × time. This indicates a balance between energy[2] input and weld time; therefore the faster the welding, the greater the clamping force. However, the engineering definition of resistance is such that the higher the clamping force, the greater the current needed to produce a constant heat.

Heat is generated by the resistance of the parts to be joined to the passage of a heavy electrical current. This heat at the junction of the two parts changes the metal to a plastic state. When the correct amount of pressure is then applied fusion takes place.

There is a close similarity in the construction of all resistance welding machines, irrespective of design and cost. The main difference is in the type of jaws or electrodes which hold the object to be welded. A standard resistance welder has four principal elements:

Figure 5.1 Automatic spot welding using robots on body framing assembly line (*Vauxhall Motors Ltd*)

146

Figure 5.2 Robot spot welder on an assembly line (*Vauxhall Motors Ltd*)

Figure 5.4 Portable spot welding machine in use (*SIP (Industrial Products) Ltd*)

Figure 5.3 Stationary pedestal spot-welding machine (*SIP (Industrial Products) Ltd*)

Frame The main body of the machine, which differs in size and shape for robot, stationary and portable types (Figures 5.2, 5.3, 5.4).

Electrical circuit Consists of a step-down transformer, which reduces the voltage and proportionally increases the amperage to provide the necessary heat at the point of weld.

Electrodes Include the mechanism for making and holding contact at the weld area.

Timing control Represents the switches which regulate the volume of current, length of current time and the contact period. Many now include adaptive in-process control units (pulsing weld timer).

The principal forms of resistance welding are classified as: resistance spot welding; resistance projection welding; resistance seam welding; resistance flash welding; and resistance butt welding.

5.2 RESISTANCE SPOT WELDING

Resistance spot welding (Figure 5.5) is basically confined to making welds approximately 6 mm diameter between two or more overlapping sheet metal panels. This type of welding is probably the most commonly used type of resistance welding. The art of production planning for spot welding is to simplify the presentation of panels in the region of mutual panel overlap. The limitation of spot welding is that the electrode assemblies have to withstand applied forces ranging from 2200 N to 4450 N for the range of sheet steel thicknesses used in vehicle construction and repair. Product design of planning must account, therefore, for the requirement that the electrodes, which are constructed from relatively weak copper alloys, need normal access to both sides of the overlapping panels to withstand such electrode forces.

The material to be joined is placed between two electrodes, pressure is applied, and the electric current passes from one electrode through the material to

147

Figure 5.5 (a) Resistance spot welding system
(b) relationship between weld formation, current and
pressure in welding

the other electrode. There are three stages in producing a spot weld. First, the electrodes are brought together against the metal and pressure is applied before the current is turned on. Next the current is turned on momentarily. This is followed by the third hold time, in which the current is turned off but the pressure continued. The hold time forges the metal while it is cooling.

Regular spot welding usually leaves slight depressions on the metal which are often undesirable on the show side of the finished product. These depressions are minimized by the use of larger-sized electrode tips on the show side. Resistance spot welding can weld dissimilar metal thickness combinations by using a larger electrode contact tip area against the

thicker sheet. This can be done for mild steel having a dissimilar thickness ratio of 3:1.

There are three kinds of distortion caused by resistance spot welding which are relevant to car body manufacture and repair. The first is the local electrode indentation due to the electrode sinking into the steel surface. This is a mechanical distortion – a byproduct of the spot welding process. Second, there is a small amount of thermal distortion which is troublesome when attempting to make spot welds on show surfaces such as skin panels without any discernible metal distortion. Last, there is the gross distortion caused when badly fitting panels are forced together at local spots. This is a mechanical distortion totally unconnected with the spot-welding process; the same type of distortion would occur with rivets or with any similar localized joining method. A combination of all these distortions contributes to the general spot-weld appearance, which is virtually unacceptable on a consumer product. The technique on car bodies is to arrange for spot-welded flanges to be either covered with trims (door apertures), or with a sealing weather strip (window and screen surrounds). The coach joint is one of the features that distinguish a cheap, mass-produced body from an expensive hand-built one.

Spot welders are made for both DC and AC. The amount of current used is very important. Too little current produces only a light tack which gives insufficient penetration. Too much current causes burned welds. Spot welds may be made one at a time or several welds may be completed at one time, depending on the number of electrodes used. One of the most significant advantages of resistance spot welding is its high welding production rate with the minimum of operator participation. Typical resistance spot-welding rates are 100 spots per minute. To dissipate the heat at the weld as quickly as possible, the electrodes are sometimes water cooled. Although many spot welders are of the stationary design, there is an increased demand for the more manoeuvrable, portable type. The electrodes which conduct the current and apply the pressure are made of low-resistance copper alloy and are usually hollow to facilitate water cooling. These electrodes must be kept clean and shaped correctly to produce good results. Spot welders are used extensively for welding steel, and when equipped with an electronic timer they can be used for metal such as aluminium, copper, stainless and galvanized steels.

5.3 RESISTANCE PROJECTION WELDING

Projection welding (Figure 5.6) involves the joining of parts by a resistance welding process which closely resembles spot welding. This type of welding is widely

Figure 5.6   Projection welding system

Figure 5.7   Continuous resistance seam welding

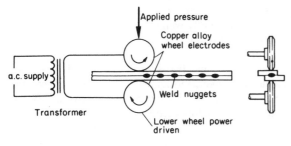

Figure 5.8   Seam welding (stitch welding)

used in attaching fasteners to structural members. The point where the welding is to be done has one or more projections which have been formed by embossing, stamping or machining. The distortion on the embossed metal face is low and is negligible on heavy metal thicknesses, although in the case of dissimilar thicknesses it is preferable to emboss the projection on the thicker of the two sheets. The projections serve to concentrate the welding heat at these areas and permit fusion without the necessity of employing

a large current. The welding process consists of placing the projections in contact with the mating fixtures and aligning them between the electrodes. The electrodes on the machine are not in this case bluntly pointed as in spot welding, but are usually relatively large flat surfaces which are brought to bear on the joint, pressing the projections together.

The machine can weld either a single projection or a multitude of projections simultaneously. The many variables involved in projection welding, such as thickness, kind of material, and number of projections, make it impossible to predetermine the correct current. Not all metals can be projection welded. Brass and copper do not lend themselves to this method because the projections usually collapse under pressure.

5.4   RESISTANCE SEAM WELDING

Seam welding (Figure 5.7) is like spot welding except that the spots overlap each other, making a continuous weld seam. In this process the metal pieces pass between roller-type electrodes. As the electrodes revolve, the current supply to each one is automatically turned on and off at intervals corresponding to the speed at which the parts are set to move. With proper control it is possible to obtain air-tight and water-tight seams suitable for such parts as fuel tanks and roof panels. When spots are not overlapped long enough to produce a continuous weld, the process is sometimes referred to as roller spot or stitch welding (Figure 5.8). In this way the work travels the distance between the electrodes required for each succeeding weld cycle. The work stops during the time required to make each individual weld and then automatically moves the proper distance for the next weld cycle. Intermittent current is usually necessary for most seam welding operations. Each individual weld contains a number of overlapping spot welds, resulting in a joint which has good mechanical strength but which is not pressure tight.

Mild steel, brass, nickel, stainless steel and many other alloys may be welded by this method, although its use is largely limited to operations on mild and stainless steel. A maximum economy is obtained if the combined thickness of sheets to be joined does not exceed 3.2 mm. Before welding, the surfaces must be clean and free from scale and this may be done by sand blasting, grinding or pickling.

5.5   RESISTANCE FLASH WELDING

In the flash welding process (Figure 5.9) the two pieces of metal to be joined are clamped by copper alloy dies which are shaped to fit each piece and which

149

Figure 5.9 Flash welding

Figure 5.10 Resistance butt welding

conduct the electric current to the work. The ends of the two metal pieces are moved together until an arc is established. The flashing action across the gap melts the metal and as the two molten ends are forced together fusion takes place. The current is cut off immediately this action is completed.

Flash welding is used to butt or mitre sheet, bar, rod, tube and extruded sections. It has unlimited application for both ferrous and nonferrous metals. For some operations the dies are water cooled to dissipate the heat from the welded area. The most important factor to be considered in flash welding is the precision alignment of the parts. The only problem encountered in flash welding is the resultant bulge or increased size left at the point of weld. If the finish area of the weld is important, then it becomes necessary to grind or machine the joint to the proper size.

5.6 RESISTANCE BUTT WELDING

In butt welding (Figure 5.10) the metals to be welded are brought into contact under pressure, an electric current is passed through them, and the edges are softened and fused together. This process differs from flash welding in that constant pressure is applied during the heating process, which eliminates flashing. The heat generated at the point of contact results entirely from resistance. Although the operation and control of the butt welding process is almost identical to flash welding, the basic difference is that it uses less current, has a constant pressure and allows more time for the weld to be completed.

5.7 RESISTANCE WELDING IN BODY REPAIR WORK

The object of car body repair is to put damaged vehicles back into a pre-accident condition. Today's chassisless bodies hold engine, suspension and steering in the right places and are designed to absorb the impact of crashes by crumpling, thus shielding the passenger compartment (and its passengers) from shock and deformation. From the viewpoint of safety as well as mechanical efficiency, proper welding is vital in this kind of repair.

Car body design demands careful choice of the sheet metal, which was, until recent years, all mild steel. Tensile strength and ductility, which are good in mild steel, are vital to 'crumplability' (the ability to absorb the impact energy), and this is why resistance spot welds are used. The average body shell is joined together by approximately 4500–6000 such spot welds. These remain ductile because the welding process does not alter the original specifications of the steel. Lighter body weight reduces the load on the car engine and therefore has a direct influence on petrol consumption.

For weight and fuel saving reasons, high strength steels have been introduced for some panel assemblies on body shells. As these steels have a different character from low-carbon steel (mild steel), which still accounts for 60 per cent of the body shell (see Figure 5.11), they cause repair welding problems. Higher-strength steels have been made specifically for motor car manufacturers to produce body shells from thinner but stronger steel sheet. These steels are less ductile and are harder. Above all, they do not tolerate excess heat from bad welding, which makes them brittle or soft or can cause panel distortion. Low carbon steel tolerates excess heat well. While older all-mild-steel bodies essentially needed only to have the welding machine set for the metal thickness, current new bodies can contain steel of up to four different strengths, hardnesses and ductilities, some coated on one side, some coated on both sides, and some

Figure 5.11 Body panels made from high-strength/galvanized steels (*Motor Insurance Repair Research Centre*)

		Material			Material
1	Hood panel, outer	SGAC35R	20	Front pillar, outer, upper	SPRC35
2	Hood panel, inner	SGACC	21	Front pillar, inner, upper	SPRC35
3	Upper frame, outer	SGACC	22	Centre pillar, inner	SPRC35
4	Upper frame, inner	SGACC	23	Centre pillar, outer	SPRC35
5	Front side member	SPRC35	24	Front floor, side sill, outer	SGACC
6	Front end gusset	SPRC35	25	Front floor, side sill, inner	SGACC
7	Front fender	SENCE	26	Side sill, outer rear extension	SGACC
8	Front skirt panel	SGACC	27	Quarter panel, inner	SENCE
9	Grille filler panel	SGACC	28	Rear pillar, inner	SPRC35
10	Front end cross member	SPRC35	29	Rear shelf panel	SPRC35
11	Side sill, inner front	SGACC	30	Trunk lid inner paneL	SGACE
12	Front upper frame extension	SGACC	31	Trunk lid outer panel	SGAC35R
13	Cowl top outer panel	SGACC	32	Quarter panel, outer	SENCE
14	Front door outer panel	SGACC	33	Rear skirt panel	SGACC
15	Front door inner panel	SGACE	34	Rear floor cross member	SGACC
16	Rear door outer panel	SGACC	35	Rear floor side member	SGACC
17	Rear door inner panel	SGACE	36	Rear floor side sill	SGACC
18	Roof panel	SGACC	37	Roof reinforcement	SGAHC
19	Front pillar, outer, lower	SPRC35			

SPRC: phosphorus added

SGACC, E ⎤
SGAHC ⎦ Galvanized steel plate

SGAC35R: phosphorus added (also galvanized)

SENCE: SPCE with electrogalvanized zinc-nickel coating

The numbers in the material codes indicate the tensile strength (kg/mm^2)

uncoated. Zinc coated sheet materials require the use of heavier welding equipment capable of producing a higher current to penetrate the zinc coating, and the electrodes must be constantly maintained by cleaning to avoid zinc pick-up when welding.

The repair of bodies incorporating low-carbon steels and HSLA steels therefore demands very different welding routines from those for low-carbon steel alone. Low-carbon steel bodies can be resistance spot welded or gas (TIG) welded or arc (MIG) welded; but higher-strength steels should not undergo the last two processes, because they involve nearly three times the heat of resistance spot welding. The temperatures generated are over 3300°C for gas or arc welding but only 1350°C for resistance spot welds, for joints of similar strength. Higher-strength steels, however, with their higher tensile strength, limited ductility and greater hardness, are particularly vulnerable to heat, and are apt to lose strength and change ductility when overheated.

Developments in welding equipment combined with the use of electronic controls have opened the way to new body repair welding techniques that help to simplify the practical problems posed by bodies made from a mixture of low-carbon and high-strength low-alloy steels. The traditional resistance welding method has had to be improved to join higher-strength steels. Because the weld current flow is hindered by the steel's coating, these may require higher temperatures to break them down before a weld can be formed. For producing consistently good welds it is necessary to use two or three stages for welding, the duration of each stage being adapted to the nature of the steel and its coating.

5.8 RESISTANCE SPOT WELDING OF HIGH-STRENGTH STEELS

The rigidity of the body and its ability to withstand high torsional and other stresses depend on the assembly method used to bring the various body panels together. Spot welding is used throughout the industry (see Figure 5.12) for two reasons: first, because it is the strongest and most reliable method of joining two pieces of metal; and second, because of the total absence of panel distortion through the welding. In order to effect a satisfactory repair, vehicle welds having the same characteristics as the original are essential.

A comparison between an electrical spot weld and a forged weld shows that in both these processes a union is formed by an amalgamation of the metal molecules. These have been consolidated in each of

the two pieces, despite the difference in the two processes employed. In the case of forge welding the pieces are heated in the forge furnace and then hammered until a homogeneous material results. In the case of the spot-welding process the gun must have a pressure device which can be operated by the user and transmits the pressure to the electrodes, and a transformer to enable current at high intensity to be fed to the electrodes.

Spot welding is the primary body production welding method. Most production welding is carried out on metal gauges of less than 2.5 mm, although greater thicknesses can be spot welded. With the introduction of high-strength steels, car manufacturers are producing body panels as thin as 0.55 mm and using gauges of between 1.2 and 1.5 mm for structural members. By using the correct equipment, two-sided spot welding can be successfully accomplished on these steels.

Weld quality
Careful control of three factors is necessary to make a good-quality spot weld:

1 Squeeze time.
2 Weld time (duration of weld flow).
3 Hold time.

The main disadvantage associated with welding in general is that any visual inspection of the weld gives no indication of the weld quality. It is therefore essential that spot-welding equipment used in motor body repair takes outside circumstances automatically into account, such as rust, scale, voltage drop in the electric main supply, and current fluctuations.

The quality of a spot weld depends on:

1 The strength of the weld must be equal to the parent metal. This is a problem of tensile strength and homogeneity of the weld nugget itself.
2 The welding heat must not in any way alter the inherent qualities of the parent metal.
3 The welding pressure must prevent parent metal separation so as not to cause panel distortion and stresses in the assembly.

Heat application
With resistance welding the welding time is controlled by either electronic or electro (electrical) devices. Hand-held pincer-type weld guns, as supplied to the car body repair trade, are usually controlled electronically with the minimum of presetting. Weld time can range from a fraction of a second for very thin gauges of sheet steel, to one second for thicker sheet steel. Weld time is an important factor, because the strength of a weld nugget depends on the correct

Figure 5.12 Weldmaster 2022 in use (*ARO Machinery Co. Ltd*)

Figure 5.13 Welding together panels of the same thickness (*Motor Insurance Repair Research Centre*)

depth of fusion. Sufficient weld time is required to produce this depth of fusion by allowing the current time to develop enough heat to bring a small volume of metal to the correct temperature to ensure proper fusion of the two metals. If the temperature reached is too high, metal will be forced from the weld zone and may induce cavities and weld cracks. In some grades of high-strength steels, cracking within the vicinity of the heat affected zone has appeared after the welding operation.

Heat balance

In the resistance welding of panels of the same thickness and composition, the heat produced will be evenly balanced in both panels, and a characteristic oval cross-sectional weld nugget will result (see Figure 5.13). However, in the welding of panels produced from steels of a dissimilar composition, i.e. conventional low-carbon steel to high-strength low-alloy steels, an unbalanced heat rate will occur. This problem will also arise when spot welding two different thicknesses of steel; more heat will usually be lost by the thicker gauges, resulting in unsatisfactory welds. To compensate, the welder must either select an electrode made from materials that will alter the thermal resistance factor, or vary the geometry of the electrode tip, or use pulse equipment.

153

Figure 5.14 Types of electrode profile (*Motor Insurance Repair Research Centre*)

Table 5.1 Recommended tip pressures according to the gauge of steel

Gauge of panel (mm)	Pressure (kg)	Length of arm (mm)
0.55 + 0.55	50	250
0.80 + 0.30	60	250
0.95 + 0.95	70	250
1.00 + 1.00	80	250
1.25 + 1.25	100	250
1.25 + 2.00	120	250

These pressures relate to HS steels: a reduction in pressure may be necessary for conventional steels

Electrodes

The functions of the electrode (chromium/copper) are to:

1 Conduct the current to the weld zone.
2 Produce the necessary clamping force for the weldment.
3 Aid heat dissipation from the weld zone.

The profile and diameter of the electrode face is dependent upon the material to be welded (Figure 5.14). The diameter of the face will directly influence the size of the nugget. The proper maintenance of the electrode tip face is therefore vital to ensure that effective current flow is produced. For example, if a tip diameter of 5 mm is allowed through wear to increase to 8 mm, the contact area is virtually doubled; this will result in low current density and weak welds. Misalignment of the electrodes and incorrect pressure will also produce defective welds.

Electrode tip dressing is best carried out with a fine-grade emery cloth. Coated steels will often cause particles of the coating to become embedded in the surface of the electrode tip face (pick-up). This necessitates frequent tip dressing; when the faces have become distorted, the profile or contour must be reshaped. Cutters are available to suit most profiles and tip diameters. Domed tips are recommended; they adapt themselves best to panel shapes and last longest. The adjustment of electrode clamping force is critical for any type of steel, particularly when long-arm arrangements are used and complex configurations of arms are used for welding around wheel arches. It should also be noted that the tip force is difficult to maintain with long arms fitted to hand-held pincer-type guns (see Table 5.1).

5.8.1 Factors affecting weld quality

The following factors can have a large influence on the final outcome of the spot weld:

1 The type of metal being welded (for example, coated metals).
2 Joint configuration.
3 Current and timing settings.
4 The type of welding equipment being used.
5 Electrode maintenance.

Clearance between welding surfaces

Any clearance between the surfaces to be welded causes poor current flow. Even if welding can be made without removing such gaps, the welded area would become smaller, resulting in insufficient strength. Flatten the two surfaces to remove the gaps, and clamp them tightly before welding.

Metal surface to be welded

Paint film, rust, dust, or any other contamination on the metal surface to be welded causes insufficient current flow and poor results. Remove such foreign matter from the surface before commencing welding.

Corrosion prevention on metal surfaces

Coat the surface to be welded with anti-corrosion agent that has a high conductivity (e.g. zinc primers). It is important to apply the zinc primer uniformly between the panel surfaces to be welded.

Minimum welding pitch

The strength of individual spot welds is determined by the spot weld pitch (the distance between spot welds). The bond between the panels becomes stronger as the pitch is shortened, but if the pitch becomes too small and the spot welds are too close together this can allow current shunting, which in effect drains away the weld current towards the previous spot weld (Figure 5.15).

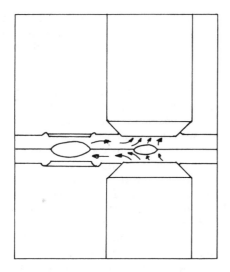

Figure 5.15 Current shunting in resistance welds positioned in close proximity

Positioning of welding spot from the edge and end of the panel

The edge distance is also determined by the position of the welding tip. Even if the spot welds are normal, the welds will not have sufficient strength if the edge distance is insufficient.

Inspection of spot welds

Spot welds are inspected either by outward appearance (visual inspection) or by destructive testing. A visual inspection is used to judge the quality of the outward appearance (tip bruises, pin holes, spatter, number of spots, spot positions), while destructive testing is used to measure the strength of a weld. Most destructive tests require the use of sophisticated equipment which most body shops do not possess. Consequently a simpler method called a peel test has been developed by general use in the workshop.

Destructive testing: peel test

After setting up the equipment a test weld should be made, using sheet metal of the same thickness and condition as the job to be done. When the test piece is completed, it should be torn apart. If the settings are correct, the joint will 'unbutton', that is the weld nuggets will be on one sheet and the holes on the other (Figure 5.16a).

Weld tests for shear and peel for HSLA steels

When shear testing spot welds produced when welding together two HSLA steels, partial spot-weld failure may occur. If the partial failure does not exceed

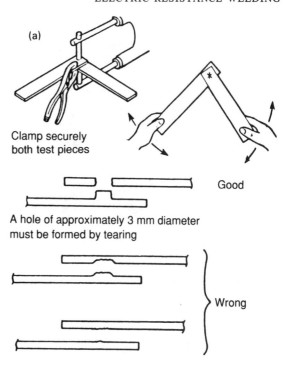

Clamp securely both test pieces

Good

A hole of approximately 3 mm diameter must be formed by tearing

Wrong

Reference value 3–4 mm

Chisel

Tap with a hammer

Figure 5.16 (a) Peel test (b) destructive test (*Motor Insurance Repair Research Centre*)

20 per cent of the total nugget area, the strength of the weld should not be impaired (see Figure 5.17).

5.9 ARO SPOTRITE PULSA RESISTANCE WELDING SYSTEM

For resistance spot welding in vehicle body repair there is now a British invention called the Spotrite (made by ARO Machinery Co. Ltd).

This is an adaptive (self-setting timing) in-process

Figure 5.17 Modes of spot-weld failure (*Motor Insurance Repair Research Centre*)

Figure 5.18 Spotrite Pulsa with gun (*ARO Machinery Co. Ltd*)

control unit which operates in several stages. Stage 1 is the monitoring stage for recognizing the material (low-carbon or HSLA steel) and for sensing through any protective coatings, while judging how closely the clamped materials are fitting between the electrodes which will form the joint. Stage 2 is automatically linked and self-setting to provide a burst of current to produce the weld nugget. Stage 3 (and 4 if needed) will provide further precise timed pulses to bring the weld to the desired size, taking into account the number of sheets of metal and their thickness and the distance of the weld from the edge of the workpiece. The adaptive part of the control decides the number of stages needed and their duration. A weld cycle which includes all these stages added together will take less than 0.75 s.

With this equipment much of the technology is transferred from the operator to the controls, only because the operator has no means of knowing which type of material he is welding. The control monitors what the welding gun is doing, and uses the information to take the decision by computing variables such as electrode tip wear, spot-weld pitch, voltage fluctuation, changes in metal thickness, and the presence of scale, dirt and rust. Consequently quality control is no longer the operator's responsibility.

Audiovisual signals warn the operator if there is overheating, if the electrode tip needs reshaping or cleaning, and if the weld arms are open too early. For difficult or unusual work, the experienced body repairer can switch to manual setting to control the unit's weld heat and time tolerance controls (see Figure 5.18).

A pincer-type welding gun with a powerful weld transformer (to maintain the very short weld times) is fitted with a strong pressure system to deal with the majority of work, which can be approached from two sides in pincer-type fashion. A range of interchangeable weld arms and electrodes of different shapes and lengths can be used to convert the standard gun instantly into the special tool that a job may require (see Figure 5.19). Special sets of arms with electrodes, specifically designed for use on individual makes of vehicles, have been designed in collaboration with most car manufacturers (Figure 5.20).

5.9.1 Setting up equipment for use

The most important points to be considered in setting up the equipment are:

1 Thickness of the sheet metal to be welded.
2 Accessibility of the parts to be welded.
3 State of the surface of the sheet metal to be welded (this must be as clean as possible, and any rust, scale or paintwork should be removed).

The setting-up procedure is as follows:

1 With the equipment switched off, check that the electrode tips are aligned and correctly shaped. If domed tips are used (these generally give the best results), the tip radii should be 51 mm and 77 mm. When truncated cone tips are used, check that the diameter is correct for the gauge of material to be used: the diameter should be $5\sqrt{t}$, where t is the thickness of single sheet in millimetres. Check that the tip force is enough without bending the electrode arms or sliding the tip one upon another.
2 Switch on mains supply and check that the mains light (red) is on.
3 Switch function selection switch to resistance spot welding.

Figure 5.19 Pincer welding gun used in different locations in repair work (*Motor Insurance Repair Research Centre*)

4 Switch on Spotrite control and check that the ready light is on.

5 Test earth leakage unit by pressing test button.

6 Set spot size to zero.

7 Make splashless welds by selecting the lowest heat and the longest time setting to make the desired size of weld nugget.

8 Make two welds approximately 51 mm apart. Peel test the second weld, i.e. tear the test piece apart and check whether the nugget is the size approximately

to the weld strength needed. The nugget size should be $4.5\sqrt{t}$.

9 Increase the spot size setting from zero in single steps, and make five trial welds in each setting. If the reject alarm is heard (a high pitched pulse note: red light illuminates) for more than three welds, reduce the spot size setting until the reject alarm is activated only two or three times.

10 Increase the heat step by step to reduce the actual weld time until splashing occurs. Then set back heat one step to stop splashing. The equipment is now fully set.

5.9.2 Welding procedure

1 Prepare the panel surface by removing any paint, primer and in general any insulating material covering the surface to be welded. This preparation is a key factor to good-quality spot welding. Paint must be removed by either paint remover or sanding. If rust is present on the panel surface, sanding is a better method of preparation as it will leave the surface with a bright metallic finish which facilitates the flow of electric current.

2 Obtain the correct adjustment of welding gun electrodes and arms.

3 Determine a suitable weld pitch for the panel assembly to be welded to obtain maximum strength.

4 Make sure that the correct distance is set from the edge of the sheet metal panel to the nearest spot weld.

5.10 SINGLE-SIDED SPOT WELDING

As a result of the operational limitations of conventional double-sided spot welding, single-sided spot welding equipment has become more widely used in the vehicle body repair industry. This system offers the benefits of conventional spot welding without the inherent problems of accessibility with double-skinned panel sections. Single-sided spot welding is therefore an alternative to conventional double-sided spot welding, or can be used in conjunction with it.

In the single-sided spot welding process the operator manually forces the single electrode against the panel, with the electrical circuit being completed by an earth clamp and the cable back to the transformer. This allows welds to be made in positions where access is possible only from one side.

Manufacturers are now using different types of steel to construct their vehicle bodies, the main three being low-carbon steel, galvanized steel and high-strength steel. This has led to confusion and difficulty

L = 125 mm
    250 mm
    350 mm
    500 mm

L = 250 mm
    125 mm

Figure 5.20 Electrode arm sets for different makes of vehicle (*SIP (Industrial Products) Ltd*)

in identification and welding. The main problem with high-strength steel is that it is heat sensitive and difficult to identify on vehicles without data (MIRRC Thatcham *Methods Manual*). In double-sided welding this problem is solved by using pulse welding, which keeps the heat in the weld as low as possible. Some single-sided equipment, especially that which operates at high current, does not require pulse control welding. Instead these machines use a massive burst of power at 8000 ADC in a very short interval, which keeps the temperature of the spot weld below the recommended temperature. The other advantage of this system is that it does not need to identify whether the steel is high strength or low carbon. The problem with galvanized steel is that it has a very high contact resistance, making it difficult to weld; therefore the high DC machines use a special preheat function for this type of steel. In the first stage of the weld the machine lowers the resistance of the steel by melting the coating, causing it to flow from the weld. Then, once the resistance is low enough, it will automatically carry out the second stage weld at the correct setting.

5.10.1 Single-sided spot welding equipment

This equipment (Figure 5.21) ranges from 2500 to 9200 amperes as follows:

1 2500 A using two phases at 415 V.
2 8000 A using three phases at 415 V.
3 9200 A using three phases at 415 V.

The equipment can be used to carry out the following operations:

Single-sided spot welding Ideal where access is difficult from both sides of the material. It is suitable for

welding on wings, front panels and rear quarter panels (Figure 5.22).

Two-electrode single-sided spot welding Suitable when unable to attach the earth clamp satisfactorily. It also allows two spot welds to be made simultaneously and is suitable for welding sill sections in place.

Pulse control roller spot welding This gives a continuous spot weld along an overlapped edge of metal. It is ideal for roof gutters and for welding patches to vehicle panels when dealing with corrosion repair without creating distortion (Figure 5.23).

Welding copper ring washers for pulling This allows rows of washers to be welded to the panel surface.

Figure 5.22 Single-sided spot welding used in panel repair (*Stanners Ltd*)

Figure 5.23 Pulse controlled roller spot welding (*Stanners Ltd*)

Figure 5.21 Single-sided and double-sided spot welding equipment (*Stanners Ltd*)

Ideal for pulling out large dints by using a slide hammer with a special hook attachment which fits through the rings, which are later broken off by twisting.

Rapid puller This is designed for pulling out small dints quickly and effectively by welding the puller to the panel, pulling out the dint, then twisting the tool to release it from the panel (Figure 5.24).

Copper shrinking of high spots This uses a copper tool for shrinking stretched panels which have been overworked by hammering (Figure 5.25).

Figure 5.24 Rapid spot puller (*Stanners Ltd*)

Carbon shrinking for overstretched panels This uses a carbon pencil rod and is used for retensioning a panel surface that is only slightly stretched (Figure 5.26).

Figure 5.25 Copper shrinking attachment (*Stanners Ltd*)

Figure 5.26 Carbon pencil shrinking attachment (*Stanners Ltd*)

Figure 5.27 Captive nuts welded on to panel (*Stanners Ltd*)

160

Welding captive nuts to vehicle This piece of equipment can be used to weld captive nuts, trim studs and threaded bolts to panel surfaces when they need to be replaced (Figure 5.27).

Single-sided spot welding equipment has a low current intensity, which ensures safety for the operator. The equipment uses direct current at a maximum of 12 volts. All electrodes can be quenched in water, without danger to the operator, when they become overheated, and this extends their life. Single-sided welding with one electrode and one earth clamp results in current loss in the metal panel, and also the metal panel is a bad conductor of electricity. To overcome this problem, Stanners Ltd use a system which gives good results by using two earth clamps positioned correctly on the panel being welded. With this system 20 per cent more current is passed through the weld, resulting in better and stronger welds.

5.10.2 Setting up equipment for single-sided spot welding

1 Set the weld timer dial.
2 Set the welding mode switch.
3 Set the welding power dial.
4 Connect the earth clamp plate to the negative side of the welding output cable holder, and the single-sided electrode to the positive side of the cable holder.
5 Connect two earth clamp plates as close as possible to the area to be welded.
6 Ensure that both pieces of metal are clean and making good contact. Also make sure that the lower piece of metal is well supported to allow pressure to be applied to the electrode by the operator.
7 Press the electrode against the workpiece to be welded. Apply pressure to both pieces of metal and press the switch to carry out the weld.
8 It is important that the electrode is quenched in water after prolonged welding to prevent it becoming hot or overheating.
9 The electrode tip should maintain its original profile if good spot welds are to be achieved. Therefore, when necessary, the electrode should be redressed back to its correct shape.

QUESTIONS

1 What is meant by the term 'resistance welding'?
2 Name and describe three methods of resistance welding.
3 Give an example where resistance welding is used in vehicle manufacture.

4 Resistance welding uses various electrodes: select and sketch one type.

5 How is a workshop test carried out on a spot weld to test its strength?

6 Suggest one application of projection welding in the assembly of a vehicle body.

7 Illustrate types of joints that would be suitable for spot-welding applications.

8 Describe the three stages in the production of a spot weld.

9 Which important points should be considered when reshaping a resistance welding electrode?

10 Explain the importance of resistance welding in the repair of vehicle bodies.

11 Which metals are used for making electrodes in resistance welding?

12 What is the difference between butt welding and flash welding?

13 Name the principal parts of resistance welding equipment that would be used in the body repair shop.

14 State the qualities required of a good spot weld.

15 Explain the term 'robotic welding'.

16 What are the important factors to be considered when spot welding high-strength steel.

17 Explain the importance of the adaptive self-setting timing control unit when welding high-strength steels.

18 Explain the working procedure of a pincer-type welding gun.

19 Describe, with the aid of a sketch, the formation of a weld nugget during the spot-welding cycle.

20 Describe a method of resistance welding that would be used on the assembly line to weld a roof panel into position.

21 What is the purpose of 'hold time' when carrying out the process of spot welding?

22 Describe typical repair situations that would use a pincer welding gun and a single-sided welding gun.

23 State where resistance seam welding could be found on a vehicle body.

24 Show, with the aid of a sketch, the principle of twin-spot welding.

25 Describe, with the aid of a sketch, the resistance projection welding process.

26 List the advantages of the resistance spot-welding technique used in the repair of vehicle bodies.

27 Sketch one type of electrode arm sets used in vehicle repair.

28 With the aid of a sketch, explain how heat is generated to form the spot weld.

29 State the treatment that should be carried out before replacing a spot-welded panel.

30 State why water cooled electrode tips are used in the manufacture of vehicle body shells.

6

TIG/MIG/MAG welding

6.1 DEVELOPMENT OF GAS SHIELDED ARC WELDING

Originally the process was evolved in America in 1940 for welding in the aircraft industry. It developed into the tungsten inert-gas shielded arc process which in turn led to shielded inert-gas metal arc welding. The latter became established in this country in 1952.

In the gas shielded arc process, heat is produced by the fusion of an electric arc maintained between the end of a metal electrode, either consumable or non-consumable, and the part to be welded with a shield of protective gas surrounding the arc and the weld region. There are in use at present three different types of gas shielded arc welding:

Tungsten inert gas (TIG) The arc is struck by a non-consumable tungsten electrode and the metal to be welded, and filler metal is added by feeding a rod by hand into the molten pool (Figure 6.1).

Metal inert gas (MIG) This process employs a continuous feed electrode which is melted in the intense arc heat and deposited as weld metal: hence the term consumable electrode. This process uses only inert gases, such as argon and helium, to create the shielding around the arc (Figure 6.2).

Metal active gas (MAG) This is the same as MIG except that the gases have an active effect upon the arc and are not simply an inert envelope. The gases used are carbon dioxide or argon/carbon-dioxide mixtures.

The following should also be noted:

Gas tungsten arc welding (GTAW) This is the terminology used in America and many parts of Europe for the TIG welding process, and it is becoming increasingly accepted as the standard terminology for this process.

Gas metal arc welding (GMAW) This is the terminology used in America and many parts of Europe for the MIG/MAG welding processes, and it is becoming increasingly accepted as the standard terminology for these processes.

6.2 GASES USED FOR SHIELDED ARC PROCESS

The shielding gases used in the MIG/MAG and TIG welding processes perform several important functions:

1 Protection from atmospheric contamination.
2 Arc support and stabilization.
3 Control of weld bead geometry.
4 Control of weld metal properties.

It is necessary to prevent contamination of the weld pool by atmospheric gases which cause deterioration of the weld bead quality, by surface oxidation, porosity or embrittlement. In the consumable electrode process, MIG/MAG, it is also necessary to consider the potential loss of alloying elements in the filler wire owing to preliminary oxidation in the arc atmosphere. In TIG welding, oxidation of the non-consumable tungsten electrode must be prevented. For these reasons most welding shielding gases are based on the inert gases argon (Ar) and helium (He). Active gases such as carbon dioxide (CO_2), oxygen (O_2) and hydrogen (H_2) may be added to the shielding gas to control one or other of the functions stated, but the gas chosen must be compatible with the material being welded (Table 6.1).

The successful exclusion of atmospheric contamination depends on the ability to provide a physical barrier to prevent entrainment in the arc area, and in the case of some reactive metals such as titanium it may be necessary to extend this cover to protect the solidified weld metal while it is cooling. The gas cover depends on the shielding efficiency of the torch and the physical properties of the gas. The higher the density of the gas the more resistant it will be to disturbance, and gases which are heavier than air may offer advantages in the downhand welding position (Table 6.2).

The shielding gas used in MIG/MAG processes displaces the air in the arc area. The arc is struck within this blanket of shielding gas, producing a weld pool free from atmospheric contamination. The type of gas used determines the heat input, arc stability and mode of transfer, as well as providing protection

Figure 6.1 TIG welding equipment AC/DC (*Murex Welding Products Ltd*)

Figure 6.2 MIG welding equipment (*Migatronic Welding Equipment Ltd*)

Few gases possess the required shielding properties, however, and those that do with certainty – the inert gases, notably argon – are relatively expensive.

6.2.1 Argon

Argon is one of the rare gases occurring in the atmosphere and is obtained from liquefied air in the course of the manufacture of oxygen. Argon is an inert gas. It does not burn, support combustion, and does not take part in any ordinary chemical reaction. On account of its strongly inactive properties it can prevent oxidation or any other chemical reaction from taking place in the molten metal during the welding operation.

The argon is supplied in steel cylinders coloured blue, a full cylinder having approximately 200 bar pressure which is reduced by a regulator to approximately 15 litres per min. when drawing for welding. Normally the cylinder should not be allowed to empty below 2 bar. This prevents air from entering the cylinder and helps to preserve the purity of the contents. Gas pressures are shown as bar: 1 bar $\approx$ 14.505 lbf/in^2; 10 lbf/in^2 $\approx$ 0.689 bar. Gas consumptions are in litres per hour (litre/h): 1 ft^3/h $\approx$ 28.316 litre/h.

Argon has been more extensively used than helium because of a number of advantages:

for the solidifying weld metal. With any gas shielded arc process the type of shielding gas used greatly influences the quality of the weld deposit, weld penetration and weld appearance. The heat affected zone can also be influenced by the composition of the gas.

One of the important functions of the shielding gas is to protect the weld zone from the surrounding atmosphere and from the deleterious effects of oxygen, nitrogen and hydrogen upon the chemical composition and properties of the resulting weld. In this capacity the gas fulfils the major function of the fluxes used as electrode coverings or deposited as an enveloping layer during welding with other processes. The obvious advantages derived from the use of gas shielding are that the weld area is fully visible; that little, if any, slag is produced; and that the absence of abrasive flux increases the life of jigs and machine tools. In the MIG welding process, gas shielding enables a high degree of mechanism of welding to be achieved.

Table 6.1 Chemical and physical compatibility of welding shielding gases and materials

Material	Gas	Compatibility
Plain carbon steel and low-alloy steel	Argon, helium	No reaction
	CO_2, oxygen	Slight oxidation of alloying elements
	Hydrogen	Porosity and HICC risk
	Nitrogen	Porosity and loss of toughness
Austenitic stainless steel	Argon, helium	No reaction
	H_2	Reduces oxide
	O_2	Oxidizing
	CO_2	May cause carbon pick-up
Aluminium and alloys	Argon, helium	No reaction
	H_2	Gross porosity
	O_2	Oxidizing
Copper	Argon, helium, N_2	No reaction
	H_2	Porosity
Nickel	Argon, helium	No reaction
	N_2	Porosity
Titanium	Argon, helium	No reaction
	O_2, N_2, H_2	Embrittlement

Table 6.2 Density of common welding shielding gases

Gas	Density (kg/m³)
Argon	1.784
Helium	0.178
Hydrogen	0.083
Nitrogen	1.161
Oxygen	1.326
Carbon dioxide	1.977

1 Smoother, quieter arc action.
2 Lower arc voltage at any given current value and arc length.
3 Greater, cleaner action in the welding of such materials as aluminium with AC.
4 Lower cost and greater availability.
5 Lower flow rates for good shielding.
6 Easier arc starting.

The lower arc voltage characteristics of argon are used to advantage in the welding of thin metals, because the tendency towards burn-through is lessened. Pure argon can be used for welding aluminium and its alloys, copper, nickel, stainless steel and also for MIG brazing.

6.2.2 Helium

Helium is a colourless, odourless inert gas almost as light as hydrogen. It is found in the United States in a natural gas and is therefore more widely used in America than anywhere else. Helium has a high specific heat, so that a given quantity requires much more heat to raise its temperature by 1°C than does air; therefore the weld temperature is reduced and so distortion is minimized. A disadvantage of helium is that, because of its lightness, two and a half times the gas flow is required for a given performance than would be needed with argon. Helium is more favourable than argon where high arc voltage and power are desirable for welding thick material and metal with high heat conductivity such as copper. Helium is more often used in welding heavy than light materials.

6.2.3 Carbon dioxide

This gas is used as a shielding gas in the MAG welding process. It is not an inert gas: when it passes through the welding arc there is some breakdown into carbon monoxide and oxygen. To ensure that the oxygen is not added to the weld, deoxidants such as silicon, aluminium and titanium are included in the welding wire, which is specially made for carbon dioxide MAG welding. The deoxidant combines with the released oxygen to form a sparse slag on the surface of the completed weld. A gas heater with an electrically heated element is used to prevent freezing of the gas regulator after prolonged use with carbon dioxide gas. Since the development of the carbon dioxide process it has become widely used for the welding of plain carbon steels.

Table 6.3 Gas mixtures available and their applications

Gas	Applications	Features
Argon	TIG: all metals. MIG: spray pulse, aluminium, nickel, copper alloys	Stable arc performance. Poor wetting characteristics in MIG. Efficient shielding. Low cost
Helium	TIG: all metals, especially copper and aluminium. MIG: high-current spray, aluminium	High heat input. Increased arc voltage
Argon + 25 to 80% He	TIG: aluminium, copper, stainless steel. MIG: aluminium and copper	Compromise between pure Ar and pure He. Lower He contents normally used for TIG
Argon + 0.5 to 15% H_2	TIG: austenitic stainless steel, some copper nickel alloys	Improved heat input, edge wetting and weld bead profile
CO_2	MAG: plain carbon and low-alloy steels	Low-cost gas. Good fusion characteristics and shielding efficiency, but stability and spatter levels poor. Normally used for dip transfer only
Argon + 1 to 7% CO_2 + up to 3% CO_2	MIG/MAG: plain carbon and low-alloy steels. Spray transfer	Low heat input, stable arc. Finger penetration. Spray transfer and dip on thin section. Low CO_2, levels may be used on stainless steels but carbon pick-up may be a problem
Argon + 8 to 15% CO_2 + up to 3% CO_2	MIG/MAG: plain carbon and low-alloy steels. General purpose	Good arc stability for dip and spray pulse. Satisfactory fusion and bead profile
Argon + 16 to 25% CO_2	MIG/MAG: plain carbon and low-alloy steels. Dip transfer	Improved fusion characteristics for dip
Argon + 1 to 8% O_2	MIG/MAG: dip, spray and pulse, plain carbon and stainless steel	Low O_2 mixtures suitable for spray and pulse, but surface oxidation and poor weld profile often occur with stainless steel. No carbon pick-up
Helium + 10 to 20% argon + oxygen + CO_2	MIG: dip transfer, stainless steel	Good fusion characteristics, high short-circuit frequency. Not suitable for spray pulse transfer
Argon + 30 to 40% He + CO_2 + O_2	MIG: dip, spray and pulse welding of stainless steels	Improved performance in spray and pulse transfer. Good bead profile. Restrict CO_2 level for minimum pick-up
Argon + 30 to 40% He + up to 1% O_2	MIG: dip, spray and pulse welding of stainless steels	General-purpose mixture with low surface oxidation and carbon pick-up. (It has been reported that these low-oxygen mixtures may promote improved fusion and excellent weld integrity for thick-section aluminium alloys)

6.2.4 Argon mixtures

Gas mixtures that are suitable for vehicle body repair work consist of 95 per cent argon and 5 per cent carbon dioxide, or 80 per cent argon and 20 per cent carbon dioxide. These mixtures give smoother results with a better, cleaner and more attractive spatter-free weld. They also improve metal transfer and weld finish. These gases can be used to weld low-carbon mild steel, high-strength steel (HSS) and very low-carbon rephosphorized steels.

6.2.5 Helium mixes

These are specially formulated for MIG welding of stainless steels. They are a mixture of high purity helium and argon, with small controlled additions of carbon dioxide. They contain no hydrogen, and are suitable for welding all grades of stainless steel including weldable martensitic grades, extra-low-carbon grades and duplex stainless steel.

6.2.6 Choice of shielding gases

Shielding gases must be carefully chosen to suit their application (Table 6.3). The selection will depend on:

1 The compatibility of the gas with the material being welded.
2 Physical properties of the material.
3 The welding process and mode of operation.
4 Joint type and thickness.

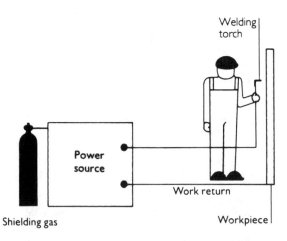

Figure 6.3 Basic principles of the TIG welding process (*BOC Ltd*)

6.3 TIG WELDING

6.3.1 Principles of operation

The necessary heat for this process (Figures 6.3, 6.4) is produced by an electric arc maintained between a non-consumable electrode and the surface of the metal to be welded. The electrode used for carrying the current is usually a tungsten or tungsten alloy rod. The heated weld zone, the molten metal and the electrode are shielded from the atmosphere by a blanket of inert gas (argon or helium), fed through the electrode holder which is in the tip of the welding torch. A weld is made by applying the arc heat so that the edges of the metal are melted and joined together as the weld metal solidifies. In some cases a filler rod may be used to reinforce the weld metal.

Before commencing to weld it is essential to clean the surfaces that are to be welded. All oil, grease, paint, rust and dirt should be removed by either mechanical cleaning or chemical cleaners.

Striking the arc may be accomplished in one of the following ways:

1 Using an apparatus which will cause a spark to jump from the electrode to the work (arc stabilizer AC equipment); or
2 By means of an apparatus that starts and maintains a small pilot arc which provides a path for the main arc.

Once the arc is struck, the welding torch is held with the electrode positioned at an angle of about 75° to the surface of the metal to be welded. To start welding, the arc is usually moved in a small circle until a pool of molten metal of suitable size is obtained. Once adequate fusion is achieved, a weld is made by gradually moving the electrode along the parts to be welded so as progressively to melt the adjoining edges. To stop welding, the welding torch is quickly withdrawn from the work and the current is automatically shut off.

The material thickness and joint design will determine whether or not filler metal in the form welding rod needs to be added to the joint.

When filler metal is added it is applied by feeding a filler rod from the side into the pool of molten metal in the arc region in the same manner as used in oxy-acetylene welding. The filler rod is usually held at an angle of about 15° to the surface of the work and slowly fed into the weld pool.

The joints which may be welded by this process include all the standard types such as square groove, V groove, as well as T and lap joints (Figure 6.5). It is not necessary to bevel the edges of material that is 3.2 mm or less thickness.

6.3.2 Modes of operation

The TIG process may be operated in one of the following modes:

DC electrode negative In this mode the electrode remains relatively cool while the workpiece is effectively heated. This is the most common mode of operation for ferrous materials, copper, nickel and titanium alloys.

DC electrode positive With DC electrode positive there is a tendency for the electrode to overheat and fusion of the workpiece is poor. The advantage of this mode of operation is the cathodic cleaning effect which removes the tenacious oxide film from the surface of aluminium alloys.

AC alternating current This offers a good compromise between plate heating and the cathodic cleaning effect and is used with aluminium and with manganese alloys.

Figure 6.4 Principles of the TIG welding process

6.4 TIG SPOT WELDING

TIG spot welding is an adaptation of the main process. This method utilizes the heat from the tungsten arc to fuse the base material in much the same way as ordinary TIG welding. The tungsten electrode is set inside the argon shield to ensure that fusion takes place in a completely shrouded atmosphere. The sheets or parts to be joined are held in close contact by the manual pressure of the gun, and fusion is made from one side of the joint only (Figure 6.6). The equipment comprises a water-cooled torch with associated cables for argon, water and power, a standard AC/DC welding set and a timer and contact unit. The arc is struck by pressing a switch on the gun activating the timer which carries the welding current to the tungsten electrode. The arc is struck automatically and fusion takes place between the top and bottom components of the joint to be made. The depth of penetration through the component part is controlled by the current and time cycle. The process is used for joining mild steel and stainless steel not exceeding 1.6 mm, but is not suitable for aluminium and magnesium base alloys. The results of spot welds differ according to the type and quality of the materials used, but providing the surfaces of the joint are clean and free from rust, scale, greases or dirt, satisfactory spot welds can generally be made.

6.5 EQUIPMENT USED IN TIG WELDING

The equipment required for TIG welding (Figure 6.1) consists of a welding torch equipped with a gas passage and nozzle for directing the shielding gas around the arc, a non-consumable electrode, a supply of shielding gas (argon), a pressure reducing regulator and flow meter, a power unit and a supply of cooling water (Figure 6.7) if the welding torch is water cooled. The individual components may differ considerably, depending on power requirements and the type of work to be carried out.

6.5.1 Power unit

Standard AC and DC welding equipment may be used, but in most cases special welding units are used which are capable of producing AC or DC, have automatic control of argon and water flow, and have fine current control switches for the stopping and starting of welding. The choice of welding current is determined by the material to be welded. Metals having a refractor surface oxide film, like magnesium, aluminium and its alloys, are normally welded with AC, while DC is used for carbon steels, stainless steels, copper and titanium. When direct current is used the electrode may be connected either to the positive or to the

167

1 Square edge close butt

T should not exceed 3 mm for manual welding or 5 mm for machine welding without filler wire. With filler wire addition, machine welds up to approximately 6 mm thick material are possible with this edge preparation

2 Flanged edge close butt

Used on material thickness up to 2 mm

3 Square edge open butt

This form of preparation is only used when filler wire is to be added. Gap should not normally exceed 3 mm and then only used when plate is to be welded from both sides. **T should not exceed 10 mm**

4 Open butt inserted strip

This method of preparation avoids the use of a separate filler wire and is suitable mainly for machine welding applications. Thickness should not normally exceed 8 mm and the thickness of the filler strips should not exceed approximately 3 mm. The edges of the plate must butt closely to the filler strip throughout the whole length of the weld seam. *H*, the height of the strip above the plate, should not exceed 3 mm for the whole range of metal thickness involved

5 Single-bevel close butt

Single-pass welds up to 10 mm *T* are possible with both hand and machine applications, but multipass welds are recommended where *T* exceeds 8 mm. Single-pass machine welds with filler wire addition and heavy currents are possible on thicknesses up to 3 mm but the preparation shown in 6 is preferred where *T* exceeds 10 mm

6 Double-bevel close butt

This preparation is recommended for *T* in excess of 10 mm, assuming both sides of the joints are accessible

Figure 6.5 Recommended edge preparation

Figure 6.6 Principles of the TIG spot-welding process

negative side of the power source, depending on the material to be welded. Usually the majority of general welding requires direct current with negative polarity, as the heat distribution and current loading are used to the best advantage and the tungsten arc electrode can carry at least four times as much current, without overheating the electrode, as an equivalent positive arc. Practically all metals other than magnesium and aluminium are suitable for this method, which gives deep penetration with a very narrow weld bead, whereas DC positive gives a shallow penetration with a wide bead (Figure 6.8).

Figure 6.7 Gas, water and power supply for TIG welding

6.5.2 Welding torch

Various types of torches are available to suit the different applications and current requirements. Torches may be water or air cooled: for currents below 150 A air-cooled torches are used, while from 150 to 400 A water-cooled torches are used (Figure 6.9). The air-cooled torches are used for welding light materials and the water-cooled torches for welding heavier materials, as the water cooling then prevents cracking of the ceramic shield at the tip of the torch. The torch is fully insulated electrically and has a quick release collet arrangement to facilitate convenient adjustment or changing of the tungsten electrodes. Tungsten having a melting point of 3400°C, is used as the electrode material owing to its refractory nature. It is almost non-consumable when used under ideal welding conditions. A ceramic shield, which is interchangeable, directs the gas so as to form a shroud around the arc and weld metal. The argon and the electric current are supplied to the torch through a combined cable and gas hose. In the water-cooled models a third cable is added to carry the water to and from the torch. A water flow switch can be provided to give complete protection to equipment and operator by shutting off the welding current if the water supply should fail. To avoid contamination of either the electrode tip or

the work, which would occur if the normal method of arc striking were employed, a high-frequency spark unit or an arc stabilizing device is used to stop the operator from having to touch the electrode on the surface of the work.

6.5.3 Gas supply

The inert gas, argon or helium is supplied to the welding torch from the storage cylinder via a gas pressure regulator and a gas economizer valve (Figure 6.7), which may be a dual-purpose valve when cooling water is used, and a special flow meter calibrated in cubic feet per hour or litres per minute of gas flow. The gas flow required varies with current setting, shroud size, material being welded, and type of weld joint.

6.5.4 Filler metals

Filler materials for joining a wide variety of metals and alloys are available for use with the gas tungsten arc welding process. Among them are filler rods for welding various grades of carbon and alloy steels, stainless steels, nickel and nickel alloys, copper and copper alloys, aluminium and most of its alloys,

169

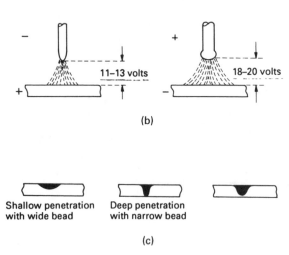

Figure 6.8 Alternative methods of DC connections: (a) theoretical distribution of heat in the argon shielded are with the alternative methods (b) average differences in arc voltages with equal arc lengths, using (left) negative polarity at the electrode and (right) positive (c) relative depths of penetration obtainable with (left to right) DC positive, DC negative and AC

Figure 6.9 A water-cooled TIG welding torch

magnesium, titanium, and high temperature alloys of various types. There are also filler materials for hard surfacing. Wherever a joint is to be reinforced, a filler rod is added to the molten puddle. In general, the diameter of the filler rod should be about the same as

Table 6.4 Electrodes for TIG welding

Electrode type	Use
1–2% thoriated tungsten	DC electrode negative Ferrous metals, copper, nickel, titanium
Ceriated tungsten	As above Improved restriking and shape retention
Zirconiated	AC Aluminium and magnesium alloys

Table 6.5 Recommended diameters and current ratings (BS 3019: Part 1) for TIG electrodes

Diameter (mm)	Maximum current (A) DC electrode (−) thoriated	AC electrode (+) zirconiated
0.8	45	–
1.2	70	40
1.6	145	55
2.4	240	90
3.2	380	150
4.0	440	210
4.8	500	275
5.6	–	320
6.4	–	370

the thickness of the metal to be welded. For sound welds, it is important that the physical properties of the rod be similar to the base metal.

6.5.5 TIG electrodes

Normally pure tungsten electrodes are used, but to improve arc striking and stability an addition of either thorium oxide or zirconium oxide is added to the tungsten. For alternating current welding zirconiated electrodes are used, while for direct current welding thoriated electrodes are used. The chosen electrode must be of a diameter which suits the current.

Improved performance can be obtained by alloying the electrodes lanthanum, yttrium and cerium, particularly in automatic TIG welding where consistency of operation is important (Table 6.4). The electrode diameter is determined by the current and polarity: recommended diameters are given in Table 6.5. The angle to which the electrode is ground depends on the application. The included angle or vertex angle (Figure 6.10) is usually smaller for low-current DC applications. In order to obtain consistent performance on a particular joint it is important that the same vertex angle is used.

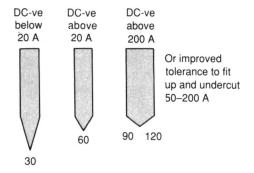

Appropiate vertex angles, degrees

Figure 6.10 Appropriate vertex angles of electrodes (*BOC Ltd*)

Figure 6.11 Recommended angles for torch and filler rod in TIG welding

Figure 6.12 Motion of torch and filler rod for TIG welding heavy sections

6.6 TIG WELDING TECHNIQUES

The normal angles of the torch are 80–90° and of the filler rod 10–20° from the surface of the horizontal plate respectively (Figure 6.11). The arc length, defined as the distance between the tip of the electrode and the surface of the weld crater, varies between 3 mm and 6 mm, depending on the type of material and the current used. The filler rod is fed into the leading edge of the molten pool and not directly in the arc core, and should be added with a slightly transverse scraping motion with the tip of the filler rod actually making contact with the weld metal. This ensures that the rod is at the same electrical potential as the plate during transfer of metal to the weld and avoids any tendency of the rod to spatter. The heated end of the filler rod should always be kept within the influence of the shrouding argon gas in order to prevent its oxidation.

Butt welds in thin-gauge materials are carried out with a progressive forward motion without weaving, but a slightly different technique is required when tackling medium and heavy section plate. As the filler rod diameter increases with increasing thickness of plate, there is a tendency for the end of the filler rod to foul the tungsten electrode. Contamination of the hot tungsten by particles of molten metal causes immediate spattering of the electrode and particles of tungsten may, according to the degree of contamination, become embedded in the weld pool. Loss of tungsten in this manner will cause the arc to become erratic and unstable, and the electrode will certainly need to be replaced before further welding is attempted. To avoid repetition of this occurrence, the arc length must be increased slightly to accommodate the insertion of the larger filler rod. This procedure cannot be taken too far, however, because there is a maximum arc length beyond which good welding becomes impossible. The upper limit is usually about 6 mm thick for aluminium, which does not allow for the free access of a 6 mm diameter filler rod. For heavier sections, therefore, a forward and backward swinging motion of the torch is employed. The weld area is melted under the arc; the torch is withdrawn backwards for a short distance from 6 mm to 3 mm along the line of the seam and the filler rod is inserted in the molten pool (Figure 6.12). The torch is moved forward and the filler rod is withdrawn from the pool simultaneously. A rhythmical motion of both torch and filler rod backwards and forwards in a progressive forward motion melts down filler rod and plate without the filler rod entering the core of the arc, and is recommended when welding plate in excess of 6 mm thick.

6.7 APPLICATION OF TIG WELDING

This process has found an application in the body building side of the industry, where it is used to ideal advantage for fabricating components by welding in materials such as aluminium and stainless steel. The advantage of the method is that materials which would normally require flux can be welded without it; therefore cleaning of the weld is minimized and the effects of distortion are greatly reduced. This process is especially adapted for welding light-gauge work requiring the utmost in quality or finish because of the precise heat control possible and the ability to weld with or without filler metal. It is one of the few processes which permit the rapid, satisfactory welding of tiny or light-walled objects.

Among the materials which are readily weldable by this process are most grades of carbon, alloy or stainless steels, aluminium and most of its alloys, magnesium and its alloys, copper, copper-nickel, phosphorbronze, tin bronzes of various types, brasses, nickel, nickel-copper (Monel alloy), nickel-chromium-iron (Inconel alloy), high temperature alloys of various types, virtually all of the hard surfacing alloys, titanium, gold, silver and many others.

6.8 MIG/MAG WELDING

The development of the MIG/MAG processes is in some ways a logical progression from the manual metal arc and TIG processes. The effort throughout has been to obtain and maintain maximum versatility, weld quality, speed of deposition, simplification of the welding operation and lower operating costs.

MIG/MAG welding has been adapted for many industrial applications, and over the past years has become widely used for car body repairs. This method of welding is an electric arc process using DC current and a continuous consumable wire electrode without the addition of flux. On account of the absence of flux, gas is used to shield the arc and weld pool from atmospheric contamination. The process can utilize argon, argon/carbon dioxide mixture or carbon dioxide as the shielding gas, the choice being dependent upon the type of material being welded and the economics associated with the selected gas. If nonferrous metals or stainless steels are to be welded, argon is the usual choice for shielding gas on grounds of compatibility. However, when mild steel, low-alloy steels or high-strength steels are to be welded, argon/carbon-dioxide mixture or carbon dioxide is generally used for reasons of overall efficiency, weld quality and economy.

Figure 6.13 Basic principles of operation of MIG/MAG welding (*BOC Ltd*)

Many types and grades of metal can be welded using this method: aluminium, aluminium alloys, carbon steel, low-carbon and alloy steels, microalloy steel, nickel, copper and magnesium. The success of this welding method is due to its capability of giving a consistently high-quality weld while also being very easy to learn. In addition it has the advantage of spreading very little heat beyond the actual welding point, and this helps to avoid distortion and shrinking stresses which are a disadvantage in the oxyacetylene process.

6.8.1 Principles of operation

Metal inert-gas or active-gas shielded arc welding (consumable) is accomplished by means of a gas shielded arc (Figures 6.13, 6.14) maintained between the workpiece and a consumable (bare wire) electrode from which metal is transferred to the workpiece. The transfer of metal through the protected arc column provides greater efficiency of heat input than that obtained in the TIG welding process. The resultant high-intensity heat source permits very rapid welding. In this process a continuously fed electrode

Wire drive may be located
in welding gun handle or at
wire reel

Wire reel

Welding
gun

Shielding
gas

Wire
drive

Gas
supply

Work

Controls

Argon

Electrode and
filler rod

d.c.
welder

Contactor

Controls for governing
wire drive, current, gas
flow, and water if used

Figure 6.14 Principles of the MIG/MAG welding process: argon, argon/CO_2 or CO_2

passes through a gun, during which it passes through a contact area which impresses the preselected welding current upon the wire. The current causes the wire to melt at the set rate at which it is fed. The shielding gas issuing from the nozzle protects the weld metal deposit and the electrode from contamination by atmospheric conditions which might affect the welding process. The arc may be started by depressing the trigger of the welding gun and scratching the electrode wire end on the work.

The equipment is designed so that the wire automatically feeds into the weld area as soon as the arc is established. Most MIG/MAG welding sets that are manufactured for the automobile repair trade are semiautomatic, the operator only being concerned with the torch-to-work distance, torch manipulation and welding speed. Wire feed speeds, power settings and gas flow are all preset prior to commencement of welding.

6.9 MIG/MAG SPOT/PLUG WELDING

An advantage of MIG/MAG welding is the ability of the process to be adopted for single-side spot-welding applications, either semi- or fully automatically. By extending the welding gun nozzle to contact the workpiece, one-sided spot welds may be performed using dip transfer conditions. Predetermined weld duration times may be employed, the gun trigger being coupled to a suitable timer and, if desired, fully mechanized. Unlike resistance spot welding, no pressure is required on the workpiece with MIG/MAG spot welding, and neither is a backing block. Mismatch of the sheets is permissible with a maximum gap equivalent to half the sheet thickness, the extra metal being provided by the electrode wire. Up to 30 spots per minute

may be welded, which compares reasonably well with the 100 spots per minute from resistance welding techniques. The deep penetration characteristics of this welding process enable spot welding of widely differing metal thicknesses to be performed successfully, together with multisheet thicknesses.

MIG/MAG plug welding differs from MIG/MAG spot welding in that the outer metal panel has a predrilled or punched hole which is filled up with the weld metal to form the 'plug'. The hole sizes used are 5–6 mm with currents of 50–60 A for panel thicknesses of 0.75–1.2 mm. Care should be taken when MIG/MAG plug welding to avoid an excess build-up of weld metal, to reduce the necessity of dressing the finished weld. This method is used to advantage in the fitting of new panel sections, where the original was resistance spot welded and access is now difficult to both sides.

Higher-strength steels are used for selected panel sections, but as they are vulnerable to heat they are not as easily welded as mild steel. MIG seam and butt welding produce hard weld joints; they will tear from the sheet metal on impact. However, MIG spot welds and particularly puddle (or plug) welded MIG spots can be made ductile. The weld time has to be short to reduce the heat affected zone around the weld.

Modern car body designs are constructed with deformation zones both front and rear, and the shear impact properties of the original welding have been carefully calculated to ensure that the energy of an impact is fully absorbed and contained within the zone. Changing the manufacturers' original welding specification could impair the safety of the vehicle. The crumplability (impact energy absorbing) design of car bodies makes new demands on welds. For its success the body design relies on the sheet metal to crumple or fold rather than tear in a collision. This protective design depends on the ductility of the metal, and the welds too have to be ductile. If they are soft they will break without forcing the assembly to crumple, but if they are hard the welds will unbutton and the assembly will fly apart instead of folding up slowly. Welds therefore must be ductile as well as large and strong.

6.10 EQUIPMENT USED IN MIG/MAG WELDING

The basic equipment required comprises a power source, a wire feed unit and a torch. The power sources commonly used have constant-voltage characteristics, and controls are provided for voltage and inductance adjustment. This type of power source is used in conjunction with a wire feed unit which takes the wire from a spool and feeds it through a torch to the arc. A control on the wire feeder enables the speed of the wire to be set to a constant level which will in turn determine the arc current.

The welding torch should be reasonably light and easy to handle, with provision for gas shield shrouding, control switch, easy wire changes and good insulation. The torch is connected to a wire feed and control unit by means of:

1 A flexible armoured tube carrying the welding wire.
2 A plastic tube carrying the shielding gas.
3 A pair of plastic tubes carrying cooling water, the return tube often carrying the welding supply to cool the welding cable (light-duty torches are air cooled).
4 The control wires for the switchgear.

The whole feed unit is bound together by a plastic sleeve, and is 1.5 m to 3 m long. The wire feed unit houses the drive unit for the wire feed, which can be varied in speed to suit current/voltage conditions. The wire reel is also carried in the unit and is loaded with some 15 kg of welding wire.

6.10.1 Power unit

DC power units are used as either rotary generators or rectifying units which are specially designed to give full versatility of arc control. The equipment is either single phase (130–240 A) or three phase (250–500 A). The principal components of most machines are welding transformer, rectifier, choke coil, wire feed unit, gas solenoid valve and electronic control box.

The welding transformer is dimensioned so as to achieve optimal welding properties. The transformer is manufactured from materials able to withstand a working temperature of up to 180°C. By way of a further safeguard against overloading, there is a built-in thermal fuse which cuts out the machine at 120°C. The thermal fuse is automatically reconnected once the transformer has cooled down.

The rectifier is constructed from a fan, thirsters, diodes and a capacitor battery. During welding, or when the machine is hotter than 70°C, the fan cools the rectifier and the transformer. The rectifier is electronically protected against overloading in the event of any short circuit between welding positive and negative, with the machine cutting out approximately 1 second after the onset of short circuiting.

The transformer converts the high mains voltage into a low alternating voltage, which is rectified and equalized into DC voltage in the rectifier module. A choke coil reduces the peaks in the welding current and thus eliminates the cause of welding spatter. When

the switch on the torch is depressed, the thirsters come on. The rectifier emits a DC voltage, which is determined by the remote control in the welding trigger and the gas/wire matching switch on the box. Simultaneously, shielding gas is turned on and the wire feed motor is started up at a speed also determined by remote regulation from the torch.

When the trigger is released the motor decelerates, and after a short time lag the gas flow and welding voltage are interrupted. This time delay is called burnback and causes the welding wire to burn a little way back from the molten pool, thus preventing it from sticking to the workpiece.

Depending on the type of equipment selected, the following functions are available: seam, spot, stitch and latching (four-cycle).

Seam Welding starts when the switch on the welding trigger is actuated and stops when the switch is released. For use in short-duration welding and tacking.

Spot Welding starts when the switch is actuated and is subsequently controlled by the welding timer for a time between 0.2 and 2.5 s. It makes no difference when the switch is released. This function ensures uniform spot welds, providing the correct setting has been found.

Stitch The wire feed motor starts and stops at intervals which are set on the welding timer and pause timer. When welding is interspersed with pauses in this way, the average amount of added heat is reduced, which prevents any melting through on difficult welding jobs.

Latching Welding starts when the switch is actuated; the switch can then be released and welding continues. By reactuating the switch, welding stops when the switch is released. For use on long seams.

A typical welding control panel (Figure 6.15) has the following features:

1 *Selection switch* This selects between the functions seam, spot, stitch and latch as described above.
2 *Power light* This lights up when the machine has been turned on.
3 *Overheating warning light* If this light comes on, the welding equipment is automatically switched off owing to overheating of the transformer. When the temperature is back to normal, the welding can be continued.
4 *Welding timer switch* With this switch the welding time is chosen, when the selection switch is in the stitch or spot position.
5 *Adjustable pause time button* With this button the pause time is chosen, when the selection switch is in the stitch position.

Figure 6.15 MIG welding control panel (*Migatronic Welding Equipment Ltd*)

6 *Burn-back button* Preadjustment of the burn-back delay button indicates the time for stopping the wire feed until the arc is switched off. This varies between 0.05 and 0.5 s.

7 *Adjustment of wire speed switch* This gives the adjustment of the wire feed from 0.5 to 14 m/min.

8 *Welding voltage switch* This sets the welding voltage of the transformer. When set at gas test, the gas flows by pressing the switch on the torch handle.

The characteristics built into the welding power supply are such as to provide automatic self-adjustment of arc conditions as the weld proceeds. Depending on the relevant current and voltage used, metal transfer between electrode and work takes place in the following distinct forms each of which has certain operational advantages (Figure 6.16).

Dip transfer (short arc)

This condition requires comparatively low current and voltage values. Metal is transferred by a rapidly repeated series of short circuits when the electrode is fed forward into the weld pool.

Metal dip transfer is the most suitable mode of metal transfer for welding on car repairs, as it offers good bead control and low heat input, thus cutting down distortion when welding in panel sections. This type of transfer will also permit the welding of thinner gauges of sheet steel, and is practical for welding in all positions.

The principle of the method (short-circuiting transfer) is briefly as follows. The molten wire is transferred to the weld in droplets, and as each drop touches the weld the circuit is shorted and the arc is momentarily extinguished. The wire is fed at a rate which is just greater than the burn-off rate for the particular arc voltage being used; as a result the wire touches the weld pool and short circuits the power supply. The filler wire then acts as a fuse, and when it ruptures a free burning arc is created. After the occurrence of this short circuit, the arc re-ignites. This making and breaking of arc interruption, takes place from 20 to 200 times per second according to the setting of the controls. The result is a relatively small and cool weld pool, limiting burn-through.

Free flight transfer

In this metal transfer a continuous arc is maintained between the electrode and the workpiece and the metal is transferred to the weld pool as droplets. There are three subdivisions of the system:

Spray transfer In this type the mode of transfer consists of a spray of very small molten metal. droplets formed along the arc column, which are projected towards the workpiece by electrical forces within the arc and collected in the weld pool. No short circuiting takes place; the welds are hotter, and the depositing of weld metal is faster. It is ideally suited for the rapid welding of thick sections in the downhand position and the positional welding of aluminium and its alloys.

Globular transfer This occurs at currents above those which produce dip transfer, but below the current level required for spray transfer. The droplet size is large relative to the wire diameter and transfer is irregular. This mode of transfer occurs with steel wires at high currents in carbon dioxide, but is generally regarded as unusable unless high spatter levels can be tolerated. The use of corded wires gives a controlled form of globular transfer which is acceptable.

Pulse arc transfer In this mode the droplets are transferred by a high current which is periodically applied

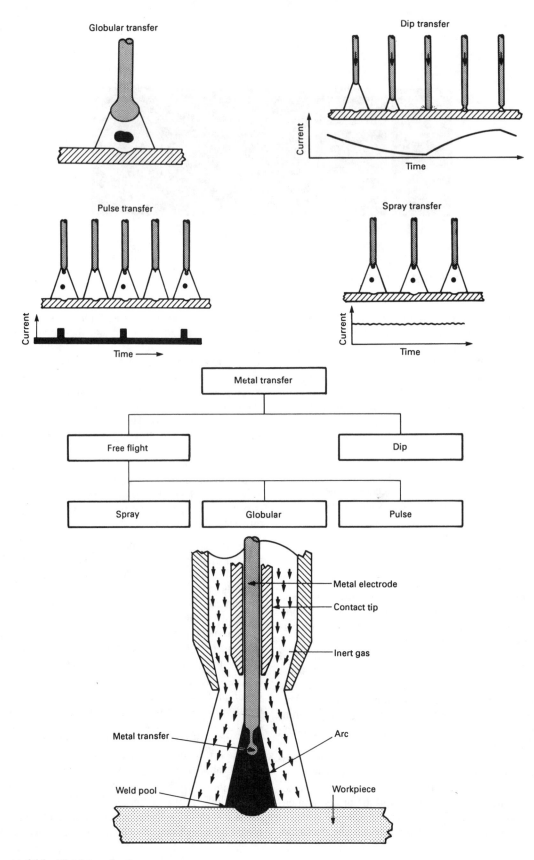

Figure 6.16 Metal transfer forms

Figure 6.17 Air-cooled MIG welding torch (*Murex Welding Processes Ltd*)

to the arc. Ideally, one drop is transferred with each pulse and is fired across the arc by the pulse. Typical operating frequencies are 50–100 droplets per second. A background current is maintained between pulses to sustain the arc but avoid metal transfer. Maximum control is obtained with this type of metal transfer, which utilizes a power supply to provide a pulsed welding condition in which the metal transfer takes place at pulse peaks. This leads to extreme control over the weld penetration and weld appearance.

6.10.2 Welding torch

Air-cooled torches are available for the various welding applications ranging from 180 A to 400 A. The design of the torch is in the form of a pistol or is curved similar to the shape of an oxyacetylene torch (Figure 6.17), and has wire fed through the barrel or handle. In some versions where the most efficient cooling is needed, water is directed through passages in the torch to cool the wire contact means as well as the normally cooled metal shielding gas nozzle (Figure 6.18). The curved torch carries the current contact tip at the front end through which the feed wire, shielding gas and cooling water are also brought. This type

of torch is designed for small diameter feed wires, is extremely flexible and manoeuvrable and is particularly suitable for welding in confined areas. The service lines consisting of the power cable, water hose and gas hose on most equipment enter at the handle or rear barrel section of the torch. The torch is also equipped with a switch for energizing the power supply and controls associated with the process. Some welding torches also have a current control knob located in the torch so that the welding current can be altered during welding. This ensures that the welding voltage is altered at the same time as any current alteration, so allowing the welder to respond immediately to variations in weld gaps and misaligned joints. Welding characteristics are excellent. Fingertip control increases both productivity and weld quality (Figure 6.19).

6.10.3 Feed unit

The consumable electrode for welding ferrous and non-ferrous materials is supplied as a continuous length of wire on a spool or reel, and the wire varies from 0.6 to 0.8 mm diameter. The feeding of the wire is achieved by the unit feed mechanism housing the

177

Figure 6.18 Range of MIG welding torches, air and water cooled, 180–600 A (*Murex Welding Products Ltd*)

Figure 6.19 Migatronic Dialog torch with current control in the torch handle (*Migatronic Welding Equipment Ltd*)

Figure 6.20 Wire feed unit (*Migatronic Welding Equipment Ltd*)

necessary drive motor, gear box and feed rolls which draws wire from the adjacent reel, or by an integrally built motor drive connected to the torch which pulls the wire in the desired direction. The feed wire unit also houses the controls which govern the feeding of the wire at the required constant speed, plus the automatic control of current and gas flow. The wire from the feed rolls is fed along a carefully designed conduit system which also carries the welding current and shielding gas. The outer end of this conduit system is connected directly to the welding torch (Figure 6.20).

6.10.4 Gas supply

The primary purpose of the shielding gas used in MIG/MAG welding is the protection of the molten weld metal from contamination and damage by the oxygen, nitrogen, water vapour and other gases in the surrounding atmosphere. However, in use there are a number of other factors which influence the desirability of a gas for arc shielding. Some of these are the influence of the shielding gas on the arcing and metal transfer characteristics during welding, on the weld penetration, width of fusion and surface shape patterns, and on the speed of welding. All of these influence the finished welds and overall results. Normal shielding gases in use are argon, carbon dioxide, and mixtures of argon and carbon dioxide, although other mixtures such as argon and oxygen can be used.

6.10.5 Welding wire

The welding wires used for MIG/MAG welding are quite small in diameter compared with those used for other types of welding. Welding wire is 0.6–1.0 mm in diameter, and is supplied in reels of 5–15 kg. Owing to the small size of the wire and comparatively high currents used for welding, the wire melts off very rapidly. Therefore the wires used must always be as long as possible, with suitable temper for being fed smoothly and continuously by motor driven mechanical means through the welding apparatus. For this reason the wire is normally provided on convenient size coils or spools.

In composition the wires are usually quite similar to those used by most other bare wire processes. As a rule the composition as nearly matches that of the base material as is practicable, while also ensuring good weld properties and welding characteristics. Steel wires are often given a light coating of copper to prevent them from rusting and to improve the electrical contact and current pick-up when passing through the welding apparatus. Welding wires are available for joining most ferrous and non-ferrous metals:

Solid wire The composition of solid filler wire is usually chosen to match the parent metal being welded. Solid wire is the most common and widely used filler material for MlG/MAG welding car body replacement panels.

Cord wires Metal and flux corded wires are available. These materials are, however, more suitable for welding thicknesses in excess of 6 mm. Metal corded wires can be obtained with additions of alloying elements to meet special requirements (HS low-alloy steels).

MIG brazing wires There are a number of compositions of filler wire that can be used in MIG brazing, but usually they are of aluminium-bronze composition. When using these filler wires, pure argon must be used as the shielding gas.

6.11 MIG/MAG WELDING TECHNIQUES

In the operation of a MlG/MAG welding machine there are two parameter settings which must match each other: the wire speed and the welding voltage. It is important therefore that the wire speed and welding voltage are adjusted to conform with each other. The wire speed gives the welding current, which must match the component panel section being melted. An increase in wire feed rate increases the welding current, at the same time reducing the length of arc, resulting in a shorter arc. When the wire speed is reduced, the current intensity is diminished, at the same time increasing the length of the arc. Raising the open circuit voltage increases the arc voltage,

though the current intensity remains almost constant. A reduced open-circuit voltage will produce a shorter arc length. A change in welding wire diameter will produce a change in current and voltage, since thinner wires require higher voltage and higher wire speeds in order to produce the same current. If the limit values are exceeded a satisfactory weld cannot be obtained.

When the wire speed setting is too low, this will cause a long, drawn-out arc and spattering and a very unsatisfactory weld condition (Figure 6.21). When the wire speed becomes too great in relation to the voltage, knocking or stubbing will be felt in the welding torch, because the wire travels to the bottom of the molten pool (Figure 6.21). Welding under these conditions will normally produce adhesion defects owing to the lack of fusion. If the voltage becomes too great in relation to the wire speed, large drops will form on the end of the wire. These will be reluctant to leave the end of the wire and will often settle as spatter beside the weld (see Figure 6.22). When the ratio between the voltage and the wire speed is correct, a highly characteristic hiss or hum will be heard from the arc.

The mutual position of the welding torch and workpiece in relation to each other is of importance to the appearance and quality of welding. In practice many different combinations of inclination, torch handling and welding position will be experienced by the body repairer (see Figure 6.23).

6.11.1 MIG/MAG welding positions

Welding positions can be as follows: flat, horizontal, vertical, overhead and, owing to the complexities of panel shapes, a combination of these (Figure 6.24). In collision repair, the welding position is usually dictated by the location of the weld in the structure or panel assembly of the vehicle. Both heat and wire speed parameters can be affected by the welding positions.

Flat welding is generally easier and faster and allows for better penetration. When welding a panel section that is off the vehicle, try to place it so that it can be welded in a flat position.

When welding a horizontal joint, angle the welding torch upwards to hold the weld puddle in place against the pull of gravity. When welding a vertical joint, the best procedure is usually to start the weld at the top of the joint and pull downwards with a steady drag.

Overhead welding is the most difficult. In this position the danger of having too large a weld puddle is that some of the molten weld metal can fall down, either into the nozzle where it can create problems, or on to the operator. Therefore always carry out

Figure 6.21 Incorrect settings for wire speed (*Stanners Ltd*)

overhead welding on a low voltage setting, which will cut down spatter while keeping the arc as short as possible and the weld puddle as small as possible. Press the nozzle of the torch against the work to ensure that the wire is now moved away from the puddle. It is better to pull the torch along the joint with a steady drag.

6.11.2 MIG/MAG basic welding processes

There are six basic welding processes used in collision repair work on vehicle bodies.

Tack weld
A tack is a relatively small, temporary MIG/MAG weld that is used instead of a clamp or a self-tapping screw, to tack and hold the panel in place while proceeding to make a permanent weld (Figure 6.25). Like the clamp or self-tapping screw, the tack weld is always a temporary device. The length of the tack weld is determined by the thickness of the metal panel to be welded and is approximately a length of 15 to 30 times the thickness of the metal panel. Tack welds must be done accurately, as they are very important in maintaining proper panel alignment.

Continuous weld
Continuous weld is an uninterrupted seam or weld bead which is carried out as one steady progressive movement (Figure 6.26). While supporting the torch securely, use a forward movement to move the torch

continuously at a constant speed, checking the weld bead frequently as you progress. The welding torch should be inclined between 10 and 15° to obtain the best weld bead shape, weld line and gas shielding effect. It is essential to maintain both the distance between the tip base and the metal surface, and the correct torch angle, otherwise a problem can arise owing to the wire length being too long. When this occurs, penetration of the metal will not be adequate; therefore to improve penetration and produce a better weld, bring the torch closer to the base metal. When torch handling is smooth and even, the weld bead will be of consistent height and width with a uniform closely spaced ripple.

Plug weld
A plug weld is used to join two metal panels together (Figure 6.27). The outer metal panel is first predrilled or punched. Next the arc is directed through the hole to penetrate the inner metal panel. The hole is then filled with molten metal to form the plug.

Spot weld
In MIG/MAG spot welding the arc is directed to penetrate both metal panel pieces through the joint position while triggering a timed impulse of wire feed (Figure 6.28).

Lap spot weld
In the MIG/MAG lap spot-weld technique, the arc is directed to penetrate equally between the edge of the

FAULT		CAUSE
Porosity		Insufficient Si, Mn in wire Insufficient CO_2 shielding because of $\begin{cases} \text{flow rate} \\ \text{frozen value} \\ \text{clogged nozzle} \\ \text{draughts} \end{cases}$
Cracking		Dirty work—grease, paint, scale, rust (i) Weld bead too small (ii) Weld too deep, greater than $1 \cdot 2 : 1$ (iii) High sulphur, low manganese, slow cooling rate
Undercutting		Travel speed too high Backing bar groove too deep Current too low for speed Torch angle too low
Lack of penetration		Current too low—setting wrong Wire feed fluctuating Electrode extension too great Joint preparation too narrow Angle too small Gap too small
Lack of fusion		Uneven torch manipulation Insufficient inductance (short circuiting arc) Voltage too low
Slag inclusions		Technique—too wide a weave Current too low Irregular weld shape
Spatter—on work on nozzle in weld		Voltage too high Insufficient inductance Insufficient nozzle cleaning
Irregular weld shape		Excessive electrode extension Wire temper excessive, no straightening rolls Current too high for voltage Travel speed too slow

Figure 6.22 Weld defects and their causes

upper metal panel and the top surface of the lower metal panel of the lap joint, and the puddle is allowed to flow on to the edges of the top piece. This is achieved by using the correct angle of the welding torch to the joint (Figure 6.29).

Stitch weld
A MIG/MAG stitch weld is a series of intermittent seam welds carried out at intervals along a lapped metal panel joint, where a continuous weld is not

necessary or would cause distortion due to heat input (Figure 6.30).

6.12 APPLICATIONS OF MIG/MAG WELDING IN VEHICLE BODY CONSTRUCTION

The continuous search for increased efficiency in production techniques in the automotive industry has

181

	Thrusting weld	Drawing weld
Width of seam	wider	narrower
Upper bead	smaller	larger
Penetration	decrease	increase
Tendency to lack of fusion	greater	lesser

Drawing weld: torch sloped in direction of weld
Thrusting weld: torch sloped away from direction of weld

Pushing weld   Pulling weld

Pushing weld   Pulling weld   Pulling weld
sloping downwards   sloping downwards   sloping upwards

Figure 6.23   Welding positions (*Migatronic Welding Equipment Ltd*)

Flat   Horizontal   Vertical   Overhead

Figure 6.24   Typical MIG/MAG welding positions

Figure 6.25   Tack weld

Figure 6.26   Continuous weld

Plug

Figure 6.27 Making a plug weld

Figure 6.28 MIG/MAG spot welding

Figure 6.29 Lap spot weld

Figure 6.30 Stitch weld

led to all major manufacturers adopting the use of MIG/MAG welding on a very wide scale. This welding process is ideally suited to flow line production processes owing to its inherent automatic characteristics. MIG/MAG welding has numerous advantages over the majority of processes likely to be encountered in automotive production. The most obvious is its capability of being used either semi- or fully automatically, this giving it virtually unrivalled versatility. In automobile construction it has almost totally replaced oxyacetylene and manual metal arc welding by virtue of its high metal deposition rates, electrode efficiency and high duty cycles. Further advantages of the process are good penetration, even without edge preparation, the ability to handle all metal thicknesses and high weld strength (618 MN/m^2 being easily achieved).

MIG/MAG dip transfer welding is a low heat input process owing to the relatively low amperages required, and it is ideal for welding fine sheet thicknesses because of the absence of distortion with minimal jigging. With the absence of flux further advantages accrue, the most obvious ones being the elimination of deslagging and chipping back when second weld starts are required. The absence of flux also means that the welder has a clear view of arc operation and weld bead appearance and is not subjected to excessive fumes. Spatter is minimal and weld bead appearances enhanced owing to the improved wetting of the parent material by the molten metal on account of the various additives present in the wire composition.

The MIG/MAG welding process can in many cases replace existing welding techniques, usually manual metal arc and oxyacetylene, to give superior welding conditions and economies. Semi-automatic and more particularly fully automatic MIG/MAG welding processes with a wide range of technical advantages have opened up new areas of production technique. Numerous companies in the United Kingdom have already adopted MIG/MAG welding to their own particular requirements. On a modern mass-produced passenger car the body shell is a relatively low-stressed unit, high stresses imposed by road conditions being carried by subframe assemblies. However, where continuous welds are required or specific components carrying high stresses are to be fitted MIG/MAG welding is employed using semi-automatic equipment. Thus components such as safety harness attachments, door hinges, jacking points, spring shackles, steering column brackets and seat frame guides are attached using the dip transfer technique which enables welds of this type to be made on thin shell panels with no distortion of the panel and deep penetration into the thicker workpiece. Where MIG/MAG welding has been introduced into automotive production lines, its value as a production process is well established.

6.13 APPLICATIONS OF MIG/MAG WELDING IN BODY REPAIR WORK

The semi-automatic MIG/MAG welding process which is used in the construction of vehicle bodies is also used for the repair of these bodies. Equipment is specially produced for thin-gauge welding in the repair of vehicle bodywork.

Welding in the repair of car bodies was mainly carried out using oxyacetylene and resistance spot-welding techniques. Both of these techniques have certain disadvantages. In the oxyacetylene method the

weld metal and surrounding panels are liable to distort owing to heat input. In spot welding if the repair is visible, the joints, which in most cases are lapped, must be solder filled to achieve an acceptable finish.

The advantages of MIG/MAG welding equipment in repair are first that it is a dual machine being capable of welding in any position, and it can weld material from 0.5 mm to 4.4 mm in thickness. Second, it can be used for spot welding from one side of the panel only, which is an advantage when welding inaccessible panel assemblies. The equipment itself is very portable, consisting of a transformer, rectifier, built-in feed wire system, lightweight welding torch with interchangeable nozzle heads for conventional welding and spot welding, earthing cable and clamp, and gas supply in steel cylinders, all of which are incorporated on a manoeuvrable trolley which lends itself to body work application in the workshop (see Figure 6.31).

Most equipment used in motor body repair usually has the following controls and functions: a weld timer which can be set from 0.2 to (usually) 2.5 seconds; some form of wire speed control which ranges from 2 to 12 m/min.; and a voltage control usually ranging from 0 to 10, the 0 setting giving the lowest welding current. On some machines the settings for wire speed and welding voltage are coupled together into one control, which can either be on the machine or positioned on the welding torch for instant adjustment. The following function controls are the most widely used: seam for continuous welding; spot, which makes use of a time setting to ensure uniform spot welds; and stitch, which is used through the weld timer and pause timer and provides intermittent welding so that the welding is interspersed with pauses, therefore reducing heat input and preventing melt-through on thin materials and gapped joints.

6.13.1 Preparing the equipment for welding

1 Select the correct dimensions of wire: 0.6 mm is best for welding thin materials and panels; 0.8 mm is used for general purposes; and 1.0 mm is used for aluminium only (using aluminium wire).

2 Select the tip for the type and dimension of wire being used and fitted to the equipment. Also select the torch nozzle for seam or spot-welding application.

3 Mount the welding wire reel on the reel holder, roll off the tip of the wire and insert it into the inlet between the feed rollers of the wire feed unit.

4 Connect the machine to the mains supply, set the wire speed selector, pull the welding torch trigger and feed the wire through the hose to the welding

Figure 6.31 MIG/MAG welding equipment (*Stanners Ltd*)

Figure 6.32 Visor-type welding screen in use (*Motor Insurance Repair Research Centre*)

torch till it appears at the end of the contact tip. (Some machines have a wire inching switch which is used when a new reel of wire is put into the machine and fed to the hose, and the wire is fed at a gentle speed to the torch.)

5 Connect the hose for the shielding gas to be used and set the gas flow regulator between 5 and 15 litres/min.

6 Set the wire speed and voltage control and select the mode of welding operation.

7 Connect the earth return clamp as close as possible to the point of welding, making sure of a secure connection to facilitate a good welding circuit.

8 Before commencing to weld, a visor-type (see Figure 6.32) or hand-held welding screen must be used for the protection of the welder. Then hold the welding torch down to the component to be welded and an arc will be struck between the wire electrode and the workpiece, thus commencing the welding.

9 Before welding on a car it is essential that the electrical connections to the battery, starter motor and generator/alternator are disconnected in order to avoid damage to the electrical equipment of the car.

For the best results for seam, spot or stitch welding, the surface of the panel should be cleaned to bare metal condition as paint or grease cause bad welds. In body work applications the heat input is limited on each side of the weld owing to the shielding gas: this has the effect of reducing possible distortion to a minimum so that adjacent parts do not get so hot as to damage trim, screen rubbers and windscreen glass. It can also be used to great advantage in repairing by sectioning or patching, as two panels can be butt welded and then the weld completely dressed off on one side with a sanding machine and finished off, using normal panel beating hand tools, to a perfect finish. As this system of welding gives a perfectly controlled penetrating weld of great strength, it will be found ideal for replacing new panel sections such as subframe (see Figure 6.33) and underframe members, where the welding is highly critical because of the stress factor present in load-bearing assemblies. The speed at which this welding can be carried out in the repair of the modern mono constructed body shell is proving itself to be an economical asset.

6.13.2 MIG/MAG welding of low-carbon steel and HSLA steels

Until the mid 1970s most if not all vehicle bodies were constructed from plain low-carbon steel, but since then there has been an increase in the worldwide

Figure 6.33 Application of MIG welding in body repair work (*Migatronic Welding Equipment Ltd*)

demand for corrosion resistance in body structures. This has led to the introduction of single-sided and double-sided coated galvanized steel, high-strength steel and aluminium. The Japanese, in particular, and the European industries have moved to the use of HSLA steels in further attempts to reduce body weight. Body skin panels have been reduced from around 0.9 mm to 0.7 mm, with structural components reduced from 3 mm to between 1.2 mm and 2.0 mm.

The use of these different materials can lead to problems for the welder. Welding galvanized steels (zinc coated) can reduce rust resistant properties around the weld areas if they are not correctly treated.

Cosmetic body panels are the thinnest panels on the vehicle, and are generally repaired by the use of butt, fillet, lapped edge or corner joints. It is therefore necessary to use as low a current as possible when using the MIG/MAG process on these thin panels.

The choice of shielding gas for the process is important as it affects not only the quality of the weld, but also the depth of penetration of the weld into the material and the amount of weld spatter that is formed around the finished weld. It also controls the temperature, which affects the suitability of the process for the thickness of materials to be welded. The choice of shielding gases commonly used can be seen in Table 6.6.

Under the right conditions, any of the gases in the table can be used for the range of thicknesses encountered in the bodyshop. However, the ideal for welding thin body panels is the colder mixture of argon with 2 per cent oxygen and 5 per cent carbon dioxide. When welding structural components and chassis members the material tends to be thicker, up to 3 mm or even more, and so it is necessary to use a hot arc in order to penetrate the material. For this reason a mixture of argon with 2 per cent oxygen and 12 per cent carbon dioxide is used to give better heat flow, greater tolerance to variation in setting, and low spatter generation. It is also a common practice to increase the wire diameter from 0.6 mm to 0.8 mm when welding these thicker panel assemblies.

6.13.3 MIG brazing

As well as being used in vehicle repair, this process is also used in vehicle production on some assembly lines as it offers increased speed and a smooth flat bead requiring little dressing after brazing. The MIG brazing process can be used with the traditional brazing filler materials of aluminium bronze, phosphor bronze and silicon bronze in the form of continuous wire on a reel. With this process the choice of filler material and shielding gas is important if the necessary flat bead is to be achieved, otherwise excessive amounts of dressing would be required. The shielding gas used is normally pure argon. However, gases that are a mixture of helium and argon produce a more fluid weld pool, which again leads to a flatter bead than with argon. A 70 per cent argon and 30 per cent helium mix is generally preferred for thinner cosmetic panels, since the richer 80 per cent argon and 20 per cent helium mix can produce excessive penetration with an increased risk of distortion, although this can be used to advantage on thicker panel structures.

6.13.4 MIG welding of aluminium

While most welding equipment is supplied primarily for the welding of ferrous metals, some can also be used for the welding of aluminium. Equipment with low amperages is really not suitable, although it can be used for short periods of welding. The larger-amperage machines (180 A and over) are better equipped to handle aluminium. The wire sizes used are 1.0 mm and 1.2 mm for the larger machines for welding thicker aluminium. The torch contact tip must be of the correct size for the wire to be used. When welding with aluminium wire a Teflon liner must be used in order to prevent the aluminium from sticking and damage occurring to the wire itself. Also, pure argon must be used as the shielding gas owing to its

Table 6.6 MIG/MAG recommended operating conditions

Application	Metal thickness (mm)	Shielding gas	Wire dia. (mm)	Current (A)	Voltage (V)	Wire feed speed (m/min)	Welding speed (mm/min)	Gas flow (l/min)
Horizontal/	1.0	Argoshield 5	0.8	66	14	3.4	900	12
vertical	1.6	Argoshield 5	0.8	130	18	9.7	600	14
fillet		Argoshield 5	1.0	160	17	5.9	563	14
	3.0	Argoshield TC	1.0	180	20	6.4	391	15
		Argoshield TC	1.2	180	17	3.8	430	15
	6.0	Argoshield TC	1.2	260	27	7.0	480	16
	10.0	Argoshield TC	1.2	290	27	7.4	430	16
Butt weld,	1.0	Argoshield 5	0.8	66	14	3.0	750	12
flat	1.6	Argoshield 5	0.8	84	18	4.0	800	14
position		Argoshield 5	1.0	125	16	4.0	640	14
	3.0	Argoshield TC	1.0	140	19	4.0	350	15
	6.0	Argoshield TC	1.2	300	28	7.6	650	16
	10.0	Argoshield TC	1.2	300	28	7.6	680	16
				320	28	7.6	580	16
Butt weld,	1.0	Argoshield 5	0.8	50	15	4.0	360	12
overhead	1.6	Argoshield 5	1.0	150	17	5.9	600	14
	3.0	Argoshield TC	1.2	180	19	4.3	520	15
Butt weld,	1.0	Argoshield 5	0.8	45	15	3.5	350	12
vertical	1.6	Argoshield 5	1.0	130	17	4.7	410	14
up	3.0	Argoshield TC	1.2	135	17	3.1	275	14

total inert characteristics, and not argon mixes or carbon dioxide.

6.14 WELDING STRESS AND DISTORTION IN THE MIG/MAG PROCESS

The MIG/MAG welding process and its effectiveness may be measured by its ability to produce joints of acceptable quality. Unacceptable joint quality may arise from a failure in the specific design or from the incident of weld defect. These problems, however, are preventable if their causes are understood and the correct operating procedures are followed.

The most common welding problems are:

1 Residual stress and distortion.
2 Incorrect bead geometry and appearance.
3 Defects.
4 Loss of properties.

6.14.1 Residual stress and distortion

The solidification and contraction of the weld bead will induce strain and consequently stresses in the joint. In the case of the contraction of the solid metal the stress will be equal to the change in temperature as the metal cools from its melting point to its ambient temperature. Under normal circumstances movement of the weld bead is restricted by the adjacent body panels in the vehicle structure, and the stress which could be generated is given by the Young's modulus of the material. This stress level often exceeds the elastic limit of the material and plastic deformation takes place. The stresses locked in the material, which may reach levels up to the elastic limit of the material, are called residual stresses, and the deformation of the material is known as distortion.

Residual stresses
In a butt weld the weld bead will tend to contract longitudinally and transversely, and this will induce tensile stresses in the weld and also balancing compressive stresses in the sheet material (Figure 6.34). In the joining processes which rely on heating or fusion, it is difficult to prevent the formation of residual stresses. If the heat affected zone is ductile and defect free (as in thin-sheet panel steel) the presence of some residual stresses may be acceptable. The most common technique used to relieve residual stress in thicker materials is post-weld heat treatment. This consists of uniform heating of the joint to a temperature at which the yield stress of the material is lowered and the residual stresses are relieved by plastic deformation.

Figure 6.34 Residual stress in a simple butt weld (*BOC Ltd*)

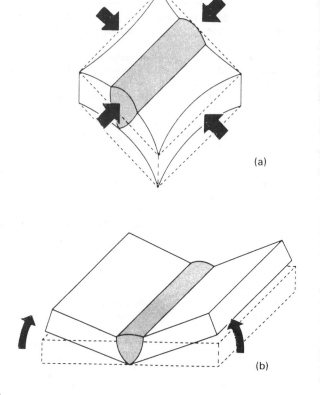

Distortion

Distortion may take the form of a change in dimensions of the joint, transverse or longitudinal shrinkage, angular movement, or out-of-plane buckling (Figure 6.35). Distortion may result in unacceptable appearance (buckled body panels), prevention of subassembly fabrication or the inability of the structure to perform its intended function (alignment of body panels after welding). The following steps may be taken to minimize distortion:

1 Use the minimum amount of weld metal. Overwelding and excessive reinforcement should be avoided in fillet welds and flat butt welds. Intermittent or stitch welding may be used.
2 Use square edge on narrow gap procedures to reduce angular distortion when welding.
3 Use high travel speed and low heat input to limit heat build-up in the panels to be welded.
4 Use the backstep weld sequence or preset the joint.

6.14.2 Incorrect weld geometry and appearance, defects, loss of properties

Overfill

Overfill or excessive reinforcement may be described as the presence of weld metal which exceeds that required for the joint (see Figure 6.36). This creates

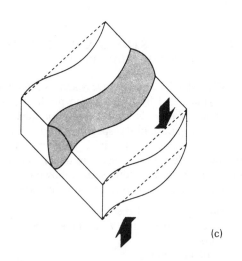

Figure 6.35 Types of distortion: (a) longitudinal and transverse shrinkage (b) angular distortion (c) out-of-plane bucking distortion (*BOC Ltd*)

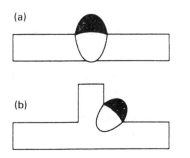

Figure 6.36 Excessive reinforcement in (a) butt weld and (b) fillet weld (*BOC Ltd*)

Figure 6.37 Root convexity: excessive penetration (*BOC Ltd*)

Figure 6.38 Root concavity: suck-back (*BOC Ltd*)

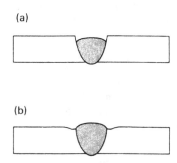

Figure 6.39 (a) Underfill and (b), (c) undercut (*BOC Ltd*)

Figure 6.40 Lack of penetration (*BOC Ltd*)

an unacceptable appearance or surface finish and would require weld dressing.

Root convexity

This results from excessive penetration on the underside of a full penetration weld. The cause of this defect is incorrect welding parameter selection (shielding gas or operating technique) (Figure 6.37).

Root concavity or suck-back

This may occur if the rear of the weld pool is too hot or large, and the combined effect of contraction and surface tension results in a root surface which is concave (Figure 6.38). The surface profile will often be smooth and less likely to produce stress than overpenetration or lack of penetration; however, it may result in unacceptable loss of cross-section. The cause of this defect is incorrect parameter selection, in particular the use of high current or slow travel speed.

Underfill and undercut

If insufficient weld metal is deposited in the joint, the parent material may remain unfused and the joint may be underfilled (Figure 6.39a). Alternatively, the weld area may be melted but the combined effect of the arc force and the flow of the molten metal may prevent complete joint filling or produce a depression in the surface at the weld boundaries: this is known as undercut (Figure 6.39b). Underfill is usually avoided by careful placement and operating technique. Undercut normally occurs at high speeds and high current, and may be avoided by reducing both current and speed.

Lack of penetration

This is classed as partial penetration and is not acceptable, particularly with respect to fatigue, loading and corrosion resistance on the joint, where full penetration is required. The defect results from poor joint preparation and unsuitable welding operating parameters, especially current settings (Figure 6.40).

Lack of fusion

Lack of fusion between successive runs or between the weld bead and the parent metal can produce serious crack-like defects. These defects reduce the load-carrying area of the joint and produce stresses, and are therefore unacceptable in welds which are subjected to fatigue loading or static loading. The cause of the defect is usually incorrect operating parameters, high deposition rate, or low heat input (Figure 6.41).

(a)

(b)

Figure 6.41 Lack of fusion (a) at sidewall and (b) inter-run (*BOC Ltd*)

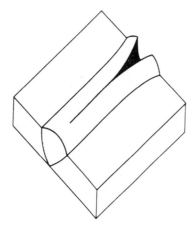

Figure 6.42 Solidification cracks (*BOC Ltd*)

Spatter
Spatter takes the form of small particles of metal which are rejected from the arc or the weld pool and adhere to the surface of the metal being joined. Spatter may be unacceptable for purely cosmetic reasons; it may also inhibit the application of surface coatings (as in vehicle painting) and may initiate corrosion. Spatter usually results from either excessive voltage or insufficient induction in dip transfer or argon enriched gas mixtures.

Porosity
Porosity results when bubbles of gas are nucleated in the weld pool and trapped during solidification. The source of the gas may be a chemical reaction such as the formation of carbon monoxide from carbon and oxygen, or the expulsion of gases which have been dissolved by the liquid metal but are relatively insoluble in the solid phase. The problem is best controlled by eliminating the source of the pore generating gas. This may be achieved by effective shielding and the prevention of leaks, the ingress of air or moisture to gas lines, and joint surface contamination from oil, grease, moisture or paint.

Inclusions
Non-metallic inclusions may be trapped in the joint owing to inadequate cleaning. Inclusions tend to be more angular than gas pores and can result in higher stress levels as well as forming a plane of weakness in the weld. The cause of this defect is usually insufficient inter-run cleaning, incorrect welding parameters or incorrect gas shielding.

Solidification cracks (hot cracking)
Solidification cracking occurs when the solidifying weld pool is exposed to transverse shrinkage (Figure 6.42). The last part of the weld pool to solidify is usually rich in low-melting-point impurity elements, and liquid films are often present at the centre line of the weld; as a result the ductility of the weld metal is lowered. The transverse contraction strain can be significant and, if the low-ductility area along the centre line of the weld is unable to accommodate this strain, cracking takes place. The problem is usually avoided by careful selection of the weld metal composition.

6.15 WELD TESTING AND INSPECTION

Weld testing and inspection can be divided into two types. In non-destructive testing, the test samples are not destroyed in the process. In destructive testing, the test samples are destroyed in the process.

6.15.1 Visible examination

This is normally carried out during and after welding and prior to any other non-destructive or destructive test being used. This visual check will usually determine the following:

Weld size
Profile or weld face shape
Surface defects in weld face
Undercut and overlap
Root defects
Weld penetration
Surface slag inclusions

6.15.2 Non-destructive testing

Non-destructive testing of weld samples is normally carried out using the following methods.

Macro examination
This method uses a low-power magnification to examine weld specimens which have been levelled, polished and etched to detect the following: lack of

190

fusion, lack of penetration, porosity, oxide inclusions, internal cracks.

Crack detection
By using dye penetrant, surface defects in both ferrous and non-ferrous metals may be detected. A solution of coloured dye is sprayed on to the weld and parent metal and allowed to soak. The dye is then washed off and the surface dried. A liquid developer is then sprayed on to the weld to give a uniform dry powder coating which is white in colour. The coloured dye oozes out of any crack in the weld into the white coating and can be seen in normal lighting conditions.

Magnetic particle method
Surface defects in mild steel and low-alloy steels may be revealed by this method. The test specimen is connected to a special power source. The magnetic test liquid is sprayed along the weld. The magnetic particles then collect along a line of crack when the current flows through the weld. Better test results are obtained if the surface of the weld has first been ground smooth.

As these penetrants and magnetic test liquids give off harmful vapours, the work must be carried out under well-ventilated conditions.

Ultrasonic inspection
This method uses sound waves which are passed through the weld. They are transmitted as pulses by a probe connected to an ultrasonic test set. Defects reflect these pulses back to the probe through a flexible cable which is attached to the ultrasonic test set, where it is displayed on an oscilloscope screen as deflections of a trace. These deflections measure the location and size of the defect. Grease is used between the probe and the work to improve sound transmission. Also light grinding of the weld or parent metal surface to remove spatter may be required before testing.

Radiography
This method uses penetrating X-rays or gamma rays which are passed through the weld and recorded on photographic film held in a lightproof container. When the film has been processed, any defect in the weld will show up as shadows in the photographic image. Only trained and radiation classified personnel may operate radiography equipment, as the equipment is extremely dangerous.

6.15.3 Destructive testing

Mechanical testing is a destructive procedure and therefore cannot be carried out on any component required for use. Representative test samples produced under similar conditions to the in-service components, for example welding procedure tests, are normally used, and accurate comparisons made.

The tests most frequently used to assess the properties of welded joints are as follows.

Tensile test
This test can be used to assess the yield point, ultimate tensile strength and elongation percentage of the weld specimen. Failure usually occurs in the parent material; therefore exact measurements are not usually obtained for the weld itself, although in this case the ultimate tensile strength (UTS) of the weld is higher than that of the parent metal. Test specimens are cut from the designated area of the weld assembly, the edges are smoothed and the corners are radiused. If an elongation value is required, then two centre-punch marks often 50 mm apart are applied one on either side of the weld; this is called a gauge length. The test equipment can vary, but the basic principles are that two sets of vice jaws are used to clamp the specimen, hydraulic power is applied to force the jaws apart, and a dial calibrated in tonnes or newtons records the load. As the load increases, the dial registers the amount of applied load until fracture occurs.

Bend test
Bend tests are carried out on butt welds and are used to determine the soundness of the weld zone. The test piece is the full thickness of the material, with the weld bead reinforcement dressed flush on both sides. It is common practice to take two specimens from a test piece: one can be bent against the face and the other bent against the root. A bend test machine consists of a roller or former connected to a ram and operated hydraulically. Unless otherwise stated, the diameter of the former should be four times the weld specimen thickness. The specimen is placed on support rollers and the centre point of the former is brought into contact with the weld face or root. Pressure is then applied to bend the weld specimen through either 90 or 180 degrees.

Nick-break test
In this test procedure the butt joint weld must first be ground flush. Then two nicks (saw cuts) are made, one on either end of the joint in the weld specimen. The weld specimen may be broken during bending, or alternatively the specimen may be placed in the jaws of the tensile test machine and struck with a hammer when tensioned.

Impact test

There are two main types of impact test, the Charpy V notch and the Izod test. Both tests employ a swinging pendulum which breaks accurately prepared specimens to which a notch has been applied. Both the tests have the same principle, which is to determine the energy measured in joules absorbed by the notched test piece at a specified temperature as it is broken from a single swinging pendulum. During fracture, energy from the pendulum will be absorbed by the specimen, more energy being absorbed by strong materials than by brittle materials. The distance the pendulum swings after fracture is measured by a pointer on a dial calibrated in joules. The lower the value indicated, the more brittle the specimen; conversely, the higher the reading, the greater the toughness.

6.15.4 Vehicle repair weld testing quality control ISO 9002 (formerly BS 5750)

Those vehicle body repair companies wishing to obtain ISO 9002 will have to conduct weld test procedures. These procedures will have to become an integral part of the company's policy on quality in the repair of vehicles while maintaining safe working practices. In addition regular testing will demonstrate the skill and ability of body technicians to maintain a high quality of weld standard in all types of crash repair work carried out by their company.

6.16 EQUIPMENT MAINTENANCE AND SAFETY

For the best results the gas and contact nozzle of the welding torch must be cleaned of welding spatter at regular intervals. Unless this is done, there is a risk of the welding current arcing between the contact nozzle and the gas nozzle to the workpiece, which could cause severe damage to the welding torch. When cleaning the gun of spatter and deposits the condition of the gas distributor should also be checked, and if it appears to be burnt and worn by spatter then it should be replaced. This is because in addition to distributing the gas it also acts as an insulator, and is of vital importance to the service life of the swan neck of the torch. It is recommended that the machine should be cleaned with compressed air once yearly, or more frequently if it is used in dusty conditions. The feed mechanism and rollers require more frequent cleaning. Regular maintenance to the following parts is important: gas nozzle, gas distributor, contact nozzle and wire guide rollers. It is never advisable to weld with a worn-out contact nozzle and deformed gas nozzle.

Any exposure to a naked welding arc, even for a fraction of a second, is sufficient to damage the cornea of the eye (welding flash). Consequently a welding screen should always be used, preferably of the helmet and visor type. By using this type both hands are free for control over the welding equipment. The hand-held type of welding screen is of course fully adequate from a safety point of view but only leaves one hand free. This could result in a shakier movement of the gun and a loss of precision in following the joint.

Wear welding gloves and suitably fitting protective clothing, especially when welding overhead so that the welding spatter does not run down the neck or sleeves of the overall worn.

Another hazard is the build-up of fumes given off by the welding process, which could be dangerous to health when welding in a confined space. When welding in a normal workshop there is no problem, but if welding in a tightly enclosed area, such as inside the boot of a car, make sure that the area is well ventilated.

Precaution must be taken when welding vehicle panels in case there are flammable materials attached to the other side of the panel which could ignite and burst into flames. Therefore always have adequate fire-fighting appliances available. (See Chapter 1.)

QUESTIONS

1 Explain the term 'MIG/MAG welding'.
2 Explain the term 'TIG welding'.
3 What is an inert gas? Explain its function in welding.
4 What are the advantages of gas shielded arc welding?
5 Name three types of gases that could be used in MIG/MAG welding.
6 What is the difference between water-cooled and air-cooled torches in TIG welding?
7 What determines the size of the ceramic nozzle to be used for TIG welding?
8 Which material are the electrodes made from in the TIG welding process?
9 State the advantages of MIG/MAG welding when compared with oxyacetylene welding for the repair of vehicle panels.
10 When MIG welding aluminium and its alloys, which type of gas would be most suitable for use?
11 Describe the difference between plug welding and spot welding.
12 Explain the mode of metal transfer used for welding thin-gauge materials.

13 Describe the three functions that most MIG/MAG welding equipment is capable of performing.

14 Explain the term 'spray transfer'.

15 Describe the purpose of a contact tip in a MIG/MAG welding torch.

16 Show, with the aid of a sketch, a repair situation where resistance spot welding can be substituted by a MIG/MAG spot weld.

17 With the aid of diagrams, describe the following defects made by MIG/MAG welding: (a) porosity (b) incomplete fusion (c) spatter on workpiece (d) poor penetration.

18 What colours are used to identify argon and argon-mix cylinders?

19 Why is it important to disconnect a battery on a vehicle before commencing any MIG/MAG welding operation?

20 List the safety precautions to be observed before and during welding.

21 Explain the form in which the electrode is manufactured for MIG/MAG welding.

22 With the aid of a sketch, show a repair application which involves MIG/MAG spot welding.

23 Describe the major features of a TIG welding torch.

24 Which mode of metal transfer uses the short arc process in MIG/MAG welding?

25 With the aid of a sketch, illustrate one method of metal transfer used in MIG/MAG welding.

26 With the aid of a sketch, explain how plug welding is carried out in repair work.

27 Describe the differences between the processes of TIG welding and MIG/MAG welding.

28 By using a sketch, illustrate a typical weld fault in MIG/MAG welding.

29 State the function of the controls of standard MIG/MAG welding equipment.

30 Explain the setting to be used when welding a large gap with MIG/MAG welding.

7

Minor accident damage

7.1 TECHNIQUES OF DAMAGE RECTIFICATION

Before a systematic approach to body repairs is possible, it is necessary to understand the characteristics of sheet metal as used for body panels. When a flat sheet of metal is bent to a wide arc or radius it will regain its former shape when released; that is, it is elastic or possesses elasticity. However, if this sheet is bent to a short arc or radius it exceeds the limits of elasticity or flexibility; the metal in the bend becomes stiff and will take on a permanent set and retain the curvature. This is the result of the stresses which have been set up at the bend, making the material work hardened. Before the sheet is formed in the press the grain structure is constant and the thickness uniform throughout (see Figure 7.1). When the metal is formed to make the body panel it is bent beyond its elastic limit. The outer surface stretches or lengthens while the inner surface shrinks or shortens (Figure 7.1). The pressure exerted on the metal by the press also changes the grain structure to work harden the surface layers. This build-up of stresses in the bend or curve is an essential factor in the design of vehicle body panels which together form the body shell. A common feature in the design and manufacture of a motor vehicle is the many curved surfaces which are normally referred to as crowns. Vehicle body panels consist of flat or slightly curved areas, sometimes quite large and elastic in nature (low crowns), such as door panels; these are held in position by stiffened, rigid sharp bends and swages which are non-elastic in nature (high crowns), such as the cant of roof panels (see Figure 7.2).

If a panel is damaged in an accident, the buckled area, being sharply bent, will create additional stiffness in the panel, whether in an elastic or non-elastic area. The slope of the buckles surrounding the sharp creases will be fairly elastic, but a greater amount of effort will be needed to reshape the sections of the panel which are made rigid either in manufacture or through accidental damage. When a panel becomes damaged due to impact, the resulting force on the metal causes buckling in the form of creases or ridges which are created because the panel has gone beyond

its elastic limits to become non-elastic, therefore establishing unwanted rigid sections within the damaged area on the panel. The characteristic stiffness of the ridges prevents the panel returning to its original shape unless additional force is applied to release the stress in the ridges in the damaged area. When these stresses in the unwanted rigid areas are released, the elastic areas will also be allowed to return to their original shape. It is important that these corrections be made in the right sequence on the individual panel, otherwise additional damage will be caused to the panels. Repairs must be performed using the reverse order and an opposing force to that of the original force which caused the damage. Consequently the correct sequence should be first to remove the last ridge which was formed, and then to work towards the first point of impact of the damaged area.

Rectification of vehicle bodies, following a true assessment of the damage, can be divided into two stages: roughing out or straightening of the reinforced sections and panels to approximately their original shape, and the finishing or preparing of the surface to a smooth appearance for repainting. Both stages are of prime importance, and many man hours can be saved if the job is processed correctly. In cases of damage where the body is distorted, the temptation is to use rough-and-ready methods depending on brute force to restore some resemblance of shape. While this may speed up the first stage of a repair, it will be found that such methods result in additional marking of panels; considerably more time will be spent on the final stage of finishing than would be required if more thought had been given to the job in the first instance, and better methods had been used to rectify distortion. Damaged panels should be restored by relieving the stresses which have been set up by the force of impact. The skill of all body repair techniques lies in the correct handling of the basic hand tools, in a variety of combinations best suited for the job in hand.

7.2 HAMMERING TECHNIQUES

Unlike most other trades, where the hammer is used with a follow-through action from a combination of

194

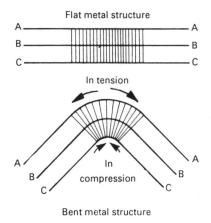

Flat metal structure

In tension

In compression

Bent metal structure

Figure 7.1 Change in grain structure during pressing (*Sykes-Pickavant Ltd*)

wrist, elbow and shoulder, in the skilled hands of a body repair worker the planishing hammer swing is a rhythmic action involving finger and wrist movement, producing a ringing blow (Figure 7.3). The hammer should not be held tensely, but during the complete cycle of movement it should be held loosely in the hand. This will achieve a higher degree of accuracy and at the same time help to reduce fatigue. This loose holding of the hammer applies equally to dolly blocks, as it permits them to bounce back naturally and to assume the correct position for striking the next blow. With practice the wrist becomes strengthened, and consequently working in restricted places becomes easier where an even wrist action is impossible. The

dolly should be allowed to lie naturally in the hand with the face to be used uppermost and, as with the hammer, should be held firmly but not tightly. Tap lightly at the dolly to obtain the feel of metal to metal, and check for control of force of blow; each blow will give a metallic ring which should be the same for each stroke of the hammer. When no metallic ring is heard the hammer is not hitting the metal in alignment with the dolly.

7.2.1 Roughing out damage

In minor repair work which can be carried out using hand tools, the first major operation is to reshape the damaged area back to its original contour. This is done by a technique known as roughing out, which must be carried out prior to any finishing process such as direct hammering or planishing. Roughing out is the reshaping of the area by hand with the aid of a heavy dolly, which forces back the damaged section to its original shape (Figure 7.4).

When repairing collision work, the normal method of correction is to reverse the process which caused the original damage. In a case of minor repair the point of impact is now the lowest part of the damage. To reverse the process this point on the underside of the panel should be struck using the same force as was originally directed against it. If this spot is hit accurately with a roughing-out dolly using the same force, the panel will spring back almost to the contour it had prior to the damage. In some cases you will be able to correct the panel damage with a single blow which will spring the panel back to its original

1 Low-crown, elastic areas
2 High-crown, rigid areas

Figure 7.2 Prepressed wing panel

Figure 7.6 The technique of direct hammering

Figure 7.3 Swing of the planishing hammer

Figure 7.4 The technique of roughing out damage

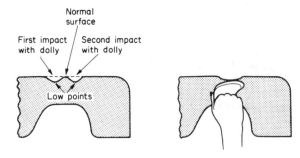

Figure 7.5 Positioning of blows in the rouging-out technique

shape. In other cases, where the repair is larger, it will be found that several blows are necessary. Hold the roughing-out dolly lightly in the hand and strike the hardest blow at the centre of what appears to be the lowest point of the damaged area, then direct the blows around the first one and gradually work outwards, decreasing the force of the blows until all the damaged area has been roughed out (Figure 7.5). However, in most cases the damage will not be completely restored to its original contour, although it will be roughed out and can be straightened to its correct contour by direct hammering or by a combination of direct hammering and indirect hammering.

The use of a heavy hammer for roughing out is not advisable, for this permits heavy blows which are concentrated in small areas and invariably results in stretching or otherwise distorting the metal, whereas a well-directed blow with a dolly that matches the original contour of the repair spreads the blow over a larger area, resulting in very little distortion of the metal. In some cases body repair workers use a boxwood mallet for roughing out, because there is less chance of stretching the metal. The technique is similar to that of using a dolly, as the mallet is used on the inside of the panel to hammer the damaged section back to its original shape; then the work is finished off by direct hammering using a panel hammer and dolly. A disadvantage in using a mallet is that on modern panel assemblies there is insufficient space to use a mallet for roughing out; therefore most body workers find a dolly more useful.

7.2.2 Direct hammering

Direct hammering is in fact the process of planishing, and the body repair worker uses it as a finishing process after the work has been preshaped and roughed out (Figure 7.6). It is the essential practice to master, and develops as a result of continuous experience.

Figure 7.7 Using a high-crowned dolly

Figure 7.8 Using a low-crowned dolly

Figure 7.9 The technique of indirect hammering

Before using the hammer and dolly together, it will be necessary to clean the underside of the portion of the wing or panel on which you will be working. Body panels and wings are covered with a sound deadening material which must be removed before starting the work. If you fail to clean the surface of this material it will not only stick to your dolly but will to a large degree destroy its effectiveness.

It is most important to choose the correct dolly block for the job, because they differ in shape, curvature and weight. In repairing the high-crowned radius of a wing you will have to use a dolly block with a high-crowned radius (Figure 7.7). In repairing large body panels and door panels which are fairly flat it is necessary to use a dolly block with a low-crowned radius (Figure 7.8). In direct hammering, by having a dolly which matches the original contour under the damaged area and striking it with a hammer, you are pushing the uneven displaced metal surface back to its original contour to give a smooth and level finish. The dolly provides support and prevents the undamaged areas that have been previously roughed out from being pushed out of place. If you do not strike squarely over the dolly, you will be hitting an unsupported area of the repair and will displace the metal, creating further damage that must be rectified later.

Direct hammering requires skill in directing the hammer blows and close observation of what you are doing so as not to hit the metal too hard, thereby displacing it. Perfect coordination between your two hands is necessary to enable you to move the dolly around under the damaged area and still continue to hit squarely over it with the hammer. Start hammering by using light blows; these will not do the job, but will show you whether or not you are hitting squarely over the dolly. Do not forget to let the dolly just lie in your hand and to grip the hammer loosely. A true ring will be heard if you are directly over the dolly, otherwise the sound will be dull. Increase the force of the blow gradually until you have found just the right force to push the raised points of the roughed-out section back without flattening the surrounding metal. The hammer should bounce back of its own accord so that it is ready for the next stroke. Likewise the dolly will spring away from the surface, and the normal resilience of your arm will bring it back, striking a blow on the metal from underneath. These things will occur normally only if you hold both hammer and dolly loosely.

7.2.3 Indirect hammering (off the dolly block)

Indirect hammering is another technique which uses hammer and dolly to level a panel surface. A low area can be raised by hammering round the outer edges in such a manner that the rebound action of the block tends to push the low area upwards to its original contour. This in fact is achieved by the sequence of hammering just off, or at the side of, the dolly block; hence the name of indirect hammering (Figure 7.9). This technique is used in conjunction with direct hammering or planishing to achieve a final finish on the panel surface. Metal that has not been excessively hammered, displaced or stretched will have a tendency to return to its original contour of its own accord. This is due to the internal strain imparted to the metal by the forming dies in manufacture. If the metal

197

is prevented from springing back by other strains imparted to it by additional bends or creases that have been formed by accident, the metal can then be restored to its normal contour by relieving whatever new strain is holding it out of position.

In direct hammering a dolly block having the correct contour to match the original shape of the panel is held under the low spot, and a series of light blows are aimed around the outer edge of this low spot, and slightly off the dolly block. The light blows will not displace the surrounding undamaged area, but the force of the downward blow will be transferred to the dolly block. As a result of receiving the hammer blows indirectly the dolly will rebound and the hand holding the block will automatically bring it back in place so that it imparts a light push upwards on the area. The centre of the damaged area will slowly rise until the original contour is restored.

7.2.4 Spring hammering

This is another technique of using hand tools to smooth and level a panel surface. In this case only a hammer is used, and it is not supported with a dolly block. The technique is used to reduce high spots which sometimes form as a panel is planished. In some cases these high spots can be reduced by careful, controlled hammering which spreads the force of the blow over the area of the metal, thus reducing the high spot. When a crown or curved surface is formed in a metal panel, it becomes strong in that it resists any change to its shape. The strength of this crowned surface can be used to support the surface being hammered without the use of a dolly. This type of hammering is called spring hammering, and can be used to correct high spots on metal panel surfaces (Figure 7.10). To take advantage of a great amount of the natural support provided by the crown of the metal, the force of the hammer blow is spread over a larger area. Once the metal is back to its original contour, additional hammering will cause the surface to sink below its original contour line, and it may not be possible to raise it readily. Always start with light blows, and as the repair nears completion, inspect the work after each blow. This will reduce the possibility of sinking the surface too low. Keep the surface of the hammer face clean and highly polished. Any marks on the surface of the hammer will be transferred to the surface of the metal and create additional work.

7.2.5 Removing low spots

Low spots can be removed in several ways, the two most common being the use of a pick hammer or a

(a)

(b)

Figure 7.10 The technique of spring hammering (*Sykes-Pickavant Ltd*)

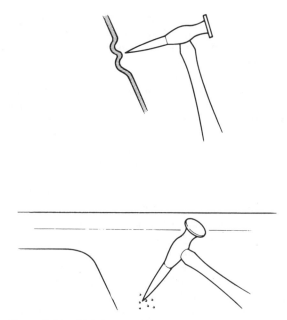

Figure 7.11 Pick hammering used to remove low spots

dolly block. When using the dolly block, start by holding it so that it can strike the underneath of the low spot on the panel with one of its rounded corners. It must be noted that if the operator does not hit exactly in the centre of the low spot, he will raise metal in some unwanted place. Accuracy is therefore essential, and can be achieved by holding a finger in the low spot and lightly tapping the underside of the panel with the rounded corner of the dolly until you feel that it is exactly beneath your finger, then strike a sharp blow and raise the metal at this point. After each low spot has been raised in this manner, these points can be filed to check that they are level with the surrounding panel surface.

The second common method of raising low spots is by pick hammering. Bringing up low spots with a pick hammer is more difficult than by the use of a rounded corner of a dolly block. With a pick hammer more accurate placing of the blow is required. Likewise greater control over the force of the blow is necessary. Start using the pick hammer in a manner similar to the dolly block. Hold the end of your finger in the low spot. Tap the under surface of the panel until the pick is directly below your finger. Then strike a light blow from beneath the panel, of sufficient strength to form a pimple in the low spot (Figure 7.11). Care must be taken to avoid overstretching the metal by using too hard a blow. These pimples represent stretched metal, but in being formed also raise the surrounding metal. When all the low spots have

been raised with a pick hammer in this manner, the pimples can then be lightly hammered level by direct hammering, and finished by filing.

7.3 FILING

Filing is one of the most important aspects of finishing a body panel. It is carried out using an adjustable file holder, fitted with flexible blades which can be adjusted concave or convex to suit most contours on the average vehicle body. Initially the file was used for smoothing off panels prior to sanding and locating high and low spots. With the introduction of body solder and later metal and plastic fillers, filing took on an even greater importance in the finishing of repairs on body panels. Filing indicates any irregularities in the repaired surface of a panel, and is carried out as the panel is planished. First of all fasten the correct file blade to the file holder with the cutting edges of the teeth facing away from the handle or operator. Adjust the contour of the file holder so that it is almost, but not quite, matching the contour of the surface on which you intend to work.

One hand is used to hold the file handle, while the other grasps the knob at the opposite end. The file should be applied with long, straight strokes, pushing it away from you along the length of the panel (Figure 7.12). Short, jabbing strokes should never be used, as these will only scratch the panel and will not indicate low spots. If the file digs in, too much pressure is being applied and hence a need for reduction is essential. At the end of the first stroke, raise the file and, without dragging it over the metal, bring it back to the starting position and make a second stroke. Repeat this procedure until the area has been covered, making the file marks parallel to one another. This is termed 'line filing', and indicates the levelness of the panel in the direction in which it has been filed. At this point both the high and low areas will show up. The high spots can be corrected by spring hammering and the low spots by direct hammering, pick hammering, or in some cases by using the corner of a dolly block. Line filing indicates curvature in one direction only, and as most panels are double curved the panel surface must be cross filed to give an accurate contour check. 'Cross filing' means a change in the direction of the file strokes so that the file is moved at an angle between 45° and 90° over the previous file strokes, thus checking the accuracy of the curvature in that direction.

After filing, and prior to refinishing the panel, the damaged area is sanded using a fine-grit sanding disc which leaves a smooth, even surface ideally suited for painting.

(a)

(b)

Figure 7.12 The technique of filing (*Sykes-Pickavant Ltd*)

Figure 13.40 Ear and eye protection when sanding (*Motor Insurance Repair Research Centre*)

7.4 SANDING OR DISC GRINDING

7.4.1 Use of grinder

Several general rules govern the use of the disc grinder. If these are observed they will enable the operator to become proficient very quickly in the use of the

grinder. The rules are considered good shop practice and are directed towards the safety of the operator. In the first instance, if the device is electrically operated see that it is properly connected and earthed. Shop floors are usually of cement; they are generally moist and, therefore, relatively good conductors of electricity. If the grinder is not properly earthed it is possible to receive a fatal electric shock when the machine is in use. Always wear goggles to protect the eyes from flying particles of metal and from small abrasive particles that come loose from the grinding disc (Figure 7.13). Always replace worn discs as soon as a tear is noticed; torn discs may catch in the work and twist the grinder out of your hands.

Always maintain a balanced position when using the grinder. This position not only permits perfect control over the machine at all times, but it will also produce less fatigue over longer periods. When operating the grinder, hold it as flat as possible without permitting the centre connecting bolt to come in contact with the surface being ground. Hold the grinder so that only 40 mm to 65 mm of the outer edge of the disc is in contact with the surface being ground. The grinder must never be tilted so that only the edge of the disc contacts the surface. Failure to observe this will cause gouges or deep scratches in the metal which will be hard to remove. Move the grinder from left to right, overlapping the previous stroke with each new stroke. Make the cutting lines as clean and straight as possible. Move the grinder in the same manner whether using it for the removal of paint, rough or finish grinding. For most grinding operations, finish grind in the longest direction possible on the repaired surface.

7.4.2 Sanding discs

The coated abrasive disc is the part of the sander that does the actual sanding, and selection of the right grit and coating for each job is important. There are five different minerals which are commonly used for manufacturing abrasives. These are garnet, flint, emery, aluminium oxide and silicon carbide. Aluminium oxide is the most important of these. Because of its toughness and durability it is used in the motor body repair trade, where it is chiefly used on metal. The abrasive is fixed on a backing which is either of paper, cloth or a combination of the two. For dry grinding or sanding, high-quality hide glues are used for anchoring the abrasive grains to the backing. For wet sanding, resins are used as the bonding agent.

Coated abrasives fall into two additional classifications based on how widely the minerals are spaced. If the minerals are close together the abrasive is close coated. When they are widely spaced it is open coated.

In close-coated abrasive discs, the abrasive is applied in such quantity as to entirely cover the backing. In open-coated abrasive discs, the backing is from 50 to 70 per cent covered. This leaves wider spaces between the abrasive grains. The open coating provides increased pliability and good cutting speeds under light pressures. Open-coated discs are used where the surface being ground is of such a nature that closely spaced abrasive materials would rapidly fill up and become useless. When grinding a body panel, always use an open-coated disc up to the time that the area being sanded is completely free of paint. Then use a close-coated abrasive to grind the metal to the point where the surface needs no further correction. The final finish is accomplished with a fine grit to get the surface smooth enough for refinishing by the painting department.

7.5 HOT SHRINKING

One of the most important skills in the repair of damaged panels is that of hot shrinking. It is important because in most cases of damaged body panels, stretching of the metal takes place. The actual process is carried out by gathering the stretched metal into a common centre or area and then heating this section. The panel steel is then at its best condition to be hammered down, thus reducing the surface area and so making shrinking possible (Figure 7.14).

The oxyacetylene flame is used as a means of heating the panel, and care must be taken to reduce the spread of heat to the surrounding area of the panel. This can be done by cooling the panel with water after every shrink. The advisable welding nozzle size for a 1.00 mm panel is a number 2 nozzle.

7.5.1 Tools required for hot shrinking

Before commencing to heat up the stretched section, it is essential that all tools and material needed to carry out the shrink should be conveniently placed so that they can be brought into use quickly. The tools required are as follows:

Wire brush The wire brush and scraper are used in preparing the panel prior to shrinking. With the scraper any anti-drum or underseal compound must be removed before applying the heat.

Mallet or shrinking hammer The mallet face has a soft surface much larger than that of a planishing hammer. If used together with a suitable dolly block it will bring the metal down to a level surface while hot, and also avoid stretching the panel as the mallet is made of wood and not metal like the panel hammer.

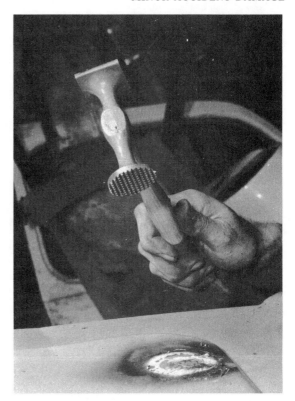

Figure 7.14 Hot shrinking panel (*Sykes-Pickavant*)

Another tool that can be used is the shrinking hammer; this is similar to a planishing hammer but the faces have cross-milled serrations which reduce the tendency for the hammer to stretch the metal because of the very small contact area between the points on the serrations and the panel.

Planishing hammer This should be used to complete the shrink after malleting, as the hammer is better for levelling out the surface of the panel than the mallet.

Dolly block This should not be fuller in shape than the actual panel being repaired. Also it should be of a rather light weight so that it forms a relatively weak backing for the malleting, thus reducing the stretching during the levelling operation. A grid dolly has a serrated face to reduce the possibility of stretching in the panel.

Damp cloth This is helpful in checking the spread of heat thus reducing the risk of panel distortion.

7.5.2 Hot shrinking process

Arrange your tools so that they are within easy reach, as it is necessary to change quickly from one tool to another when performing a shrinking operation (Figure

201

Stretched area on the panel surface

Heat spots

The first heat spot is placed in the centre of the stretched area

Welding torch flame held perpendicular to panel to make heat spot

Dolly held to form a light backing for malleting thus gathering stretched metal in towards heat spot

Location of blows of mallet thus forcing excess metal into small heat spot

Final blow to be placed on this spot

Area shrunk by first heat spot

Before hot shrinking

After hot shrinking

Figure 7.15 The technique of hot shrinking

7.15). Locate the highest point in the stretched section of the panel with which you are working. Light the torch and heat the spot to approximately 10 mm diameter in the centre of the high spot or stretched area to a cherry red, using a circular motion when heating the spot. Be careful not to burn through the metal by overheating. As soon as the spot is cherry red place the shrinking dolly (grid dolly), which is usually fairly flat, under the spot and strike several

sharp blows with a mallet around the heat spot; this will force the surplus stretched metal into the heat spot. Then the blows are directed on the centre of the heat spot, which pushes the metal down while it is still red hot. At all times the dolly block must be held loosely against the underside of the panel, exactly centred under the heat spot. After four or five mallet blows, the last being on the centre of the heat spot, the heat spot will turn black, and should be quenched immediately with a water filled sponge. Repeat this operation taking the next highest spot in the stretched section of the panel, until the bulge or fullness is finally shrunk down below the level of the surrounding surface. It can then be brought up to its correct level by planishing with a hammer and dolly and then finishing with a panel file.

The following points should be noted:

1 Never quench a red hot heat spot; wait until the metal has turned black.
2 Never heat an area greater than that which can be hammered with mallet and dolly.
3 Never use anything but an oxyacetylene welding torch for heating a stretched section.
4 Never attempt to shrink a panel until it has been roughed out.
5 Always hammer the stretched section outwards before applying heat.
6 If the stretched part of the surface is small, make a smaller heat spot.
7 It is possible to shrink metal without quenching each spot. However, the shrinking operation is much faster when each spot is quenched with water, as fewer heat spots are required if the heat expansion is drawn out by quenching than by additional spots.
8 In some panels it is possible to use a spoon for the backing tool for the hammering operation, especially on door panels or over inner constructions.
9 When performing a shrinking operation, take care to avoid overshrinking the panel. This will cause the metal to warp and buckle both in and out of the stretched area, owing to overheating of the stretched section. If this does arise, heat a small spot in the area where the panel is buckling, apply a dolly block or spoon with enough pressure to hold the buckling section up, then allow the metal to cool. Do not use the mallet or water in this case. In extreme cases like this it may be necessary to repeat this operation in several different places in the buckled section.

7.5.3 Shrinking aluminium

Sheet aluminium can, with the application of heat, be subjected to shrinking. The process is similar to that used for sheet steel except that the work should be carried out faster than when shrinking steel. This speed is essential because aluminium is a good heat conductor and the spread of heat must be prevented from distorting adjoining panels. Unlike steel, aluminium does not change colour when heated and, because of the melting temperature differences, great care must be taken not to melt holes in the panel while it is being heated.

7.5.4 Shrinking equipment

Shrinking can also be carried out using shrinking equipment, which can be either a specialized piece of equipment or an attachment to a MIG welder. Basically the equipment consists of a power source to which two cables are attached: one is to the shrinking torch fitted with a tungsten or carbon electrode (which is interchangeable), and the other is to the earth return clamp for completing the circuit.

To use the equipment, first position the earth clamp, making sure of a good connection. Switch on the power source, which in some cases has a built-in timer, and then apply the tip of the electrode to the highest point on the surface of the stretched panel to be shrunk. The resulting arc will produce an extreme concentration of heat to the small area on the panel surface.

Heat until bright red or to the preset time, then immediately cool with water. This high concentration of heat in one area together with rapid cooling is extremely effective in reducing high spots by heat shrinking in vehicle repair.

7.6 COLD SHRINKING

Cold shrinking is another method of repairing stretched sections on vehicle body panels. In this case a hammer and special dolly block are used in conjunction with one another. This dolly block is a shrinking dolly and is shaped like the toe dolly but has a groove running along the full length of its top face. The dolly block is placed under the high spot formed by the stretched metal of the damaged panel and the panel is hammered down into the groove with hammer or mallet to form a valley, care being taken not to make the valley any longer or deeper than is necessary to draw the stretched metal back to its original contour. The valley formed is then filled using body solder, which is filed to give a good finish. From the reverse side of the panel it will be seen that a rib has been formed, which will in effect give strength to the damaged area should this be required. This method is also most useful in reducing welds: the weld on the face

of the panel is depressed into the channel of the dolly to form a valley below the line of the face of the panel, and the valley is then filled by the body soldering method.

7.7 BODY SOLDERING

Body soldering (or loading, filling or wiping, as it is sometimes termed) is a general practice where owing to the structural design of the all-steel body, the use of normal panel beating methods of repair using hand tools is not possible. It is ideally used to hide a lapped joint in the construction of a body shell, and is very useful to the panel beater repairing a windscreen or door pillars, or when a dent or crease is backed by a bracket or is double skinned, which prevents the placing of a dolly behind the panel and beating the section out. Body solder was first used in the motor trade in the mid 1930s and was introduced into the repair industry by the car manufacturers who were using it on the mass production of car bodies. It was during this period that the all-steel body was developed, along with rapid advances in streamlining. To finish a panel in the area of the production welds, which in most cases were lapped, spot-welded joints, body solder was used and found most useful. This method has been continued, and today solder filling plays a major part in the finish and repair of the modern car body.

7.7.1 Composition and requirements of body solder

Body solder consists of 68.5 per cent lead, 1.5 per cent antimony and 30 per cent tin. The solder has to possess the following characteristics:

1 It must remain plastic over a large temperature range, so that it stays workable.
2 It must wipe with the solder stick and not crumble, thus providing a clean surface finish.
3 The lead and tin must not separate, as it is worked in vertical or overhead positions.
4 It must be capable of being reheated and reworked without forming hard spots.

7.7.2 Process of body soldering

During the repairs of body damage, some means of reproducing the normal contour of the damaged area is necessary when it cannot be restored by normal panel beating methods. This is a case where body solder can be used to advantage so the area can be filled and then dressed down to a smooth and perfect finish.

Body soldering requirements are soldering blocks, which are usually hardwood blocks shaped to suit the panel being soldered; a suitable grease or light oil which is rubbed on to the surface of the blocks to stop them sticking to the solder, resulting in a smoother surface finish (tallow is the optimum substance for this purpose); a sanding machine, files and emery cloth for cleaning purposes prior to tinning the metal for soldering; a welding torch or similar heating appliance which produces a low-temperature flame (if a welding torch is used the flame should be feathered, which means slightly carbonizing, resulting in a soft flame); a quantity of body solder and a suitable tinning paste complete with a tinning brush for ease of application; and a clean rag for rubbing off the tinning paste. The operator must also use a self-contained air-fed mask together with a fume extractor for his own protection and to conform with health and safety regulations. Before commencing work make sure that the appropriate tools and other materials are within easy reach, thus avoiding a delay during working operations.

The first step in body soldering is to clean the surface to be soldered to a bright metallic finish. This can be done by using a sanding machine with the right type of sanding disc until the area to be soldered is cleaned to the bare metal. Any small particles of paint which the sander will not remove can be cleaned off by using emery paper and a file; this precleaning is very important, as the tinning paste will not tin the surface unless it is perfectly clean and free from paint. Apply the tinning compound by brushing it over the cleaned section so that an area slightly larger than that to be soldered is covered with tinning paste. Using the welding torch with the flame set in the carbonizing condition, which is slightly feathered and gives a very soft flame, heat the tinning compound until it becomes fluid. Then with a clean rag wipe the tinned area to spread the tinning over the cleaned surface, making sure that every part to be soldered is perfectly clean and completely tinned. An important point at this stage is not to overheat the tinning paste when tinning or the surface will turn discoloured, usually blue, and the tinning will be burnt; solder will not then adhere to this surface unless it is recleaned and tinned again.

Hold the welding torch in one hand and a stick of body solder in the other and play the flame over the tinned section, heating it just sufficiently to cause the tinning to begin to flow. While doing this, hold the stick of body solder near the work and apply the flame over both the tinned area and the solder stick so that the melting stage of each coincides. When the end of the solder stick begins to melt, press it against the tinned section, thus causing a quantity of body solder

to adhere to the tinned surface of the work. After sufficient solder has been deposited on the surface of the work, select a suitably shaped solder block, which should have previously been greased or dipped in oil or tallow, and commence to push the body solder over the damaged section of the panel. From time to time the flame should be played over the solder to keep it in a plastic or movable state; then, using the solder block, the solder should be moulded to the general contour of the panel. The solder blocks must be kept continually coated with oil or grease to allow them to slide over the surface of the solder without sticking and picking up pieces of solder while it is in the plastic state. This coating also produces a very smooth surface on the face of the area being soldered. It is very important to make sure that the tinned surface is heated to the melting point as the solder is smeared across the area being built up; unless this is done a poor bonding between the solder and the panel will result and the solder may fall out.

After the required shape has been formed and the solder built up to a level slightly above the existing panel, the final finish is gained by filing the body solder with a flexible panel file, being careful to ensure that the level does not fall below that of the surrounding area. After filing, the solder can then be rubbed down with emery paper to give a finer surface finish for painting. The sander should never be used for dressing down the solder except as a last resort, because it is too severe and tends to cut deeply and unevenly into the solder. The dust given off from the sander when using body solder is also injurious. When the final shaping and smoothing of the loaded area is complete it is essential to remove all traces of soldering flux, oils and grease which may have been used during the loading operation. If these were not removed they would have a harmful effect when the section is finally spray painted.

Figure 7.16 a–f illustrates the stages of body soldering.

Safety points

1 Avoid skin contact with fluxes.
2 Use applicators of some form when necessary.
3 Do not inhale fumes from heat/flux application.
4 The use of a sanding machine in finishing produces injurious lead dust.
5 Health and safety regulations demand protection for the operator in the form of a self-contained air-fed mask.
6 A fume extractor reduces the risk of adjacent working areas being contaminated and protects the operator.

Figure 7.16 Body soldering: (a) panel preparation
(b) applying the tinning paste (c) heating the tinning
paste ready for soldering (d) applying the solder
(e) forming the solder to shape (f) dressing and filing
the finished solder (*Motor Insurance Repair Research
Centre*)

7.8 CHEMICALLY HARDENING FILLERS (PLASTIC FILLERS)

Although body soldering still provides the best quality of filling for a repair, there are cases where an alternative method is required. Much research on this matter has led to the development of plastic fillers which would come up to the standard of body solder. These fillers are used in the body repair trade as an alternative method to body soldering. They are based on the polyester group of thermosetting resins and require a catalyst or activator to cure them. Therefore the fillers obtainable are of a duo-pack type containing paste and hardener. When they are mixed together a catalytic action takes place, resulting in the filler hardening very quickly. As this plastic filler does not require heat during its application it has certain clear advantages. Its use eliminates fire risk, especially when filling next to petrol tanks or any inflammable material. It also eliminates the problem of heat distortion which can occur when solder filling flat body panels. It is cheaper than body solder and much easier to apply. The first of these fillers were released some years ago and many disappointments were associated with their use; problems encountered were poor bonding to panels, too much delay in hardening and too hard to file when dry. Several fillers now available have been vastly improved; they will harden in as short a period as 12 minutes provided the quantities are correct and the two chemicals thoroughly mixed. When hard these fillers have excellent bonding qualities and will feather out to a fine smooth edge. Filler materials can be dispensed either from wall mounted, air operated filler dispensers or from portable dispensers. These dispensers take a 10 kg tin of polyester filler together with a matching cartridge of benzoyl peroxide hardener (Figure 7.17).

Portable dispensers offer the user the advantage of being able to take the filler from repair to repair or from workshop to paint shop. In some bodyshops it is the normal practice to use a general-purpose filler for the main filling operation; then, once shaped and flatted, it is surfaced with a fine filler (30 per cent unsaturated polyester resin plus 70 per cent inert filling material) to bring the repair up to prepaint condition. Alternatively a bodyshop may require different types of filler such as a general-purpose filler, a glass fibre reinforced filler (with added fibreglass strands, which provide great strength for bridging holes and strengthening weakened areas in metal and GRP), a fine surfacing filler (a filler with very fine surface finish to fill fine pinholes, shallow scratches, file marks or sanding marks) and, where repairs are being made to galvanized panel surfaces, a filler suitable for zinc (a

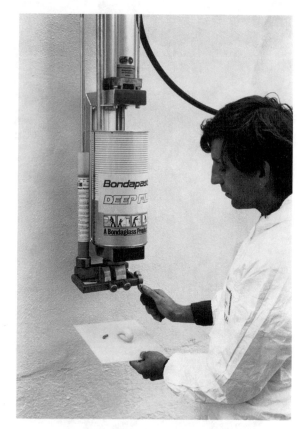

Figure 7.17 Wall mounted, air operated, filler dispenser (*Bondaglass-Voss Ltd*)

filler possessing high adhesion to coated steel surfaces). Aluminium metallic fillers are body fillers containing aluminium. The aluminium content makes them particularly easy to mix and apply. Unless the bodyshop is very large it would not be cost effective to have many wall mounted dispensers, and the portable dispenser offers a viable alternative.

The portable dispenser is operated by pushing the handle down; the filler is then extruded together with the correct amount of hardener for that quantity of filler (Figure 7.18). With most fillers this is normally 2 per cent by weight. Using a dispenser ensures that the correct proportion is added, making it impossible to overcatalyse the filler, and thus eliminating or very much reducing the possibility of spoilt paintwork. With overcatalysed filler there is a risk, particularly with metallic paints, of the repaired area showing through owing to the action of the peroxide in the hardener bleaching the paint. Another major advantage of using filler dispensers is that the filler is kept clean and uncontaminated from the beginning to the end of the

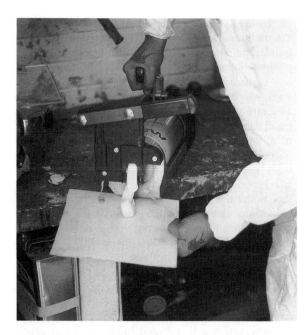

Figure 7.18 A portable dispenser extruding correct amounts of filler to hardener (*Bondaglass-Voss Ltd*)

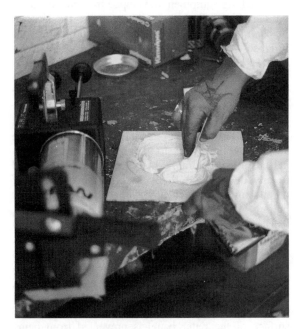

Figure 7.19 Mixing the filler and catalyst (hardener) on a non-porous surface (*Bondaglass-Voss Ltd*)

tin because there is no need to replace the lid every time the filler is used. This is a feat which is commonly accepted as impossible in most bodyshops owing to the rim of the tin becoming encrusted with filler as the applicator is cleaned off, or simply owing to forgetfulness.

In any event, even with the lid being replaced every time the filler is used, there is exposure to air, and therefore a tendency for the filler to lose its styrene content and thus to become stiffer and less spreadable. The technique of repair using this plastic filler is carried out first by roughing out the damaged area to as near the original shape as possible, or, if the area has been patched, by hammering the patch down below the original level of the panel. The area is then ground using a sander to remove all rust and paint present. A coarse-grained sanding disc should be used for this operation as this will provide better adhesion for the plastic filler. Next mix the paste with its hardener on a flat surface using a stopping knife or flexible spatula, making sure that the materials are mixed in accordance with the maker's instructions (Figure 7.19). The filler can then be applied to the damaged area after making sure that the surface is absolutely clean and free from any trace of oil (Figure 7.20). If the area to be filled up is deep, make several applications, allowing each layer to dry before adding more filler. After the filler is applied and allowed to set, it can be shaped to the contour of the panel using a plastic filler file with an abrasive paper backing, or sanded using a sander (Figure 7.21).

Plastic filler should never be used over rusted areas without patching the area with new metal so that the filler is applied to a solid base. It should not be used in areas on a panel or body surface which are continually in direct contact with water. Never drill holes in a panel to give the filler a better grip, as the holes will allow water or dampness to work in between the filler and the metal surface, leading eventually to the separation of filler from the metal surface. The filler should not be applied in any great thickness, especially where excessive vibration occurs, or the surface will crack and fall out. A good standard of finish can be achieved using these plastic fillers if the correct working procedure is adopted.

7.9 BODY JACK (HYDRAULIC)

7.9.1 Development and principles

The evolution in motor car bodywork design and construction has called for many changed methods of handling repairs. This in turn has demanded an

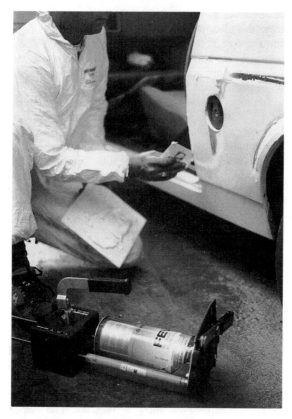

Figure 7.20 Applying filler to damaged area (*Bondaglass-Voss Ltd*)

Figure 7.21 Shaping panel contour with abrasive paper and backing block (*Bondaglass-Voss Ltd*)

increasing amount of repair equipment to augment the traditional hand tools and equipment of the body builder, panel beater and sheet metal worker. Modern equipment has been made necessary by the chassis-less construction of modern mass-produced cars and vans, which require careful alignment of the complete structure following any serious impact in addition to panel damage rectification. An essential piece of equipment for repair work is the hydraulic body jack, which is used to push and pull body shells and component body parts into alignment following an accident. Blackhawk Automotive Ltd markets a hydraulic body jack under the name of Porto Power. A range of kits of various sizes is available to suit the needs and capital expenditure of various repair shops. Kits are made up in carrying cases (Figure 7.22), on wall-board storage, and on trolleys incorporating a small press or in the form of a bench rack (Figure 7.23). Attachments and fittings have been developed to use with the body jack equipment.

The use of hydraulic body jacking equipment is not new, nor was it invented suddenly. It has developed to its present sophisticated state over many years. At one time the only type of jack available was the ratchet or screw-type body jack. The use of hydraulic body jacking equipment developed from the use of an ordinary hydraulic jack for this purpose. The hydraulic hand jack had all the advantages of providing tons of closely controlled torque-free power for the minimum of effort by the operator. It soon became apparent that the hydraulic jack was ideally suited to repair work because it could be operated in any plane and controlled from outside the car. In the essential repair of collision work, a large percentage of the work will require the use of the body jack to push or pull large areas or sections back to, approximately, their original positions. Hydraulic body jacks can be extended to any desired length by incorporating a number of attachments which are available for pushing or pulling.

The outer skin, or panels, of a body is made from light-gauge metal, placed over a framework of heavier, stiffened metal which is reinforced with various types of supports and braces. In addition to damage as a result of a collision to the outer panels of the body, the inner construction which is attached to the outer panels also becomes damaged, which means that the surface of the outer panel is prevented from being restored to its original contour; hence the inner construction must be restored to its original shape and position either before or at the same time as the outer panel metal is corrected. In some instances it will be found that once the inner construction has been restored to its normal position, the outer one will have

Figure 7.22 Snap 4 tonne standard set supplied for carrying case (*Blackhawk Automobile Ltd*)

1 Manual pump with hose
2 4-T Bantam hydraulic hose, 18 m
3 4-T ram toe
4 Extension tubes
5 Snap flex head
6 90°V base
7 Tube connector

8 Serrated saddle
9 Wedge head
10 Plunger toe
11 Chain pull collar
12 Spread ram
13 Flat base

been corrected at the same time. Before any correction can be made of such damage it is necessary to restore this inner construction. This is generally done by applying pressure to the damaged member or members. Where sharp kinks or creases have been formed at any point in the inner construction, it may be advisable to use heat while the pressure is being applied, but only on low-carbon steel and not on high-strength steel. This permits the metal to return to its original shape with little danger of cracking.

In using the body jack, it is important to understand that pressure is being applied at both ends of the jack simultaneously; therefore there could be a danger of distorting adjacent undamaged panel assemblies during the jacking process if the pushing points are not carefully selected. Such pressure can if necessary be applied either locally or spread over larger areas by the introduction and use of pressure pads, which are usually hard wood blocks. The body jack is also useful for providing support or pressure at otherwise inaccessible portions of the outer panels, as well as applying controlled pressure in a higher degree than is possible with hand tools on the various panels.

7.9.2 Basic equipment

A body jack consists of three basic units (Figure 7.23): a pump, a flexible hose connecting pump to ram, and the ram unit. The pump comprises reservoir, pump handle and hose, and is controlled by a simple open and close release valve. The handle can be screwed into the pump in two different positions for ease of operation. The hose is connected to the ram by a simple quick-release coupler which needs to be only finger tight. Pressure is applied by closing the pump release valve and operating the pump handle. The pump will build up sufficient pressure only to overcome the external resistance against the ram. The need to apply excessive pressure to the pump handle indicates that the ram has reached the limit of its movement. The ram is designed with a snap-on system to enable extension tubes and attachments to be positioned to harness the hydraulic power for any desired type of application.

All collision damage repair work which makes use of the body jack equipment is carried out by using one or another of a number of simple set-ups or, in the case of more complicated repair, a combination of

Figure 7.23 Body jack kit on a mobile trolley (*Blackhawk Automobile Ltd*)

1 Slip lock extension
2 Pump
3 10 tonne ram
4 10 tonne short ram
5 Wide-angle wedge head
6 Pull plates
7 Pull ram
8 Midget ram
9 Pull rings
10 Lock-on extension tubes
11 Male connector
12 Lock-on tube connector

13 Lock-on female and male connectors
14 Pull clamp
15 Wedgie ram
16 Flat base
17 Serrated saddle
18 Spreader plunger toe
19 Clamp toe lock pins
20 Pull chain
21 90° 'V' base
22 Wedge head
23 125 mm flex head
24 Trolley and press stand

set-ups (Figure 7.24). The first important step therefore is to understand the set-ups that can be built with this equipment, the attachments required and their application; then it is a question of breaking down a job into its basic set-ups and applying the corrective force in the correct sequence. The corrective force should be applied as near as possible in the direction opposite to the force which caused the damage. The body jack set-up should be applied so as not to push at the deepest point on the damaged section; instead work round the outer edges in ever-decreasing circles which will tend to spring the remaining damage into the final position. If the body jack set-up is applied

directly against the lowest part of a damaged section without relieving the strain, then as the pressure is applied the metal surface may become kinked and stretched and require further attention to return it to its correct level.

7.10 APPLICATION OF THE BODY JACK

7.10.1 Pushing

Pushing (Figure 7.26) is the simplest operation of all and is achieved by inserting the ram between two

1. Hydraulic pump
4. High-pressure hose
7. 4-ton midget ram
10. 10-ton hollow ram

2. Release valve
5. Speed-coupler
8. 20-ton ram
11. 7-ton shorty ram

3. Pump handle
6. Spread ram
9. 10-ton ram
12. Wedgie

1. Thread cap protector
2. Protector ring
3. Spring protector

A section of the
high-pressure hose

Rubber Fabric Interwoven wire Rubber

Figure 7.24 Hydraulic body jack (*Blackhawk Automotive Ltd*)

points and operating the pump. The plunger extends until it touches the point at which the load is to be applied, and as pumping is continued pressure is built up to overcome the resistance of the metal at the point of application. Movement of the damaged area will take place as long as pumping is continued.

Care must be taken when selecting a ram anchor; for example, if a ram was placed between two chassis members and it was intended to push from the undamaged member to straighten the damaged member, the force applied would not rectify the damage but would distort the undamaged member! The first essential is to ensure that the pushing anchor point is stronger than the point which is receiving the corrective force. This can be done by attaching a base plate to the bottom end of the ram to spread or distribute the load, which can be spread over an even larger area by putting a piece of solid hardwood timber between the base plate and the pushing point. It is seldom that a pushing application can be achieved using the ram only, because of its limited travel; therefore there are available various combinations of extension tubes, couplings and pusher heads to cater for any repair requiring a straightforward push.

1. Bantam pulling
2. Bantam pushing
3. Dozer pulling
4. Bantam spreading
5. 10-ton pushing
6. Bantam clamping
7. Bantam pushing
8. 10-ton pushing
9. 10-ton spreading

10. 10-ton clamping
11. 10-ton pushing
12. 10-ton pushing
13. 10-ton pulling
14. Wedge spreading
15. Spread ram
16. Bantam pushing
17. Bantam pulling
18. 10-ton pulling

Figure 7.25 Body jack combinations (*Blackhawk Automobile Ltd*)

211

Figure 7.26 Pushing with body jack (*Blackhawk Automotive Ltd*)

Figure 7.27 Pulling with body jack (*Blackhawk Automotive Ltd*)

7.10.2 Pulling

Pulling (Figure 7.27) is also a simple operation but uses a slightly different type of ram. With the standard equipment a pull converter set is available to enable the one push ram to fulfil both functions, but it gives an off-centre pull and is less convenient to use than the separate pull ram. With the direct set-ups using the pull rams, the tubes are under tension and there is no risk of bending. The thread sections of tubes and couplings are now under tension and it is the threads themselves that carry the load, so it is essential to ensure that they are kept clean, free from dirt and damage and are securely mated. The pulling combination obtainable makes use of the pull rams and direct pulling attachments, though it is also possible to use chain plates and chains for obtaining a pull with a push ram. The latter method is quite convenient in such cases as pulling across the width of a body from an undamaged door pillar to a door pillar which has been bowed outwards. It would be necessary to reinforce the undamaged pillar with timber to prevent distortion and to protect both pillars from marking by the chains with suitable packing material.

7.10.3 Spreading

Spreading (Figure 7.28) is a similar application to pushing except that in the latter case there is sufficient room for access for the ram and extension between the two members to be moved apart to permit a direct push. When this is not possible a means must be found of inserting jaws or attachments which are capable of applying an indirect thrust. The most obvious means of spreading is provided by the wedges and spread rams.

This is an off-centre load once more, and even under the most favourable conditions it is not possible to apply a force of more than about 7 tonnes with the 10 tonne ram, or 2.5 tonnes with the 4 tonne ram.

7.10.4 Stretching or tensioning

The technique of stretching or tensioning (Figure 7.29) is another means of obtaining a pull using a push ram. It is different from the type of pulling previously described, which was a method of applying force to pull sections towards one another which have been forced apart. Here the reverse takes place and an

Figure 7.28 Spreading with body jack (*Blackhawk Automotive Ltd*)

Figure 7.29 Stretching with body jack (*Blackhawk Automotive Ltd*)

Figure 7.30 Clamping with body jack (*Blackhawk Automotive Ltd*)

external pull is applied to pull apart or draw outwards areas that have been pushed or drawn in towards each other. The combination used to obtain this external pull employs toes, links and clamps on the end of the push ram and extension tubes. Two types of clamps are used, pull clamps for attachment to flat edges and wing clamps which have deep throats or lipped edges. Both clamps have an alligator type of action and are first tightened down on the centre bolt until the jaws are parallel and in contact with the surface of the panel to be gripped. Pressure is then applied by tightening the rear bolt, which cants the jaws forward and causes them to bite into the surface of the metal. It may well be that the time taken to set up this combination is greater than the time to pull out the damage once it is in position. On flat panels where it is not possible to get at the edges or where there is not an edge to locate a clamp, the same result can be achieved by locating the toes in the bosses of a pair of solder plates which have been sweated on to the panel. A roof panel or car door is a typical example of this. To get at both edges of a car door it is usually necessary to remove the door, but this can be eliminated by

using a clamp at the free edge of the door and a solder plate at the hinged edge. If properly used the solder plates will withstand a pull of 13 800 kN/m². The plates should be sweated on with a layer of body solder about 3 mm thick, using the minimum of heat, and quenching with a wet rag to prevent distortion. The same technique may be applied to boot lids, front wings, bonnets and rear quarter panels, and can be the means of repairing a panel in a position where direct pressure from inside would not have achieved a satisfactory result. Another combination, which is less popular in use, is clamping (Figure 7.30).

7.10.5 Example of use of body jack

Figure 7.31 demonstrates the jack being used diagonally to rectify a door opening. Pressure is applied until the clearance round all sides of the door is equal and it opens and closes freely. Note the use of a pull ram fitted with chains and connected to a swivel clamp at the upper corner and a pull ring and clamp at the lower corner. Figure 7.32 shows rectification to a door opening using a push ram connected at both ends to

213

Figure 7.31 Repair to a door opening (*Blackhawk Automotive Ltd*)

Figure 7.32 Repairs to a door opening using push ram (*Blackhawk Automotive Ltd*)

push-pull clamps, which are bolted on to the door flange edges. The doors are left suspended on their hinges to act as templates during the operation.

Figure 7.33 shows a twin-linked aperture restraint holding the door opening in shape while pulling or pushing takes place, so that the door aperture does not go out of alignment as the repairs are carried out. The centre screw jack allows preloading to put the re-straining unit in tension. The door may be left in its correct position and closed with the restraint in place.

Where the rear end of a car becomes accidentally pushed in, the panels can be returned to their correct alignment in the manner illustrated in Figure 7.34. The jack is placed across the aperture of the boot lid, with a wedge head attached to one end and the rubber flex head to the other. This is to spread the force of the pressure evenly over a larger area. The boot lid, when repaired or replaced, is fitted in position and will act as a guide for alignment when pushing out the surround panel.

A rear windscreen opening can be restored to its original shape by placing the body jack diagonally across the corners which are out of square, as shown in Figure 7.34. Where the standard rubber flex head does not suit the shape of the body, the wide-angled wedge head must be used, as it will automatically adjust to fit the corner. The rear windscreen glass

Figure 7.33 Repairs to a door opening using aperture restraint (*Blackhawk Automotive Ltd*)

Figure 7.34 Repairs to boot lid aperture and rear windscreen (*Blackhawk Automotive Ltd*)

7.11 CARE AND MAINTENANCE OF BODY JACK

As with all hydraulic equipment, little trouble is experienced with the working of the jack provided the unit is kept free from oil leaks. When topping up with oil it is necessary to use the correct type of oil, taking care not to allow any dirt or grit to enter the oil track while adding or checking the oil level. Air sometimes becomes trapped in the oil track, in which case it is necessary to bleed the pump.

may be used as a template, but this must be handled with great care in case of breakage.

Figure 7.35 shows a rear end collision and the body jack being used to straighten the subframe and wheel arch sections of the underbody while also correcting the tension on the D-post, thus allowing the rear door to open.

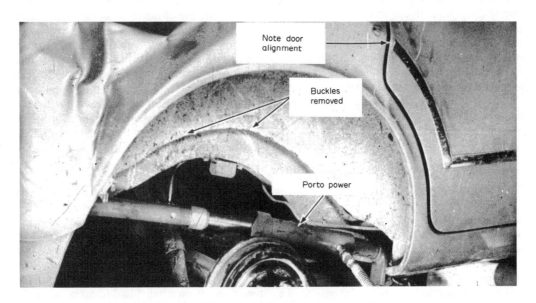

Figure 7.35 Repairs to a wheel arch and subframe (*Blackhawk Automotive Ltd*)

7.11.1 Bleeding the body jack

Clamp the pump in a vice. Close the release valve and operate the pump handle until the ram plunger is fully extended. If the plunger will not move by pumping, withdraw it by hand. Remove the filler plug from the end of the pump and release the valve. Place the plunger on the floor and slowly push down until it collapses, expelling all the air. Pump the handle rapidly then close the release valve and replace the filler plug. The unit is now ready for operating.

7.11.2 Care of the hose

On remote control jacks, where the hydraulic pressure is supplied to the ram through a hose, it is well to exercise care so that the hose does not become damaged. The hose is made from oilproof rubber reinforced by woven steel wire which is covered on the outside by a fabric and rubber combination (Figure 7.24). Do not permit heavy objects to fall or drop on the hose, as a sharp, hard impact may kink the wire strands in the hose. Because of the rubber covering, the kink may not be noticeable, and the application of pressure will eventually cause the strands to break and the hose will leak. In making set-ups with the jack, always be careful to anchor the ram unit so that its pushing force will not tend to bend or break the hose fittings.

7.11.3 Care of threads on ram and attachments

When the ram is not in use, attachments provided for protection of the plunger thread and ram body should be in place. Use all of the threads to make connections, and always turn the attachments until they are tight. Always keep the threads in all attachments clean and free from grease. Whenever threads become bent or damaged, they should be repaired so that the proper fit can be obtained when connections are made. Most attachments are now snap-on connections and therefore have no threads and need no maintenance.

7.12 REPAIR OF COMPONENT MOTOR BODY PANELS

To repair damaged motor body panels requires great skill in the use of hand tools and repair techniques, and an ability to assess the cause, extent and sequence of the damage sustained. Damage by accident and its subsequent repair covers a wide range of incidents from minor scratches and cosmetic damage to the write-off. The repair will only be approved by an insurance company after considering the car's age, condition and relevant market value.

Vehicle body repair work can be divided basically into two groups: minor accident repair work and major accident repair work. Body repair workshops vary in their opinions as to the dividing line between the two assessments. Generally they can be defined as follows.

Minor accident repair work
To be able to carry out minor repairs, a good level of ability with hand tools and all types of power tools, both electrical and air operated, is essential to the body repair worker. He or she needs a knowledge of body construction, an appreciation of materials and their properties, and a practical expertise in appropriate repair techniques, including the use of all types of welding equipment.

Minor repair work can be classified as: the simple cosmetic repair requiring the use of hand tools only; the cutting out of damaged panel sections and their effective replacement; the replacement of complete panels such as wings, bonnets, boot lids, doors and sill panels; and the finishing of these panels to a point where paint can be applied. A minor repair can also involve adjustment to door locks and window mechanisms, the restoration of body apertures, and the use of hydraulic equipment to realign body panels and apertures to their original shape.

Major accident repair work
Major repair work can be classified as a repair which involves the use of manufacturer's replacement parts, and the reconstruction of the body or parts of the body on an approved body jig. A major repair will normally involve all the features listed for minor repairs. In addition it will include: the rectification of any misalignment of the underbody and body shell using conventional hydraulic pulling equipment, together with either a fixed bracket jig or a universal jig with measuring system; the realignment of the body shell, correcting damage with a combination of pulling and pushing equipment; and the cutting out of panels and reinforcing members which are damaged beyond repair, and the welding in of replacements. Major repairs are dealt with in Chapter 8.

The conclusion of all repairs must restore the vehicle to its original safe, roadworthy condition to the satisfaction of the owner and the insurance company. In order to achieve this the repairer needs to use his acquired skill and knowledge and, while each accident repair has its own individual features, he or she must be able to assess the damage and make the choice of appropriate methods of repair and the best equipment to effect a speedy first-class result.

7.12.1 Repairing rust damage

In this work the body repairer relies on his own judgement, skill and experience. Rust is a corrosion, known chemically as iron oxide, which occurs on the surface of iron and most of its alloys when they are exposed to air and moisture. The designs of all-steel body shells over the past years have provided many pockets which could be termed water or moisture traps, thus creating suitable conditions for the rusting process. In particular, rust attacks wings, sill panels, wheel arches, floors of luggage compartments and bottoms of doors, the worst being the sills because of their close proximity to the road. During the past few years some manufacturers have made improvements which have reduced the rusting of bodies. In some cases this has been achieved by good design and in other cases by treating the metal prior to painting.

When the body repair worker is faced with rust problems, he has a choice of two methods of repair, depending on the extent of the damage. The best possible results are obtained by cutting away the corroded panel or section and replacing it with a hand-formed section or a factory-pressed panel. The replacement panels can then be fitted by welding them into position and finishing by planishing, filing and sanding. In the case of the older vehicle where new panels are not available or where the vehicle's age or condition make it uneconomical to fit new panels, the method of fabricating or patching these areas, by cutting out and replacing the sections from flat sheets fabricated by hand, is adopted. In many cases if the original sections are carefully cut out and not too distorted, they can be used as an excellent guide to the manufacture of the new sections. Templates can also be made up before the old sections are cut out to check alignment and curvature when fitting the new section. Often double-curvature panels such as wheel arch fabrications must be made up in three or four parts for ease of patching on to the original body. The main difficulty experienced in this type of repair is the welding of the new metal on to the old; this is one of the reasons why it is important to cut away all the rusted section so that the new metal can be welded to a rust-free section. In cases where the sections are very badly corroded and welding is difficult, the section can be cleaned of surface rust and sometimes brazed to form the joint.

The second method of rust repair, which is only a temporary measure and not recommended for longevity, is to fill the corroded section with either body solder or a chemically hardening filler. If the corrosion is only very slight, giving a pinhole effect, the area can be sanded down to bare metal, hammered down carefully to below its original level and then filled up with body solder and filed to a finish. Plastic filler should not be used in this case because the moisture would seep through, parting the filler from the panel. Where the corroded area has turned to holes it can only be repaired by placing a patch over the corrosion and welding or brazing it in place. This patch must be tapped down below the panel level, then filled with body solder or plastic filler to obtain the final finish. In some cases where it is difficult to weld a patch, the perforated section can be reinforced by using glass-fibre matting impregnated with resin and bonded to the underside of the repair. The surface can then be filled with plastic filler and finished by filing.

7.12.2 Repair of minor accident damage

Repairs arising from minor accidents are usually of a relatively straightforward nature, as the damage is either a dent, a scratch or a scruff to the outer panel surface of the body and does not always involve structural distortion.

When repairing it is essential to know the nature or properties of the sheet metal used in body panels. When a flat sheet of metal is bent to a wide radius it will regain its former shape when released; in other words, the metal is flexible. If this metal is bent to a small radius it exceeds the limits of its flexibility, and the metal in the bend becomes stiff and retains its curved shape. These are known as rigid sections. Therefore a body shell and panels are a combination of rigid and flexible areas. The rigid areas are assemblies such as door posts, sill members, roof cantrails and flanges around wing edges and bonnets. The flexible areas are large areas of mainly flat or slightly curved sections such as bonnet tops, outer door panels, sections of wings and centres of roof panels. In the main after a collision if the stresses are removed from the rigid areas first, then the flexible areas (except where badly creased in the impact) will regain their former shape. If a panel is damaged in an accident then the buckled area, being sharply bent, will create additional stiffness in the panel, whether in an elastic or a non-elastic area. The slopes of the buckles surrounding the sharp creases will be fairly elastic, but a greater amount of effort will be needed to reshape the sections of the panel which are made rigid either in manufacture or through accidental damage. The theory of repair is that areas which are elastic in manufacture, and remain so after damage, can generally be reshaped by their characteristics once the rigid areas in the surrounding buckles are forced back into position.

In general the method of repair is to analyse the crash, establish the order in which damage occurred, and reverse the order when correcting the damage. The majority of repairs to minor accident damage requires the skill of the body repair worker in the use of hand tools and general repair techniques. Although every panel assembly has its own individual repair procedure, the basic approach is the same for all minor repairs and is as follows:

1 Carefully inspect the damaged area and analyse the severity of the damage and its ease of accessibility for repair using hand tools.

2 Decide if the repair can be carried out using hand tools only or whether the hydraulic body jack is required.

3 Select the necessary hand tools and, if using the hydraulic body jack, decide which basic set-ups and attachments are best suited to the job.

4 If the repair is carried out using hand tools only, then the back of the damaged section under repair, if accessible, must be cleaned of anti-drum compound.

5 If the accessibility for the use of hand tools is difficult owing to the presence of brackets behind the panel or double-skinned sections, rough out the damaged area either by cutting out the back and using spoons to lever the damage out, or by using a panel puller on the front of the damaged section to pull out the damage. The area should then be cleaned, filled with the appropriate material and finished.

6 When using hand tools only, the damaged area should be roughed out to its original shape, although this operation can also be carried out using hydraulic equipment to push the damaged section back to its original shape.

7 Once the damaged section has been reshaped, either by hand or hydraulic means, planish it using a combination of direct and indirect hammering and filing.

8 Then check the low spots, if any, by cross filing and raise them by further planishing or pick hammering. At this stage high spots may develop due to stretching of the metal, and hot shrinking of these points will be necessary.

9 Sand the panel surface over the damaged area using a very fine sanding disc.

7.12.3 Minor repairs to wings

Removal of a small dent from a wing is one of the simplest of repair jobs. The first step is to check the underside of the wing to ensure that it is free from road dirt and anti-drum compounds; then the damaged area is roughed out and the wing reshaped to its original contour. The reshaping is done with a rather heavy hand dolly of a similar shape to that of the contour of the damaged wing section. The blows should be heavy with a follow-through action which will speed up the roughing out operation. It is very important, while roughing out damage, that full-shaped or very curved dollies and heavy ball pein hammers are not used, as they cause excessive stretching of the already damaged metal. Metal that is returned to its original pressed shape during roughing out will smooth out more quickly and evenly.

When the roughing out is complete, the next step is to planish the roughed area. In the case where the wing has been heavily coated with cellulose, it is advisable to remove this coating using the sander fitted with an open-coated disc suitable for paint, or with paint remover; the latter must be neutralized to stop the burning action on the paint. The first step in smoothing is to try to level out the uneven surface by working the high areas into the low areas. This can be done by holding the dolly block under the low area and tapping down the adjacent high spot with a planishing hammer. In some cases there may be no high spots and no adjacent low areas, in which case the high spots, if any, can be tapped down often with just the planishing hammer and without the dolly block backing. These high and low areas are found by passing the hand over the section under repair. As planishing continues, filing will show up any low and high areas, which will need correcting by tapping down high areas and lifting the low areas by further planishing with hammer and dolly or using a pick hammer. The final finish is achieved by cross filing the original file strokes; this is a double check on curvature and smoothness of the panel surface.

7.12.4 Minor repairs to door panels

When repairing door panels the main difficulties rise through the fact that most door panels are nearly flat sheets of metal, which means that even the slightest stretching due to over-hammering will produce a fullness which will stand out after the repair has been painted. The greatest care must be taken.

The first step is to strip the door of interior trim and window. The amount of stripping necessary depends on the extent and position of the damage. With most door repairs it is quicker to remove the door from the vehicle by releasing the check strap and then taking out the set screws in the door side of the hinges, or, if the hinge is welded, by knocking the hinge pin out. Having prepared the door and the work bench, an inspection can then be made of the door frame to determine the accessibility for the use of hand tools and hydraulic equipment. When carrying out the repairs it is often necessary to cut the back of the door frame and bend it, thus permitting greater freedom of movement for the use of hand tools. The thorough removal of all anti-drum material is essential before any actual planishing is commenced.

The shape is gained by roughing out with the mallet and dolly block, after which the finish is attained with the planishing or pick hammer in conjunction with the file. In selecting a dolly it is advisable to choose one that is rather light and slightly flatter than the panel being planished. This will reduce the risk of stretching the panel. In some cases where the door panel is badly creased and is inaccessible for the use of hand tools, it would be better to rough out the damage with the aid of the body jack or spoon acting as a lever, smooth it over with hammer and dolly, then fill it with body solder and file the area to obtain the final finish.

7.12.5 Reskinning door panels

This process affords considerable saving in time and cost compared with the practice of replacing complete door assemblies. The technique of this process is the same regardless of the shape or type of door to be reskinned:

Removal of a damaged skin panel This is achieved by drilling out the spot welds around the flanged areas of the door using either a Zipcut or cobalt drill or Spotle tool and also, on some types of door, using a power saw to make joints across the pillars (Figure 7.36a). The flange can be then eased up using a flange removing tool (Figure 7.36b), or in some cases the outer edges of the flange are ground through using a sander (Figure 7.36c). If this method is used, care must be taken not to damage the door frame. The damaged panel skin can then be removed using a hammer and chisel and easing up the flange strips that are left (Figure 7.36d).

Preparing door flanges The door flanges should now be straightened up using a hammer and dolly and the face of the flanges sanded to make a smooth surface for the attachment of the new skin panel.

Preparing the new surfaces The door flanges should now be painted with a zinc-rich interweld primer to stop any chance of corrosion between the door flange and the new skin (Figure 7.36e).

Fitting the new skin panel The prepainted skin panel is now placed over the frame and aligned using the door lock holes as a guide, and MIG tacked on to the joint pillars if necessary. The edges of the skin are now hammered over the door frame using a hammer and dolly until the flange is folded over completely. During this operation great care is essential if the panel face is not to be marked (Figure 7.36f).

Welding in the new skin panel The spot welds should now be replaced to fix the new skin panel to the frame taking care to use the correct electrodes, especially on the face side of the panel. Adhesive is used on certain doors to fix the skin panel to the door frame. Where joints have been made in the pillars they must be MIG welded, ground flush and soldered (Figure 7.36g).

Final cleaning and inspection The soldered joints must be filed and sanded with a DA sander. Finally, inspect the skin panel for any defects, which will need correcting by filing and sanding (Figures 7.36h and 7.36i).

7.12.6 Pulling out double-skin panel damage

When inaccessible body panels are damaged, a method of repair for the removal of the damage, without leaving holes or having to remove interior trim, is to use a special pin welding gun. Also pin welding attachments can be fastened to spot welding equipment (Figure 7.37). The welding gun attaches pins, screws, washers or studs to the surface of any damage so it may be pulled out. There are two sizes of pins: small (2 mm) which are normally used for skin panel damage, and larger (2.5 mm) which are used for chassis legs or thicker-gauge metals.

First the damaged area must have its paint removed and be sanded down to a bare metal finish in order to give a good electrical contact between the pin and the welding gun. Insert the pin into the spring-loaded nozzle of the gun. The two points of contact are the tip of the pin and the outer copper ring on the welding gun, which should, when pushed down, make as even a contact as possible with the panel surface under repair. Press the gun to the surface of the metal, press the trigger for 1–2 seconds only and remove the gun from the pin, which now should be welded to the panel. The number of pins which need to be welded on to the panel will vary in accordance with the depth and extent of the damage, starting at the deepest section of the damage and working outward.

The dint is then gradually pulled out using a slide hammer, which tightens on to both sides of the pin by the rotating action of the chuck. The dinted area is

(a)

(b)

(c)

(d)

(e)

(f)

(g)

(h)

(i)

Figure 7.36 Reskinning door panel: (a) removing spot welds (b) removing flanges (c) grinding through flanged edges (d) removing damaged skin panel (e) priming door frame (f) folding door edge flanges (g) soldering the pillar joints (h) finishing panel edges (i) completed reskinned door (*Motor Insurance Research Repair Centre*)

then pulled out by using the slide hammer action, on one pin at a time, beginning at the deepest part of the damage and working outwards. The pins are removed by breaking them from the panel surface and sanding down their residue.

When the damage is a crease and very deep, ring washers may be used instead of pins to facilitate a stronger pull. A clamp may be fastened to these washers and attached by chain to pulling equipment which would then pull out the damage. Alternatively a hook is inserted into the slide hammer to pull out each washer individually (Figures 7.38, 7.39).

When the damage has been completely pulled out the area may be filled using body solder or plastic filler according to the position and extent of the damage. The filled area is then sanded and filed down to an acceptable finish for painting.

7.12.7 Minor repairs to bonnets

The bonnet of a car is firmly fastened when closed. Many models have spring-loaded hinges so that the tension of the springs holds the bonnet firmly in place at the hinge side. At the point of locking a sturdy catch holds the bonnet down under spring tension. When open the bonnet is virtually unsupported as it is only held in place by the hinges. This means that only minor repairs can be carried out with the bonnet in place, and if hydraulic power tools are necessary it is advisable to remove the bonnet from the car. Large areas of almost flat sections running into gradual return sweeps are incorporated in the designs of most bonnets. The flat panel and the return sweep are both shapes that need careful repairing to avoid stretching of the metal.

Figure 7.37 Pull pin kit used with a spot welding gun (*ARO Welding Ltd*). (a) Clean the damaged area with an abrasive disc. (b), (c) Set the spot welding gun controls. In case of doubt, perform a trial weld on a section similar to the dented one to help you select the best setting. Weld the pins at the selected positions on the damaged section. (d) Once the pins have been welded to the section, use the inertia weight tool to pull the dented section back into its proper shape. (e) Make sure you do not exercise more pull than is needed to bring the panel back into its correct position, to avoid bulging. (f) Use your normal shearing tool to cut off the projecting portion of the pins. (g) For a smooth finish, go over the area with an abrasive disc in the usual way.

Figure 7.37 (continued)

Figure 7.38 Fastening ring washers to the damaged area ready to pull (*Stanners Ltd*)

Figure 7.39 Pulling damage out using hook and slide hammer (*Stanners Ltd*)

A rather common problem that arises when repairing bonnets is the development of a loose edge. This looseness usually occurs along the back edge of the bonnet, which in most cases is a raw edge, and even the slightest stretch will cause a buckle. It is essential that this buckle be removed, and the best way of carrying this out is by hot shrinking the edge. Another characteristic of bonnets is that the edge flanges crack, and these should be welded as early as possible to prevent the extension of the crack and to keep the bonnet in its correct shape.

The repair procedure for minor, accessible dents is first to rough out the damaged area using a mallet to minimize stretching, and then to planish the area using a beating file in conjunction with a dolly block which will also reduce the possibility of stretching. If the repair is in such a position as to make the use of hand tools difficult because of the strengthening struts,

the area should be roughed out using very thin body spoons and then filled with plastic filler, as the heat produced when soldering might distort the panel. The prominent position of the bonnet requires its finish to be perfect because ripples and low spots can be easily seen when painted.

7.12.8 Minor repairs to sill panels

The sill panel on a car is attached to the door pillar and floor, and is of double-panel box-like construction having both inner and outer panels. Because of its position it is one of the most likely places to receive damage.

Two methods of repair can be used for double panel assemblies. First, cut away part of the inner panel, or in the case of the sill, along the top. Then bend the panel or top section upwards to make the outer panel accessible for the use of hand tools. Push out the damage using the spread ram which acts as a wedge, or force it out using body spoons as levers, then planish and file. Bend the top section or back panel back into position and weld. Care should be taken here to avoid overheating the repaired area.

The second method, which is less time consuming, can be used if the dent is small and not very deep. The area can be sanded clean to bare metal and filled using body solder. If the damage is very deep it will need pulling out, and this can best be done using a panel puller on the outer panel surface. The holes needed for using this tool should then be welded up and the damaged area should be sanded, filled with body solder and filed to achieve the final finish.

7.12.9 Minor repair of body panels using adhesives

With the advancement of adhesive, technology, Permabond have developed an adhesive called Autobond specially formulated for car repair applications. This is a two-part product which has been developed to meet the specific requirements of the car repairer. It is designed to replace panel welding with a minimum of surface preparation; it will also protect against corrosion. It provides substantial labour saving in avoiding the necessity to remove fuel tanks and soft trim required before any welding repair. The adhesive not only bonds metal to metal but is also suitable for bonding GRP components.

For ease of use the adhesive is supplied as a layer of resin on top of a layer of hardener inside a plastic tub; the two layers will not react until mixed with the stick provided. The resin and hardener are coloured light grey and black respectively to provide a visual check that thorough mixing is achieved. After mixing is complete, setting begins at a rate depending on the ambient temperature. The best performance is achieved by heating the bond area to 40°C for 1 hour; however, at 60°C full hardening is achieved in 30 minutes. Curing at normal ambient temperature will give joints of reduced strength and is not recommended. Figure 7.40 a–f shows the application sequence.

7.12.10 Removal and replacement of exterior and interior soft trim and hard trim

Body exterior mouldings are attached by weld stud-retaining plastic clips; weld stud-retaining plastic clips with attaching screws; an adhesive bond using either tape or sealant; a self-retaining spring clip or clinch-type clip; or special attaching screws.

During repairs, observe the following:

1 Adjacent paint surfaces need protecting with masking tape to help prevent any possible damage.
2 Always use the correct tools for the job, and take great care with mouldings.
3 Water can leak into the interior of the body through any body panel holes made by screws, bolts and clips unless they are securely sealed.

Door trim
The door trim pieces are normally assembled in one-piece or two-piece trim pads. Removal of door trims is carried out in the following order: door lock handle and door locking knob; mouldings; window regulator handle and door latch handle; arm rest assembly; mirror remote control bezel nut; and door trim retaining screws (if any). Then lift the trim panel retaining clips from the door inner panel, and disconnect all wiring so that the trim panel may be removed. Prior to reinstallation of the trim pad, always make certain that the watershield is in position and correctly sealed.

Quarter trim panel
This is the panel which fits over the interior of the quarter panel. Removal of the quarter trim panel is carried out in the following order: rear seat cushion; rear seat back; rear window handle (if any); and any screws or mouldings. Then unfasten the panel retaining clips and pull the trim panel away from the quarter panel.

Floor carpet
Carpet for car floors is made either in one piece which is moulded to fit the shape of the floor, or in two pieces to fit the front and rear sections of the floor respectively. In order to remove the one-piece carpet

it is necessary to remove everything in the way, including seat belts, seats, centre console, and door sill scuff plates. However, the two-piece carpet can be removed with the seats still in place because they are made with cut-outs to allow for easier removal. In some cases the floor of a car is covered with heavy rubber flooring instead of carpet, and this can be removed and replaced in a similar manner.

Headlinings
Headlinings are of two types. The first is soft and made from cloth or vinyl coated. The second is harder, being formed from moulded hardboard coated with foam or cloth which has a vinyl facing. The replacement of the moulded headlining is a simple, straightforward operation because of its one-piece rigid structure. The soft type is more complicated in its removal owing to the necessity of removing a large amount of trim in addition to the windscreen and rear window in some cases.

7.13 THE REMOVAL OF MECHANICAL COMPONENTS

The repair of collision damage to monoconstructed vehicles often involves removal and replacement of the mechanical parts. In many cases major drive parts such as engines, transmissions and drive axles are mounted directly to structural panels of the vehicle body. In other cases, these parts are mounted to supporting cross members, subframe assemblies, or cradle assemblies that are mounted directly to structural panels. These structural panels provide support for the static load of the mechanical parts mounted to them. Structural panels must also withstand dynamic loads developed by the mechanical components. Engine and transmission mounts must withstand severe torsional loads of acceleration and braking. Correct alignment and mounting of mechanical parts is critical to the operation of the car, its road holding ability and the safety of the car after repair.

7.13.1 Engine assembly removal

The term 'drivetrain' is sometimes used when discussing European or American monoconstructed type vehicles. A drivetrain (engine assembly) in a front wheel drive car includes engine, transmission, drive shaft, and suspension systems all assembled together, and are usually located in the front end of the car. They are supported by cross members or subframes that are bolted directly to the body.

Many mechanical parts such as engine mounts and transmission supports are through-bolted. The position

Figure 7.40 Minor panel repair using adhesive: (a) preparing surfaces (b) cleaning with solvent (c) applying adhesive (d) assembling joint with rivets, tack welds or clamps as appropriate (e) removing excess adhesive, heating bond area, buffing joint (f) completed panel (*Permabond Adhesives Ltd*)

of these through-bolted mountings must be maintained parallel to each other to allow for the correct movement of the mechanical parts. When these mechanical mountings are not in correct alignment due to collision damage, free movement of the mechanical parts will be impaired and therefore must be correctly realigned when replaced after the body damage has been repaired.

In some collision damage repair situations it is necessary to completely remove the engine assembly from the vehicle to make repairs to the body possible. Removal of these mechanical parts allows ready access to the structural panels for repair or replacement. At the factory these assemblies are usually installed from the underside of the car and therefore should be removed in a similar way either by lifting the vehicle away from the engine assembly or by dropping the engine assembly from the vehicle.

It is essential that the usual safety precautions are always observed when working on the vehicle. Car manufacturers' service manuals contain specific precautions that must be followed when dismantling or rebuilding any of these parts, for example fasteners must be retightened to their assigned torque values.

Start by disconnecting the engine and suspension assembly from the top of the engine compartment. Before disconnecting any vacuum lines or electrical lines, attach a piece of masking tape to both sides of the parts disconnected marking the same code letter on both sides to facilitate later reconnection.

Care must be taken when removing the engine assembly by continually checking for wires or hoses that might have been overlooked and not disconnected.

While the body structure is being repaired the mechanical units can be checked and repaired if necessary. Reinstallation of the engine assembly can be accomplished by reversing the removal procedure. After the body structure has been accurately repaired the cradle can be quickly and correctly positioned by using the line-up holes located in the cradle mountings. The body technician must be aware of the specifics of removal and replacement for particular vehicle models by using manufacturers' service manuals.

7.13.2 Suspension and steering systems

A vehicle's suspension steering system performs three basic functions:

1 It acts as the connection between the wheels and the vehicle body.
2 It dampens and controls the ride by absorbing road shock and sway.
3 It provides directional control of the vehicle.

Quality bodyshop repairs on a vehicle must include the return of the steering and suspension systems to their original factory location. This is especially important in monoconstructed vehicles as structural body panels provide the critical mounting positions for the suspension and steering. In some vehicles the steering equipment is bolted directly to a structural body panel. When this is done, the body panel must hold the steering equipment in its correct location. The body structure must maintain the proper relationship of steering and suspension.

Rear suspension components are also mounted to body structural panels. The proper relationship of the rear suspension parts to each other and to front suspension parts depends on the position of the vehicle's structural panels. All vehicles, not only those of monoconstruction, require an inter-related suspension and body design. It is generally accepted that safe, efficient collision repairs demand that both body and suspension be corrected in relationship to one another. Correct collision repairs of suspension systems and supporting structural body panels must restore the ability of these panels to support the high dynamic loads experienced during operation of the suspension systems. Body repair technicians must restore traditional wheel alignment angles to manufacturers' specifications when repairing collision damage to suspension systems. Manufacturers have designed certain suspension, steering and alignment features into a monoconstructed vehicle and when any repairs are made the manufacturers' specifications must be followed. If these specifications are changed or tampered with, they will change the handling and safety features designed and built into the vehicle (see Section 8.4.3 in Chapter 8.)

7.14 COOLING SYSTEMS

The cooling system includes such parts as the radiator, water pump, drive belt, radiator hoses, thermal switch-operated electric fans, heater hose and heater. In addition water is used as the coolant in the radiator. The radiator is sometimes called a heat exchanger. There are two basic types of radiator designs: in a downflow radiator the coolant flows from the top tank downwards to the bottom tank, while in the crossflow type the tanks are located at either side and the coolant flows across the radiator core from tank to tank.

The radiator provides a large cooling area for the water and exposes it to the air stream. A reservoir of water is held in a header tank, often made from thin steel, brass sheet or plastic. The header tank and lower tank are connected by numerous brass, copper or

Figure 7.41 Electrical harnesses in a motor vehicle

aluminium tubes surrounded by cooling fins; this assembly is known as the matrix, block, stack or core.

The most vulnerable component in the cooling system with respect to collision damage is the radiator. Sandwiched between the engine and the grille, it is frequently a casualty in frontal impacts. On vehicles with inline engines the fan is pushed into the radiator. Depending on the severity of the crash, the fan might only do cosmetic damage to the core or totally destroy it.

Sometimes a radiator might have no visible damage yet the impact has created hairline cracks around the hose connectors along the core header or tube seams. Problems may arise later if the system is not checked thoroughly during the repair process.

7.15 ELECTRICAL SYSTEMS

Electrical systems are an essential part of the motor vehicle. The car is threaded with a great number of wires, most of which are bundled together in harnesses (Figure 7.41). These harnesses route the wires from the battery to all electrical body parts; interior lights, headlights, electric door locks, electric mirrors, etc. These harnesses are fitted inside body panels or underneath body trim such as along the pillars, sill

panels, doors, quarter panels and roof panels. Damage in these panel areas often cuts or abrades insulation protecting the wires, resulting in a short or open circuit. Collision forces can also pull wires from their connections, and corrosion damage can loosen earth wire connections, again breaking the electric circuit thereby causing a fault.

Before any collision damaged vehicle is returned to its owner every electrical component should be checked to verify that it works when it is switched on and off. If not working properly the problem must be traced to its source and the faulty wire or loose connections repaired. Often the problem is simply a blown fuse or a loose connector, for example when repairing the outer door skin, the door is removed from the vehicle and any electrical components are disconnected from the relative wiring harness, but if the connectors are not properly reconnected when the door is replaced, the window, lock or exterior mirror will not operate. Always double check connectors, make sure harnesses are secured in their clips and that the earth wires are tightly secured to the body panel.

Some workshops have specialist auto-electricians to deal with the many complicated electric/electronic components used in cars, particularly damage to starter, ignition and computerized systems. The testing of the major components in these systems often requires expensive diagnostic equipment, but there are many minor problems in the lighting and accessory circuits that could be quickly diagnosed and repaired. Minor electrical trouble shooting requires a basic knowledge of electrical theory and correct diagnostic tools.

7.15.1 The battery

The battery is the power plant or power source of the vehicle, therefore it must be treated with respect as well as being protected. Always disconnect the battery earth cable as soon as the vehicle is received at the workshop because of potential electrical problems which may have occurred in the collision.

A low amperage shortage will gradually drain the vehicle's battery. A disconnected battery will avoid possible damage to electrical components through which the current might flow. Also disconnecting the battery's earth cable before recharging a battery on a vehicle will avoid damage to electrical components on the vehicle, such as transistors and microcircuits, which are very sensitive to high current levels. The high amperage charges can burn out these expensive components.

QUESTIONS

1 Explain the terms 'direct hammering', 'indirect hammering' and 'pick hammering', as applied to body repair techniques.
2 Describe the technique of cross filing.
3 Describe, with the aid of sketches, three different methods of using a portable hydraulic body jack in the realigning and straightening of vehicle body damage.
4 Explain each of the following stages of repairing a front wing which has received minor damage: (a) the analysis and assessment of the extent of the damage (b) selection of the appropriate tools needed to carry out the repair (c) the repair techniques required (d) the alignment and final check.
5 Explain the process of body soldering when used in the repair of a damaged body panel, and list the necessary equipment.
6 Describe, with the aid of sketches, the technique of hot shrinking to restore a panel to its original contour.
7 Explain the difference between hot shrinking and cold shrinking techniques.
8 When is it considered necessary to fill with body solder, in preference to any other method of repair?
9 Describe a method of repairing a sill panel which is showing signs of corrosion.

10 What precautions must be taken, after body soldering a repair, to prevent subsequent paint defects?
11 Explain the importance of tinning a panel before commencing body soldering.
12 State the disadvantages associated with the use of hydraulic push rams when used on the inside of a vehicle.
13 Give one practical application of the body jack when being used for each of the following operations: pushing, pulling and spreading.
14 Describe a suitable method of removing the damaged skin during the repair process of reskinning a door panel.
15 Explain how a new door skin is secured to the door frame, and list the tools required.
16 Indicate the type of welding necessary when securing a new door skin to the door frame.
17 Why is it important to clean the underside of a damaged panel before commencing repairs?
18 Illustrate a tool which could be used in the removal of damage from a double-skinned section.
19 When, and how, would a pin welding gun be used in repair work?
20 What type of attachment would be used on the end of a body jack to spread the force of the load during a repair?
21 Explain the differences between a hydraulic push ram and a hydraulic pull ram.
22 The lower section of an A-post has suffered corrosion damage. Explain a suitable method of repair.
23 Describe a suitable process for the removal of spot welds from a body panel without distorting the flanges.
24 Describe the sequence of repair (not replacement) to a rear quarter panel which has received minor accident damage.
25 With the aid of a sketch, show how a body jack can put a door panel in tension.
26 A small corroded area of a wing needs a patch repair. Explain how this process will be carried out.
27 Describe, with the aid of sketches, how the hydraulic system of a body jack works.
28 With the aid of a sketch, show the techniques involved in the manufacture of a small double curvature panel by hand.
29 Describe, with the aid of a sketch, a vector pull for correcting vehicle body alignment.
30 Explain why careful study of accident damage is important before any stripping or repair work is carried out.
31 Explain the importance of correct alignment when fitting new body panels and state how this is achieved.
32 Explain the term 'drivetrain'.

33 Explain the three basic functions that suspension and steering systems perform.

34 Explain the importance of alignment between suspension components and the body structure when repairing a vehicle which has been involved in collision.

35 Explain the two types of radiator systems used on motor vehicles.

36 Explain the safety precautions to be taken to protect the electric systems and battery when working on collision damage.

8

Major accident damage

8.1 DAMAGE CLASSIFICATION AND ASSESSMENT

Damaged bodywork is corrected by first observing the extent of the damage, then deciding how it as caused and the sequence in which it occurred. The resulting damage can be classified into two groups:

Direct or primary damage This results from the impact on the area in actual contact with the object causing the damage. This will result in the largest area of visible damage and is the cause of all other consequent damage. Primary damage is identified by first determining the direction of the primary impact. This knowledge will help in the search for concealed damage.

Indirect or secondary damage This is usually found in the area surrounding the direct damage which causes it, although in certain cases it may be some distance from the actual point of impact. After the impact, internal damage is caused by the forced movement of objects and passengers towards the point of impact, and can be seen in the form of damaged dash panels, broken seat frames and twisted steering wheels.

These two groups can each be subdivided in two further ways:

Visible damage This is damage that can be readily seen in the area of actual contact, such as a vehicle having suffered frontal impact causing damage to the bumper, grille, bonnet and front wings. A detailed examination may discover distortion of the inner wing valances, which would indicate visible indirect damage.

Concealed damage This is indirect damage, but is not easily detected by visual examination unless the vehicle has been partially dismantled to allow a detailed inspection. In most situations measuring equipment in the form of body jigs must be used to detect concealed damage, because complicated monoconstructed vehicles may hide further damage such as misalignment, which could therefore affect the steering and roadworthiness of the vehicle.

Direction of damage
Direction of damage, or line of impact, is particularly important to the body repairer. It is used to identify the sequence and direction in which the damage occurred, and consequently the reverse sequence to be followed for the repair. Direct damage marks are usually scratch marks where the paintwork has been damaged; they are an excellent guide to what happened, and indicate the possible location of any hidden damage. By careful study of the damage sustained it should be possible to ascertain the direction and strength of the impact force, and this is always the preliminary stage of a detailed assessment.

Methods of describing major damage
Parallel side damage is caused by the impact object moving parallel to the vehicle and causing substantial damage along the full length of the side of the vehicle, e.g. wing, doors, rear quarter panel.

Direct side damage is caused when the vehicle is struck at an angle to its side, causing substantial damage at the point of contact.

Front-end damage is the result of head-on collision, collapsing panels from the bumper to the front bulkhead.

Three quarter frontal damage is the result of an angled front end collision, sustaining damage to one front wing, the grille and bonnet.

Rear-end damage is the result of an impact direct or slightly angled to the rear end of a vehicle and causing substantial damage to bumper, rear panel, boot lid, boot floor panel and quarter panels.

Roll-over damage is caused by the vehicle rolling completely over and returning to its wheels. In some cases this type of movement could cause damage to almost every panel.

Total write-off is damage so extensive that the vehicle is either unrepairable or the total cost of repair would be greater than the value of the vehicle.

The proportions of damage sustained in different directions is shown in Figure 8.1.

Figure 8.1 Proportions of damage sustained in different directions in UK accidents (*Motor Insurance Repair Research Centre*)

8.2 PULLING, ALIGNMENT AND REPAIR SYSTEMS USED ON MAJOR ACCIDENT DAMAGE

Since the monocoque construction of car bodywork based on engineering principles took the place of coach-built bodies mounted on a separate chassis, the whole concept of repair work has undergone radical changes in both methods and the equipment employed. Repairs to damaged body shells mean a great deal more than the beating out of a few dents, or even the cutting away of a damaged portion and welding in a new pressing.

The majority of motor cars on the road today are of unit or mono construction. Instead of a body built on to a chassis, the whole unit is constructed round a framework of light sheet metal box sections which provide an overall rigidity of exceptional strength and twist resistance. Owing to this construction, collision damage usually is confined to the area of impact; the box sections tend to crumple or concertina, thus absorbing much of the shock and rarely permitting end damage to travel beyond the centre of the car.

In order to deal with the major damage which occurs to the mono constructed vehicle, specialist equipment has been developed. The equipment consists of frame and body straighteners to pull the damaged body shell back into alignment. These are used in conjunction with body repair, alignment and measuring jigs and thus provide accurate location points where exact positioning becomes critical, especially when the panel assemblies carry major mechanical components and suspension units.

The new generation of pulling and pushing equipment began in the 1950s with the introduction of Dozer equipment, which enabled the repairer to use external hydraulic pulling to aid the repair. Then came the idea of repairing a vehicle on an alignment jig using attachable/detachable brackets, so that it was unnecessary to check the repair after every pull. Next came the universal measuring system or bracketless jig, which involved a measuring bridge or in some cases laser measurement. Multipulling repair systems were introduced, which were either static or mobile and which used the vector pulling principle. Later came mobile jig benches and lift operated systems with pulling attachments. Finally, dual repair systems give the repairer the advantage of precision measuring allied to the use of brackets.

The types of pulling, alignment and repair systems described in this chapter include the following:

1 Portable pulling equipment (Dozer system).
2 Stationary pull-post systems (floor anchored).
3 Stationary floor mounted rack (Korek system).
4 Stationary floor mounted rails.
5 Floor anchored or anchor pot pulling systems (Mitek).
6 Stationary bench-type jig mounted pulling systems (universal or brackets).
7 Mobile bench-type jig mounted pulling systems (brackets, mechanical measuring, electronic measuring, laser measuring).
8 Mobile bench-type jig mounted pulling system using universal brackets.
9 Centre-post hoist jig system with pulling equipment (brackets/measuring).
10 Four-post hoist jig system (brackets/measuring).
11 Scissor-type hoist jig system with pulling equipment (mechanical or electronic measuring).
12 Drive-on bench systems with tower ram pulling (mechanical or laser measuring).
13 Multifunctional repair systems with pulling and measurement systems.

Pulling equipment: general description
Pulling equipment available for major accident damage can range from a single mobile pulling unit to multipulling units; these may be arranged around a bracket jig system or a measuring bridge system; they may be set up on mobile benches, centre-post or four-post lifts; and they may incorporate brackets, or measuring systems or a combination of the two. The choice of systems is varied and wide and depends on the cost involved in the initial outlay, the requirements of the individual workshop and the workload of the shop (based on the number of vehicles repaired each week).

8.2.1 Dozer equipment

Blackhawk Automotive Ltd have a portable pulling frame that can be taken to the car in any part of the

Specification of AEK-614:
Pivot arm, Ht.: 1.67 m (65¾ in.)
Length: 3.00 m (118⅛ in.)
Caster Dia.: 100 mm (4 in.)
Weight: 274.2 kg (605 lb)
Capacity: 10-ton

Figure 8.2 Damage dozer (*Blackhawk Automotive Ltd*)

1 Basic frame assembly
2 Air hydraulic unit
3 Extension beam
4 Support stands and cross tube (set)
5 Underbody clamps (pair)
6 Cross tube clamps (pair)
7 Chain positioning loop
8 Multi-direction, self-tightening clamp
9 Pull clamp
10 Pull ring
11 Multiposition anchor post
12 Multipull dozer hook
13 Frame horn puller
14 Chain with two hooks 2.70 m
15 Chain with one hook 2.70 m
16 Tram track gauge

body repair shop and then moved on to the next job once straightening has been completed. This frame is called a Dozer, and is designed to cater for various classes of repair work. The Dozer (see Figure 8.2) is designed for heavy major frame and body damage, for light frame and body straightening, and for use in conjunction with a repair bench.

Basically the Dozer consists of a base beam which is the backbone of the unit, an upright beam pivoted to the base beam, a hydraulic ram across the angle and an adjustable rear anchor post. The secret of this equipment's success lies in its anchorage to the car, using body anchor clamps in pairs, either standard for cars with vertical pinch welds (Figure 8.3) or right-angled clamps for those with horizontal pinch welds (Figure 8.4). These clamps each have two sets of jaws so that the thrust of the equipment is spread over four points at the strongest part of the car's underframe, and should be fixed as near to the damaged area as possible to restrict the stretching action to this area only. The support cross tube with reinforcing pipe is slid through the bosses in the body anchor clamps, thus providing a rigid thrust point for the rear anchor post (Figure 8.5). The ends of the cross tube provide a lifting point for the adjustable safety stands, enabling the car to be raised to give access underneath. The stands are adjustable to compensate for uneven flooring. The hydraulic ram may be actuated either by

233

Figure 8.3 Standard body anchor clamps (*Blackhawk Automotive Ltd*)

Figure 8.4 Right-angled body anchor clamps (*Blackhawk Automotive Ltd*)

a manual pump or by the air/hydraulic pump, which is quicker and easier to use and leaves the operator with free hands. The pull is made by a chain taken round the pivot post, located by means of the sliding chain guide, and passed through the selected clamp or attachment. The chain then is hooked back on itself, thus providing a double chain. A range of self-tightening clamps and accessories is available (Figure 8.6) designed to clamp on to or be fixed to the wide variety of sections which may require to be pulled.

With this equipment and a little ingenuity it is possible to get a direct pull to the front or rear, or to either side by altering the position of the equipment, an upward or downward pull by varying the height of

the chain, and a side pull, so that by varying these set-ups it is possible to pull over a full 360°. This technique also can be applied for panel tensioning to correct indentations in boot lids, bonnets and doors. In the majority of straightening operations it is also necessary to use a hydraulic ram with special attachments in conjunction with the frame and body straightener to keep the metal moving in the correct direction and to remove secondary damage and stresses set up in bent metal. This equipment overcomes the limitations of the body jack in three ways. First, it takes the reaction to more than one of the strongest points on the car underframe, so that the problem of a single point strong enough to push from is overcome. Second, the Dozer can be lined up to pull in any direction, so that the problem of direction of pull does not arise. Finally all connections are made externally so that there is no necessity to strip interior trim or move assemblies to provide access (Figure 8.7).

8.2.2 Korek body/frame straightening system

The system commences from a flat base area which is actually a high-tensile steel, box section modular frame with a slotted upper face. It can be installed in the workshop either by concreting it into a suitable position in the floor or by siting it on a level area of the floor. If the latter method of installation is used, approach ramps are provided for positioning the car. The equipment uses multiple anchorage and hook-up points which provide tremendous versatility in the direction of pull available (Figure 8.8). Four automatic air/hydraulic pumps with 10 tonne rams are used for the pulling. These are connected to the base frame by special ram foot clamps and are secured by a tapered steel wedge that is hammered into position through the clamp, forcing it tight on to the frame.

To repair a damaged car it must first be positioned over the main frame and raised on safety stands, which are fastened through tubes and pinch-weld clamps to the underside of the vehicle. At this point the vehicle should be anchored to the main frame using chains and clamp attachments to hold it against the corrective pulling forces. On selecting the appropriate pulling positions, clamps are attached to the damaged section and chains are hooked on to the clamps and placed in line with the required direction of pull. The ram units are positioned at the correct angle for pulling by setting the bottom into a ram foot clamp which has been secured to the frame, and at the top by the use of a cross-pin through the chain. The loose end of the chain is then fastened to another ram foot anchorage point. This procedure is repeated with each of

Figure 8.5 Anchor clamps in position on body sills

Figure 8.6 Self-tightening clamp attachments

Figure 8.7 Dozer in position

Figure 8.8   Korek system with accessories, including P188 Mk2 measuring system (*Blackhawk Automotive Ltd*)

the four hydraulic units when a multipull set-up is required. The foot pumps actuate the ram units which in turn tension the chains and slowly pull out the damaged section to its original position.

The advantage of this system is that cars can be repaired singly, or several vehicles can be straightened at the same time using the rigid base (see Figure 8.9). Multiple pushes and pulls can be delivered by the vector-type rams, singly or simultaneously, thereby equally distributing the forces applied in repairing damaged components. The system can also be used with various measuring systems, for instance a mobile bench or Blackhawk's P188 Mk2 universal measuring and correction system.

8.2.3   Mitek anchor pot collision repair system

The Mitek is a transportable floor-based hydraulic pulling system using anchor pots set into the workshop floor (see Figure 8.10). These anchor pots are like long plugs with chains attached to the base and a cap on top which leaves a flat floor when the system is not in use. The anchor pot is pretensioned to expand the pot sleeve and give a firm anchorage point.

These pots, to which the vehicle and Mitek power unit are secured by the use of tie-down chains, can be fitted into any workshop floor, usually to form a working bay ranging from 12 anchor pots to as many as 28 according to the type of repairs to be carried out. The system uses the vector principle of exerting pressure on chains to pull or push in any direction to carry out repairs on any part of the vehicle.

The vehicle is secured to the anchor pots using tie-down chains and wedge anchors which are fastened to the anchor pots by pulling each chain tightly by hand to remove excess slack and then inserting it into the fork of the wedge anchor. The anchor pot chain is then placed in the slot of the wedge anchor base, driving the wedge into the anchor to take up any slack which remains in the chain. Single or multiple Mitek pulling units are then also secured to the anchor pots using tie-down chains and wedge anchors and siting them in the direction of the pull or push required.

Pulling heights can be adjusted by using various attachments to push or pull in all directions up to a height of 2.5 metres. The Mitek can be used with a measuring system so that repairs can be checked as they are pulled (see Figure 8.11).

Figure 8.9 Korek system straightening two cars at the same time (*Blackhawk Automotive Ltd*)

8.2.4 Celette UK 5000 pulling system

This is a powerful pulling system which is equally suitable for cars or light commercial vehicles. It can be used with any Celette mobile bench.

The system 5000 consists of one or more mobile pulling towers, which can be easily moved in any direction on six retractable wheels. The tower can be instantly held in position using chains and self-tightening eccentric anchoring blocks, which fit into slotted channel sections set into a concrete floor in such a way that they form rectangular shapes, thus enabling pulls to be made on four sides of any repair. A special anchoring beam attached to the tower ensures complete safety when the system is in use by locking it into the channel section. The maximum pulling force on the system is 6 tonnes and it can be used at any height up to 3 metres, which is particularly useful for pulling out damage at roof level on a car or a commercial vehicle. The ram stroke has a length of travel of 500 mm, which has the advantage of speeding up the pulling operation and hence the repair. The angle of pull can be controlled throughout the traction.

The system can also be used for pushing or as a crane using optional accessories. Several simultaneous pulls can be carried out using a number of towers. The equipment can be used with a mobile bench, which can be anchored to the slotted channel sections using chains and anchor blocks. The vehicle itself is then held in place using individual jacking sill clamps attached to the bench (Figure 8.12).

8.2.5 Alignment and repair systems

Jig brackets: general development

Vehicle design and manufacture have progressed considerably over the years. The development of crash repair systems has likewise mirrored these changes. When cars were chassis built, the chassis tended to be relatively flat, so that the repair was mainly two dimensional. The change to lighter monocoque construction introduced one other dimension which demanded further consideration. First, the height of the critical points on the vehicle's underside were controlled relative to an imaginary datum line, and so height became of vital importance. Second, accuracy became a far more critical consideration than in the past, as suspension systems became less adjustable and more complex.

Figure 8.10 Mitek system with accessories (*Blackhawk Automotive Ltd*)

Jig brackets were introduced to serve as simple go/no-go gauges, providing a continuous visual indication of the extent of damage. During repairs brackets were found to yield further benefits. They provided progressive anchorage, meaning that once a critical point had been repaired and locked in place with the jig bracket, it would not be disturbed by subsequent repairs. In addition, during building the jig bracket acts as a welding jig to ensure that new parts are correctly installed and that the positions of important steering and suspension pick-up points are not disturbed by welding heat.

Concurrent with these developments, vehicle manufacturers were concentrating on particular aspects of car design. They were attempting to improve body weight by the introduction of high strength steels and vehicle safety by incorporating strong passenger compartments with front and back end crumple zones to absorb impact on collision. These two developments mean that cars are more susceptible to damage in the crumple zone areas at the front and rear ends as a direct result of the built-in safety characteristic of deformation of structures. Consequently more cars now need alignment and repair requiring the use of jig equipment. In particular there has been a growth in the number of cars sustaining damage which, while not major, still requires the use of proper diagnostic and repair systems to effect a repair. The repairer must therefore choose the repair system most appropriate to the degree of damage present. Consequently there has been a growth in the development of measuring systems which can be used in a wide variety of repair situations with speed and accuracy. With dual systems, which combine both brackets and measurement, the repairer can carry out fast and accurate repairs whatever the degree of damage. However, with any body alignment system, whether jig brackets or a measuring system, it is vital that the completion of repair should be followed by a full suspension and wheel alignment check to make sure that the car is completely roadworthy.

Since the early 1950s there has been considerable progress surrounding jig brackets. On the technical side, developments mean that the jig brackets are now available for a wide range of vehicles, are lighter, easier to use and more readily available. For ease of use and to prevent possible errors, integral brackets fit to a regular-spaced hole pattern on top of five integral beams which are common in all integral bracket sets. The front integral beams run longitudinally, as

Figure 8.11   Mitek system in use, with P188 Mk2 measuring system (*Blackhawk Automotive Ltd*)

Figure 8.12   System 5000 pulling tower and frame (*Celette UK*)

do chassis legs, thus allowing first improved access to the engine compartment, and second the production of stronger, simpler brackets. All integral sets incorporate a number of check brackets which are fitted without stripping out mechanical components. Each integral bracket carries a plate which shows a

reference number, which side of the jig it fits to and which edge points forward.

8.2.6   Celette UK alignment and repair systems

Celette UK offers a wide range of fixed or mobile jigs, from the mobile bench to the four-post jigs lift.

Celette benches

The Celette bench (Figure 8.13) is mounted on four heavy-duty wheels, two of which are fitted with brakes to allow the bench to be locked in position during use. Being completely mobile, it can be moved to wherever it is most convenient and the space cleared after use. It can also be fitted with four bench legs, which allow it to be used with existing in-ground pulling systems. The vehicle can be fastened in place on the bench using either four sill clamps or the modular cross beams. These cross beams are bolted directly on to the bench and have the MZ bracket system attached above them. Once the tops and towers of the bracket system are fitted they give an immediate visual indication of the location and extent of damage, and continue to do so throughout the course of the repair (see Figure 8.14). The brackets also act

239

Figure 8.13 Mobile bench showing pulling system and MZ bracket system (*Celette UK*)

as a solid welding fixture, clamping new parts in their correct position at the critical points during welding up (see Figure 8.15). The most important feature of the brackets is that they provide progressive anchorage, locking newly repaired areas in place so that they are not disturbed by subsequent pulls to other areas.

A hydraulic push and pull unit can be quickly clamped to the jig bench at any point. Its double adjustments at the base of the vertical arm and on the horizontal beam allow the push or pull to be widely adjusted to any angle or height without the need to relocate the unit. In addition this equipment can be used for vector pulling and pushing and upward or downward pulls. The bench can also be used with the Metro 2000 measuring system.

Celette jig lifts
The jig lifts (Figure 8.16) are of wheel-free design which enables rapid loading and anchoring of damaged vehicles. The wheel-free system allows the vehicle to be moved easily lengthways and sideways for easy bracket or sill clamp location. The design of the decking plate enables the sill clamp outriggers to be left permanently in place which gives the benefit of a drive-on and drive-off pulling facility.

When not in use as a body repair system, the jig makes an ideal general service lift, as the vehicle can be supported either on its own four wheels or on its underside using the wheel-free system. The lifting capacity of the jig lifts ranges from 2.5 tonnes to 3 tonnes, and so large cars and light commercial vehicles can be worked on. The jig bed can be fitted with the full range of Celette brackets, including the MZ repair system and the Metro 2000 measuring system. The hydraulic push and pull unit and adjustable sill

clamps can be used for anchorage and pulling, providing a dual repair system (see Figure 8.17).

Celette UK MZ system
This system for crash repairs incorporates all the traditional benefits of jigs and brackets, but, in addition, has been designed to reduce the model specific content of the system to a minimum while maximizing the number of brackets which can be fitted, without the need to strip out the mechanical parts first. It consists of 22 universal lower brackets called 'base towers', into which upper brackets called 'tops' are fitted that are specific to the model being repaired. These tops are much smaller and lighter than the conventional brackets, and so are easier to insert or remove when the vehicle is on the jig. This system was made possible by the use of computer-aided design (CAD) equipment. Details of vehicles currently in production were inputted on to the computer; it then identified the most common reference points and evaluated a number of alternative arrangements. From this a set of universal towers was developed to suit the wide range of different vehicle models. The CAD system is also being used to produce manufacturing and user drawings for the top sets, resulting in the faster introduction of tops for newly designed vehicle models.

The basis of the MZ system is in effect a two-piece bracket set. A model-specific top slides under a piston action into the universal tower unit, and a locating pin holds the two together at the correct height. The top locates into the bodywork of the vehicle in the same way as a conventional bracket, and likewise the base of the tower is fitted to the jig using four bolts into the modularly spaced holes. The towers come in five different heights to cater for various requirements. A complete set comprises 22 units, with between two and six of each height depending on the frequency of use. To cater for variations in width or length, the tower unit is mounted offset on its base. It can therefore be set in one of four mounting points. In so doing the area within the 100 mm modular grid spacing can be covered; any further variations are covered by additional offset on the model-specific top unit.

The choice of tower, plus its required location and rotation, is clearly marked on the information sheets which accompany all MZ sets, showing both plan and three-quarters view. To simplify identification and rotation, each tower has a coded arrow which corresponds with arrows on the sheet (see Figure 8.18). When the tower has been fixed, the required top unit can be slid in and held in place by pushing in the locating pin. To cater for mechanicals in requirements,

Equipment

Accuracy =
jig bench
brackets

Safety =
anchoring
clamps

Ease of working =
multidirectional
hydraulic straightener

Method

1 Fit brackets

2 Place vehicle on
brackets with or
without removal
of mechanical units
Level jig bench
Fit brackets in
non-distorted zones
Remove mechanical
units only from zones
which need
straightening

3 Clamp vehicle with
anchoring clamps
Attach straightener
to jig bench
Straighten distorted
zone
Brackets allow a
permanent check
Rebuilding: new
components position-
ed on brackets

Figure 8.14 Use of the Celette bench (*Celette UK*)

two sets of holes are drilled in some towers and tops, the upper set being for mechanicals out and the lower set for mechanicals in.

Celette UK Metro 2000 measuring system
This is a universal diagnostic and repair measuring system based on simultaneous three-dimensional verification of important points of the vehicle. The measuring system is dual purpose as it fits directly to any Celette bench or jig lift, and there is a choice of using brackets or measurement. Thus any degree of damage can be repaired using the most appropriate system. A complete damage diagnosis can be carried out without any stripping of mechanical components, facilitating speedy and effective repairs.

The system is calibrated using points on the

241

Figure 8.15 Car fixed on M8 mobile bench (*Celette UK*)

Figure 8.17 Bodymaster 2000 with Metro 2000 measurement system (*Celette UK*)

Figure 8.16 MUF 61 Bodymaster jig lift with Cobra 3 puller and MZ brackets (*Celette UK*)

vehicle's underbody which are accurately jigged during manufacture. The jacking sill clamps ensure that the vehicle's underbody is brought parallel to the measurement frame; this is vital if height measurements are to be accurate. To ensure accuracies, either the vehicle or the measuring frame must be adjusted so

that they are parallel. The calibration procedure is that the vertical scale built into the sill clamps and telescopic pointers set the vehicle at the correct height. The pointer carries slides on transverse rules with their own scales to allow width positions to be set. A tape runs along each side of the frame, and slides within its housing for instant setting. Three or four datum points are selected on any undamaged area, and the system is calibrated to the height, width and length position of these points. The frame can be bolted down after calibration. All eight pointers are available for taking measurements, since none needs to be left in the calibrated position; therefore all eight locations are available for simultaneous checking during repair.

One data sheet is usually required for each vehicle, giving published dimensions from manufacturer's drawings. These data sheets show the initial sill clamp settings, and the critical dimensions for all mechanical units in place and removed. They also give the MacPherson strut data, which enables a check on the position of the front suspension fixing from above without any stripping of suspension components. The checks include the length, width and height positions of the strut fixings and also the angle of the flitch plate, these are all vital to the correct steering geometry of any vehicle under repair (see Figure 8.19).

Celette UK Bodymaster 2000 drive-on repair system
The Bodymaster 2000 drive-on system is easy to operate. Faster repairs are achievable, as vehicles can be loaded and off-loaded very quickly. In order to facilitate the loading and unloading of a damaged vehicle that cannot be driven on to the bench, a winch is provided.

Figure 8.18 Example information sheet for use with the MZ bracket system (*Celette UK*)

Figure 8.19 Metro 2000 measurement system (*Celette UK*)

The system has other features which make it attractive to bodyshop operators because they greatly facilitate the work on crash repairs. These features include a hydraulic adjustable platform and an integral high-capacity twin pulling tower system. The hydraulic platform provides easier and speedier loading and off-loading of a vehicle and allows the operator to set the bench at any suitable working height to a maximum of 700 mm.

Bodymaster 2000 is particularly versatile owing to its 5 metre long tubular steel rigid base. As a result the system is suitable for the repair of passenger vehicles, vans, four-wheel-drive vehicles, and light commercial and chassis-based vehicles. The design of the system enables it to be used with Celette's Metro 2000 measuring system and also with Celette's MZ diagnostic and repair bracket system (Figure 8.17).

Celette UK Metro 90 measurement system
The Metro 90 is a complete crash repair system based on both bracket and measurement methods of repair. Centred around the Celette MT10 mobile bench and Metro 2000 measuring system, Metro 90 is a complete package including a pulling and clamping system, loading kit and full range of accessories (Figure

Figure 8.20 Metro 90 measurement system (*Celette UK*)

Figure 8.21 The ECO 2000 mobile lifting trolley (*Celette UK*)

8.20). Pulling capacity is provided by the Caiman pulling unit, which also provides extra adjustment, making the system easy to use. An additional wide range of checking accessories also allows more points on the vehicle to be checked, and a telescopic measuring gauge can be used in such areas as engine, upper body compartments, and screen apertures.

The Metro measuring system consists of a rigid alloy frame with eight trolleys that run along the frame. Each trolley is fitted with a half-bridge carrying the vertical pointers and measuring adaptors which allow

location on various points of the vehicle's underbody, including horizontal axis locations. Thus asymmetric points can be checked and repaired simultaneously.

The vehicle is supported on four three-way adjustable sill clamps and is calibrated in all three dimensions – height, width and length – on an undamaged area of the vehicle underside. With conventional structural sills being increasingly replaced by aerodynamic skirts, the clamps can use swivel jaws that clamp on to the lower sill panels where conventional clamps cannot be used. The jaws of the clamps rotate through 360 degrees, ensuring that damaged vehicles can be securely held in place, enabling structural alignment to be guaranteed.

The unit is supplied complete with a full set of laminated colour data sheets, and regular updates are available.

Another advantage of the system is that, with the use of beams and towers, it can be used simply as a bracket system, as this mobile bench has also been specifically designed to accept the MZ diagnostic repair system. The Metro 90 can also be used in conjunction with Celette's ECO 2000 mobile lifting trolley.

Celette UK ECO 2000 mobile lifting trolley

This unit is a mobile lifting trolley which operates using a compressed air supply at a pressure of 7 bar. Capable of lifting weights of up to 2000 kg to a height of 1 m, it provides a simple and effective means of loading damaged vehicles on to a mobile bench, thus creating a comfortable and adjustable working height for various mechanical and servicing work. It is very manoeuvrable in any workshop area. With its controlled lowering speed and integrated safety system it is ideal for any shop needing a mobile lifting unit, not just the bodyshop but also the general workshop, workbays and mechanical lifting bays (Figure 8.21).

8.2.7 Car Bench alignment and repair systems

There is a wide range of body repair equipment available from Car Bench. This equipment is both flexible and versatile, covering a full range of systems designed to suit each individual workshop and all repair situations. It is dual-purpose equipment, suitable both for jig repair using brackets and for repairs using a measurement system. The equipment is described in the following sections.

Mobile bench

The mobile bench (Figure 8.22) is the simplest of all the Car Bench models. It was primarily introduced into the range of equipment for those bodyshops with

Figure 8.22 Mobile bench with autocontrol measuring system and swivel pull post (*Car Bench International*)

Figure 8.23 Mobile lift with mini bracket support system (*Car Bench International*)

limited working space and height restrictions. It is mounted on four robust wheels, allowing it to be easily moved around the workshop. This allows the repairer to utilize valuable workshop space. The wheels are completely detachable, allowing the bench to be lowered directly to floor level. This enables a damaged car to be mounted on to the jig frame with the minimum amount of effort. Separate support legs are included for workshops with uneven floors, and they can be adjusted until the jig bed is perfectly levelled. The hydraulic pulling unit can be mounted in any position, so pulls can be made from any angle around

the frame at the front, the back or either side. This bench can be used with the autocontrol measuring system, the minibracket system and the traditional bracket system. It can also be converted into a hoist by using the scissor-action lift.

Mobile lift
The lift is an extremely versatile unit which can be easily moved around the workshop (Figure 8.23). It is unique in that the frame may be disengaged from the lifting mechanism, allowing a repaired vehicle to be wheeled away. It incorporates the same hydraulic pulling equipment and jig/measuring facilities as the mobile bench.

Scissor-action lift
The scissor-action lift is quite unique in that once the frame has been lowered to rest on its wheels, the base unit can be automatically raised from the floor so that it retracts directly into the frame. This gives the necessary clearance needed to enable the mobile bench to be moved freely around the workshop. It is raised by using a mobile control unit with a lifting capacity of 3.5 tonnes which allows adjustment to height levels to secure the frame in any comfortable working position.

Standard Car Bench four-post lift
The jig itself is a rectangular steel frame incorporated within a four-post 2.5 tonne lift (Figure 8.24). The

245

Figure 8.24   Four-post lift with autocontrol measuring system (*Car Bench International*)

damaged vehicle can be either driven or pushed on to the bench using a trolley jack.

A special trolley is placed under the damaged vehicle, enabling it to be moved easily along the frame to meet the locating points on the jig bed. Once mounted to the vehicle the anchorage brackets are bolted to the predetermined holes in the frame as specified on the jig charts. This ensures that the strongest part of the vehicle is securely anchored to the jig bed and that it remains so throughout realignment and repair. The anchorage bracket incorporates hollow bolts fitted over spring hanger bolts on the front mounting of the rear suspension, enabling the vehicle to be pivoted. This allows further brackets to be fitted to specific points on the vehicle, which may then be used as checking locations. Further brackets, for repair and panel assembly, are provided for fitting to the front and rear suspension and mechanical pick-up points of any type of vehicle. The swivel pull post can be positioned at any point around the frame and locked to it, to allow pulling to be carried out at any angle.

Alignment can be precisely checked at any stage of the repair while pulling is in progress. This is done by relating the jig brackets to the corresponding holes on both the cross beams and the frame. No further measuring of any kind is required. Therefore the repairer can see how far to push or pull to realign the section under repair. The essential function of this system is to pull and realign simultaneously and rebuild the

damaged sections with absolute precision while they are held in place by the brackets. This four-post lift allows work at any comfortable height, giving complete freedom and access around and under the bench.

Centre-post bench
This is suitable for workshops with an existing centre piston installed. It has all the characteristics of the standard Car Bench system.

Mini bracket/support system
This system, although greatly reduced in size and weight, still retains the main features of the Car Bench system. The special support arms, to which modified brackets are fixed, are mounted on the cross beams in the same manner as the original bracket system (see Figure 8.23). They can be moved both laterally and longitudinally in order to locate the pick-up points on the underbody of the vehicle. They may also be extended vertically and horizontally to achieve unlimited positions for the attachment of brackets. By doing this, Car Bench has transformed the idea of a traditional bracket, fixed and rigid, to a more functional system which can be adapted to suit each individual repair regardless of the make or model of the vehicle. Mini cross beam plates have consequently been designed to attach to the special support arms and have exactly the same function as the original cross beams, although they can now be moved nearer the car for the attachment of this style of bracket.

Unified support system

The unified bracket system enables Car Bench users to repair any vehicle using a bracket repair technique but without the necessity for hiring brackets. Because of their universal anchorage, this functional system may be used in any repair situation, regardless of the make or model of vehicle being repaired. The unified system may be applied for use with all the models in the Car Bench range of equipment. It consists of four specific anchor points and eight modular base blocks. These modular blocks can be moved both vertically and horizontally to obtain unlimited positions. Once the unified brackets are attached to the base units, they are positioned according to the technical data sheets provided. Because the base blocks, incorporating unified brackets, are fully adjustable, they give total accuracy in all measurement readings. The data sheets provide accurate measurements of vital control points for mechanical parts both in position and dismantled. The system has been designed in such a way that it may be used in conjunction with the Car Bench measuring system and mini bracket system using the base modular blocks as starter packs.

Autocontrol measuring system

This system can be used with any Car Bench model. It gives the repairer the dual advantage of precision measuring allied to the use of brackets. It is designed for use when damage occurs which is not severe enough to necessitate jigging. The system incorporates graduated rails for longitudinal measurements, four sliding cross members for external and internal measurements, and varying lengths of tube with built-in millimetre scales for obtaining height measurements. Four adjustable sill clamps are also supplied to ensure a quick and easy centralization and anchorage of the car to the frame, while a special bridging device enables the repairer to check for external damage to the body shell. The system includes a wheeled storage trolley to hold the measuring rods and adaptors, and a catalogue of data sheets.

8.2.8 Globaljig universal bracket system

The Globaljig universal bracket system is manufactured in Italy and is available as a mobile (Figure 8.25), four-post lift or centre-post lift unit (Figure 8.26). It is also available with a side lift, making positioning of the vehicle on the bench very simple; and, because of the mobility of the side lift, the vehicle can be easily moved around the workshop area (Figure 8.27). Conversion sets are also available for other jig benches. It is a universal bracket system, comprising one set of jig brackets that are designed to fit any type of vehicle and light commercials, eliminating costly hire or purchase of specific vehicle model brackets. Each bracket is designed as a fixing point, providing anchorage throughout the vehicle, with mechanical parts in or out. With the Globaljig there is an option of brackets or sill clamps, providing a precise and progressive anchorage. Precision and strength are the main features of this system: accuracy is guaranteed to within 1 mm. The brackets included in the system are strong and truly universal; each has a single bolt fixing, providing quick and simple assembly. All calibrated scales are easy to read, and are attained by sliding the beams and base blocks to their specific location.

The pulling unit is a multivector system, easily positioned around the jig bed. When placed at the front or the rear of the jig, the puller will pivot through 220 degrees, allowing pulls to be obtained from both sides of the vehicle without removing the unit from the jig bed. This unique design allows the pulling capacity to remain constant at any given height or angle.

The overhead measuring bridge is a standard feature of the Globaljig. It provides a strong, accurate measuring device for suspension mountings and is also used for checking the upper body measurements (Figure 8.28). Once measurements are satisfactorily achieved, the accurate positioning of new panels can be made prior to welding.

Two types of data sheet are supplied. One is for quick diagnostic checks with mechanical parts in position, and the other is for more detailed repairs with mechanical parts removed.

The system can also be used as a building jig for classic cars or tubular framed sports cars, or as control equipment for estimation or diagnosis of damaged or previously repaired vehicles.

In the case of anchor points varying from their engineering specifications owing to manufacturers' tolerances, this system can still carry out the repair because of the total adjustability in all dimensions and the capability to handle tolerances, even allowing for positioning and movement during repair.

8.2.9 Universal Bench car body repair systems

Universal Bench offer a wide range of mobile benches, a four-post jig lift, and a scissor bench. The repair system offers specific anchorage that can guarantee a precise and reliable repair. The UB Modular system gives positive repair with jig brackets. This offers quick and easy mounting on to cross beams and allows the possibility of checking and anchoring up to 22 points on the underbody of a vehicle (four anchorage

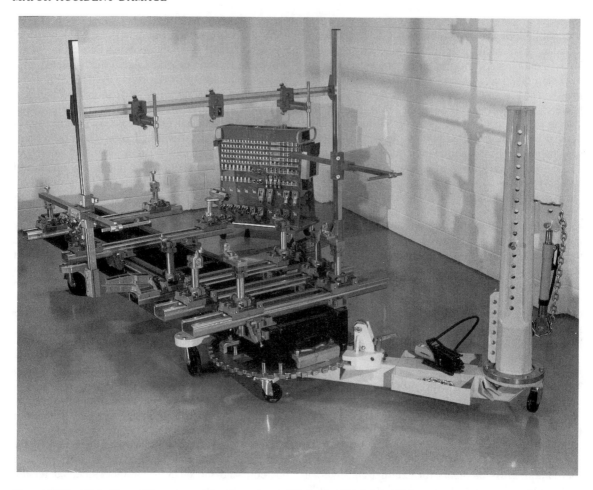

Figure 8.25 Globaljig mobile universal bracket system (*Globaljig, Tri-Sphere Ltd*)

Figure 8.26 Globaljig centre-post lift unit (*Globaljig, Tri-Sphere Ltd*)

Figure 8.27 Globaljig mobile side lift jib loader (*Globaljig, Tri-Sphere Ltd*)

be used for repairs which require the replacement of body panels because of the totally accurate positioning of the panels to be replaced. Data sheets for the system use manufacturers' specifications and measurements. UB Electronics is a measuring system with digital readout. This allows quick and accurate reading of longitudinal, transverse and vertical measurements. The measuring system can be used with all Universal Bench units.

Bracketless universal systems: general description
Bracketless universal systems offer certain advantages over the traditional fixed bracket systems. The universal jig does not require the attachment of special mounting brackets, and therefore may be used in the repair of any vehicle model. Each system is a self-contained unit, with its own measuring system for checking body distortion and its own pulling and pushing equipment for the repair of any damage, whether minor or major.

8.2.10 Dataliner repair system

Dataliner: general description
The Swedish company Nicator has developed a universal alignment jig combined with a special measuring method. The system is called Dataliner (see Figure 8.29). The straightening bench, around which the system is designed, eliminates model-specific brackets altogether. It allows the repair of collision damage without the extensive dismantling and reassembling of components. Its most outstanding feature is the precise measurement obtainable (±1 mm) with the use of a laser beam in conjunction with comprehensive data charts suited to different makes and models of vehicles.

The bench is made from strong hollow beams, known as the mainframe, to which transport beams are attached in a transverse manner. These transport beams with chassis clamps are first positioned under the vehicle, which is raised from the floor by the use of a high-lift trolley jack. Then the four chassis clamps are positioned and tightened, to the bottom edge of the sill on the vehicle and the top edge of the transport beams, by using quick-release and snap-on bolts. Once the transport beams have been fitted in place and tightened, their wheels allow the vehicle to be moved to any convenient area in the workshop.

The mainframe of the bench has two wheels which are centrally located. This allows the frame to be pushed under the vehicle. Using the jack support on the mainframe, the frame is lifted and anchored to the transport beams, after which four floor stands are placed under the frame. The floor stands are

Figure 8.28 Globaljig overhead measuring bridge (*Globaljig, Tri-Sphere Ltd*)

Figure 8.29 Complete Dataliner repair system showing laser equipment and pulling equipment (*Dataliner, Geotronics Ltd*)

and 18 mini brackets). The pulling equipment can be attached to the bed, giving a pulling facility all round the vehicle. There is a standard four-post bench incorporating lifting facilities, and a four-post lift with a disengageable jig frame. This unit is ideal for busy workshops with fast throughput of work, giving easy mounting and positioning of the vehicle and the possibility of rotating the vehicle on the frame. Disengageable frames allow other frames to be used with the same lift. Universal Bench have developed a universal repair system that can be mounted to any jig frame by using an adaptor. This is a positive system which allows the repairer to check and hold the most important underbody points on a vehicle. It can also

Figure 8.30 Laser beam passing through the transparent scales underneath a vehicle (*Dataliner, Geotronics Ltd*)

Figure 8.32 Beam splitter and laser guide (*Dataliner, Geotronics Ltd*)

Figure 8.31 Transparent scales hung in position for alignment (*Dataliner, Geotronics Ltd*)

individually adjustable to raise the vehicle to the most suitable working height for the repair.

Measuring system

The measuring system of the Dataliner is based on the principle that a laser beam can act as an optical square, creating a perfect right angle. By means of transparent scales the plane of measurement is transferred under the vehicle (Figure 8.30). This provides a clear view of all measuring points and allows measurements to be taken and alignment work to be carried out simultaneously. The main components of the measuring system are: a set of measuring rails; a laser unit, which emits a low-power safe laser beam; a beam splitter; and laser guides and transparent scales.

When the measuring equipment has been connected to the bench, the long rail is positioned on the least damaged side of the vehicle and the short rail on the front or rear of the vehicle. The transparent scales are hung under the vehicle in accordance with information on the data charts (see Figure 8.31). The transparent scales transfer the measuring point on the vehicle to a level which can be illuminated with the laser beam. The scales are mounted on special yokes designed for bolt heads and fixture holes. The centre of the scale has a target area through which the laser beam passes when the measuring point is at the correct position. As soon as the scales are in place, calibration can be carried out. This is done by using the laser guide to deflect the light on scales on two undamaged measuring points under the vehicle, vertically adjusting the measuring rail and angling the laser beam using a wheel on the top of the laser guide (see Figure 8.32). The laser guide is equipped with a self-levelling system, which automatically repeats the height angle of the deflected beam when the unit is moved to other locations on the rail. Calibration is complete when the laser beam passes through the target areas on the scales on three undamaged measuring points. The beam splitter is designed to make it possible for measuring height, width and length at the same time (Figure 8.32). It is sited in front of the laser unit and splits the beam to travel simultaneously along the two rails. It can also be used for the alignment of upper body measurements by deflecting the beam at the appropriate angle. Using the other laser guide on the short rail, the centre line of the vehicle and the width of the underbody can be checked from the front or back of the vehicle (Figure 8.33).

Figure 8.33 Checking the centre line of a vehicle (*Dataliner, Geotronics Ltd*)

Figure 8.35 A downward pull using a chain wheel (*Dataliner, Geotronics Ltd*)

Figure 8.34 A counter-support (blocking arm) in use (*Dataliner, Geotronics Ltd*)

Figure 8.36 Simultaneous multipulling (*Dataliner, Geotronics Ltd*)

Straightening equipment

The straightening equipment is designed on the vector principle using hydraulic rams and chains. Pulling and pushing can be carried out at all possible angles, both lengthwise and crosswise, and at any height. The basic Dataliner kit includes two complete 10 tonne pulling units. A counter-support (blocking arm) prevents the vehicle from moving in the direction of pull, and holds the vehicle so that the pulling forces affect only the damaged zone of the vehicle (Figure 8.34). This blocking arm can be used anywhere on the bench, and with extension tubes it can reach both high and low points of a repair. Downward pulls can be carried out using a chain wheel

which can be mounted on the bench frame. As this wheel is pivoted it automatically adjusts itself to the angle of pull (Figure 8.35). On severe major damage several independent hydraulic units can be used simultaneously at any angle round the bench frame (see Figure 8.36).

A major feature of the Dataliner is that measurement and pulling can be carried out at the same time. This guarantees complete control over the straightening operations from the first pull to the final adjustment of the damaged area. Measuring and alignment also takes place at the same time, which means that a continuous check on the measuring during the whole repair is possible. The position of the laser spot on

Figure 8.37   Dataliner drive-on rack system (*Dataliner, Geotronics Ltd*)

the transparent scale shows when the correct alignment point has been reached.

Accessories are available to measure the MacPherson suspension strut tower without any dismantling (Figure 8.29). A flex lock arm will fix and hold panels in position during assembly and welding.

Dataliner drive-on rack system

This system has been designed to repair cars and small commercial vehicles. It is a complete workstation that can also be employed for body preparation, mechanical work and as a platform for wheel alignment. The system features versatility as a multifunctional piece of equipment. The construction of the rails permits limitless tie-down points. Chassis clamps for unibody vehicles can accommodate vehicles of all widths. The working height of the track is adjustable, and the work platform makes it easy to reach all points of vehicles being repaired. This equipment is used in conjunction with Dataliner's laser measuring system, and has multipulling facilities (see Figure 8.37).

Dataliner laser check

Dataliner laser check has introduced a system for checking car chassis. This system is faster, more reliable and more accurate than conventional measuring methods. The laser check is based on Dataliner's laser measuring system in combination with a computer

programme for fast entry and checking measurements. The equipment consists of:

1 Laser guide with electronic calibration and digital measurement display.
2 Hand unit with a memory capacity for four different car models.
3 Personal computer (PC) for connecting to hand unit for registration of data and specifications.
4 Printer for printout of measurements.
5 Modem with access to central register and specification for all car models.

With this system, calibration of laser measurements has been simplified considerably. Measurements are made electronically and are accurately displayed digitally on the laser guide. It is not possible to obtain incorrect readings. With the hand unit connected, measurements appear immediately on the unit display. The hand unit has a storage capacity for data and specifications for up to four different car models (Figure 8.38).

The test car measurements can be quickly compared with specifications, with deviations displayed in millimetres. When measurements and deviations need to be documented, the hand unit can be connected to a printer for printout.

All marketed car models will be found digitally registered in the company's main computer. Measure-

Figure 8.38 Hand-held unit with memory (*Dataliner, Geotronics Ltd*)

Figure 8.39 Blackhawk PB 31/8 mobile straightening and measuring system (*Blackhawk Automotive Ltd*)

ments are available either on disk or via modem from the main computer. All data and specifications can be stored in the PC and are easily transferred to and from the hand unit via an adaptor. The programme is simple to understand and requires no special knowledge of computers.

8.2.11 Blackhawk mobile repair system PB30

The Blackhawk mobile repair system PB30 offers a completely portable repair system that can easily be moved around the workshop. This ensures ease of access to the most difficult repair job even in a limited space. The equipment is available in a single-pull or a two-pull version. Easy working access is ensured by the absence of lift corner posts. It provides a bodyshop with a versatile and comprehensive means

of undertaking crash repairs accurately and efficiently, with minimal disruption to vehicle components.

The complete repair system consists of a base frame and two main elements: a totally independent measuring system allowing complete flexibility of operation, and a pulling system using the Vector principle for precise directional pulling and pushing. The base frame is manufactured from polarized steel. It supports the vehicle, the pulling arm and the measuring system. The vehicle is attached to the frame using sill clamps which are wedged into lateral beams. The vehicle may be loaded on to the sill clamps using a high-lift trolley jack, a two-post lift or a side loading lift (Figure 8.39).

The measuring system works on the principle that a measuring scale can locate vital alignment points in the length, width and height on every vehicle model. These measurements are taken from the zero plane or datum line. The zero plane is the most basic but accurate of all available references, and is used by the vehicle manufacturers to establish vehicle dimensions. The extension scale not only measures height, but when installed on a telescopic cross slide it also measures width. These cross slides glide backwards and forwards on a longitudinal beam to record length measurements. Data sheets provide the necessary information to identify the car's main measuring points. Pneumatic activators (air bellows) align the system to key datum points on the vehicle using respective adaptors from the range supplied. These adaptors rise to contact the car underbody and are held firmly in position by air pressure. They stay with the vehicle owing to the elasticity of the air bellows, and any pressure changes on the measuring unit are controlled by internal regulators. The measuring unit is then perfectly located and parallel to the zero plane and the manufacturer's datum line. These adaptors are engineered to locate precisely and in use are selected according to the information given on the vehicle's data charts which show adaptor type, datum points and their coordinates (see Figure 8.40).

The hydraulic repair system includes a multi-directional push–pull facility together with accessories. The measuring system can be used with ground anchorage collision repair systems as well as mobile repair systems.

8.2.12 Car-O-Liner repair and measuring systems

Car-O-Liner have introduced the Mark 5 alignment system together with a drive-on collision repair system called BenchRack and an electronic measuring

Figure 8.40 Blackhawk PB30 measuring system (*Blackhawk Automotive Ltd*)

Figure 8.41 Mark 5 collision repair system (*Car-O-Liner (UK) Ltd*)

system called Car-O-Tronic which can be used on both jigs.

The Mark 5 collision repair system
This is a universal measuring system developed from the Mark 4 system. It can be either mobile, static or with a built-in lift. The Mark 5 is capable of lifting a

car to a height of 1.4 metres using the scissor lift, thus allowing the bodyshop staff to work standing up, and therefore reducing stress and increasing speed and productivity. It provides increased working room between the jig and the vehicle therefore allowing ease of access for movement and tools. Positioning the vehicle is achieved with the help of rolling ramps. After the ramps have been used, they can be folded up and used as stands or as a work stool, thus helping to keep the workshop free from additional equipment. The correct pulling angle is essential for successful alignment work. The Draw aligner finds the pulling angles easily with almost continuous adjustment and has a built-in telescopic extension arm which allows for repairs needing high pulls.

The Mark 5 equipment consists of the following: alignment bench, Draw aligner, measuring system (Figure 8.41).

The base frame of the alignment bench is a welded structure built from square cross-section tubing, and can be fitted with an integral scissor lift or a single column lift. The upper surface of the frame is milled flat to serve as a reference plane, and there are milled tracks on all four sides for attachment of bench wheels, bench mountings and jack plates. The bench mountings

Figure 8.42 Mark 5 bench showing the scissor lift and Draw aligner (*Car-O-Liner (UK) Ltd*)

Figure 8.43 Mark 5 measuring system (mechanical) (*Car-O-Liner (UK) Ltd*)

are located in the side tracks of the base frame and can be adjusted for height. The mounting arms can be turned either inwards or outwards to suit the width of the vehicle. The chassis clamps are bolted to the arms of the bench mountings and are fitted with tooth jaws which grip the sill flanges of the vehicle.

The dolly sets consist of a number of components which can be used in various combinations and are mounted on the bench frame. Any required point on the vehicle can be fixed in position by the use of these dolly combinations. They can also be used for controlling the pull in certain directions during alignment and as a welding fixture when new parts are to be welded in.

The Draw aligner is used with a 10 tonne hydraulic ram operated by a pneumatic foot pump, and can be

placed at any position along the four sides of the base frame, being locked on to the base frame by the locking wedge. The Draw aligner pivots in the sideways direction and is locked in the required position by a peg. Next the arm can be inclined in the sideways direction to give the optimum pulling angle, then locked in position. The arm is fitted with an extension for high pulls. A safety wire is fitted between the arm and the hydraulic ram mounting in order to limit the outward movement of the arm (Figure 8.42).

The measuring system can be either mechanical or electronic. The mechanical system consists of a measuring bridge which is made of aluminium and is provided on both sides with movable measuring tapes for length measurements. It is designed to be placed on the flat milled surface of the base frame. The measuring slides decide the width measurements and run along the measuring bridge. There is a pull-out slide on each side of these which is provided with three mounting holes for height tubes. Readings are made on scales on the side of the tubes. These height tubes are of various lengths and marked with sliding scales with millimetre graduations for reading height measurements. There are various measuring adaptors such as sockets, cones and angle blocks which are fitted into the top of these height tubes. The combination of height tube and scale adaptor that should be used at the point to be measured is shown in the data sheet for the particular vehicle (Figure 8.43). Equipment is also available to measure the upper anchor points of MacPherson struts together with the dimensions of the engine compartment and the whole of the upper body (Figure 8.44).

The data sheet files contain checklists for most car models and show height, length and width dimensions at a number of measuring points on the vehicle. The data sheet also gives information on the correct points for placing the chassis clamps for locating the vehicle on the bench.

Drive-on collision repair system: BenchRack

The BenchRack can be used on passenger vehicles and light transport vehicles. The ramp system enables the vehicle to be secured to the bench quickly. The BenchRack is equipped with a built-in hydraulic scissor lift which can lift a weight of 3 tonnes to a height of 1.4 metres, allowing the operator to select quickly a suitable height for any type of repair undertaken. The 12 removable ramp sections are made from lightweight alloy and fitted in the tracks on the side of the bench. The ramps can be removed when necessary to facilitate access when measurements are taken or alignment work is carried out. Adjustable chassis clamp arms may be raised or lowered as needed, or can also

Figure 8.44 MacPherson strut measuring equipment (manual) (*Car-O-Liner (UK) Ltd*)

Figure 8.45 Car-O-Tronic electronic computerized measuring system (*Car-O-Liner (UK) Ltd*)

be turned in for use on pick-up trucks and other narrow framed vehicles. Chassis clamps hold the vehicle secure while pulling is taking place. Two 9 tonne Draw aligners provide the pulling force, 360 degrees around the BenchRack. The side support system is used to hold undamaged and already repaired components in place while pulling other areas. The measuring can be carried out using the Mark 5 mechanical system or the Car-O-Tronic electronic system, for fast and accurate measurements of any vehicle damage.

Car-O-Tronic measuring system
The Car-O-Tronic is a universal electronic computerized measuring system. It is designed primarily to measure and check the dimensional correctness of vehicle chassis. Car-O-Tronic measures either with reference to the Car-O-Liner data sheet or on an absolute basis. Advanced mathematics and computer technology mean that this system can be used without any other special equipment. All that is needed to make the system operational is a flat smooth surface, a measuring bridge, the electronic measuring arm and a hand terminal (Figure 8.45). The system is easy to operate: the measuring arm is moved along the bridge underneath the vehicle and simultaneously measures

the length, width and height at the precise data measuring points, displaying this on the hand terminal and then comparing the results with the manufacturer's data stored in its data bank. This immediate, accurate information regarding the extent of the distortion sustained by the vehicle determines whether or not the vehicle will need straightening and subsequently pulling. This information is then fed back to a remote computer terminal upon which it is displayed. A hard copy can be taken via a printer linked to the computer. The measuring system can be left in place while the pulling process is being carried out and can be used to determine the amount of overpull required to bring the vehicle into alignment with its specific manufacturer's data (Figure 8.46).

The Car-O-Tronic can also be linked into the Autoquote management control computer package. This effectively allows for complete computerization of the entire bodyshop operation.

8.2.13 Chief E-Z Liner 11 universal alignment and straightening system

The Chief E-Z Liner 11 system consists of all the equipment necessary for damage analysis and repair

Figure 8.46 Pulling and measuring using the Car-O-Tronic (*Car-O-Liner (UK) Ltd*)

Figure 8.47 Chief E-Z Liner II system showing the gauge measuring equipment (*Chief Automotive Ltd*)

to current vehicle models. It uses a precision universal gauge measuring system and special pulling and anchoring attachments in conjunction with the main frame platform (see Figure 8.47). The equipment consists of a main frame platform which tilts down at the back to form a ramp, up which a vehicle can be driven

or winched. Once the car is in position the platform can be raised hydraulically to a horizontal plane and locked into place.

The platform has 200 tie-down boxes which provide unlimited holding positions for any type of car or light commercial vehicle. Four special anchor clamps are supplied. These lock into tie-down boxes to locate the vehicle. The clamps themselves rotate through 360 degrees and have height adjustment. At the front of the unit are three independent pivoting towers. These between them can be swung in an arc of 180 degrees, providing a wide range of pulling angles. Each tower is equipped with a 5 tonne hydraulic ram to provide the pulling power, and an adjustable collar to enable precise pulling angles to be achieved. Two portable hydraulic rams are also supplied for lifting, pushing and pulling, thus providing the means for unlimited pulling capacity at any point on the damaged vehicle. Power for the pulling equipment is supplied by a heavy-duty hydraulic pump operated from a remote control handset.

The universal gauging system gives a fast positive visual alignment analysis before and during repair. Six alignment gauges feature vertical and horizontal calibrated scales, and a variety of hanging attachments. These self-centring gauges form a skeleton image of the damage extended below the vehicle. Each gauge measures width from the centre line as well as interacting with the gauge system. Width is compared with specifications by reading the scale through a convenient window on the top of the centre housing (see Figure 8.48). The attachments are calibrated to show the actual distance from the datum plane to the attachment point. Special colour treatment on each side of the gauges provides easy analysis of the datum plane; yellow stripes on one side and orange stripes on the opposite side can be alternated to provide contrasting colours for siting.

With all the gauges in position, the simultaneous multipull hook-ups are made and the pulling process begins. Throughout the pulling process the gauges show the centre line and datum plane gradually becoming aligned until they read central. When the centre line and datum are aligned and the correct length is achieved, the vehicle structure is then in total alignment.

8.2.14 The Genesis electronic measuring system

The Genesis electronic measuring system, developed by Chief Automotive Ltd, integrates the precision of laser scanning with a computerized data base for accuracy in collision repair analysis (Figures 8.49, 8.50).

Figure 8.48 Self-centring gauge showing measurement window (*Chief Automotive Ltd*)

Figure 8.49 The Genesis electronic measuring system (*Chief Automotive Ltd*)

The Genesis system begins with the vehicle specification data base. For each vehicle specification there are graphic displays, both overhead and side view of the vehicle's underbody structure (see Figure 8.51). In addition to showing the extent of collision damage, the Genesis system is designed to monitor progress throughout the repair and verify that the vehicle structure is correctly aligned. Throughout the repair the

computer compares vehicle specifications with the manufacturer's current reference point measurements. Computer printouts verify the vehicle's structural condition by showing overhead and side view diagrams.

The Genesis system measures using the principle of triangulation. The system's electronic body scanner houses two spinning hubs, each of which emits a laser beam. These two rotating laser lights project towards light reflective targets, which are suspended from the vehicle's underbody reference points. Each laser beam strikes a reflective material in the end of the body scanner housing, which activates a counter when the laser light is reflected back to the hub. The beam also strikes a target, which has retro-reflective material on one side, and which is attached at a control point on the underside of the vehicle. The beam is reflected back to its source, the laser hub, which is then reflected up to a detector above the centre of the hub, which again activates or turns off the counter.

The number of counts the counter has made, from when it was turned on by the beam striking the end of the housing to when it is turned off by the beam striking the target, can be used to calculate the angle of the beam to the housing. The same process occurs with the other hub, which also determines another angle. The body scanner housing and the two laser beams striking the target form a triangle.

Figure 8.50 Genesis electronic system components (*Chief Automotive Ltd*)

1 Computer	5 Workstation	9 Target attachments
2 Display monitor	6 Body scanner	10 Upper body bar
3 Keyboard	7 Scanner tray	11 Lower body bar
4 Printer	8 Targets	12 Scales

Since the spinning hubs are a known distance apart, the counters have determined two angles of the triangle: therefore the length of the sides of the triangle can be mathematically determined by trigonometry (triangulation) (Figure 8.52). This can then be further converted mathematically into length and width measurements for the target locations.

The body scanner automatically reads all reference points simultaneously, from strategically placed targets positioned on the vehicle underbody. These readings are then compared with published data and are displayed in colour on the monitor screen.

Upper body and strut tower positions are similarly located to provide height, width and length specifications relevant to the lower body. Genesis first displays

visual guides, showing where to place each target. It then graphically illustrates how existing positions compare with vehicle specifications and provides direction and distance information for planning the repair. The entire system stays in place while repairs are being made.

Setting up the equipment, hanging the targets in position, entering the vehicle's information, and positioning the body scanner, take a qualified bodyshop technician approximately 10 minutes. Calibration of the vehicle is then carried out automatically by Genesis in a few seconds.

To check progress at any moment the computer can provide either a visual display or a printout verification of the vehicle's structural condition. This can

Figure 8.51 Computer measuring screen (*Chief Automotive Ltd*)

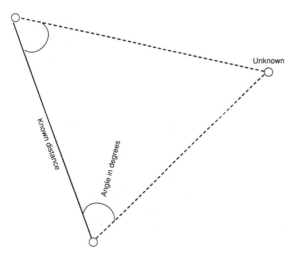

Figure 8.52 Triangulation (laser measurement) (*Chief Automotive Ltd*)

be of great benefit for insurance companies for quick approval of additional repairs and also for customers requiring verification of repairs.

8.2.15 Kroll Autorobot multifunctional system

Kroll Autorobot of Finland have developed a multifunctional system for alignment, repair and straightening. It can be added to as a workshop expands, thus catering for both small and large bodyshops (Figure 8.53).

Autorobot L

For the small bodyshop wishing to invest in a crash repair system, the system begins with the Autorobot L (Figure 8.54). This is easily and quickly loaded using the unique patented sill clamps. The pulling tower can be used 360 degrees around the vehicle to be repaired. Multiple pulling positions around the Autorobot L mean that two or more pulling towers can be used at any one time for both minor and major repairs. This system is mobile and can be moved to any work area in the workshop easily and quickly. The short bed allows access for repair and the engine can be removed while the vehicle is still mounted on the bed.

Figure 8.53 Autorobot XLS II showing liftpack servicing four top frames (*Kroll (UK) Ltd*)

Figure 8.54 Autorobot L using lifting crane (*Kroll (UK) Ltd*)

Figure 8.55 Autorobot XLS II system (*Kroll (UK) Ltd*)

Autorobot XLS II

By adding to the Autorobot L with a lift, extra pulling towers and a measuring system it becomes the Autorobot XLS II (Figure 8.55). The lifting unit of this system makes many phases of the job comfortable, such as the removal of mechanical parts and the alignment and repair of a damaged chassis. In addition to this the lifting unit assists the mounting of the vehicle.

It takes only a few minutes to mount a vehicle on to the Autorobot XLS II. The four operations are as follows:

1 The vehicle is brought up above the bench on the drive-on ramp with or without the aid of a winch.
2 The sill clamps are then moved into place.
3 The straightening bed is hydraulically lifted.
4 Finally the sill clamps are tightened.

The design of the Autorobot allows maximum accessibility under the front and rear of the vehicle; therefore

261

Figure 8.56 Autorobot measuring system used on the XLS II (*Kroll (UK) Ltd*)

Figure 8.57 Autorobot III Super complete system (*Kroll (UK) Ltd*)

all dismantling, measuring and straightening operations can be carried out with ease.

The measuring system (Figure 8.56) is interchangeable with all Autorobot benches. A damaged vehicle body can be straightened to its original measurements with accuracy and ease using this system. Mechanical measuring rods are used to remeasure the chassis and body. All necessary measuring information for various vehicle models can be found on the data sheets provided. The overhead measuring system can help restore the upper part of the vehicle body to its original shape as on the data sheets. The system traverses the full length of the vehicle, allowing measurements to be taken at any point along its length.

III Super

The III Super features five pushing–pulling towers and multifunction robot arm, all operated by remote control electrohydraulics. This system of multitowers

allows straightening and counterpushes combined with holding positions so that the straightening work becomes easier for the operator. The straightening system works on a sliding tower base, allowing the most difficult of repairs to be carried out (Figure 8.57).

8.2.16 Choice of systems

The design concept of monocoque construction with its crumple zones which absorb energy through deformation of panel structures, and the increasing use of high-strength steels, have made essential the use of repair and alignment systems even for minor damage repairs. This has been encouraged by the research carried out at the Motor Insurance Repair Research Centre, Thatcham, and by the promotion by the VBRA and the AA of improved standards throughout the vehicle body trade.

Owing to the wide range available of repair and alignment systems, it is increasingly difficult to select any one system, as they each have many differing advantages. The following are some of the important criteria to be considered in the selection of suitable equipment.

1 Suitability for the type of repair work normally handled.
2 Suitability for the volume of work handled.
3 Availability of initial training and further training as required.
4 Adequate service and back-up by the manufacturer.
5 Availability of accurate data information which should be constantly reviewed and updated.
6 Expected lifespan of the equipment, and the possibility of it becoming outdated.
7 Mobility, portability and ease of storage.
8 Firm securing of vehicle during repair.
9 Good system of alignment that can be used without too much dismantling of mechanical components (dual systems are sometimes preferable).
10 Multipulling facilities for simultaneous repair over 360 degrees, and enough pulling power to cope with HSS.
11 Adjustable working height positions.
12 Adequate holding facilities to allow the welding in of new panel assemblies.

8.3 ALIGNMENT OF THE MODERN INTEGRAL BODY

8.3.1 Misalignment and vehicle control

Any serious impact on any part of the all-welded body of the mono constructed vehicle will cause distortion throughout the structure, which will not necessarily be adjacent to the damaged area. Since the front and rear suspension units are connected, either directly or through the medium of a front or front and rear subframe, distortion of the body shell means a disturbance of the relationship of the running wheels one with another. When this occurs the result will be crabwise running in which the car seems to travel in a sideways manner, commonly called dogtracking. It is often necessary for the driver of such a vehicle to struggle constantly to maintain a straight course, and this becomes greater as the speed increases.

Misalignment of car underbody can also cause tyre wear and may affect the brakes and steering control, which will not be cured however much checking and adjustment is carried out. These faults can render a car outside the uniform standards required by law in respect of the fitness of the car for use on the road. A car with a damaged or weakened underbody can be a menace to safety on the road. Aside from the effects it has on steering control and tyre wear, it can also place undue stress on other mechanical parts of the vehicle. The alignment of the engine with the clutch and transmission may be affected. This could cause a manual transmission to jump out of gear and might result in permanent clutch failure. Any radical change in the angle of transmission to the rear axle may cause excessive wear in the universal joints, noise in the rear axle or axle failure. Moreover, whenever the underbody has been damaged by collision there is a possibility of a broken hydraulic brake line which could lead to complete brake failure. Electrical connections also may become broken. There are a number of modern cars where the rear track varies substantially from the front to the back and there are several which have up to 25 mm variation in track; these points are taken into consideration when checking for distortion.

8.3.2 Checking a mono constructed body shell for underframe alignment

In order to make an alignment check of a mono constructed underbody, the first step is to assess the extent of the damage, the probable amount of force involved which caused it, and the direction of that force. This information will act as a guide by indicating where to look for possible distortion. With this knowledge a visual check should be made of doors, bonnets, boot lids, roof and centre pillar positions for any distortion which may be visible. Inconsistent gaps around these panels show that the panel assembly has been moved during the collision.

The underbody should be checked next. This can only be done by jacking the car up and inserting safety stands, or by using lifting equipment in the form of a hoist which will allow a more thorough examination of the underside of the vehicle. The subframes and cross members can now be examined for kinks or buckles with the aid of a portable light, but where sighting is difficult or impossible the members are examined by touch. This is not conclusive evidence of distortion, but will generally be sufficient to convince the repairer whether a more precise check should be made by using the dropline method, the gunsight gauge method, or a jig alignment system.

8.3.3 Dropline method of checking underbody alignment

For many years in the body repair trade the dropline method was the basic means of checking the alignment of both composite and mono constructed vehicles. When a car has been damaged the relationship of the vital points, such as rear suspension spring hangers, front hub centres, and front suspension centres, must be checked on a flat floor surface with the vehicle jacked clear of the floor, all four road wheels removed, and safety axle stands in position.

With a plumb bob and length of cord, plot on to the workshop floor a series of points common to both right- and left-hand underbody members. At least eight such points should be selected, four on each side, which could include front and rear spring shackle bolts, bumper bar bracket bolts, or any factory formed holes, rivets, bolts, or intersection of cross members common to both side members. On a composite designed body the body bolts provide ideal locating points. Variation in wheelbase can be checked by plotting the centres of each of the four wheels. The plumb bob line should be held against the centre of each point selected and the position where it strikes the floor should be marked with a pencil cross. The pencil is more easily seen if the floor is previously chalked in the approximate area where the plumb bob will fall.

After all the points have been plotted and the wheels replaced, the car can then be rolled away, leaving the chalked pattern on the floor. These points are joined diagonally by using a chalked length of cord which is held tight and then flicked to the floor, leaving a chalked straight line between each pair of points. These lines will indicate if any variation has occurred in the diagonal measurements. The next stage is to establish a chalked centre line through the diagonals. This is done by bisecting the lines joining the front and rear pairs of points and using the chalked cord to mark the centre line. If the underbody is in perfect alignment,

Figure 8.58 Dropline check on front and rear subframes of a Mini (*Rover Group Ltd*)

A-A	660.40 mm	Front subframe front mounting set
	26.0 in	screws
B-B	412.75 mm	Front subframe rear mounting set
	16.25 in	screws
C-C	1282.70 mm	Rear subframe front mounting set
	50.50 in	screws
D-D	977.90 mm	Rear subframe rear mounting block
	38.50 in	set screws

All dimensions taken at centre line of set screw or set screw hole.

this centre line should then pass where each diagonal intersects the centre line. When the centre line does not pass within 3 mm of these intersecting points, measurements must be taken to establish which member is distorted. A further check can be made by joining the sets of points transversely. These transverse lines will be at right angles to the centre line if the underbody is in correct alignment (Figure 8.58).

Owing to the inaccuracy of this system, the increase in the complexity of design structure of vehicles, and their critical suspension geometry, the dropline method has been superseded by the use of alignment jigs, using either a bracket alignment check system or a universal measuring system.

8.3.4 Gunsight gauge method of checking underbody alignment

Another method of checking underbody alignment for distortion is that of using gunsight frame gauges (Figure 8.59). These gauges consist of two sliding bars which can be adjusted by either pulling out or pushing in to make them fit correctly across a chassis frame or underbody. At the middle of the gauge is a sighting pin which always remains central irrespective of the distance to which the gauge is extended, and which is used to establish the datum line (the vehicle's centre line). There are adjustable hanging rods on both ends so that the gauge may be raised or lowered. These hanging rods are also used to attach

Figure 8.59 (a) Gunsight gauge frame (b) diamond detector gauge (*Blackhawk Automotive Ltd*)

the gauge to the underbody or frame at symmetrical points on it, which may be factory formed holes, mounting points, or any part of the underframe which has identical positions on both sides of the vehicle (Figure 8.59a). Never hang gauges on movable parts such as control arms, springs, torsion bars, or any mechanical moving parts, as false readings will be obtained. A minimum of three gauges is essential, but the more gauges used the easier it will be to determine

Figure 8.60 Frame gauges showing distortion (*Blackhawk Automotive Ltd*)

exactly where the distortion is located, as sighting along four or five gauges is quicker than relocating three gauges back and forth along the length of the vehicle.

When setting up the gauges to check underbody alignment, the in-line condition will be when all sighting pins are in line and all gauge bars are parallel. If one gauge must be lowered to clear some obstruction on the underbody, all other gauges must be lowered a corresponding distance to maintain a level sighting. The condition where the gauge bars are not parallel (Figure 8.60a) indicates that the underbody has moved up or down at some point along its length. The condition where the sighting pins are not in line, while the gauge bars are still parallel (Figure 8.60b), indicates that the underbody members have moved to one

side only (sway). A twisted underbody is recognized by the gauge condition where sighting pins are out of line in addition to the bars not being parallel (Figure 8.60c).

As well as these basic checks an additional gauge is available, known as a diamond detector gauge (Figure 8.59b), which is specially made to fit on the top or bottom of the self-centring gauges. This provides extra sighting pins to help to detect sideways movement (sway) and diamond damage (when the underbody has been forced into a diamond shape), which may not be evident when using self-centring gauges only. The only indication of a diamond condition would be that the two pins of the diamond detector gauge would be out of line with all other self-centring pins. Having determined the type of damage, the actual location is found by visual inspection. The main advantages gained by using this system of alignment check are the speed at which it can be set up to diagnose distortion, and the convenience it offers in making regular checks during repair procedure.

Chief precision alignment gauge system
The principle of the self-centring siting pin is used by Chief in their alignment gauge system. These gauges are hung underneath the car from specific data reference points, giving an instant alignment check according to the siting on the pins (see Figure 8.61 and Section 8.2.13).

8.3.5 Vehicle alignment checks using a digital measuring tool

This is a lightweight aluminium measuring tool which can be used to check body alignment on any part of a vehicle body. By extending the tool, its measuring range covers from 2 mm up to 3683 mm. The measurements are displayed on an LCD digital readout, in either metric (millimetres) or imperial (feet and inches), and are accurate to 1 mm. It is supplied with pointers, cones and magnetic bases so that accurate measurements can be taken on various parts of the vehicle without difficulty (Figure 8.62). This measuring tool is used for comparative measurements when checking a vehicle for damage and when estimating a repair. While a vehicle is on a jig, the tool can be used to double check measurements taken by the jig's own measuring system. It also can be used for measuring a vehicle's wheelbase and comparing it with manufacturer's data (Figure 8.63). In addition it can be used to check the critical suspension points before, during and after repair (Figure 8.64).

Figure 8.61 Chief E-Z Liner II showing hanging gauges, self-centring (*Chief Automotive Ltd*)

Figure 8.62 Digital measuring tool with accessories (*Stanners Ltd*)

Figure 8.63 Checking a vehicle's wheel base with a digital measuring tool (*Stanners Ltd*)

8.3.6 Underbody alignment using jig fixtures

Using an alignment and repair system is the only method of guaranteeing a comprehensive and accurate check on the alignment of the underbody of a vehicle. The monocoque body is produced on a production line using a series of quality controlled jigs and fixtures for holding all panels in the correct position for spot welding. To the production engineer this is the only way of consistently reproducing a basic shell fitted with all its mechanical parts in the correct places. When it comes to repairing a body which has been damaged or distorted in an accident it is only logical that accurate alignment jigs should be used to

ensure a safe, roadworthy repair and one which has the appearance of a new vehicle. The introduction of systems of body jigs was a major step forward in body repair techniques. These systems were designed and developed to cope with the ever-increasing call on the accident repair trade. Every vehicle presented a different problem but, equally, every body shell had certain points which always could be relied upon to

Figure 8.64 Digital measuring tool being used during repair to check vehicle suspension points (*Stanners Ltd*)

be accurately controlled during factory production (Figures 8.65, 8.66), and it was around these points that all manufacturers of alignment equipment designed their products. This approach and the enthusiastic cooperation of the vehicle manufacturers at all stages ensured that when a car was mounted on the equipment, the damage of distortion showed up in an unmistakable fashion. The products now available to the body repairer include the following:

1 Alignment systems that incorporate bracket mounting (see Figure 8.67).
2 Alignment systems that incorporate either a mechanical (see Figure 8.68) or a laser light measuring system (see Figure 8.69).
3 Dual equipment, which incorporates both measurement and bracket systems.
4 Cassette-type multifunctional alignment and repair systems (see Figure 8.70).
5 Alignment systems that incorporate either a mechanical or an electronic measuring system (Figure 8.71).

Manufacturers are continuing their research to develop appropriate body repair equipment as car design and methods of assembly are influenced by technological progress.

8.3.7 Vehicle body alignment: upper structure

Damage to the inner construction of a car body might be quite severe although not obvious. In some cases the damage to the outer panels of the body can be repaired and the original damage will appear to have been corrected although it has not. Failure to check the correction of the internal damage by alignment

methods can result in incorrectly fitting doors, bonnets and boot lids.

The alignment methods are based on comparative measurements in which one distance is compared, by means of a trammel, tram-track gauge or measuring equipment incorporated in an alignment measuring system (such as in Figure 8.70) to another which should be the same. Comparative measurements are universally used and are regarded as the easiest and quickest method of measuring collision work. These measurements are supplied by most manufacturers on data sheets or in body alignment manuals. Body measurements are made in the same way in both composite and mono constructed vehicles. Checking body measurements is done by a system of diagonal comparisons, commonly called X checking. The location and extent of the damage is determined by measuring the body. Further measuring during the repair will indicate when alignment is restored.

In this system of measuring the body is divided into two basic sections: the front section, which is the area from the centre pillar forwards (Figure 8.72); and the centre/rear section, which is the area from the centre pillar backwards to the rear boot compartment (Figure 8.73). In addition to these sections, there are special sets of measurements for the alignment of the bonnet lid, the boot lid, and the front and rear doors. Some alignment systems incorporate upper body alignment measuring equipment (see Figures 8.74–8.77).

8.3.8 Door alignment

The doors of a car body are said to be misaligned when they do not fit the contour of the body or when they do not fit in the door opening correctly. Doors must provide a good seal against dust, water and air, and in order to do this they must match the contour of the body at all points. When closed, doors must fit correctly into the opening provided for them, because if the door is incorrectly positioned it will not close properly and the gap around the door will not be uniform. In some cases where the door appears to be misaligned the door itself is not the cause of the fault, and so it is advisable to X check the body at the forward and centre positions to determine whether the reason of the failure to match the body contour is due to distortion of the body or distortion of the door itself. In some cases lack of uniform clearance at the front of the door might be due to mispositioning of the front wing.

Door alignment is checked by making a visual close inspection of the door and its relation to the surrounding body panels. First, open and close the door and

The following data applies to Saloon and Estate models.

Reference	Dimensions	Location
A	920 mm 36.22 in	Jig location hole centres on bonnet locking platform

Figure 8.65 Manufacturer's alignment points: vertical and longitudinal (*Rover Group Ltd*)

	mm	in	
A-D	785	30.9	Front chassis leg forward jig locating hole to subframe rear locating hole
B-D	294 ± 3	11.57 ± 0.12	Front damper upper mounting hole to subframe rear mounting hole
C-D	184 ± 3	7.24 ± 0.12	Front subframe forward mounting hole to rear mounting hole
D-E	280 ± 2	11.02 ± 0.08	Front subframe rear mounting hole to centre chassis leg front jig location hole
D-J	3033	119.41	Front subframe rear mounting hole to rear chassis leg rearward jig location hole
D-F	1220 ± 3	48.03 ± 0.12	Front subframe rear mounting hole to rear suspension cross member jig location hole
G-H	827 ± 3	32.56 ± 0.12	Rear chassis leg forward jig location hole to rear suspension cross member jig location hole
G-J	1363 (Ref.)	53.66	Rear chassis leg front to rear jig location holes
K-M	501.5 ± 3	19.74 ± 0.12	Trailing arm mounting to rear damper upper mounting centre hole
K-H	537 ± 3	21.14 ± 0.12	Trailing arm mounting to rear suspension cross member jig location hole
H-J	536 ± 3	21.10 ± 0.12	Rear suspension cross member jig location hole to rear chassis leg rearward jig location hole
a	150 ± 1	5.9 ± 0.04	Datum line to front chassis leg forward jig location hole
b	607 ± 5	23.89 ± 0.2	Datum line to front damper upper mounting centre hole
c	286 ± 3	11.26 ± 0.12	Datum line to front subframe forward mounting hole
d	151 ± 2	5.94 ± 0.08	Datum line to front subframe rearward mounting hole
e	40.6	1.59	Datum line to centre chassis leg front jig location hole
f	55	2.16	Datum line to centre chassis leg rear jig location hole
g	86	3.39	Datum line to rear chassis leg forward jig location hole
h	256.3	10.09	Datum line to rear suspension cross member jig location hole
j	284	11.18	Datum line to rear chassis leg rearward jig location hole
k	145.5	5.72	Datum line to trailing arm mounting
m	607 ± 5	23.89 ± 0.2	Datum line to rear damper upper mounting centre hole

Figure 8.66 Manufacturer's transverse alignment points (*Rover Group Ltd*)

	mm	in	
A1-A2	1034	40.71	Front chassis leg jig location holes
A1-CL	513	20.20	LH front chassis leg jig location hole to centre line
A2-CL	521	20.51	RH front chassis leg jig location hole (offset) to centre line
B-B	961 ± 3	37.83 ± 0.12	Front damper upper mounting centre holes
C-C	870 ± 3	34.25 ± 0.12	Front subframe forward mounting holes
D-D	800 ± 2	31.5 ± 0.08	Front subframe rearward mounting holes
E-E	800 ± 2	31.5 ± 0.08	Centre chassis leg front jig location holes
F-F	800 ± 2	31.5 ± 0.08	Centre chassis leg rear jig location holes
G-G	1066 ± 1	41.97 ± 0.04	Rear chassis forward jig location holes
H-H	760 ± 1	29.97 ± 0.04	Rear suspension cross member jig location holes
J-J	1024 ± 1	40.31 ± 0.04	Rear chassis leg rearward jig location holes
K-K	1200 ± 1	47.24 ± 0.04	Trailing arm mounting brackets
M-M	1050 ± 3	41.34 ± 0.04	Rear damper upper mounting centre holes

Figure 8.67 Alignment and repair using a jig bracket system (*Globaljig, Tri-Sphere Ltd*)

Figure 8.68 Alignment and repair using a measuring ridge system (*Blackhawk Automotive Ltd*)

269

Figure 8.69 Alignment and repair using a laser measuring system (*Dataliner, Geotronics Ltd*)

Figure 8.70 Autorobot L using full measuring system (*Kroll (UK) Ltd*)

Figure 8.71 Alignment system using electronic measuring for both underbody and upper body structures (*Car-O-Liner (UK) Ltd*)

should be taken on the damaged door, working from points that can be easily established on an undamaged door, and the readings compared to determine whether the damaged door requires further attention. Always be sure to take measurements from the same points on both doors.

8.3.9 Bonnet alignment

Bonnet alignment can be easily checked by visual inspection. When the bonnet is closed the gap all around it should be uniform; if it is not, misalignment exists. Manufacturers' specifications concerning this gap are available; however, a good general rule is that this clearance should be between 3 mm and 6 mm wide. Correct bonnet alignment with the wings and front grille preserves the streamlined contours of the front end of a car. A uniform gap should exist between the sides of the bonnet and the wings. At the rear end of the bonnet the body is recessed to form the scuttle panel into which the bonnet fits to give a continuous flowing line. If the bonnet is too high or too low a recognizable step occurs at this point. If the

observe any movement at the edge of the door at the lock pillar; if there is any up and down movement, the door is out of alignment but is being corrected by the dovetail of the lock as the door closes. Look for signs of rubbing or scraping by the bottom edges of the door on the sill panels or centre pillar. Scrub marks are evidence of a condition known as door sag. In cases where the door is severely damaged and a good deal of straightening is necessary, it is essential to check the door before any attempt is made to reinstall and to align the door with the body. Measurements

Figure 8.72 Front diagonal alignment check (*Rover Group Ltd*)

A	920 mm 36.22 in	Jig location hole centres on bonnet locking platform	F	1326.3 mm 52.22 in	Front door aperture
B	640.3 mm 25.21 in	Bonnet locking platform to front spring mounting, top	G	1648 mm 64.88 in	From centre of cut-out on front seat mounting cross member to trim edge of cantrail and BC-post intersection
C D	1187.5 mm 46.75 in	Bonnet locking platform to front spring mounting, top			
E	1423.5 mm 56.04 in	Front windscreen aperture	H	1128 mm 44.41 in	Between BC posts at intersection of cantrail and post trim edge

bonnet is too far forward a large gap will exist between the rear of the bonnet and the raised portion of the scuttle panel; however, if the bonnet is too far back this gap will be too small and there is a possibility that when the bonnet is opened it will catch the scuttle panel and chip the paint on either or both of these panels. When a condition of misalignment exists that affects the bonnet opening, it will be necessary to X check the opening before deciding whether to move either the wings or the grille panel. In some cases this can be done by adjustment; in other cases, where these assemblies are fully welded, hydraulic equipment must be used. The bonnet hinges on most cars are also constructed to give adjustment; therefore the bonnet can be moved forwards, backwards and sideways.

8.3.10 Boot lid alignment

Correct boot lid alignment exists when the boot lid matches the contour of the body surrounding panels.

Misalignment of the boot lid is checked visually by an inspection of the gap all round the boot lid between it and the body. It is often necessary to check more closely for boot lid alignment, because an incorrectly aligned boot lid could allow the entrance into the luggage compartment of water and dust which might cause damage to anything being carried there. A simple check is to chalk the edges of the body flanges which contact the weatherstrip on the boot lid, then close and reopen the lid, thus transferring the chalk to the weatherstrip at each point where contact is made. If this chalk line is visible around the entire weatherstrip, the boot lid sealing is perfect. Where the chalk line does not appear, the boot lid is not sealing properly and realignment will be necessary. Realignment may be possible by adjustment of the latch or hinges, but in some cases it may be necessary to bend or twist the boot lid back to its correct alignment. When the boot lid opening is at fault it must be carefully X checked, and it can only be realigned by the use of hydraulic equipment.

Figure 8.73 Centre and rear alignment check (*Rover Group Ltd*)

A	974.5 mm 38.37 in	Rear door aperture	D		1309 mm 51.54 in	Boot aperture
B	1398 mm 55.04 in	Between trim edge at base of BC-posts	E	estate	1315 mm 51.79 in	Tail door aperture
C	1959 mm 77.13 in	Rear screen aperture				

Figure 8.74 Complete upper body measuring system (*Kroll (UK) Ltd*)

Figure 8.75 MacPherson strut measuring (*Kroll (UK) Ltd*)

272

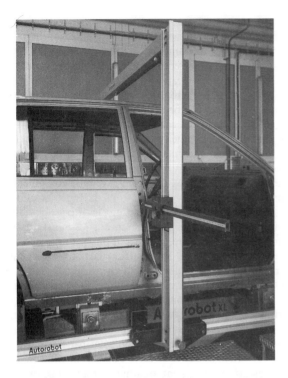

Figure 8.76 Upper body measuring system measuring door aperture (*Kroll (UK) Ltd*)

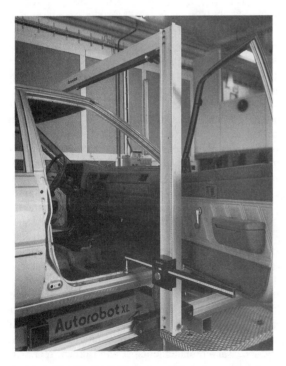

Figure 8.77 Upper body measuring system measuring sill panel (*Kroll (UK) Ltd*)

Figure 8.78 Pulling equipment being used to realign underframe members (*Car-O-Liner (UK) Ltd*)

8.4 MAJOR REPAIR TECHNIQUES

In major repair work the method of repair is to analyse the crash, establish the order in which the collision damage occurred, and reverse the order when correcting the damage. Distortion of the vehicle's underframe in the case of mono constructed vehicles, or of the chassis in composite constructed vehicles, must be rectified first before any other part of the repair is attempted. Any vehicle body under major repair will never hold its correct alignment unless underframe damage has been completely repaired first. This essential stage in the repair of the vehicle is carried out by first inspecting the damage and checking its alignment by recognized methods to locate the exact position and extent of the damage. Correction is carried out by using alignment and repair equipment in conjunction with hydraulic pulling and pushing equipment to realign any underframe members which do not align with the specified locating points (see Figure 8.78). Any members which are beyond economical repair can be cut out and replaced with new sections by using a combination of power tools and MIG welding equipment. The use of this hydraulic equipment together with the alignment and repair system will ensure precise accuracy of the complete underbody.

The next stage of the repair is the realigning and reshaping of the body shell structure, and is normally known as roughing out the damage. After alignment checks have been made, hydraulic equipment is used to push and pull the body shell back to its correct shape (Figure 8.79). It is advisable to rough out all damaged sections, even though some of these may

273

Figure 8.79 Realignment of the body shell using simultaneous push and pull hydraulic equipment (*Kroll (UK) Ltd*)

Figure 8.80 Welding in new panel sections while vehicle remains located on alignment and repair bench (*Dataliner, Geotronics Ltd*)

eventually need replacing with new panels. The reason for this is that the successful fitting of a replacement section will depend on the correct alignment of the surrounding areas, which can best be achieved by restoring them to as near the true shape as possible before the removal or cutting away of the sections beyond repair. It has been found that the use of multiple hydraulic pulling equipment used simultaneously is the most effective method when dealing with the majority of major collision work, together with standard hydraulic body jack equipment as a secondary pushing/pulling facility to aid the repair of the damage. The main advantage is the fact that the pulling is done externally from any angle while the car is

anchored securely. In cases where there is a tear in the damaged section, this must be welded up before any pulling or pushing is attempted, otherwise the tear will hinder the rectification and possibly become greater on the application of force.

An important factor is that heat can be used to relieve stresses in correcting damaged sections that have been badly creased or buckled as a result of impact. In this case the stress resulting from the buckle helps to retain the metal in its damaged state, and even after it has been restored to its correct shape by the application of pressure from hydraulic equipment, the section will tend to return to its damaged position if pressure is released. Therefore it is of considerable importance that before the pressure is taken off, these buckles or creases are hammered out with the use of heat and hand tools. When using heat for relieving stresses, it is important not to overheat the section beyond dull red, and wherever possible never to heat any point more than once as excess or repeated heating on one spot causes surface oxidation and annealing, both of which weaken the member or panel area. Heat can only be used on low-carbon steel panels and not on high-strength steels, because heat weakens the latter by disturbing the heat treatment which originally strengthened them. This is particularly so in the case of frame members, where part of the strength of the member is derived from internal stresses set up during the forming operations in the manufacturing processes.

When the roughing-out stage is complete and any major body misalignment has been corrected, then the panel assemblies which are beyond repair must be cut out in such a way that the remaining connecting flanges are left intact. These are then straightened with the use of hand tools to facilitate the locating of the new panel section, which after positioning must be checked for alignment with its surrounding panels. When the alignment of the new piece is correct it is welded into position; since the vehicle is still in the repair equipment, correct alignment is maintained (Figure 8.80), check that all doors, the bonnet and the boot lid fit and operate in the appropriate body shell openings. Minor damage such as small dints and scrapes in the original panels should now be repaired using hand tools and the conventional techniques of planishing or filling.

On completion of all repairs to structural and panel damage, the vehicle can be removed from the alignment and repair system. All dismantled mechanical and body trim parts can be reassembled, including any necessary replacements to windscreen, rear window and door windows. It is imperative that after repairing all major accident work the vehicle's steering

Figure 8.81 Vehicle showing front-end damage being lifted to be positioned on the jig (*Motor Insurance Repair Research Centre*)

Figure 8.84 New inner wing and chassis section ready to be welded in place (*Motor Insurance Repair Research Centre*)

Figure 8.82 Vehicle on jig being pulled before cutting out damaged sections (*Motor Insurance Repair Research Centre*)

Figure 8.83 Vehicle on jig showing damaged sections removed (*Motor Insurance Repair Research Centre*)

geometry is checked with optical alignment equipment and a road test carried out to assess its road worthiness and handling capabilities. When the repairer is satisfied with the vehicle's performance and that all repairs have been completed, the vehicle will need refinishing to return it to its original factory finished condition (Figures 8.81–8.88).

Although every vehicle receiving major collision damage must be individually treated, the following is a basic approach to repair procedure:

1 Inspect and check underframe or chassis for alignment using conventional equipment.
2 Rectify any misalignment of underframe or chassis using hydraulic pulling and pushing equipment, hydraulic body jack, and alignment and repair system.
3 Realign body shell, correcting damage with a combination of pulling equipment and body jack, and the use of heat and hand tools (not HSS). Also cut out and weld in any replaced buckled panels and reinforcing members which are beyond repair.
4 Repair doors, fit glass, and body trim to doors and check for ease of operation and alignment of the door in the opening in the body shell. Also check alignment of bonnet and boot lid and ease of operation.
5 Smooth and finalize minor damage to body panels with hand tools.
6 Replace all mechanical, trim and body parts.
7 Replace windscreen and rear windows if necessary.
8 Make an optical check on the vehicle's steering geometry.
9 Road test the vehicle.
10 Refinish to original factory condition.

Figure 8.85 New inner wing section welded in place (*Motor Insurance Repair Research Centre*)

Figure 8.88 Panel repairs completed (*Motor Insurance Repair Research Centre*)

Figure 8.86 Front panel positioned and welded in place (*Motor Insurance Repair Research Centre*)

Figure 8.87 Bonnet and wings positioned (*Motor Insurance Repair Research Centre*)

11 Valet car's interior and exterior.
12 Final bodyshop check for quality control of completed work, prior to returning vehicle to customer.

8.4.1 Repairs to monocoque bodies by pulling

The method of correcting damage by pulling from the outside is not new, but the application of this principle has developed into two main methods. These are direct and vector pulling.

Direct pulling
This is achieved by using systems which are designed around a base beam, sometimes mounted on castors for easy movement, with an upright beam pivoted at one end. A hydraulic push ram is mounted across the angle between the two beams. When the ram is extended, the upright beam is pushed in an arc backwards, thus putting tension on to the chain attached to the damage. This produces a direct pull between the repair and the beam (Figure 8.89).

Vector pulling
This is achieved by attaching a chain to the damaged area, then passing it over a hydraulic ram set as near to 45 degrees as possible, and anchoring it to either a rack, a tie-down system or a special clamp. Pressure is applied to the chain by extending the ram; this puts tension in the chain, which in turn creates a pulling force on the damage. As pressure is increased the angle will continuously change in response to the pressure applied (Figure 8.90).

The principle involved in a pulling repair is to apply force to the car body that is opposite to the force that originally damaged it. With a monocoque body, the engine, suspension and steering rack all contribute to

Figure 8.89 Direct pulling (*Kroll (UK) Ltd*)

Figure 8.90 Vector pulling (*Dataliner, Geotronics Ltd*)

the final strength and shape of the vehicle, so it is important not to remove them unless absolutely necessary for the type of repair being carried out.

Before beginning actual pulling, establish exactly the nature and type of damage sustained. This can only be achieved by the use of alignment and repair equipment; visual inspection is not satisfactory and can lead to inaccuracies. However, the vehicle must still be considered as a unit and the pulling force applied must act on the whole of the body and not just on the damaged parts.

The development of pulling systems has meant that in dealing with major body repair work it is possible to get a direct upward or downward pull to the front, rear or either side of the vehicle using single or multiple pulling equipment.

When repairing mono constructed bodies, basic body repair methods and a knowledge of panel beating is absolutely essential. The combination of methods always necessary in repairs is as follows: heavy external pulling, use of body jack, use of heat (only on low-carbon steels and not on high-strength steels), use of power tools and cutting out buckled sections or reinforcing members. Before any pulling commences, the angle of the pull is already known, but difficulties can arise in setting up the precise angle with the equipment. This problem can be solved by using the principle of parallel lines. First, examine the damaged parts carefully and take accurate measurements to see in which direction, and by how much, the damaged parts have moved. This means that both lateral and vertical movement must be determined to make sure the correct reversal of this damage can be achieved. When this is known, the first pulling must always start as near to the major impact as practicable.

Heavy external pulls are a must for all severe mono constructed body damage because the impact has stressed the body metal. It is important when pulling damaged sections back to their original shape not to apply all the force at one place at the same time. Spread the restoring forces by using multipulls, which will allow the pulling forces to be activated from several points on the damaged section simultaneously. This method of pulling is more effective than single pulls on severely damaged vehicles (Figures 8.91, 8.92). The body jack can also be used to assist by applying additional forces at the same time so they help each other in working the panel back into place.

With all mono constructed bodies, special attention must be given to certain load-bearing or structural members such as frame side members, inner wheel arch panels, cowl areas, cross members and the floor pan that form a part of the cross members or box sections. These must be brought back to the equivalent of their original condition, which means returned to their original shape without wrinkles or excess thinning of the metal.

The first step in making any hook-up is to anchor the pulling equipment into anchor pots, a rack system, or an alignment and repair system. Next, a pulling attachment such as a sheet metal clamp or pull hook is secured to the damaged part. Work the damage out of the metal with a hammer and dolly while the metal is under tension from the pulling equipment. Use heat sparingly as required to remove severe wrinkles. Where sheet metal damage is widespread, several hook-ups may be required to bring the damage out gradually to prevent tearing and further damage.

With the vector method of pulling, parallel pulling can be carried out in the following way. First, connect

Figure 8.91 Simultaneous multipulls on two vehicles (vector pulling) (*Blackhawk Automotive Ltd*)

Figure 8.92 Simultaneous multipulling using direct pulling (pulling towers) (*Kroll (UK) Ltd*)

the chain to the damaged part of the car, then hold the chain tightly in the direction you wish to pull and adjust the pulling unit or ram to the measured angle. It is not necessary to have the chain vertically in line with the direction of pull, but it is important that the ram should not be set at an angle lower than 45 degrees; that the chain links are set in line without any twist; and that the chain between the ram and chain anchor point should always lean towards the car. As soon as tension is applied to the chain, safety wires must be fitted in case the clamp or chain tears away from the main structure of the car.

Rectification of various damage types
Although every accident is different and must be treated individually, it is possible to generalize and divide accident damage into several types.

Each type can be pulled and pushed straight in a number of ways. For instance, if a vehicle has been in a head-on collision, and has suffered a straightforward crumple, secure the undamaged part of the underbody or chassis leg and pull out the crumple section in the direct line of damage. If the vehicle was struck by another, or if it has hit a low obstacle, it will have sagged. To repair this, secure one end of the vehicle, provide a support at the point of the bend, and pull down the raised end. With a twist, hold and support the undamaged part and apply a downward force to the front while allowing the other end to pivot up. A diamond can be difficult. Hold one side of the vehicle and, pull along the line of the diagonal. The tendency will be for the whole of the vehicle to move, so hold the opposite corner to the pull. To repair severe side damage, push out and stretch the crushed side. It will also help to pull from the outside; this is because the passenger compartment is very strong, and repairing damage to it requires considerable force.

8.4.2 Repairs to underbody damage of monocoque vehicles

The underbody is the foundation on which the vehicle is built. It is of the utmost importance, therefore, first to determine the extent of the collision damage to the underbody and then to correct it. The repairer must be able to determine what, if any, damage exists before attempting a repair. It is also necessary to determine whether any underbody misalignment exists which requires repair before attempting to correct body alignment and damage. The majority of body repair shops have alignment and repair equipment capable of handling this type of repair. Although at present the majority of British manufacturers are producing motor vehicle bodies designed and built on mono or unitary construction principles, there are still some special sports models which have independent chassis construction, in addition to the available European and American vehicles which are based on composite construction. Consequently body repair establishments must make provisions to deal with any such vehicles which may be brought in for repair.

The main idea of straightening underbody damage is to exert force in the reverse direction from that of the collision impact. Alignment and repair equipment permits several pulling set-ups to be made at one time. This type of equipment allows the vehicle to be aligned using either brackets or a measuring system. Repairs are carried out using a combination of pulling equipment, body jacks, chains, clamps, wood blocks and welding equipment. The severity of the damage decides the method of repair and techniques to be used. In the case of a vehicle which has received extreme damage, and in which the underbody has twisted badly, the method of repair is that the vehicle must be mounted on to the repair system and the exact amount of distortion established by using either brackets or a measuring system. While the vehicle is still mounted on the system, the underbody must be pulled back into alignment first and then checked against the manufacturer's data, especially the critical suspension and engine mounting positions.

First, rough out the damage but do not remove any panels unless it is necessary. Body damage and alignment should, wherever possible, be corrected at the same time as any underbody damage. Work can be made easier by stripping off any body panels or mechanical parts which might interfere with accessibility to the damaged area. As side and cross members are usually formed from low-carbon steel, heat may be used to relieve stresses in badly creased areas. However, when these members are made from high-strength steel, heat must not be used because of its weakening effect; the metal must be repaired in a cold state. For low-carbon steel, heat may be applied with an oxyacetylene welding torch. Only a very little heat is required to bring the colour of the heated member to a dull red, at which time it is at a proper temperature to be worked. Start to heat the buckled portion or damaged area well out near the edge. Pan the flame over the entire buckled area so that it is heated uniformly. Best results can be obtained by moving the flame in a circular motion until the entire area is heated. Heating well out towards the edges of the damaged area first will remove the chill from the surrounding area, thus preventing the damaged area from cooling too rapidly.

Pulling equipment can be used for heavy external pulling by anchoring it to the underbody members using special bolt-on clamps or chain attachments and pulling the damaged section back into line. Where it is difficult to obtain an anchor point owing to inaccessibility, a substantial metal tab is welded on to the member; this can be used for pulling and later removed. In some cases a combination of pulling and pushing is needed when correcting damage, and this requires a heavy-duty body jack to be used in conjunction with pulling equipment. Wood blocks can be used to spread the load to prevent distortion. As the repair proceeds with a combination of pulling, pushing and heating, continuous checks should be made for alignment, as it is sometimes necessary to overcorrect to allow for springback in the metal structure. A final alignment check should be made after the tension is released.

8.4.3 Wheel alignment (steering geometry)

Over the years there has been increased awareness of the importance of wheel alignment, and particularly four-wheel alignment, as an integral part of the major crash repair procedure. Straightening a vehicle involves two separate alignment operations. First, the body must be aligned, making sure that suspension mounting points are in the correct position. Once the vehicle is jigged, in many cases a mixture of old and new suspension components is fitted. Second, a full geometry check must be undertaken to satisfy the repairer that the car is within the manufacturer's tolerances after the repair.

Wheel alignment has an important role to play in the overall safety of the modern vehicle, and proper testing equipment in this area is now vital. Much of the new technology caters for what is now regarded as four-wheel or total alignment. Modern vehicles have become far more sophisticated. They may have active rear suspension, which can also be computer controlled. These set-ups have an element of steering built in to complement the work done by the front wheels: the system is commonly known as rear wheel steering or four-wheel steering. Rear wheel alignment with a fractional variance from the manufacturer's setting can now be critical to a car's handling and steering. It is not normal for cars to veer to left or right: suspension systems are designed and set up by the manufacturer so that the car will travel straight, regardless of road crown.

The main purpose of wheel alignment is to allow the wheels to roll without scuffing, dragging or slipping on the road. The proper alignment of suspension and steering systems centres around the accuracy of six control angles: camber, caster, steering angle inclination (SAI), scrub radius, toe (in and out), and turning radius (Figure 8.93).

Inspection and test drive

Thorough visual inspection and a test drive on a straight flat road should show whether the car needs to go for wheel alignment. The basic checks are:

1 Measure ride height.
2 Does the vehicle appear level or is there any sagging?
3 Are the tyres properly inflated and of correct size and specification?
4 Is there any uneven wear on the tyres?

(Facing page)

Figure 8.93 Wheel alignment (*Sun Electric UK Ltd*)

(a) Front wheel toe

The individual front wheel toe angle *A* is the angle of the front wheel from the straight overhead. The total toe is the sum of angles *A* and *B*. The term 'toe-in' is used when the wheels are closer together at the front, and 'toe-out' is when the wheels are closer at the rear. The purpose of toe is to ensure that the wheels are in the straight ahead position when driving. An incorrect setting would cause excessive tyre wear.

(b) Castor

The castor angle is the forward or backward tilt of the king pin or ball joints, and is measured as an angle from the vertical. A positive castor is when the top ball joint is behind the bottom ball joint. A negative castor is the opposite. The purpose of castor is to cause the front wheels to maintain a straight ahead position and to return to the straight ahead after making a turn. Incorrect castor will not cause tyre wear but would cause the vehicle to wander on the road and not return to the straight ahead after cornering.

(c) Camber

The camber angle is the inward or outward tilt of the wheel when looking from the front of the vehicle. A positive camber is when the top of the wheel tilts away from the vehicle. A negative camber is when the top of the wheel tilts towards the vehicle. The purpose of camber is to bring the centre point of the steering in the centre of the tyre so the tyre turns on one point. This will decrease the effort required to turn the steering. Incorrect camber will cause the tyres to wear on the inside or outside, heavy steering and poor directional control.

(d) KPI (SAI)

The KPI or SAI is the angle formed by a line drawn through the king pin or ball joints with a line drawn vertical. The purpose of KPI is the same as for camber. The KPI will reduce the need for large camber angles, and therefore reduce the tyre wear by allowing the wheel to be near vertical.

(e) Included angle

The included angle is the sum of KPI (SAI) and camber. The point of intersection of KPI and camber gives the point about which the wheel rotates when the steering is turned. This point should be in the centre of the tyre where it contacts the road. Incorrect included angle would cause heavy steering and excessive tyre wear.

(f) Toe on 20° turns

The toe on turns angle allows the front wheels to follow different arcs when cornering, and is measured when the inner wheel is at 20° from the straight ahead. The purpose of toe on turns is to allow for the greater distance of travel of the outer wheel when cornering. Incorrect toe on turns would cause excessive tyre wear.

(g) Set back

Front wheel set back is the amount that one front wheel is ahead of the other. Excessive set back would cause the vehicle steering to pull.

(h) Rear wheel reference toe

The front to rear wheel alignment measures the amount of out of alignment of the front and rear wheels. If the wheels are out of line the vehicle will 'crab', which means that the vehicle will appear to be driving sideways.

(a) A   B   Front

(b) A = castor angle   Front   A

(c) Top   A   A = camber angle

(d) Top   A   A = KPI (SAI)

(e) Top   A   A = included angle

(f) A   20°   A = measured value

(g) Front   Set back

(h) A   Front   A = Measured value

Figure 8.94 Four-wheel alignment: steering wheel straight ahead (*Sun Electric UK Ltd*)

5 Low-speed wobble may show up a separated tyre tread.
6 High speed may reveal steering wear and odd noises, indicating loose or damaged parts.

Pre-alignment check
This breaks down into two areas: tyre inspection and steering component inspection. Tyre inspection, front and rear, is as follows:

1 Check for any unusual wear patterns: camber, toe wear, inflation wear, cupping.
2 Check for any physical problems: ply separation, dry rot.
3 Check tyre size and type: same size side-to-side, same brand and tread pattern. Do not mix radial-ply and bias-ply tyres.
4 Tyre pressure and wheels: check pressure and set to specifications; check for bent or eggshape rims.

Steering component inspection is as follows:

1 Tie rod assemblies.
2 Idler arm and bushings.
3 Centre link and joints.
4 Manual steering gear: check for excessive play and leaks, check U-joint at steering shaft.
5 Power-assisted steering (run engine): check for excessive play; inspect all hoses and seals; check fluid level and belt condition; check power-assisted balance.
6 Ball joints and wheel bearings.
7 All bushings, front and rear.
8 Coil springs, torsion bars and shock absorbers.
9 Calibrate alignment equipment.

Wheel alignment procedure
Two-wheel alignment is still used in many workshops as it takes less workshop time, is easier and requires less expensive equipment. However, its efficiency relies on the car having two parallel axles, and front and rear wheels perfectly in line with each other. Four-

wheel alignment owes much to computer technology, which can instantly check and define the alignment of a vehicle. As full wheel alignment starts from a centre-line reference on the rear axle and then checks all steering geometry angles on all four wheels, a simultaneous four-wheel check will speed up the entire operation. Computer-based alignment systems use computer power to carry out the calculations, so that you can be certain of centralizing the steering wheel and alignment of the vehicle. This ensures that the steering wheel spokes are horizontal when the car is travelling straight ahead (Figure 8.94).

8.4.4 Replacement of damaged panels

Damaged panels can be removed from vehicles by using:

1 A hacksaw and metal cutting snips.
2 A hammer and thin narrow-bladed chisel.
3 Either a conventional drill, a Zipcut tool, or a spot-welding removal tool (air operated) to drill out each spot weld.
4 An air chisel with appropriate cutting tools.
5 A power saw having either a rotary vibrating blade or a straight reciprocating blade.
6 A plasma arc cutting torch.
7 A combination of any of the above methods.

A severely damaged inner panel such as a wheel arch can be cut out using the oxyacetylene torch. However, this method is not recommended because of the very ragged, uneven cut edge left by the torch. A better method would be the plasma cutting torch, which leaves a fine cut edge for panel replacement. With both of these methods it is important to be aware of the fire risks.

Lapped and spot-welded joints of panels must be drilled first and carefully separated with a narrow-bladed cold chisel (Figure 8.95). The positions of the spot welds are indicated by small circular dis-colourations of the metal. These are centre popped, then drilled 4.8 mm or 5.6 mm sufficiently far to break the joint; it is not always necessary to go right through both parts of the panel, as in most cases if the top panel is drilled the joint will break. Alternatively a cobalt drill specially designed for cutting out spot welds can be used, either in a conventional air or electric drilling machine, or fitted to an air attachment designed specifically as a spot-welding removal tool. Another alternative is the Zipcut tool, which again will fit into a conventional drilling machine and which cuts round the spot weld leaving a hole in the top panel surface (see Figure 8.96). In some cases a fine-toothed hacksaw blade, fitted in a padsaw handle, and

Figure 8.95 Drilling out spot welds for the removal of damaged panels (*Motor Insurance Repair Research Centre*)

Figure 8.97 Cutting out damaged panels with a power saw (*Motor Insurance Repair Research Centre*)

Figure 8.96 Zipcut tool for the removal of spot welds (*Sykes-Pickavant Ltd*)

Figure 8.98 Alignment of new panel sections (*Motor Insurance Repair Research Centre*)

a pair of snips or shears can be used to remove damaged sections of panels. A tool for removing damaged panels is the power chisel set, which comprises a compressed air gun having interchangeable chisel heads. This sheet metal cutter is capable of speedy and accurate removal of panels or parts of panels that have to be replaced. Power saws can also be used in the removal of damaged sections: either the rotary saw with a vibrating blade, or the straight reciprocating blade (see Figure 8.97). Both of these tools give an excellent fine cut edge suitable for instant rewelding without any dressing.

The bodywork having been straightened and aligned as much as possible, the new panel should be positioned and held in place by two or three clamps and all adjacent panels checked for alignment with the new panel (Figure 8.98). To ensure a perfect fit it is often necessary to trim the adjoining panels of ragged edges, and to straighten out the locating flanges using hand tools (Figure 8.99). When making a close butt weld, exact alignment is ensured by positioning and

Figure 8.99 Cleaning up the locating flanges (*Motor Insurance Repair Research Centre*)

Figure 8.100 Welding-in new panel section (*Motor Insurance Repair Research Centre*)

clamping the new panel outside the old so that a scriber can be run down the edge of the old panel where the joint will come. Excess metal then being carefully trimmed and the edge dressed up with hammer and dolly, the new panel is ready to be welded into place. Always brush on weld-through anticorrosive primer before welding. The panel should be aligned, clamped and checked. It should next be tack welded at several points; then the clamps should be removed and the panel rechecked for alignment. If this is not satisfactory the tack welds are easily broken. When alignment is correct, further tack welds may be placed between the first set. To avoid distortion only short sections between the tack welds should be welded at a time and the metal allowed to cool (Figure 8.100). In some cases it is helpful in confining the heat, and thus reducing the chance of distortion, to place wet cloth packing either side and a little distance away from the weld; alternatively there is a foam type of material which will act as a heat barrier (Section 8.4.7). Panels that were originally spot welded, but cannot be spot welded back, can be MIG welded in the course of

repair; the welds are made in the same place by welding through the holes in the adjacent panel which were left when the original spot welds were drilled out. This method is known as plug welding. Another method of securing panels is to MIG braze them in place, but one must remember that although MIG brazing will cause less distortion than MIG welding, it is not as strong. Therefore if the particular panel is a load-bearing panel, it must be welded in fully to obtain the maximum strength for the particular panel assembly. MIG welding has the advantage of reducing distortion to a minimum, owing to the effect of the inert gas shielding the spread of heat around the weld zone. This makes butt joints in panel assemblies more easy to accomplish, as less dressing up and planishing is required than in gas welding. Another advantage arises from the automatic feeding of filler material into the weld pool, which results in better penetration in all weld positions. As this equipment can be used both to weld and to spot weld, it is widely employed as a means of welding in new panel assemblies.

8.4.5 Partial panel replacement

The reason for replacing only part of a panel can vary according to the type of repair. Usually it is quicker and therefore less expensive than full replacement. If sectioning does not save on time or money, then the part is completely replaced: that is, when the repanelling and straightening reaches the cost of the complete new panel. Some manufacturers design repair panels specially for these purposes.

Part panel replacement has long been established as an effective way of repairing body damage on all cars. Depending on the type of damage involved, it used to be common practice to replace an entire sheet metal panel; by means of a part panel repair it is possible to replace only those panel sections which are actually damaged. The possibilities for sectional repairs to load-bearing and non-load-bearing parts have been taken into account during the initial phase of development by manufacturers. All instructions given regarding the locations of cut lines for sectional repairs to load-bearing parts must be strictly adhered to. Sectional repairs to vehicles damaged in an accident should be confined to body parts in which the damage has not produced any loss of strength sufficient to jeopardize safety. Only welding materials reaching the design weld strength should be used. Moreover, a body alignment and welding jig must always be used for repair operations such as sectional replacement of the side-member/apron-panel assembly. This ensures satisfactory repairs and adherence to the specified dimensions. Manufacturers have also carried out numerous strength tests, and extended trials (crash tests) have proved that part panel replacement is just as effective as replacing complete new panels. Provided repairs are expertly carried out, all repair procedures using part panels will result in the same standards of strength and operational safety being maintained as for a new vehicle.

To carry out this type of repair (see Figures 8.101a–f), the initial procedure is to make certain that the sections to be joined are from identical models. Then determine the most suitable point at which to make the joint: this will be influenced by the length of the weld, the amount of distortion likely to occur in making the weld, and the ease with which it can be dressed up. Remove the bulk of the unwanted section by cutting it away with a power saw, leaving an allowance of about 20 mm from the joint line, which can be trimmed to size when the pieces of the panels are separated. Where it is possible to fit the two sections on the vehicle, it is considered good practice to trim only one edge and to set the panels up with one section overlapping the other, as this enables a check to be made on the alignment of any surrounding or adjacent panels such as bonnet edges and door edges. A good butt joint is achieved by cutting through. When the alignment is correct, the two sections are tack welded along the length of the joint. The joint is then hammered level and fully welded. After this it is planished using normal techniques to achieve a smooth, undetectable joint. If this is impossible owing to inaccessibility, the weld should be hammered in using a shrinking dolly and the weld area filled.

Vehicles that have undergone an extended corrosion prevention treatment to prevent body perforation by rust must be repaired using replacement panels coated by the new (cathodic) priming process. These panels are identified by corresponding stickers. Therefore remove as little as possible of the cathodic primer coating on replacement panels during sanding or other abrading operations, e.g. on spot-weld flanges or in areas where welds are to be made later. When repairs are being carried out in the underbody area, the zone in question must then be treated with underbody wax. The areas outside the side members and the wheel houses must also be treated with underbody protection material.

8.4.6 Repairing extensively damaged panels

Whenever possible it is best to repair severely damaged panels while they are still attached to the body shell. One advantage of leaving the panel in position is that it remains rigid while being processed. As already explained, it is difficult to hold a panel firmly when it is not attached to the body, and to beat a panel that moves with each blow is most unsatisfactory. Second, the shape is maintained while the panel is in position, and this allows the edges of the panel to be lined up with such parts as bonnets, doors and boot lids. In addition the use of the body jack, while the panel is fixed to the body, allows full use of the attachments designed for roughing out such parts.

Having decided whether the panel will be repaired on or off the job the actual repair can then be roughed out, keeping in mind the fact that the shape needs reforming with as little stretching of the metal as possible. The original damaging force could have stretched the panel and, while reshaping, further stretching should be reduced to a minimum by the use of such methods as pushing out the damage with a body jack fitted with suitable rubber flex head; or using a hardwood block between the body jack and panel; or using hardwood blocks in conjunction with the hammer to eliminate the metal-to-metal contact. Where necessary, anneal creased sections with the oxyacetylene welding torch prior to removing them. As the roughing out proceeds, weld any tears in the metal so as to gain a rigid panel as soon as possible. Very stretched sections can be shrunk by the use of heat spots during the roughing out. A boxwood mallet, in conjunction with a suitable dolly block for the shape of the panel being repaired, should not be used as an initial smoothing or levelling step prior to the final planishing. The actual smoothing with the planishing hammer and dolly should never be started until the correct shape is formed in the panel. At this stage the normal processes of planishing, dressing up, filing and picking up low spots should not be adopted until the job is completed. Either because certain parts of the repair are inaccessible or because of their overstretched condition, it may be necessary to use solder filling or plastic filler to achieve a smooth finish.

8.4.7 Repair methods using heat barrier material

This is a method of repair using a specially formulated compound where heat would cause a problem of distortion or overheating of adjacent materials when welding.

The Cold Front heat sink chemical compound was originally developed for the American space programme. This heat barrier material, based on a chemical formula of magnesium aluminium silicate, prevents the conduction of heat through metal, thus eliminating the risk of distortion to panels, or damage to areas immediately adjacent to any welding operation. When the material is applied to a metal panel on a vehicle

Figure 8.101 Replacement of part panels:
(a) clamping new panel section into place (b) cutting in
(c) tack welding (d) section fully welded in (e) dressing
the welded joints (f) soldering the joint and filing to a
finish (*Motor Insurance Repair Research Centre*)

body undergoing repair, it prevents the transfer of heat past the Cold Front barrier, giving complete protection to glass, rubber, plastic, paint and any material likely to be damaged by close proximity to the high temperatures which are generated during the processes of welding, brazing or soldering.

The method of application is as follows:

1 Apply generously, as using too little can allow heat damage. Apply to one side of the metal in light gauge work (20 SWG) and both sides of the metal when working with heavy gauge (above 3 mm) for maximum protection.
2 When the mound of material begins to warm up, it becomes saturated with heat. Once saturated, it will allow heat to be conducted through the metal. If there is still work to be carried out, place more Cold Front material on top of the existing mound to delay the conduction of the heat.
3 Always apply the material as close to the area of repair as possible.
4 Damage can be caused by radiant heat as well as conducted heat. The material acts as an effective heat shield against radiant heat when it is applied over the surface to be protected. Be sure not to leave any cavities or depressions when spreading.
5 It is safest to protect the repair area completely around the heat zone. However, if protection is only needed in one direction, the heat barrier should be spread five to six times as wide as the area to which the heat is being applied.
6 Metals have different conducting characteristics: copper, brass and aluminium conduct heat more rapidly than steel. Therefore the better the metal is as a conductor, the more heat barrier should be applied when working with that metal.

Cold Front heat barrier is odourless, non-toxic and harmless to skin. It will not stain surfaces, and any residue can be washed off with cold water once the repair is completed.

The ability of Cold Front to act as a total heat barrier is demonstrated by holding a strip of 20 SWG metal in the bare hand after applying a line of Cold Front halfway along the strip, then heating the portion of the strip above the line to red heat. The part of the strip being held in the hand remains completely cold (Figure 8.102).

8.4.8 Door hanging

Door hanging requires particular care, as the fitting of doors is one of the most essential features of crash repair work. The most important aspect when dealing with the hanging of doors is that a door which is

Figure 8.102 Application of Cold Front heat barrier material (*Gray–Camping Ltd*)

known to be the correct shape should never be altered to fit a door opening that is out of alignment. In addition, the resetting of door hinges must not be used as a method of rehanging doors without first checking for and correcting any misalignment.

Hinges used on the modern vehicle can take a good deal of force without altering their settings. In cases where hinges have been subjected to collision damage, the hinge transmits the damaging force to the pillar or door frame, causing twisting and misalignment. Sometimes hinges are so excessively damaged that they need replacing, although this is not the complete answer to correcting misalignment troubles arising from such damage. Where new hinges are necessary a close inspection and comparison should be made with the identical hinge mounting on the opposite side of the car, and any misalignment of this mounting position should be rectified before fitting the new hinge.

When it is considered that the hinge mounting points are correct, the doors should be hung in their respective positions and all screws or hinge fixing bolts placed loosely to allow the door to be realigned according to the car manufacturer's adjustments. The fixing bolts should be tightened if possible while the door is in its closed position. In most cases this is not possible, which means that the doors have to be held open while at the same time endeavouring to keep alignment correct while the bolts are tightened. If the door aperture is correct and the door is not twisted, with slight adjustment to the hinge position the door can be made to fit into its appropriate opening.

When the door will not fit into the body opening, the hinges should be tightened in the main adjustment position and the striker plate of the lock mechanism should be removed from the locking pillar to allow the door to swing freely. This gives a truer indication of the swing of the door as the opening is being corrected with the use of hydraulic equipment. The door should then be closed as far as possible, and the points stopping the door from entering the door aperture should be noted. Correction in most cases can be made by diagonal pushing with the body jack within the aperture. Measurements should be taken both before and after applying the pressure so that the effectiveness of the realignment of the door opening can be assessed. This checking and pushing must continue until the door is a good fit inside the door aperture.

8.4.9 Motor vehicle glazing systems

Since the introduction of legislation on the compulsory wearing of seatbelts for front seat passengers in the early 1980s, both the type and style of glass fitted into windscreens have changed. Prior to 1980, toughened glass, which shatters into tiny, relatively harmless pieces when broken, and which can dangerously obscure a driver's vision, was used by many vehicle manufacturers. This glass was indirectly glazed on to the body and secured using a self-tensioning rubber weather strip fitted to the aperture. With the seatbelt legislation in force, however, safety standards were improved, bringing an increased use of laminated glass, which is the type that remains in place when broken and therefore allows the driver to continue the journey.

This resulted in a change in glazing methods, with laminated glass being increasingly secured by the process of direct glazing. This is a method of fitting a glass unit to a vehicle by chemically bonding it to the prepared aperture using specialized compound sealants. This method provides two definite design benefits. It gives an aerodynamic profile, and also increases the strength of the windscreen, thus making it safer and more weather resistant. As well as being easier to fit on the production line, the majority of direct glazing is now done by robots. A direct glazed windscreen can also be replaced to its original specification without affecting the structural integrity of the vehicle.

Indirect glazed windscreen removal and replacement

The two basic types of safety glass used in the car windscreen are laminated and toughened. Laminated glass is of a sandwich construction and consists of

Figure 8.103 Laminated glass

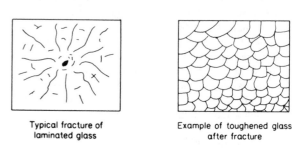

Typical fracture of laminated glass

Example of toughened glass after fracture

Figure 8.104 Characteristic breaking pattern of laminated and toughened glass

two pieces of thin glass one on either side of, and firmly united to, a piece of transparent reinforcing known as the interlayer (Figure 8.103). Although such a glass may crack, forming a spider's web pattern (Figure 8.104), it holds together and the panel remains in one piece except under conditions of the most violent impact. Toughened glass is produced by the process of heating a solid piece of glass and then rapidly cooling it so that its liability to fracture is greatly reduced and its strength increased to about six times that of untreated glass. If fracture should take place, the resulting fragments consist of very small, comparatively harmless particles (Figure 8.104).

In major accident damage, removal and replacement of the windscreen is an essential feature of the repair. Many windscreens and rear windows are held in place by a rubber weatherstrip which is usually of single-piece construction. Both glass and any outside trim mouldings, if used, are recessed into the weatherstrip. It also has a recess which fits over the body flanges all round the opening for the glass. It is this portion of the weatherstrip that holds the entire assembly in place.

Indirect types of glazing systems can be identified for each specific model by referring to the body section of the relevant manufacturer's repair manual. The rubber weather seals used are either mastic sealed, dry glazed, self-sealing or push fit (Figure 8.105). The self-sealing types are held in place by a removable centre filler strip and can be either mastic sealed

(a)

(b)

(d)

(c)

Figure 8.105 Indirect glazing system: (a) mastic-sealed (b) dry glazed (c) self-sealing (d) push fit

or dry glazed (Figure 8.105c). All the systems are used with either a rubber weather strip moulding with a sealing compound (Figure 8.105a) or a rubber weather strip moulding without a sealing compound (Figure 8.105b). The rubber weather strip has two rebates, one for the glass and one to seat over the metal flange of the body aperture. It is the contact area of the aperture that requires careful attention whenever the glazing is disturbed or removed. In all cases it is essential that the aperture is correctly painted prior to refitting any of the weather seals.

In order to remove a windscreen which is fitted with a self-tensioning weatherstrip, the following procedure must be carried out. First, cover the bonnet to protect the paintwork. Then, working from the inside of the car, remove any instrument panel mouldings or trim which may interfere with the removal of the windscreen. Also, working from the outside of the

Figure 8.106 Using pull cords to fit windscreens

vehicle, remove any windscreen chrome mouldings which may be fitted into the weatherstrip. Again working from the inside and starting from one of the top corners, pry the rubber weatherstrip off the body flange with a screwdriver. At the same time press firmly against the glass with your hand adjacent to the portion of the rubber lip being removed, or bump the glass with the palm of the hand; this should force the entire assembly over the body flange. The windscreen can then be removed from the body opening.

To replace the windscreen, first clean the glass channel in the rubber weatherstrip to be sure that all traces of sealer and any broken glass are removed. Place a bead of new sealing compound all round the weatherstrip in the glass channel. Work the glass into the glass channel of the weatherstrip and be sure it is properly seated all the way round. Lay the windscreen on a bench, suitably covered to prevent scratching, so that the curved ends are pointing upwards and in this position the pull cords used to seat the rubber lip over the body flange can be inserted into the metal channel on the weatherstrip (Figure 8.106). One or two cords may be used. Where two cords are normally used they can be pulled in opposite directions, which will make the fitting of the windscreen easier. Commence with one cord from the bottom right-hand side of the windscreen, leaving about one foot spare for pulling. Start the second cord from the bottom left-hand corner and proceed to the right, following round up to the top left-hand corner. Apply sealer all round the

metal lip on the body aperture. Place the entire unit in the windscreen opening with the cord ends hanging inside the vehicle. An assistant can help by pressing against the glass from the outside while each cord is pulled out of the groove. As the cord is pulled out, the rubber lip is seated firmly over the body flange. A rubber mallet can be used to tap the unit around the outside so as to seat the entire windscreen assembly firmly in place. Any surplus sealer can be cleaned off with white spirit.

The procedure for removing a windscreen fitted with a self-sealing weatherstrip is first to locate the joint in the filler strip which runs right through the centre of the weatherstrip. The strip is then carefully eased up and pulled out slowly around the entire assembly. This relieves the tension on the glass which can then be lifted out of the weatherstrip by easing one corner first. To replace this type of windscreen the metal lip on the body aperture is sealed with a sealer, the appropriate channel in the weatherstrip is then placed over this lip and seated all the way round the body aperture. The windscreen is fitted into the glass channel on the weatherstrip with the aid of a special tool which enables the glass channel lip to be lifted, thus allowing the glass to slip easily into position. A small brush is used to apply a solution of soap and water to the filler channel. This assists the filler strip installation. A specially designed tool is used to insert the filler strip into its channel.

Direct glazed windscreen removal and replacement
The method of direct glazing of windscreens, also known as bonding, is very popular with motor manufacturers. This process involves the bonding of glass into the aperture. Some of the advantages claimed for direct glazing are as follows:

1 Increased rigidity and strength caused by integration of the glass into the body of the vehicle, reducing the need for supporting members and improving visibility with enlarged glass areas.
2 Weight reduction.
3 Improved aerodynamics by the deletion of rubber surrounds, aiding fuel economy.
4 A better seal against the weather, eliminating the need for resealing.
5 Increased protection against car and contents thefts.

Various bonding materials are used in direct glazing. Some require heating to induce a chemical reaction to create adhesion, while others will cure at room temperature.

Polyurethane and silicone materials are usually supplied as a pumpable tape. They are cold cured and the material is dispensed on to the glass through a specially formed nozzle out on the end of a cartridge. This can be done with the aid of a hand operated or compressed air cartridge gun. These materials are highly viscous in their uncured state, enabling a high degree of manoeuvrability within the glass aperture to ensure a good seal.

The sealant itself is either one- or two-component polyurethane. The latter contains an accelerator compatible with the adhesive; this is applied evenly to the perimeter of the windscreen (Figure 8.107). Once this is achieved, the glass is placed into the aperture using glass suckers and aligned before securing. When a one-component polyurethane is used the car can be driven away in four to six hours: if a two-component polyurethane is used it takes only 30 minutes to cure, allowing the vehicle to be back on the road within an hour of the repair starting.

To remove the glass from the vehicle, the bonding material has to be cut. This can be achieved by using a piano wire, a special cutter or a hot knife, as follows:

Piano wire Before using this method of removal there are certain safety precautions that should be observed. Gloves should be worn to protect the hands, and safety glasses or goggles should be used for eye protection in the event of the wire or glass breaking. When the finishers or mouldings have been removed to expose the bonded area of the glass, the wire has to be fed through the bonding. This is done by piercing a hole through the bonding and feeding the wire through with the aid of pliers. Handles can be fixed to the ends of the wire to allow a pulling action (Figure 8.108).

Pneumatic or electric cutter (oscillating) This is an air or electric powered tool to which special shaped blades to suit specific vehicle models are fitted. The tool removes windscreens that have been bonded with polyurethane adhesives (see Figure 8.109).

Hot knife The hot knife can be used by one person cutting from the outside of the vehicle. It can cut round the average bonded windscreen and clean off the excess remaining adhesive while minimizing the risk of damaging the car bodywork. Before use, all trim around the windscreen, both inside and outside, should be removed (see Figure 8.110) The cutting medium is provided by a heated blade which is placed under the edge of the glass and pulled around the perimeter, melting the bonding to release the windscreen. It is used in conjunction with an air supply, which constantly blows on to the cutting area of the blade. This prevents the heat dissipating along the blade and gives a constant temperature as well as eliminating smoke and fumes emitted from the cutting

Figure 8.107 Direct glazing with moisture-cured urethane

Figure 8.108 Removing direct glazing using a piano wire

Figure 8.109 Electric windscreen cutter (*Fein/George Marshall* (*Power Tools Ltd*))

Figure 8.110 Welwyn hot knife (*Welwyn Tool Co. Ltd*)

operation. Overheating can result in toxic fumes being given off and a charcoal filter mask should be worn as a safety precaution.

Before glazing can be replaced, the bonding surfaces must be prepared correctly. The residue of the original sealer left in the aperture has to be trimmed to ensure there is a smooth layer for the new sealer to adhere to, and to allow the glass to seat in the correct position. Various sealants for windscreen replacement are available.

The surfaces are then prepared with the materials included in the individual manufacturer's glass replacement kit, that is sealer application gun with bonding material, suction cups and leak test equipment, following the instructions provided. There is little variation in the sequence of operations, which is typically as follows:

1 Using a sharp knife, trim and level off sealer remaining in the vehicle windscreen aperture. Remove loose sealer. Areas where bare metal is exposed must be treated with etch primer.
2 If the original windscreen is to be refitted, level off the remnants of the old sealer. Take care not to damage the black ceramic edging.
3 Apply the cleaning solvent provided in the repair kit to the windscreen aperture and the inboard edges of the screen, then wipe both aperture and screen with a clean cloth.
    Warning: when working with solvents and primers, use PVC gloves or apply barrier cream to hands.
4 Take the spacer blocks from the repair kit, remove the adhesive backing, and fit them in the original position on the windscreen aperture. Ensure that the differently shaped blocks are located correctly.
5 Fit the suction cups to the outer face of the windscreen and place the screen in the vehicle. Centralize the screen in the body aperture. Take strips of masking tape and attach them across the join between the body and the screen. These strips afford a guide when finally fitting the screen after sealant has been applied. Cut the masking tape strips at the glass edges and remove the screen.
6 Shake the tin containing the glass primer for at least 30 seconds. Then, using the felt swab, apply the primer evenly along the screen perimeter. When dry, wipe with a clean cloth. Repeat the above process, this time by cutting the applicator head and using it to apply a coat of primer 17 mm (0.7 in) wide to the windscreen aperture.
7 Immerse a cartridge of sealer in water at a temperature of 60°C for approximately 30 minutes.

Pierce the sealer cartridge in the centre of its threaded end and fit the precut nozzle. Remove the lid from the other end, shake out any crystals present and install the cartridge in the applicator gun.

8 Apply the sealer in a smooth continuous bead around the edge of the windscreen. The sealer bead should be 12 mm (0.5 in) high and 7 mm (0.25 in) wide at its base.

9 Lift the screen using the suction cups and offer it up to the vehicle, top edge leading. Carefully align the masking tape strips, then lower the screen into position. Remove the suction cups. Testing for leaks, using either leak testing equipment or spraying with water, may be carried out immediately. **Caution**: if a leak or leaks are detected, apply sealer to the area and retest. Do not remove the screen and attempt to spread the sealer already applied.

10 If leaks are not present, fit the windscreen finishers. Heat the windscreen finishers to 45°C and, commencing at one end of the screen lower corners, press into position around its entire perimeter. Remove the fascia's protective covering. Trim the lower spacer blocks.

11 Fit retaining clips as necessary. Fit the windscreen wiper finisher panel and air intake mouldings and the wiper arms and blades.

Caution: do not slam the vehicle's doors with the windows fully closed until the screen is fully cured.

Warning: the integrity of the vehicle's safety features can be impaired if incorrect windscreen replacement bonding materials and fitting instructions are used. The manufacturer's instructions should be adhered to at all times.

8.4.10 Water leak detection

The general principles for searching for the location of water leaks on the vehicle are not specific to any particular model and can apply to all vehicles.

First, start by obtaining as much information as possible from the customer as to when, where and how the leak occurs, and also whether the water appears to be clean or dirty. If these facts are not known, considerable time could be spent checking the wrong areas of the vehicle.

Tools and equipment
The following tools and equipment are recommended:

Garden spray (hand pump pressure type)
Wet/dry vacuum cleaner
Torch
Mirror
Seal lipping tool
Trim panel removing tool
Small wooden or plastic wedges
Dry compressed air supply
Hot air blower
Sealant applicator
Ultrasonic leak detector

Locating the leak
Locating the source of the water leak involves a logical approach together with a combination of skill and experience. For the purpose of locating the leak the vehicle should be considered in three specific areas: the front interior space, the rear passenger space, and the boot space. From the information provided by the customer the body repairer should be able to determine which area is the right one on which to concentrate.

Having identified the area of the leak, the repairer must find the actual point where the water is entering the vehicle. An ordinary garden spray, of the type which can be pressurized and adjusted to deliver water in the form of a very fine spray or a small powerful jet, has been found to be very effective in helping to locate most leaks. Using a mirror and torch will help to see into any dark corners.

Testing
The sequence of testing is particularly important. Always start at the lowest point and work upwards. The reason for this is to avoid masking a leak in one place while testing in another. If for example testing was to commence around the windscreen, water cascading down could leak into the car via the heater plenum or a bulkhead grommet. However, it could be wrongly assumed that the windscreen seal was at fault.

The visible examination of door aperture seals, grommets and weather strips for damage, deterioration or misalignment, as well as the actual shut of the door against the seals, are important parts of identifying an area where water can pass through.

Leak detection using ultrasonic equipment
When the vehicle is in motion, the body shape may produce eddy currents and turbulence which can force air and water through the smallest orifice. When the vehicle is stationary, it can be difficult to reproduce these conditions to a realistic level.

The ultrasonic equipment works on the principle of a transmitter creating ultrasonic waves which penetrate the smallest orifice in the vehicle body and are then picked up by a receiver fitted with a suitable probe, which can in turn pinpoint the exact leak point.

The transmitter is placed in a base plate which automatically switches it on via a reed switch in the base of the transmitting body. Ultrasonic waves will then penetrate out through the unsealed area, including the front windscreen, wiper spindle and washer jet fitment, roof seams, bulkhead seams and grommets, A-post area, door seals, front wheel arch seams and heater air intakes, to the receiver.

An important feature of this equipment is the incorporation of a sensitivity control which enables the operator to check a wide range of fitments. For example, a boot seal is a very light touch seal, whereas a urethane screen fitment is at the other end of the scale setting of the equipment and would need a high setting to determine a leak.

To ensure satisfactory leak location and testing, it is recommended not to use a leak detector on a wet vehicle, which should be blown dry prior to the test. As with any equipment it is important to read the instructions to enable the equipment to be used to its full potential.

Sealing

Having located the point of entry of the water, it is then necessary to carry out satisfactory rectification. Door aperture seals and weather strips should be renewed if damaged or suffering from deterioration. Alternatively the seals can be adjusted by carefully setting the mounting flange after making sure the fit of the door is correct.

Leaks through body seams should be sealed from the outside wherever possible to ensure water is excluded from the seam. First, dry out with compressed air or a hot air blower.

When leaks occur between a screen glass and the weather strip, or in the case of direct glazing between the glass and the body, avoid removing the glass if possible. Use recommended sealers to seal between the glass and the weather strip or the body.

If the vehicle is wet then it should be blown dry prior to sealing. It is difficult to seal a wet vehicle because, if a fault is found, it cannot be rectified quickly before moving to another area.

8.4.11 Windscreen repair: Glass-Weld Pro-Vac

This system of repair involves extracting all the air from the damaged glass and replacing the void with a resin which, when cured with ultraviolet light, is optically clear and is stronger than the glass that has been replaced. The system is widely accepted, and repair to Glass-Weld standard would not cause the vehicle to fail the statutory Department of Transport test for windscreens: 80 per cent of stone damaged windscreens can be repaired by this method (Figure 8.111).

When glass breaks, an air gap opens up. Sometimes crushed glass may also be present. There are also flat surfaces present inside the glass on either side of the air gap. These three things result in the possibility of the damaged area being affected. The damage will eventually spread further as the temperature changes and the vehicle flexes in normal use (Figure 8.112).

The system works, as follows:

1 All foreign materials and crushed glass are carefully removed from the centre of the damaged area to open up an airway into the break. Certain types of damage may need to be precision drilled (Figure 8.113).
2 The patent Pro-Vac injector is filled with the appropriate resin, depending on local temperature and humidity, before being mounted on the screen. The injector is then threaded through the stand until the outer seal makes airtight contact with the screen (Figure 8.114).
3 The Pro-Vac injector is capable of creating a total vacuum within the damaged area, which is essential for top quality repairs. Using alternating vacuum and pressure cycles, all of the air in the break is withdrawn and the void is filled with resin. Once the damage is optically clear, curing can commence.
4 Using a special ultraviolet lamp, the resin is cured. Once the curing process is complete the repair area is not only optically clear but also structurally sound; in fact it is stronger than the glass it replaces (Figure 8.115).

8.4.12 Automobile plastics welding

The car manufacturing industry, in its endeavours to reduce weight and improve fuel economy, forecasts a greater use of plastics in future designs (see Section 4.12). Considering the extensive use of plastics on current models, coupled with an even greater anticipated usage, it is therefore important that engineers and repairers are knowledgeable in the various types of plastic that are being used and are aware that some plastics can be repaired. Many body components are manufactured in a variety of plastics. Bumpers, grilles, light surrounds and even complete body panels have enabled designers to enhance vehicle aerodynamic styling and cosmetic appeal while retaining impact resistance and eliminating corrosion from these areas.

Plastic offers the same structural strength as steel in a body component because of its greater elasticity.

Figure 8.111 Before and after repair (*Glas-Weld Systems (UK) Ltd*)

Figure 8.112 Damaged windscreen (laminated safety glass) (*Glas-Weld Systems (UK) Ltd*)

Minor impacts that could deform steel beyond repair can be absorbed by plastic. Where damage is incurred it is capable of repair by welding. Cracks, splits, warping and even the loss of material from plastic components can be remedied with the aid of the Leister Triac hot air welding equipment. Where a steel component with equivalent damage would be replaced at some cost, the repair of the plastic part can save time and expense, particularly when winter accident periods make great demands of the vehicle repairer's parts stock. Welding plastics does not produce fumes when

Figure 8.113 Cleaning the damaged area (*Glas-Weld Systems (UK) Ltd*)

295

Figure 8.114 Fitting injector to the windscreen (*Glas-Weld Systems (UK) Ltd*)

Figure 8.115 Using ultraviolet lamp to cure resin (*Glas-Weld Systems (UK) Ltd*)

the correct procedure is followed. In a short time a plastic component can be restored to an 'as new' condition without the need for fillers or special treatments. The combination of welding and recommended paint procedures will show no trace of a repair that should last the life of the vehicle.

Identification of the material

There are two basic types of plastic used in cars: thermosetting and thermoplastic (see Section 4.12.3). Thermosetting plastics are cured by heat during manufacture. They cannot be welded; any more heat applied to them will break down their molecular bonding. The way to repair them is by using adhesive. Thermoplastic materials can melt without breaking down, so they can be manipulated like steel. With the right amount of heat they can be bent, softened and welded. The skill is in the selection of the appropriate temperature. The majority of plastics employed in vehicle manufacturing are thermoplastics. There are different types of thermoplastics, each having a specified temperature for welding operations.

Experienced repairers of plastic may recognize broad types of plastic by the degree of hardness or softness of the component surface. A quick test for identifying to which group a plastic belongs can be made by cutting a very thin sliver off the component. The thermoplastic curls right back on itself, but the thermoset stays straight.

In their body repair manuals, some vehicle manufacturers give details of plastic parts, while others mark all plastic parts with code letters. However, when no information or coding is available, identification can be carried out in two ways. The first is the method of combustion testing, where a small strip of material is held in a butane flame and the flame colour is noted. The other method, which works on the majority of the most common plastic materials, is to use an organic solvent test kit. These kits, produced by an automotive paint manufacturer, work by a process of solvent application to the material surface. A normally concealed area should be chosen and degreased, and any paint applied to the surface should be removed from the test area with the aid of an abrasive. Identification is confirmed by reaction between the plastic and test solvent in accordance with the test kit manufacturer's instructions. Gloves and face masks should always be worn when using solvents.

The usual plastic identification codes are as follows:

ABS	acrylonitrile butadiene styrene
ABS/PC	polymer alloy of ABS
PA	polyamide (nylon)
PBT	polybutylene terephthalate (POCAN)
PC	polycarbonate
PE	polyethylene
PP	polypropylene
PP/EPDM	polypropylene/ethylenediene rubber
PUR	polyurethane (not all PUR is weldable)
PVC	polyvinyl chloride

Figure 8.116 Leister Triac electric welding tool and accessories (*Welwyn Tool Co. Ltd*)

Figure 8.117 Rotary control on rear of hot air tool for temperature setting (*Welwyn Tool Co. Ltd*)

GRP/SMC glass fibre reinforced plastics (not weldable)

Equipment for plastic welding
The Welwyn Tool Company supply the Leister Triac welding guns (see Figure 8.116). These blow hot air out of their nozzles, and sophisticated electronics make sure that the temperature of this air is exactly right. A potentiometer is set to control the power (Figure 8.117), a photo-electric cell monitors the colour of the heating element and, as a failsafe, a thermocouple double checks the output. The guns can maintain a critical temperature setting to ±5°C, independent of any mains voltage fluctuations. It is important to use

Figure 8.118 Split bumper (*Welwyn Tool Co. Ltd*)

a welding rod of the same material as the component: hence the importance of correct identification. The welding rods come in various profiles, and there is a speed-weld nozzle available to suit each rod.

Repair method
Suppose a bumper has suffered a long, straight crack which makes it particularly suitable for repair by welding (see Figure 8.118). When carrying out the repair process, thorough preparation of the surfaces is important. When working on a painted bumper it is necessary to sand off any paint in the vicinity of the area to be welded; a mask for facial protection is then necessary. To minimize the risk of damage spreading, the ends of the crack are drilled out with a 2 mm drill. The edges of the crack are then shaped into a V with a burring bit which has a cutting edge on both its circumference and its face (see Figure 8.119). This will allow the welding rod, which in this case is supplied in a V shape, to fit snugly into the crack. Care should be taken not to penetrate more than two-thirds into the depth of the material. The extent of the damage should now be clearly visible.

In any welding operation it is important that the two surfaces to be joined should remain in alignment, so they should be tacked together using a tacking nozzle (see Figure 8.120). The section of the temperature chart relating to this nozzle must be consulted to determine the correct gun setting; the temperature can then be adjusted on the potentiometer. After allowing the gun to heat up for at least two minutes, the tacking operation can be carried out. The nozzle is held at an angle of about 20 degrees and is run along the crack without applying any pressure.

Figure 8.119 Rotary burring tool cutting a V-groove (*Welwyn Tool Co. Ltd*)

Figure 8.121 Welding rod trimmed to a point (*Welwyn Tool Co. Ltd*)

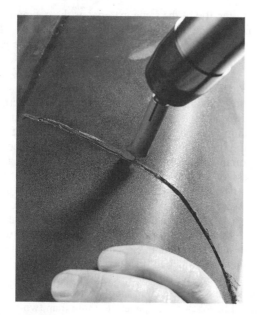

Figure 8.120 Tack welding split in bumper (*Welwyn Tool Co. Ltd*)

Figure 8.122 Main plastic welding operation (*Welwyn Tool Co. Ltd*)

The speed-weld nozzle is fixed to the gun, and the temperature is again adjusted prior to carrying out the weld. The end of the welding rod is trimmed into a point to ensure a smooth start to the weld (see Figure 8.121). The welding rod is inserted into the speed-weld nozzle, and as soon as the edges show signs of melting the weld can be carried out (see Figure 8.122). Contact should be maintained between the nozzle and the workpiece but, as with the tacking operation, no pressure should be applied with the gun. The welding rod, however, should be pushed well into the crack. The rate at which the welding rod is fed into the gun should match the distance travelled. It is also important to operate the gun at the correct angle. When the weld is finished, the gun is pulled away leaving the

Figure 8.123 Weld dressing (*Welwyn Tool Co. Ltd*)

welding rod attached. The excess rod is then trimmed off.

The bumper is allowed to cool, and the welded area can then be sanded down with an 80 grit disc before being passed on to the painter (see Figure 8.123). The bumper has a non-textured painted finish, which will be reinstated. After normal preparation and priming have been carried out a filler is applied. After flatting the filler, two further coats of primer are sprayed on and flatted. The usual cleaning procedures should be carried out between each process. The colour can now be applied. Painting should always be carried out according to the paint manufacturer's instructions.

If the repair method is carried out correctly, the component should achieve up to 90 per cent of its original strength.

When repairing plastic materials there must always be strict observance of health and safety requirements, so the operator should work in a well-ventilated environment. Using the gun at an abnormally high temperature does not assist the welding operation, and can cause dangerous fumes.

Welding defects
A tack weld can be broken and restarted if panel alignment is not achieved on the first attempt. To prove main weld strength, allow it to cool then attempt to pull it from the groove by the attached welding rod. If the weld stays firmly in place then the weld has been successful.

Typical welding defects and their causes are as follows (see Figure 8.124):

Figure 8.124 Defective plastics welds and their causes (*Welwyn Tool Co. Ltd*)
(a) Weld started correctly but completed too quickly: no wash, indicating haste or welding temperature too low
(b) Hot air tool not allowed to attain the correct welding temperature before starting, and weld finished too soon, leaving a hole
(c) Weld started too late with an unprepared welding rod end: hole and protrusion of plastic result
(d) Too much pressure applied to the welding rod, leaving a low and deformed weld bead: filling may be necessary
(e) Welding temperature too hot for the material, blistering the sides of the weld: repair area may be brittle

Poor weld penetration or bonding Incorrect weld site preparation; welding speed too fast; temperature too low; weld attempted with dissimilar materials; poor technique.

Uneven weld bead width Welding rod stretched; uneven pressure applied to welding rod.

Charred weld Welding speed too slow; temperature too high; repair area overheated.

Warping Parts fixed under tension; poor site preparation.

8.4.13 Plastic repair

Duramix combines the tremendous strength and durability of a plastic weld system with the flexibility of

Figure 8.125 Wet bay (*Autoglym*)

chemical curing products, thus eliminating the need for a filler or stopper to create the complete cosmetic finish. It is compatible with all plastics, fibre-glass and metal surfaces. Repairs can be carried out on flexible plastic bumper bars, semi-rigid plastic panels, ABS plastic grilles, polycarbonate bumper bars, and thermoplastic bumper bars.

Duramix is a urethane composition. It applies easily to vertical surfaces, resists sagging, contours with a spreader to the original surface shape, sets within three minutes, and is easily sanded to a high-quality repair within 15 minutes. It produces a tenacious bond while maintaining flexibility, even in cold temperatures. The repair procedure is as follows:

1 Material and equipment required: plastic cleaner, heat gun, reinforcement patches, 3 in grinderette, DA sander, plastic spreader, masking tape, rubbing-down paper and the Duramix filling material.
2 Identify the plastic to be repaired. Most of the semi-rigid plastics on vertical panels on today's vehicles are urethane, Xenoy, or other repairable materials. A small percentage are thermoplastic polyolefin (TPO), and these must be repaired using a slightly different procedure.
3 Clean the plastic panel surface and back of the repair thoroughly to remove all road dirt, oil and grease.
4 Remove any deformations in the plastic panel. If the panel has undergone a severe impact it may have some residual distortion. To remove any distortion, warm the stretched or distorted area with a heat gun. The warm air will allow the panel to return to its original shape.

5 Apply a structural support to the back of the repair using a Duramix reinforcement patch. This will provide some firmness so that the repair area can be V-grooved and feathered back around the repair.
6 V-groove the area using a coarse 3 in disc, then feather back the paint around the V-groove.
7 Apply Duramix to the plastic panel. First, select a length of contouring plastic which will cover the entire repair area. Then mask off the area surrounding the repair to reduce the sanding and clean-up time. Apply Duramix directly to the V-grooved area, slightly overfilling the area; then within 30 seconds overlay a sheet of contouring plastic and use the flat side of a plastic spreader to compress and smooth the Duramix into the V-grooves. Duramix will start to set within 50 seconds after it has been dispensed, so the body repairer should work quickly to apply the contouring plastic.
8 Sand the repair using a DA sander: start with a coarse grit disc and finish with a smooth grit disc, feather edging the whole repair.
9 Apply a sealer, then primer surfacer, then finishing coats to suit the plastic panel or bumper bar being repaired.

8.4.14 Valeting of repaired vehicles

After repair work has been completed, the vehicle should be presented to the customer in a first-class, clean condition. All repaired vehicles should be thoroughly inspected for quality control. The repairs should be guaranteed for a specific mileage or period, as required by the Code of Practice for the Motor Industry and by the VBRA Code. Many insurance companies now make an allowance for valeting within their agreed repair price, and this provides the opportunity for the bodyshop to produced a first-class factory finish to both the exterior and interior of the repair.

Premises, equipment and chemicals used in cleaning and valeting
When cleaning and valeting a vehicle it is essential to organize a standard method of working to ensure that nothing is inadvertently missed. The ideal premises and equipment should be set out in separate purpose-designed working areas.

The cleaning process should be undertaken in a wet bay with effective drainage, good lighting and adequate working space all round the vehicle when its doors are open. Compressed air and high-pressure cold and hot water should be available (Figure 8.125).

Valeting should be carried out in a well-lit, dry bay with adequate working space all round the vehicle.

Figure 8.126 Dry bay (*Autoglym*)

Figure 8.127 Degreasing engine (*Autoglym*)

Compressed air, electrical power points, warm water, a workbench and storage cupboards should be available (Figure 8.126).

Equipment, details are as follows:

1 High-pressure hot and cold washer, 70–100 bar (1000–1500 psi), with chemical throughput facility to ensure that engine cleaners and traffic film removers work quickly and effectively.
2 Electric/air polisher, 1500–2000 rpm, with polythene foam and lambswool polishing heads.
3 Fine grade, 100 per cent cotton, polishing cloths.
4 Vacuum cleaner and/or shampoo vacuum cleaner with assorted upholstery brushes and crevice tools.

5 Hand-pumped, pressurized sprays for dispensing engine cleaners and traffic film remover.
6 Trigger spray dispensers for interior cleaning, together with wheel, engine and carpet brushes.
7 Good-quality chamois leather, sponges, polishing cloths (100 per cent cotton, knitted stockinette type), steel wool, spatula, glass scraper, buckets, hot air gun (useful for removing PVC stickers, self-adhesive design trims).

There are many manufacturers and suppliers of valeting and cleaning chemicals. The wide range of valeting and chemical cleaners available is broadly divided up as follows:

Exterior detergents and solvents

Interior detergents and solvents

Interior/exterior rubber, PVC, plastic cleaners and conditioners

Glass cleaners, paints, lacquer and protectorants

Paintwork polishes and conditioners

Cleaning and valeting process
Prior to commencing work, check that the vehicle is ready. All body repairs, paintwork and mechanical work should be completed. Be aware of areas which have been newly painted as they may be chemically or water sensitive. Individual chemical products carry their own instructions, and health and safety procedures must be adhered to at all times.

Autoglym recommend the following step-by-step procedure for cleaning and valeting.

Cleaning: wet bay

1 Remove spare wheel, rubber mats and wheel trims if fitted.
2 Protect engine air intake and sensitive electrical equipment (distributor cap, fuse box) with plastic sheet.
3 Apply degreaser to engine and compartment. Brush heavy soiling. Alternatively use hot-pressure washer with appropriate detergent (Figure 8.127).
4 Apply degreaser to door apertures and edges. Brush heavy soiling. Alternatively use hot-pressure washer with appropriate detergent.
5 Clean wheels, trims, spare wheel with alloy cleaner. Brush brake dust deposits. Treat bright metal and motifs. Rinse all items well (Figure 8.128).
6 Pressure wash engine compartment to remove degreaser. Commence with lower areas. Work methodically upwards (Figure 8.129).
7 Pressure wash door apertures and edges to remove degreaser. Carefully angle water jet away from the vehicle interior.

301

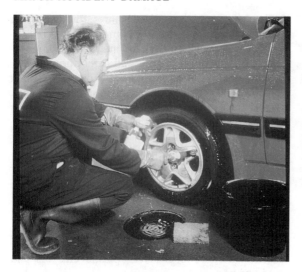

Figure 8.128 Cleaning wheels (*Autoglym*)

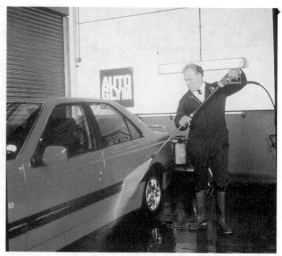

Figure 8.130 Cleaning bodywork (*Autoglym*)

Figure 8.129 Pressure washing engine compartment (*Autoglym*)

Figure 8.131 Drying engine (*Autoglym*)

8 Apply traffic film remover to engine compartment. If necessary, sponge or brush to remove grime.

9 Pressure wash engine compartment to rinse away traffic film remover.

10 Pressure wash wheel arches to remove mud and debris. Plain water is normally adequate.

11 Pressure wash and rinse bodywork, grilles, tyres. mudflaps. Pay particular attention to difficult to polish areas behind bumpers (Figure 8.130).

12 Apply traffic film removed to rubber mats. Clean with high-pressure washer.

13 Use air line to dry engine. Remove plastic sheeting. Check engine starting. Use water dispersant if necessary. Run engine to aid drying (Figure 8.131).

14 Use air line and chamois leather to remove excess water from bodywork or trim strips which may trap water (Figure 8.132).

Valeting: dry bay

1 Finish engine compartment. Clean hoses, wiring, plastic and paintwork with appropriate dressings.

2 Repaint deteriorated black areas. Use fine jet matt black aerosol or small spray gun.

3 Clear lacquer engine if required to enhance and preserve appearance. Close bonnet.

4 Before interior cleaning, remove all loose carpets, tools, ashtrays and personal items to the bench.

Figure 8.132 Removing water (*Autoglym*)

Figure 8.134 Cleaning carpets (*Autoglym*)

Figure 8.133 Brushing and vacuuming (*Autoglym*)

5 Use glass scraper to remove all labels from windows. Residual adhesive can be removed with adhesive remover or water.

6 Remove all plastic labels from bodywork using hot air gun. Residual adhesive can be removed with adhesive remover.

7 Vacuum clean all interior surfaces. Slide front seats forward. Use brushes with vacuum nozzle to clean crevices and air vents (Figure 8.133).

8 Clean luggage compartment first. Use interior cleaner by spraying and wiping clean with cloth rinsed frequently. Check body channels and rubbers.

9 Wash interior. Start with headlining and use interior cleaner. Heavily soiled carpets or seats may require shampoo vacuum treatment.

10 Removed carpets should be thoroughly brushed, vacuumed and washed on the bench. Use shampoo vacuum if necessary. Allow to dry (Figure 8.134).

11 Tools and jack should be cleaned, and repainted if necessary. Wash out ashtrays.

12 Plastic coated fibreboard may be painted or stained to cover damage or scrape marks. Check body sides for tar, and top surfaces for industrial fallout. Use appropriate cleaner before polishing.

13 Restore paintwork. Start with roof panel. Use paint renovator with polisher, or appropriate cleaner/polish. Hand polish small areas, corners, edges (Figure 8.135).

14 Apply protective wax coating by hand, ensuring total coverage of all panels. Leave polish applied at this stage.

15 Clean all external body rubber and plastic mouldings with appropriate dressings.

16 Check all door apertures and rubber seals. Polish door aperture paintwork with clean cloth. Treat rubber seals with appropriate dressing.

17 Check all wheels. If required, clean with steel wool and thinners. Protect tyres with dressing or mask. Respray wheels and clean tyres.

18 Glass cleaning. Lower side windows. Clean top edges completely. Close windows. Polish outside first, then inside. Clean surrounding seals and mirrors.

19 Interior plastic can be dressed to enhance and protect appearance.

Figure 8.135 Polishing (*Autoglym*)

20 Replace all carpets, mats, spare wheel, ashtray, tools, wheel trims.
21 Check interior for remaining imperfections. Check under all seats, glove box, door pockets. Finally vacuum clean. Place protective paper on floor mats.
22 Remove polish. Methodically check all edges, valances, glasses, lights, grilles. Crevices and motifs may be lightly brushed to remove polish.

Checklist

1 Check exterior mirrors, all glass and surrounding seals. Check reverse of interior mirror.
2 Check polish smears, wheel arch edges, front and rear lower pillars, side sills, door handles, grilles. Touch in stone chips.
3 Check windscreen wiper arms and blades, air grilles.
4 Check all light lenses, motifs, number plates and spot lights.
5 Check door edges and apertures, engine and luggage compartment, body channels and seals.
6 Check control pedals and foot wells, especially under front seats.
7 Check instrument glasses, switches, control levers, interior air vents.
8 Check all ashtrays, glove box, door and seat pockets.

8.5 ESTIMATING AND COSTING

8.5.1 Repair or replacement

The repair of all collision damage can be divided into three categories:

1 Repairing by realigning and reshaping the damaged section which can be economically repaired.
2 Repairing by removing sections beyond economical repair and replacing them with new sections.
3 Repairing by using a combination of realigning and reshaping together with the replacement of appropriate sections.

Before deciding whether to repair or replace, consideration must be given to the extent and type of damage, whether it is possible to repair a particular panel or not (this fact is influenced by the equipment which is available), and also whether it will be cheaper to repair or replace any one section. A good body repair worker would probably be able to repair almost any part of a car damaged in a collision; however, the labour and time cost involved in attempting to repair extensively damaged panels would be an uneconomical proposition. Only experience in body repair work will give the ability to estimate the time required to do a particular job. Therefore the final decision depends on what is possible to repair and what is economical to repair.

As the construction of the modern vehicle advances, body panel assemblies are becoming very complicated and therefore their cost is constantly increasing. The cost of replacement parts differs between one manufacturer and another and even between models. In most cases the following parts are usually replaced rather than repaired:

1 All chrome exterior trim. Owing to the intricate design and nature of the materials from which they are made, trims do not lend themselves to re-straightening, and the cost of replating is greater than the cost of a new part.
2 Interior trim which is difficult to clean and repair, especially tears and gashes.
3 Certain mechanical components which it would be ill advised to repair and reuse owing to their critical alignment and strength factors.

On mono constructed vehicles the correct positioning of new panels, which may incorporate reinforcing members, becomes increasingly important and calls for expensive jigging to ensure the accurate alignment of panels which will have to be fitted with major mechanical components and suspension units. The highest proportion of any repair bill is made up of the cost of labour involved in stripping out to gain access to the damaged area, and rebuilding after replacement is effected. In certain cases, therefore, it can be more economical to repair a damaged panel than to replace it because of the time and labour cost involved for the amount of work over and above that required to repair the part. Consequently in any body repair workshop the dividing line between repairing and replacing is determined not only by what it is possible to repair and what it is economical to repair, but also by the availability of the most up-to-date equipment to deal with all types of major collision damage.

8.5.2 Costing

The determining factor when deciding whether to repair or replace lies in the comparison between the cost of repairing the damaged part as against the cost of a new replacement part. When the owner of a car is personally paying the cost of repairs, the repairer will need to come to an agreement with him concerning an acceptable standard of repair for the amount of money the owner is able to pay. When it is an older car the extra cost involved in striving for perfection in the repair is not always justified, since these costs could be more than the current value of the vehicle under repair. In cases of this nature a compromise must be arrived at between the repairer and owner as to the quality of repair and cost of repair.

Where an insurance company pays for repairs to the damage of a new or nearly new car, the quality of the work must be such that when the repair is finished there is no indication of the damage having occurred. When an insurance company is paying for repairs to an older car, and the condition of the car (in many cases due to corrosion) affects the quality of the repair, the possibility of achieving perfection of appearance is limited and a mutual agreement must be reached between the owner and the insurance company on a satisfactory quality of repair. Time is always an important factor in the repair of collision damage; however, the majority of car owners are not willing to sacrifice quality of repair for speed of repair.

8.5.3 Estimating

The ability to estimate can only be gained through practical experience in the field of body repair work. An estimate must be competitive to be acceptable to both the private car owner and the insurance company, for the majority of collision jobs are paid for by an insurance company. In estimating, the financial gain for the bodyshop will depend on the estimator's skill in assessing the damage, his knowledge and experience in repair techniques, and the capabilities of the equipment available.

Small body repair establishments have no separate estimator and therefore it is usual for whoever prepares the estimate to be responsible for carrying out

the repair work as well. The larger establishments employ one member of staff who is responsible for all estimating, while the actual repair work is carried out by the tradesmen on the shop floor. Consequently there must be no lack of coordination and understanding between these two and the jobs they perform. The decisions of the estimator are all important as they instigate the organization of work on the shop floor. Moreover, no matter how skilled the tradesmen are, with bad estimating the financial profits can be drastically affected.

In collision work the estimate is considered as a firm commitment to do the work involved for the amount of money shown, and should be detailed so that insurance companies or private owners can determine from the estimate exactly what it is proposed to do to the damaged vehicle. The estimate must include cost of parts and labour costs at the recognized retail rate of the bodyshop establishment (Figures 8.136, 8.137).

In the preparation of an estimate, the crash damage should be itemized into the number of damaged panel sections and assemblies, and therefore it is important to have a knowledge of vehicle body construction. The outer panels which make up the body shell should be referred to by the manufacturer's recognized names, such as:

Near-side front door (NSF door)
Near-side rear door (NSR door)
Off-side front door (OSF door)
Off-side rear door (OSR door)
Roof panel
Boot lid
Bonnet
Near-side centre pillar (NS centre pillar)
Radiator grille
Near-side front wing (NSF wing)
Off-side front wing (OSF wing)
Near-side sill panel (NS sill panel)
Off-side sill panel (OS sill panel)
Front bumper bar assembly with valance
Rear bumper bar assembly with valance

In addition this can be further broken down to all internal panel structures according to the position of the damage.

It is essential to determine the exact amount of stripping necessary for either the repair or the removal and replacement of a damaged section. To calculate the actual cost of a job it is necessary to establish a set rate per hour for all repairs done in the repair shop, and therefore an accurate total repair time can be calculated on the time taken to repair each section of the body. This then provides the actual cost

Repair Estimate № 000713

OWNER _____

ADDRESS _____

TEL: HOME _____ BUSINESS _____

MAKE & MODEL _____

REG. No. _____ YEAR _____

PAINT CODE _____ TRIM _____

ENGINE No. _____

CHASSIS No. _____

INS. No. _____

INSPECTING ENGINEER _____ TEL. _____

CLAIM No. _____

WE HAVE PLEASURE IN SUBMITTING OUR ESTIMATE. V.A.T. EXTRA **£**

LABOUR _____	
PARTS (At manufacturers list prices)	see attached
COLLECTION & TOWING _____	
STORAGE PER DAY _____	
CAR RENTAL from £ _____ per day (unlimited mileage)	

ESTIMATE PREPARED BY: _____ DATE _____

Any additional damage found on dismantling will be the subject of a supplementary estimate.

REPAIR OPERATIONS	REMOVE & REFIT	REPAIR	RENEW	HOURS PANEL	PAINT
FRONT SECTION					
BONNET					
WINGS					
DOORS/FRAMES					
ROOF					
REAR SECTION					
SCREENS/GLASS					
LIGHTS					

	REMOVE & REFIT	REPAIR	RENEW	HOURS PANEL	PAINT
UNDERSIDE/FLOORS					
ACCESSORIES					
INTERIOR					
JIG WORK					
MECHANICAL REPAIRS					
SUSPENSION					
STEERING					
WHEELS					
ENGINE COMPARTMENT					
TRANS./FINAL DRIVE					
FUEL SYSTEM					

WING HEADLIGHTS DOOR DOOR WING
BONNET WINDSCREEN ROOF WINDOW SPARE BOOT
HEADLIGHTS DOOR DOOR WING
WING

© STANDARD FORMS LTD. Romsey Hants   OFFICE COPY   Stock Form No. M 26

Figure 8.136 Repair estimate

Bodywork Invoice B 01144

OWNER			Cash ☐		
			Account ☐		
ADDRESS			Retail ☐		
			Int. ☐		
			Wty. ☐		

TEL. HOME: BUSINESS

Is Owner VAT Registered? Yes/No

PART No.	DESCRIPTION	Qty.	UNIT PRICE	TOTAL

DATE IN   DATE OUT   INVOICE DATE

MAKE

MODEL

SPEEDO READING   FUEL   E   ¼   ½   ¾   F

REG. No.   YEAR

PAINT CODE   TRIM

ENGINE NUMBER

CHASSIS NUMBER

INSURANCE COMPANY

INVOICE ADDRESS

INSPECTING ENGINEER

TEL.

ESTIMATE No.   CLAIM No.

I/We have read and accept your terms of business. I/We agree to pay all sums due on completion of work prior to collection of vehicle. Where applicable I/We agree to pay any Owner's Contribution or Excess Charge specified by the insurance company.

Owner's Signature _____ Date _____

LABOUR AS PER ESTIMATE No.

TOTAL LABOUR CHARGE

	INSURANCE COMPANY TO PAY	OWNER TO PAY
LABOUR		
PARTS		
SPECIALIST MATERIALS		
TOTAL EXCL. VAT		
LESS PARTS DISCOUNT %		
SUB-TOTAL		
VAT at %		
SUB-TOTAL		
EXCESS £		
OWNERS CONTRIBUTION £		
DUE FROM INS. Co.➤		
DUE FROM OWNER———➤		
TOTAL INVOICE VALUE £		

COLLECTION NOTE

I certify that repairs to the above vehicle have been completed and that the vehicle has been made available to me for collection.

Owner's Signature .... Date ....

STANDARD FORMS LTD. Romsey, Hants   Stock Form No. M.16

Figure 8.137 Bodywork invoice

estimate for repairing each section or part of the job. The retail rate or set rate per hour is the amount of money that the repairer charges the customer for labour, and is made up of: wages paid to the tradesmen; the cost of overheads, which should include items such as supervision, depreciation of equipment, rent, heat, light, electrical power, advertising, telephone accounts, cleaning, office staff, stationery and postage, and workshop materials; and also a reasonable amount of profit.

8.5.4 Computer estimating

Computers are rapidly losing their mystique, and are becoming as indispensable to the bodyshop as the spray booth and chassis jig. Offering benefits in all aspects of bodyshop operation, there are computers and software packages dedicated to quick and easy repair estimates, stock control, invoicing and management accounts, paint and materials, parts list, mixing and colour matching, job cards, workshop loading, booking in, job efficiency reports, invoice production, reports and letters (Figures 8.138–8.141). Costs have tumbled and the benefits can be reaped by all bodyshops, regardless of size.

The key to success in any bodyshop is the production of an accurate, well-presented estimate. An estimate has to be a clear, concise statement of what you consider to be a fair return for the care and work you carry out on a crash damaged vehicle. By utilizing the memory capacity of the computer you will have readily available all necessary details to help you draw up an estimate quickly and accurately.

Your computer system will have the facility to prepare not only a detailed document for the customer, but also a comprehensive breakdown for the insurance company. The documents produced will be tailor made to your own letterhead stationery. The insurance estimate can often be sent direct by fax to the company involved, thereby further reducing the time gap between estimating and authorization by that company. Apart from the major bonus of speed, a computerized estimating system will greatly enhance your company's image as a professional organization. You will have instant access to the progress of any job: most systems include this as standard. The more time and money you spend at the outset, the more control you will have over staff movement and job completion.

8.5.5 Insurance procedure

Under the Road Traffic Act the car owner is obliged to insure his vehicle either under third party insurance cover or fully comprehensive insurance cover. As a direct result of this, most accident damage is covered by insurance and is therefore repaired in bodywork establishments.

The procedure for dealing with repairs carried out under an insurance claim is in four stages, as described in the following sections.

Claim form
When involved in an accident which has resulted in vehicle damage, the owner should obtain and complete an insurance claim form and immediately return it to his insurance company, or make a written report on the accident and damage received.

Itemized estimate
According to the extent of the damage, and if the vehicle is still road worthy, the owner takes the vehicle for inspection of the damage. The repairer will make a visual inspection of the assessed damage, and from the knowledge gained complete a written itemized estimate which he will submit as a tender to the insurance company. This estimate will show the total cost of repairs, and where the estimated amount is under a certain figure set by the insurance company, the owner has the right to authorize the repairer to do the work. However, in most repair cases this figure is exceeded, and the insurance company's assessor is the only person authorized to allow the repairs to proceed.

One of the important factors when estimating for insurance claim damage is to examine carefully every section of the vehicle, especially those parts which are a known weakness in the construction and therefore liable to be affected directly or indirectly by a collision. A methodical system of estimating is essential to avoid missing any damage, and is usually carried out by noting in order all removal and replacement items, all repair items, all respray items and all items to be supplied new at cost, including mechanical parts and any trim. Supply items are usually difficult to price because of the makers' fluctuating prices, and therefore they should be listed 'at cost'. Spray painting can be quoted either by itemizing each part separately or by a complete price for the total spray operation. While in the owner's presence, the repairer should point out any rusted sections which may affect the repair work, or any previous unrepaired damage which is not covered under this insurance claim.

Authority to repair
It is essential to obtain the authority to repair from the insurance company involved before any work is started on the damaged vehicle. On receiving the

dyMaster House
rch Cross
rest Row
st Sussex
18 5LJ
: (0342) 826001
x: (0342) 826002

ACCIDENT REPAIR CENTRE
FULL JIG FACILITIES
SPRAY BOOTH
ALL INSURANCE WORK

Engineers Estimate

s. M. Jones,
2, Kings Road,
arpthorne,
. East Grinstead,
ast Sussex,
123 4LB.

31st March 1992

timate No: 10010
hicle   : Ford Escort 1.6L,
g No.   : F376 AFG
assis No : 11-H7-SLBN43/87
int Type : Solid colour

int & materials	£	112.61
ncludes dry goods etc.)		
g bracket hire	£	
covery charge	£	

mments :
ee separate list for parts)

Estimate Details	Hours
Remove and refit :	
Front Bumper	1.00
O/S/F Headlamp	1.00
O/S/F Indicator	0.50
Front Grille	0.20
Fog Lamps	1.00
Mouldings	0.50
O/S Mirror	0.50
Repeater Lamp	0.10
"Ford" Decal	0.10
O/S/F Door and Trims	1.00
Radiator	1.00
O/S/F Tyre	1.00
Repair and make good :	
Front Panel	1.00
O/S/F Door	2.50
O/S Front Chassis Leg end	2.00
Cut out and weld in :	
New O/S/F Wing	5.00
Hang and align :	
O/S/F Door	1.00
New Bonnet	1.00
Wheel Alignment	1.50
Load onto Jig	4.00
Prepare and paint :	
O/S/F Door	3.00
New Bonnet	4.00
Front Panel	2.50
New O/S/F Wing	3.00
O/S Front Chassis Leg end	1.00
Total Hours	**39.40**

Total labour cost @ £14.50 per hour £571.30

Figure 8.138 Customer's estimate (*Bodymaster UK*)

BodyMaster House
Wych Cross
Forest Row
East Sussex
RH18 5LJ

Tel: (0342) 826001
Fax: (0342) 826002

Mrs. M. Jones,
42, Kings Road,
Sharpthorne,
Nr. East Grinstead,
East Sussex,
RH23 4LB.

Estimate No :   100

Dear Madam,

Re; Ford Escort 1.6L, Registration Number: F376 AFG.

We have pleasure in submitting our estimate for repairs to the above vehicle.

Repairs:
Remove and refit:
Front Bumper, O/S/F Headlamp, O/S/F Indicator, Front Grille, Fog Lamps,
Mouldings, O/S Mirror, Repeater Lamp, "Ford" Decal, O/S/F Door and Trims,
Radiator and O/S/F Tyre.

Load vehicle onto jig.

Repair and reshape:
Front Panel, O/S/F Door and O/S Front Chassis Leg end.

Cut out and weld in:
New O/S/F Wing.

Hang and align:
O/S/F Door and New Bonnet.

Check and set wheel alignment.

Paintwork:
Prepare, prime and topcoat:
O/S/F Door, New Bonnet, Front Panel, New O/S/F Wing and
O/S Front Chassis Leg end.

Labour;   £   571.30

Plus Parts :- (To be supplied at MRP)
New Bonnet   Front Bumper
O/S/F Headlamp   O/S/F Indicator
O/S Mirror   Repeater Lamp
New O/S/F Wing   Clips etc
Radiator (Not discountable)   O/S/F Tyre

Paint, materials and sundry items.

Yours faithfully,

Bodyshop Manager.
Please Note: All Prices Subject To 17.5% VAT.
            Please ensure your radio code is recorded before repair.

Figure 8.139 Engineer's estimate (*Bodymaster UK*)

...dyMaster House
...ch Cross
...est Row
...st Sussex
...18 5LJ

...: (0342) 826001
...: (0342) 826002

ACCIDENT REPAIR CENTRE
FULL JIG FACILITIES
SPRAY BOOTH
ALL INSURANCE WORK

Vehicle Job Card

...stomer   : Mrs. M. Jones,   31st March 1992
...hicle   : Ford Escort 1.6L,   Reg No : F376 AFG
...assis No : 11-H7-SLBN43/87
...int Code : B1
...b/Estimate No : 10010

...pair Format	Est Time	Actual Time
...move :Front Bumper, O/S/F Headlamp, O/S/F Indicator, Front Grille, Fog Lamps, Mouldings, O/S Mirror, Repeater Lamp, "Ford" Decal, O/S/F Door and Trims, Radiator, O/S/F Tyre.	7.90	
...pair :Front Panel, O/S/F Door, O/S Front Chassis Leg end.	5.50	
...ld in :New O/S/F Wing.	5.00	
...ng and align :O/S/F Door, New Bonnet.	2.00	
...eck and set wheel alignment.	1.50	
...ad vehicle onto jig.	4.00	
...int :O/S/F Door, New Bonnet, Front Panel, New O/S/F Wing, O/S Front Chassis Leg end.	13.50	
TOTAL	39.40	

Date	Operation	Initial	On	Off	Total
				TOTAL	

Signed ....

Figure 8.140   Vehicle job card (*Bodymaster UK*)

BodyMaster House
Wych Cross
Forest Row
East Sussex
RH18 5LJ

Tel: (0342) 826001
Fax: (0342) 826002

ACCIDENT REPAIR CENTF

FULL JIG FACILITI

SPRAY BOO1

ALL INSURANCE WOF

Vehicle Checklist

Customer   : Mrs. M. Jones,
Vehicle   : Ford Escort 1.6L,
Chassis No : 11-H7-SLBN43/87
Paint Code : B1
Job/Estimate No : 10010

31st March 19
Reg No : F376 A

Workshop :

CHECKLIST	TICK
Lights	—
Headlamp beam	—
Door workings	—
Trims and fixings	—
Security of parts	—
Brake fluid level	—
Water level/antifreeze	—
Aperture gaps	—
Wax injection	—
Underseal	—
Coachlines	—
Masking tape	—
Blow - ins	—
Overspray	—
Paint finish	—
Cleanliness interior	—
Cleanliness exterior	—
Wheel nuts	—
Roadtest	—

signed

. . . .

Comments on general condition

Office Use :

Satisfaction Notice	
Excess Invoice	

signed

. . . .

Figure 8.141 Vehicle repair checklist (*Bodymaster UK*)

repairer's estimate, the insurance company will instruct their own engineer assessor or an independent assessor to examine the vehicle and satisfy himself that the claim is in order and that the estimate submitted by the repairer does not include any labour or material necessary as a result of any other than the accident report. The engineer assessor then agrees the cost of repairs, particularly the labour charges, with the repairer while inspecting the vehicle, and decides whether or not damaged parts shall be repaired or replaced.

After this inspection the assessor will send written instructions on behalf of the insurance company; these constitute the authority to repair. A condition of these instructions is that the repairer is restricted to repairing the damage as seen and estimated for. Any additional damage disclosed when dismantling the vehicle must have a separate estimate submitted, and work cannot be carried out on this damage until the extra estimate has been agreed and the necessary work authorized by the insurance company.

Clearance certificate
This certificate is provided by the insurance company for the vehicle owner to sign when he has seen that all the agreed repairs have been completed satisfactorily, and the damaged parts reinstated to their original condition. When this certificate has been signed by the vehicle owner, it releases the insurance company from any liability in respect of the claim for damage caused by this particular accident. It is to the repairer's advantage for him to ascertain that the clearance certificate has been duly signed before the vehicle is returned to its owner.

The duty of the repairer is to see that the damaged car is reinstated to its original condition. He is expected to make full use of his skill and knowledge to effect the best possible repair, as the owner relies on his reputed skill.

8.5.6 Motor Insurance Repair Research Centre (Thatcham)

In the 1960s the motor insurance industry became concerned about the escalating cost of vehicle accident damage repair work and its effect on motor insurance premiums. To have some direct influence on these costs it was recognized that motor insurers required a means of researching the cost of repairing accident damaged cars and light commercial vehicles.

In 1969, motor insurance company members of the British Insurance Association and motor syndicates at Lloyd's joined in a scheme to create a research centre. The result was Thatcham, named after the small Berkshire town where it is situated, and the only centre of its type in the UK. Thatcham is unique in that it represents an entire motor insurance market. It has been granted research status by the government, and is funded by levies on the members of the Association of British Insurers and Lloyd's Motor Underwriters Association.

The aims of the centre are as follows:

1 To advise on repair methods and prepare accurate job times for panel replacement.
2 To minimize the effects of road accident damage and liaison with manufacturers in the interests of better vehicle design.
3 To pioneer quicker, more cost-effective methods of damage repair.

Thatcham exists to promote cost-effective methods for motor vehicle repair. This includes demonstrating the types of equipment and techniques which are available to the repair trade. This effort is backed by a professional approach using skilled workshop personnel and engineers recruited from the repair trade and manufacturers. They are able to provide insurance engineers and repairers with essential repair information, often as soon as new vehicle models become available at the dealers.

Research at Thatcham is divided into two stages.

Stage 1 research determines the best method of removing and replacing the outer cosmetic panels of undamaged vehicles, and the time taken to do this.

Stage 2 research is more advanced; it relates to vehicles that have been subjected to controlled structural damage, and is concerned with the repair methods and times associated with such damage. Because most research concentrates on prelaunch or recently launched vehicles, accident damage is simulated on the crash test facility. This provides uniformity of impact, irrespective of the model, and provides data based on constant factors, thus making model damage comparison more meaningful. Vehicles can be propelled into a static crash barrier or impacted by a 1000 kilogram mobile crash barrier.

Both stage 1 and stage 2 research is observed by a work study engineer, who determines the most effective method of repair. This is achieved through consultation with the vehicle manufacturer, other specialist engineers and very often the experienced skilled tradesman carrying out the work. Subsequently, repair methods are established before publication. The evolution of manufacturing and repair techniques inevitably means the introduction of new materials, tools and techniques which could have a significant impact on repair methods. Specialized research projects are set up to establish the effect of such materials, tools and equipment on repair methods, times and costs. From time to time, research into specific aspects of vehicle engineering is undertaken for manufacturers.

The results of the Centre's research are published in methods manuals, special reports, newsletters and in the form of parts pricing information. Once the work study engineer has evaluated the information obtained through observation and consultation, the data is published in a methods manual. These contain comprehensive data on repair methods and times, welding tables and diagrams, and technical information supplied by the vehicle manufacturer. The results of the specialized research are published through special reports. Newsletters supplement published data, providing information for immediate action within the vehicle repair industry.

Training is seen as an essential and increasingly important part of the work done. Thatcham provides courses for insurance company staff engineers and independent consultant assessors, concentrating on the latest developments in jig technology, welding and refinishing. Help is also offered to develop potential repair talent by encouraging educational institutes, such as technical training colleges, to visit the Centre.

Overall, the staff are working towards enhanced low-speed impact performances; quicker and more cost-effective repairs; and a better understanding between those who do the repairs and those who pay for them. Thatcham continues to influence and improve repair technology, keeping pace with the ever-increasing sophistication of the modern motor vehicle to the benefit of the motoring public.

QUESTIONS

1 Define the terms 'primary damage' and 'secondary damage'.
2 Explain the theory of collapsing metal panels when they are involved in a collision.
3 Define the terms 'visible damage' and 'concealed damage'.
4 Define the term 'direction of damage'.
5 Describe what is meant by direct damage to metal panels.
6 With the aid of a sketch, explain the difference between a single- and a double-crowned panel surface.
7 Use a sketch to explain the principle of the Mitek system.
8 Describe, with the aid of a sketch, the principle of the Korek system.

9 State two advantages of Dozer equipment when used in repair.
10 Describe how the vector principle is applied in repair work.
11 With the aid of a sketch, describe pressure areas and tension areas on a damaged panel section.
12 Explain the basic use of the pulling tower system in the repair of vehicle bodies.
13 Draw a sketch to show how a Dozer can be used to repair a front end damaged by collision.
14 What are the comparable advantages of portable and fixed body jigs?
15 Explain the term 'bracketless jig systems'.
16 What are the advantages of using bracketless jig systems?
17 State the procedure to be followed in order to mount a vehicle on a bracket-type jig system.
18 State the advantages of a dual alignment and repair system.
19 Explain how the measurement system works on Dataliner equipment.
20 How can misalignment of a car body affect the control of the vehicle when it is being driven on the road?
21 Use a simple sketch to show how the dropline method of alignment is carried out.
22 Use a simple sketch to show how gunsight gauges are used in repair.
23 State the factors which determine whether damaged panels should be repaired or replaced.
24 List, in logical sequence, a basic approach to the repair procedure adopted in major collision damage.
25 What is meant by repairing using partial panel replacement?
26 List four methods of panel removal and the tools used.
27 Why is a vehicle road tested following major repair work?
28 Describe a method of repair by replacement of a front wing which has received major accident damage.
29 What is the importance of care of customer's vehicles when received for repair in the workshop?
30 Describe the difference between a laminated glass windscreen and a toughened glass windscreen.
31 With the aid of a sketch, describe the fitting of an indirect glazed windscreen.
32 Describe the removal of a direct glazed windscreen, and the type of equipment that would be used.
33 Describe in detail how to check for door aperture alignment.
34 Explain the method of repairing and aligning a

damaged body shell, when using a jig and hydraulic pulling equipment.

35 Explain why a careful study of accident damage is necessary, before any stripping or repair is carried out.

36 State the advantages of having a body jig system incorporated in a lift system.

37 Why is it essential to check the steering geometry of a vehicle after major repair work has been carried out?

38 Describe the four stages of the procedure for dealing with repairs carried out under an insurance claim.

39 How are material costs established on an estimate?

40 State the importance of the clearance certificate.

41 A suspension frame member is to be replaced by welding; explain the correct method of achieving its alignment before hand.

42 A vehicle is to have the rear boot floor, wheel arch and quarter panel assemblies removed. State the repair procedure to reinstate these panel assemblies.

43 With the aid of a sketch, show the position of a pull-dozer to realign a centre pillar after side impact.

44 Explain the repair procedure necessary for part panel replacement on the quarter panel assembly of a four-door saloon.

45 With the aid of labelled sketches, show the difference between direct glazing and indirect glazing.

46 Outline the procedure for mounting a vehicle on a jig using the MZ bracket system.

47 Show, with the aid of a sketch, how the laser on Dataliner equipment can achieve a 90 degree angle.

48 State the advantages of the use of split measuring bridges on a jig measuring system.

49 Explain what is meant by the term 'universal jig bracket'.

50 State the safety precautions necessary when carrying out pulling in repair.

9

Company administration and personnel

9.1 THE COMPANY

9.1.1 Company structures

The company's size will dictate its structure according to the number of employees. Additional factors which will also influence the structure are whether the company is a dealership within a chain of companies, or an independent bodyshop, or a one man owner/employee.

A large company is usually headed by a board of directors, and immediately below the board comes the person responsible for the running of the company (managing director).

A smaller company could be run by an owner, a director, or manager, or one person fulfilling all these roles.

The managing director
From the managing director should emerge a structure that would ensure the effective use of all resources and a suitable place for every member of the company. Without such a structure, organization will be unsatisfactory and control impossible.

Company structure is usually based on a simple line organization which shows the various staff levels from higher management down to office and workshop. At each level the person in charge is answerable to the figure of authority immediately above him/her, and thus graded levels of authority are laid down.

Below senior management come middle managers, then second and third line supervisors, who interpret rules and policies. The first-line supervisors oversee rather than perform work, while the second-line supervisors, for example the chargehand, are still performing an operator's job but also have some responsibility. Next we reach the operators who are skilled tradesmen, then the apprentices trained by the tradesmen and finally semi-skilled or unskilled operators responsible for their own task.

Many activities are undertaken within the vehicle bodyshop. Bodyshops range in size from the one man business, to very large groups employing many hundreds of staff. The average bodyshop is relatively small with between 10 and 30 employees. This is due chiefly to the requirements of the area in which the company is based (Figures 9.1a, 9.1b, 9.1c).

Bodyshops can be classified as:

1 Sole trader. A one man business trading under his own name with or without employees.
2 Partnership. Two or more individuals trading under their own names.
3 Firm. A one man business or partnership trading under a name which is not their own: such a business must be registered. It should be noted that in partnerships, each partner is responsible for all the debts even to the extent of his own private assets.
4 Limited companies – private or public. Shareholders put up the original capital and become risk-takers only up to the amount of their shareholdings. Every business registered under the Companies Act becomes legal, with rights and duties subject to their constitution and the law.

9.1.2 Staff responsibilities

Duties and responsibilities of staff
In order to ensure comprehensive cover of all duties it is essential to define clearly the work of each person in charge. Job descriptions for skilled and unskilled personnel are not usually written down since they know what is expected from them.

Companies of all kinds will have fixed areas of responsibility that consist of clearly defined jobs. The person in charge of each area of responsibility should have a clear knowledge of what is required of him/her in order to prevent an overlap of duties. A written job description in the form of a contract can achieve this.

A job description usually includes the following:

1 Title of job. Job location, main purpose of job.
2 Duties and responsibilities. Limits of authority, scope of job and its responsibility.

3 Skill and knowledge required. Desirable modifications.
4 Working conditions. Dangerous and hazardous conditions should be mentioned.
5 Economic conditions. Rates of pay, bonus payments, holidays, sickness benefits.

Bodyshop manager – vehicle repair

1 To be directly responsible to owner/director/board of directors. Also to interpret policy decisions and have them implemented.
2 To achieve an agreed return on the company's investment on its workshop facilities.
3 To promote customer satisfaction by providing good customer care, high quality repairs and workmanship.
4 To supervise all personnel connected with work, to ensure their safe working conditions at all times and to ensure that company safety policies are applied.
5 To be responsible for all other parts of the workshop.
6 To relate with insurance assessors, other repair establishments, MIRRA and VBRA.
7 To control department costs and supervise all paperwork including invoices, monthly statements and profit and loss accounts.
8 To ensure that apprentice training programmes meet the company requirements and see that apprentices attend a College of Further Education.
9 To hire or dismiss staff according to company policies.

Foreman

The foreman must be a good supervisor and have first-class practical experience and knowledge of the vehicle body trade, but most important he must have the ability to handle the workforce. His duty is to allocate work to various tradesmen in the workshop, and he is directly responsible to the bodyshop manager for the quantity, quality and safe performance of the work carried out by each employee under his supervision. He is also responsible for team building and providing any training and development needed by the employees to update their individual knowledge and expertise and consequently improve their efficiency and productivity.

Reception engineer/receptionist

It can be the reception engineer or a receptionist who meets the customer and finally hands back the car upon completion of the repair. The attitude and behaviour of the reception engineer must reflect the image of the company. This could be the customer's first contact with the company and it must be a favourable one.

In the case of the receptionist, he/she is not technically trained and therefore is there only to welcome the customer in a friendly, professional manner and take details of the vehicle.

The receptionist engineer must be fully trained both in handling the public and technically, having acquired written qualification and practical expertise.

Skilled vehicle repairers/painters and body fitters

The quality of labour and the high standard of workmanship are two of the most important assets to any bodyshop establishment. It is important that the trained personnel are kept up to date with proper training and manufacturers' short courses, especially in paint, car repair jig equipment and welding techniques.

Companies wishing to acquire the Quality Standard ISO 9002 (formerly BS 5750) are required to train their operatives to carry out welding tests to an acceptable standard.

Semi-skilled and unskilled personnel

These personnel should have their work checked by the foreman as he is directly responsible for them. They are usually employed on polishing, car valeting and general cleaning duties.

Apprentices

It is essential that a company should have a number of apprentices so that there will be a constant supply of skilled tradesmen who have been trained by the company to their own high standards. Apprentices are normally taken straight from school and every opportunity must be provided for them to continue their technical training at local colleges through courses such as the NVQ, while also continuing their in-house experience.

9.1.3 Company management

Traditional management structure

Traditional management is based on management by personal experience and technical ability, and quite often lacks any logical method or system or specific managerial qualifications.

Organized management systems
(quality procedures)

This is based on a combination of technical ability and managerial skill and has largely superseded the traditional management methods. The principle is based on work study methods which were developed to aid management plan efficiency and productivity into every job within the company.

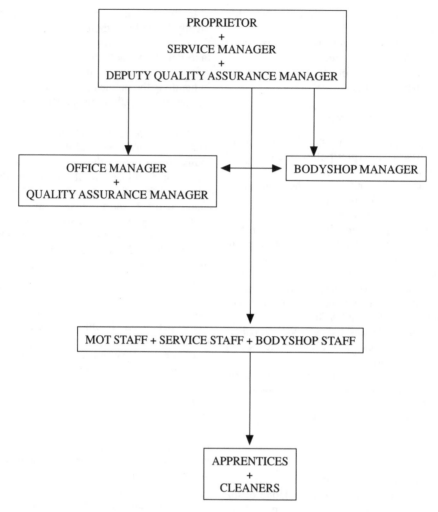

Figure 9.1a Quality assurance organization chart (Parkway Consultancy)

By operating a management system according to the defined criteria of a standard, then the company has taken all reasonable steps to guarantee quality to their customers, and provided evidence of their commitment to do so.

The assurance of quality is needed to illustrate failures and complaints and their associated costs as far as possible.

Quality Assurance Systems provide the mechanism for ensuring that a business satisfies the needs of its customers by identifying basic disciplines, procedures and criteria to ensure that products and services meet the customer's requirements.

Management functions

Planning Should cover: the establishment of objectives to determine the end results; a programme to

establish sequence and priorities of action steps to be followed in researching objectives; a schedule to establish the time sequence for programming steps; budgeting to allocate the necessary resources to achieve objectives; establishing procedures to develop and apply standardized working methods; developing policies to make decisions which apply to the problems of the enterprise as a whole.

Organization To develop an organizational structure; delegation, entrusting authority to others and creating accountability; establishing relationships creating conditions for cooperation.

Directing Selection, to choose people for positions in the organization; appraising evaluation performance and capabilities; training and development, helping people to improve their knowledge aptitudes and skills;

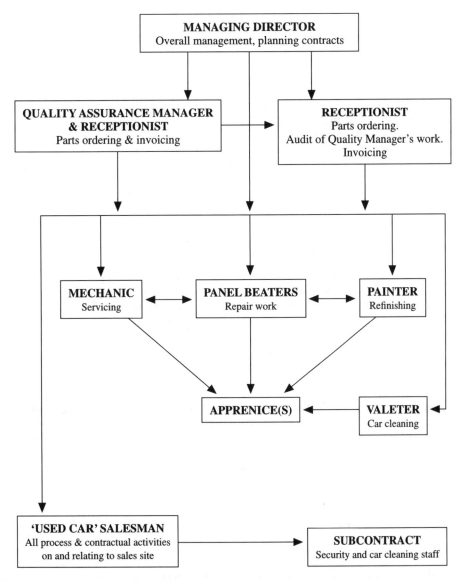

Figure 9.1b Quality assurance organization chart (Parkway Consultancy)

salary review, to determine a fair day's pay for work carried out; decision making, arriving at conclusions and judgements; dismissing staff.

Controlling The establishing of performance standards, measuring, evaluation and correcting.

Principles of organization

1 Objective.
2 Specialization.
3 Coordination.
4 Authority.
5 Responsibility.
6 Unity of command.
7 Span of control.
8 Chain of command.

9.1.4 Staff selection

The correct selection of staff is very important because of the Employment Protection Act which gives employees considerable protection against wrongful dismissal.

When selecting staff for new appointments the following areas should be considered:

319

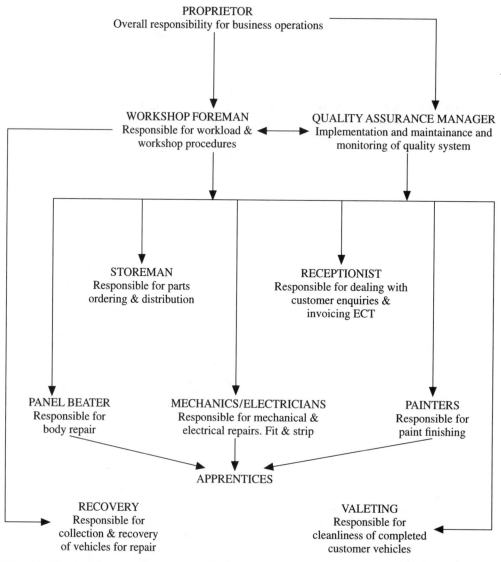

Figure 9.1c Quality assurance organization chart (Parkway Consultancy)

1 Physique – General health. Special fitness requirements for the job (e.g. colour blindness would be a disadvantage for a refinishing operator).
2 Attainments – Special qualifications required for the job.
3 General intelligence – Apprentices should be of at least average intelligence, while managerial posts will demand higher intelligence.
4 Special aptitudes – Special dexterity required for the job.
5 Interests – Any particular constructive hobbies or lively interests that could be potentially useful.
6 Disposition – Would the applicant work well as part of a team?

7 Circumstance – A wide range of factors come under this heading: age, race, mobility, qualifications, experience.

Job evaluation

This is a logical method of working out the relative values of jobs which may be graded according to a particular skill, training or qualifications needed, to physical requirements, to responsibilities involved or to working conditions. However, the establishment of a fair rate of pay does not usually involve the body repair establishments in evaluating jobs which require skill of a specialist practical nature as well as the cooperation of trade union representatives.

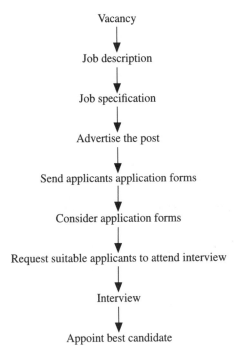

Vacancy

↓

Job description

↓

Job specification

↓

Advertise the post

↓

Send applicants application forms

↓

Consider application forms

↓

Request suitable applicants to attend interview

↓

Interview

↓

Appoint best candidate

Figure 9.1d Sequence of staff appointments

Manpower forecasting
This involves attempts to forecast the number and types of personnel that will be required in an organization. The figure obtained will depend on the replacement needs to maintain staff numbers and will be affected by any future technological or organizational developments that call for special skills or qualifications. An effective manpower plan will anticipate such developments and take into consideration the career structures offered by the organization. Manpower planning is a management function and each manager should be familiar with his/her own existing requirements and future needs. Staff may retire or leave for other jobs, new techniques or new equipment comes into use, and thus existing staff must be retrained or new staff recruited.

Personnel training
The training of personnel requires a careful study of the objectives related to a particular job before the relevant skills and competences are taught. Continual assessment must be maintained throughout the training programme to ensure that the trainee will be able to complete the required work to the standard needed, thus progressive assessment tests should form part of the skill training (Figure 9.2).

Training and safety are synonymous and the highly skilled worker is usually a safe worker.

9.2 THE CUSTOMER

9.2.1 Types of customer/client

Customer care is important in any company bodyshop if customers are to be retained. Customers must feel satisfied with the service offered from the moment they arrive on the premises at reception where they expect to be treated with respect and listened to with patience and courtesy. Then the work should be completed with skill and to the safety and technical standards laid down by the vehicle manufacturers, ready for collection of the repaired vehicle.

Some companies now assure the quality of their service by achieving ISO 9002, formerly BS 5750, which is the British Standard mark of quality. Customers are also protected by the Motor Manufacturer's Code of Practice and for those bodyshops which are members of the VBRA, their code of practice (see Section 9.3.6).

Customers can be divided into different categories, and the relationship with and approach to the customer will depend on this.

Categories can be broadly divided into the following:

Private customers Those whose work is covered by insurance and those who pay for any work not covered by insurance will both require the same high standard of customer care and service and quality of work.

Business customers who use a company car, who contract all their work, or are part of a dealership which would subcontract work will expect the same standard of customer care and service as they themselves offer to their clients.

Established customers will expect consistency in the quality of work and the maximum of personal attention.

New customers who are attracted by the quality of work done and the service offered by the company and therefore require these to meet their expectations.

9.2.2 Customer relations

A pleasing approach to customers is essential. Courtesy costs nothing but can mean so much. A smart, clean appearance and ability to instil confidence into the customers by demonstrating a good knowledge of operations are essential parts of customer relations. Enquiries should be dealt with promptly and courteously. Visitors to the premises should be offered directions to the appropriate department.

NAME	START DATE	DATE of BIRTH	EMPLOYEE REF No.
ADDRESS	TELEPHONE	JOB TITLE	HOLIDY ENTITLEMENT PAYMENT TERMS
QUALIFICATION AND RESPONSIBILITY (see reverse side of copy)		NOTICE REQUIRED	
		ASSESSMENT	

TRAINING SCHEDULE	DATES: SCHEDULED/ COMPLETED	EMPLOYEE/ TRAINER	SIGNATURE TRAINEE

STAFF PERMITTED TO:

Road Test	
Final Inspect	
Deliver	
Move vehicle on company premises	
Issue stock from stores	
Handle customer complaints	
Estimate/Contract/Amendments to Contracts	
Recovery (Ordering–Controlling)	
Recovery (Operating)	
Calibration (In house)	
Welding	
Painting	
Disposal of Scrap	

√ = Allowed to carry out procedure
No mark = Not allowed to carry out procedure
Other work specified:

Figure 9.2 Personnel training record (Parkway Consultancy)

Date:	Person taking current details:	Job/Ref No:

Customer and Vehicle details	Details of complaint (continue overleaf if required).

Corrective Action (Include comment from person responsible for area of complaint).

(Note what you are going to do to solve the complaint)

Signature of person responsible for corrective action ....

Date scheduled to complete corrective action ....

Date "closed off" ....
Signature ....

Figure 9.3 Customer complaint and corrective action form (Parkway Consultancy)

Handling customer complaints

In spite of tight quality control, a company can occasionally find a disgruntled customer on their hands with complaints about work carried out. All complaints must be dealt with purposefully and it is the responsibility of senior management to ensure that staff are trained in dealing with complaints (Figures 9.3 and 9.4).

Staff dealing with complaints should observe the following points:

Be a good listener and remain courteous

Allow the customer to express his feelings

Show genuine interest in the complaint no matter how small

Never contradict the customer (remember the customer thinks he is right)

Never lose your temper as this can aggravate the situation

To resolve any complaint:

Obtain all facts about the work done on job cards, invoices, quality control checks

Determine what needs to be done to rectify the complaint

Explain to the customer exactly what will be done to remove the cause of the complaint

Follow up correction of the fault by contacting the customer in two or three weeks to ensure that he is now totally satisfied with the work carried out

Where cases cannot be resolved customers can use the conciliatory services of an independent examiner, for example RAC, AA, VBRA or the Institute of Automobile Engineer Assessors, which will endeavour to achieve a settlement based on the facts at their disposal and an examination of the vehicle.

If a genuine interest and concern is demonstrated by the staff involved, the reputation and prestige of the company will be upheld. Quality work in itself is a powerful promotion for the company.

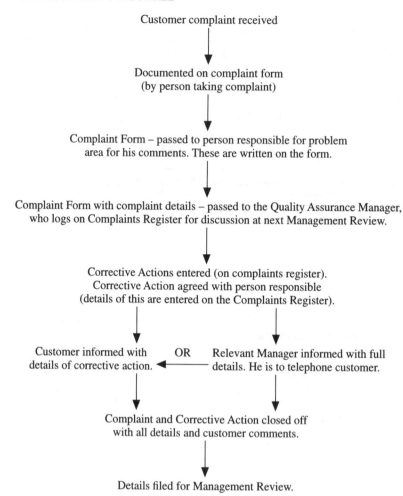

Customer complaint received

Documented on complaint form
(by person taking complaint)

Complaint Form – passed to person responsible for problem
area for his comments. These are written on the form.

Complaint Form with complaint details – passed to the Quality Assurance Manager,
who logs on Complaints Register for discussion at next Management Review.

Corrective Actions entered (on complaints register).
Corrective Action agreed with person responsible
(details of this are entered on the Complaints Register).

Customer informed with   OR   Relevant Manager informed with full
details of corrective action.   details. He is to telephone customer.

Complaint and Corrective Action closed off
with all details and customer comments.

Details filed for Management Review.

Note: When customer complaint is not settled we accept arbitration by any *mutually* acceptable neutral party (e.g. AA, RAC, MVRA, IMI, SMMT, RMI, or Insurance company assessor.

Figure 9.4   Customer complaint procedure chart (Parkway Consultancy)

9.3   THE LAW RELATING TO COMPANIES AND CUSTOMERS

9.3.1   Construction and Use Regulations

The Road Vehicles (Construction and Use) Regulations 1986

The motor vehicle Construction and Use Regulations govern the construction and use of motor vehicles on the roads in Great Britain. These regulations are constantly being amended and updated. They also require, in some instances, that the vehicles or parts of vehicles should bear a mark confirming that the vehicle conforms to certain specific requirements. Furthermore certain vehicles must be type approved

before they can be registered for use on the roads in Great Britain. These requirements are for both private vehicles and vehicles which carry goods.

Provisions covered by the regulations

A motor vehicle and all parts and accessories shall be at all times in such a condition that no danger is caused or likely to be caused to any person in or on the vehicle or on the road. The vehicle must also be suitable for the purpose for which it is used. The following are a list of the provisions covered by the regulations:

1 Brakes and braking efficiency.
2 Tyre loads and speed ratings.

3 Mixing of tyres.
4 Condition and maintenance of tyres.
5 Steering gear.
6 Windscreen and window glass.
7 Mirrors.
8 Windscreen wipers and washers.
9 Speedometers.
10 Audible warning instruments.
11 Petrol tank.
12 Power to weight ratio.
13 Rear under-run protection and side guards (commercial vehicles).
14 Silencers and smoke emission.
15 Spray suppression devices (commercial vehicles).
16 Towing.
17 Testing and inspection.
18 Ministry plates.

Type approval
Before a passenger car or dual purpose vehicle can be licensed for use on the roads in Great Britain, there must be an approval certificate in force for the vehicle unless it is specifically excluded from the type approval requirements.

'Type Approval' is the name given to the system which allows components and vehicles to be tested against prescribed standards. If the tests are successful each component or vehicle manufactured to that specification will carry the type approval.

There are two main type approval systems:

Economic Commission for Europe (ECE) The ECE agreement on type approval limits itself to setting standards for vehicle components and equipment but not entire vehicles. In the UK a number of ECE regulations have been incorporated into the standards laid down in legislation such as Construction and Use Regulations. The ECE type approved components are identified by a type approval mark which incorporates a circle enclosing an 'E' together with a number, for example, (E11)

European Economic Community (EEC) EEC type approval directives are concerned with vehicles in an assembled state and member states are obliged to incorporate specific standards into their own national legislation. EEC type approval vehicles and vehicle systems are identified by a type approval mark which incorporates the letter 'e' together with a number, for example [e11]

Vehicle Type Approval in the UK Vehicle type approvals in the UK are based on the EEC system. Once a vehicle has been type approved the manufacturer or importer will issue a Type Approval Certificate of Conformity (TAC) for vehicles manufactured within the EEC (of which the UK is a member) and which therefore allows vehicles to be used on roads in the UK.

In the case of vehicles manufactured outside the EEC a Minister's Approval Certificate (MAC) must be obtained.

9.3.2 Road Traffic Act 1988

This Act has very wide ranging powers covering most of the elements surrounding road transport. These include major offences such as driving under the influence of alcohol or drugs to offences concerning construction and use of vehicles. In some cases the act empowers local authorities to create special legislation tailored to suit the needs of their particular areas, that is speed limits, restricting access of certain vehicles to congested city centres.

Example: D purchased a car from company P, then a week later D complained about the vehicle's performance and steering. Company P's foreman stated that there was nothing wrong with the car. An independent inspection of the vehicle showed the steering was faulty and the vehicle was unroadworthy and had been in this condition at the time of the sale.

Company P is guilty under the Road Traffic Act where it is an offence to sell an unroadworthy vehicle, unless its condition is known to the buyer at the time of the sale.

9.3.3 Trade Description Act

The purpose of this Act is to protect the consumer by imposing criminal liability on traders who apply a false description to goods or make misleading statements about services. It does not alter the consumer's contractual rights. To be liable under the Act, the person applying the false description must do so within the course of trade or business.

The term 'trade description' means any statement relating to quality, quantity, size, composition, method of manufacture, production, processing, or reconditioning, fitness for purpose, place or date of manufacture, other history including previous ownership of goods.

False description of goods
The Act provides that any person who is in the course of trade or business shall, subject to provision of this Act, be guilty of an offence if he/she:

1 Applies a false trade description to any trade or goods.

2 Supplies or offers to supply any goods to which a false trade description is applied.

Example 1: A motor vehicle which was manufactured in 1990 and first registered in 1993, was later advertised by company X as a 'used 1993 model'.

Company X was guilty under this Act.

Example 2: A second-hand car was advertised for sale by D and described as a 'beautiful car'. Although it looked beautiful, it was mechanically unsound and unroadworthy.

D argued that his statement was true and referred only to the appearance of the vehicle. He was guilty because the description was false to a material degree. A reasonable person would have taken the description to refer to the vehicle as a whole, not just its appearance.

9.3.4 Law of Contract

The purpose of a contract is that the contracting parties each undertake to do something, and the failure of either to carry out his/her part of the contract renders him/her liable to a legal action by the other party.

Most simple contracts are oral agreements, for example buying petrol, buying motor vehicle components, etc.

A contract may be defined as an agreement which is legally enforceable.

The contract should include four essential components as follows:

1 An agreement between the contracting parties.
2 The provision of consideration to support the contract.
3 An intention to become legally bound by the contract.
4 Legal capacity held by each of the contracting parties.

The absence of any one of the above will prevent the making of a contract.

A contract cannot be created without the parties reaching an agreement. The idea of an agreement is therefore central to an understanding of the Law of Contract.

In the business context there are two legal questions which arise in respect of all transactions. These are whether a legal, enforceable agreement has been made and what are the terms upon which it is based. In other words, agreements are arrangements to do, or sometimes refrain from doing, specific things, and these specific things are the terms of the contract.

The law requires that certain contracts should be made in writing because in some cases it provides the consumer with a measure of protection, while in other cases it provides the means of recording their respective obligations, especially in technical transactions.

Contracts that are commonly expressed in writing include, for example arranging for credit facilities in order to purchase a new car.

9.3.5 Supply of Goods and Services Act 1982

The Act sets out terms which will be implied both into contracts for the supply of services and into contracts for work done and materials supplied.

In a contract for the supply of a service where the supplier is acting in the course of a business, there is an implied understanding that the supplier will carry out the service: (a) with reasonable care and skill – in a contract for the supply of a service where the supplier is acting in the course of a business, there is an implied term that the supplier will carry out services with reasonable care and skill; (b) within a reasonable time – where under a contract for the supply of a service by a supplier acting in the course of a business, the time for the service to be carried out is not fixed by the contract, there is an implied term that the supplier will carry out the service within a reasonable time; (c) for a reasonable charge, where no prior agreed payment has been made – where under a contract for the supply of a service, the consideration is not determined by the contract, there is an implied term that the party contracting with the supplier will pay a reasonable charge.

Example: P recovered damages for D's unreasonable delay in performing a contract. D took eight weeks to repair P's car when a reasonably competent repairer would have completed the repairs within five weeks. If a reasonable time has elapsed within which the contract should have been performed, the customer is entitled unilaterally to serve a notice fixing a time for performance of the contract (making time of the essence). The new time limit must be reasonable and if the supplier fails to meet it the other party may rescind the contract.

9.3.6 Warranty/guarantee

Both of the above words, warranty and guarantee, are used to refer to the promise given by a manufacturer or retailer when he sells goods or services, that he will meet the cost of correcting defects in those goods or services within a stipulated time or an amount of usage.

With all kinds of work in the vehicle repair industry a warranty against failure due to workmanship must be given for a specific mileage or time period. This should be stated on customers' invoices. All companies should be insured against loss claims arising from such failure. A manufacturer's warranty offers the customer a simple and straightforward way of having manufacturers' faults appearing within certain times put right at little or no cost. Different warranty dates of certain parts must be clearly stated on the warranty form to prevent misunderstanding by the customer.

The useful life expectancy of manufactured products and consumer rights are increasingly being determined by legislation.

The Motor Industry Code of Practice requires that the following inclusions are made in a guarantee:

1 A statement that it does not alter or affect any of the consumer's rights against the retailer under the Sale of Goods Act.
2 The terms of the guarantee must be easily understood, especially any inclusions or exclusions.
3 Manufacturers should give advice about what to do if a problem arises regarding parts and accessories not covered by the guarantee.
4 The manufacturer should allow any unexpired portion of a guarantee to be transferred to a subsequent owner.
5 The manufacturer should make clear that necessary rectification work may be done by any of his franchised dealers whether or not they were the original seller.
6 When a car is off the road for an extended period due to rectification of guarantee faults the manufacturer must operate fair policies to allow the extension of the original time covered.

Code of Practice operated by VBRA (Vehicle Body Repair Association Ltd)

The Code covers the conduct of VBRA members engaged in vehicle body repair and their relationship with their customers. It reflects the high standards adopted by VBRA members and the protection that the customer has in using the facilities offered by a VBRA member. The Code's provisions are subject to regular review by VBRA and the DGFT (Director General of Fair Trading).

The following gives a summary of this Code of Practice:

1 To ensure that repair work is carried out at a cost which is fair to both customer and repairer.
2 The repairer shall be responsible for the merchantable quality, fitness for purpose and the description of goods he sells (Sale of Goods Act 1979 and Supply of Goods and Services Act 1982).
3 The repairer shall be responsible to ensure that all repair work is carried out in a proper and workmanlike manner to the safety and technical standards laid down by the vehicle's original manufacturer.
4 The repairer should provide a written estimate for the cost of a repair. Also, if necessary, the customer's express permission for any increase in an agreed estimate.
5 The repairer shall state the estimated time for the repair of a vehicle and shall make every effort to inform the customer if this estimated time cannot be met.
6 The repairer shall supply a detailed invoice including the breakdown of costs, labour charges, parts and materials.
7 The repairer shall provide a written guarantee to exchange or repair any defective parts which need replacement or repair by reason of defective materials or workmanship during the repair.
8 The guarantee shall be for a period of not less than 24 months' or 24 000 miles' use, whichever occurs first from the date the repairs were done. This time should be extended to cover any prolonged period a vehicle is off the road due to rectification of faults caused by previous work done during the guarantee period.
9 The repairer should allow the transfer of any unexpired portion of a guarantee to a subsequent owner.

Vehicle manufacturers' guarantees

Some manufacturers give a three year cosmetic paintwork warranty. This warranty covers eligible vehicles against the eruption, peeling, cracking, discolouration or staining of visible surfaces of all painted body panels as a result of faulty manufacture or materials.

In addition six year anti-corrosion warranties are given which cover vehicles against perforation due to rust-through of the body panels. The term 'rust-through' means the rusting through from the inside or outside of body panels as a result of faulty manufacture or materials, and does not cover corrosion caused by neglect, accident damage, stone chips or other influences.

QUESTIONS

1 Explain the role and responsibility of the works manager.
2 With the aid of a flowchart show the organizational structure of a typical body repair establishment.
3 Explain the term 'manpower planning'.
4 Explain the term 'job description'.

5 What is meant by the term 'job specification'?

6 What is meant by the term 'technical receptionist'?

7 Explain what is meant by traditional management.

8 Explain the difference between traditional and organized management systems.

9 State four basic management functions.

10 Explain the meaning of the term 'work study'.

11 With the aid of a flowchart explain the sequence for the appointment of new staff.

12 Discuss the need for a personnel training programme.

13 Explain the importance of customer relationships within a bodyshop.

14 Explain the importance of quality control within a bodyshop.

15 What is meant by 'warranty work'?

16 Name four of the provisions covered under the Construction and Use Regulations.

17 Explain what is meant by 'type approval'.

18 Which Act would effect the use of an unroadworthy vehicle on the public highway?

19 What is the purpose of the Trade Description Act?

20 List the four essential elements which should be included in a contract.

Glossary

(Note: Words in italics are specific terms used in NVQ terminology)

Abrasive   A substance used for wearing away a surface by rubbing.

Accelerator   A constituent of synthetic resin mix which hastens a reaction.

Accessories   Optional extras not essential to the running of a vehicle, e.g. radio, heater.

Accreditation   A scheme which identifies the competence skills or knowledge acquired by an individual for which credit can be given.

Acetone   A liquid hydrocarbon capable of dissolving 25 times its own volume of acetylene gas at atmospheric pressure.

Acetylene   A combustible gas which is mixed with oxygen and used in oxyacetylene welding.

Adhesion   The ability to adhere to a surface.

Adhesive   A substance that allows two surfaces to adhere together.

Adjustments   Necessary alterations to improve tolerances in fit.

Air bags   A passive safety restraint system that inflates automatically on vehicle impact to protect the driver.

Alignment   The operation of bringing into line two or more specified points on a vehicle structure.

All-metal construction   Generally this applies to those body shells of both private cars and light commercial vehicles in which the construction is in the form of steel pressings assembled by welding, thus forming a fabricated unit.

Alloy   A mixture of two or more metals with, or without, other metallic or non-metallic elements.

A-post   A structural pillar on which the front door is hung.

Assessment   Procedure for determining the extent to which an individual has reached a desired level of competence.

Awarding body   An examining or validating body.

Backfire   In arc welding, a momentary return of gases indicated in the blowpipe by a pop or loud bang, the flame immediately recovering and burning normally at the blowpipe.

Backhand welding   Sometimes classified as 'rightward welding'. A technique in which the flame is directed backwards against the completed part of the weld.

Back light   A central window in the rear panel of the driving cab, or the rear window of a saloon body.

BC-post   Central pillar acting as a central roof and side support between the rear and the front of the car.

Bevel angle   The angle of a prepared edge creating a bevel prior to welding.

Billet   An oblong piece of metal having a square section.

Binder   A resin or cementing constituent of a compound.

Blowpipe   A tool used for welding known as a welding torch.

Body   The structured part of a vehicle which encompasses the passenger, engine and luggage compartments.

Body hardware   Functional accessories of vehicle body, e.g. door handles.

Body lock pillar   A body pillar that incorporates a lock striker plate.

Body mounting   Conventional body mounted on car chassis in composite method of body construction.

Body panels   Pressed metal panels, or plastic moulded composite panels, which are fastened together to form the skin of a car body.

Body side moulding   The exterior trim moulding fastened to the exterior of the body in a horizontal position.

Body sill   The panel directly below the bottom of the doors.

Body spoon   A body repairer's hand tool.

Body trim   The materials which are used in the interior of the body for lining and upholstery.

Bonnet   The metal cover over the engine compartment.

Boot   A compartment provided in a car body which takes the luggage and often the spare wheel and fuel tank. It may be at the front or rear of the body depending on the location of the engine.

Boot lid   Door covering luggage compartment.

Bottom side   The frame member of the base of the body extending along the full length of the main portion of the body.

Brazing   A non-fusion process in which the filler metal has a lower melting point than the parent metal(s).

Buckles   The resulting distortion of body panels after collision.

Bulkhead   A transverse support in a body structure.

Bumping   Reshaping metal with a hammer and dolly.

Burr   The resulting condition left on a metal edge after cutting or filling.

Bursting disc   A type of pressure relief device which consists of a disc, usually of metal, which is so held that it confines the pressure of the cylinder under normal conditions. The disc is intended to rupture between limits of over-pressure due to abnormal conditions, particularly when the cylinder is exposed to fire.

Butt joint   A welded joint in which the ends or edges of two pieces of metal directly face each other.

Calibrate   To check irregularities in measuring instruments.

Cant panel   The curved section of the roof top running between the comparatively flat top and the rain drip or gutter.

Cantrail   The longitudinal framing of the roof at the joint.

Carbon dioxide   A heavy, colourless and incombustible gas which results from the perfect combustion of carbon.

Carbon fibre   An extremely strong, though expensive, reinforcement which can be used in conjunction with fibreglass. It gives increased rigidity to the laminate.

Carbonizing flame   An oxyacetylene flame adjustment created by an excess of acetylene over oxygen, resulting in an excess of carbon in the flame.

Case hardening   This is the process of hardening the outer case or shell of steel articles, which is accomplished by inducing additional carbon into the case of the steel by a variety of methods.

Catalyst   A chemical substance which brings about a chemical change to produce a different substance.

Catalyst dispenser   A purpose-designed container for measuring and dispensing liquid catalyst without splashing.

Centre pillar   The centre vertical support of a four-door saloon.

Certification   The means by which achievement in terms of competence, skills or knowledge is recorded or documented.

Chassis   The base frame of a motor vehicle of composite construction to which the body is attached.

Check valve   A safety device that controls the passage of gas or air in one direction, in order to prevent the reversal of gas flow and a consequent accident.

Chemical reaction   The resulting change when two or more chemical substances are mixed.

Chopped strand mat   Chopped strands bonded into a mat to produce a popular economical general-purpose reinforcement.

Chopped strands   As the name suggests, glass fibre strands chopped into short (about 12 mm) lengths. They can be used as fillers. Useful for bodywork repairs.

Circuit   The path along which electricity flows. When the path is continuous, the circuit is closed and the current flows. When the path is broken, the circuit is open and no current flows.

Client   The person or organization employing the services offered, e.g. employer, sponsor, learner.

Cold curing   Generic term for materials which harden at room temperature, after the addition of a catalyst.

Collapsible steering column   A safety feature in the form of an energy-absorbing steering column designed to collapse on impact.

Compartment shelf panel   The horizontal panel situated between the rear seat back and the back window.

Competence   The ability to perform activities to a required standard in an occupation.

Competence element   A statement that describes what can be done, an action, behaviour, or outcome which an individual should be able to demonstrate.

Compressive strength   The ability of a material to withstand being crushed. It is found by testing a sample to failure: the load applied, divided by the cross-section of the sample, gives the compressive strength.

Condensation   A change of state from a gas to a liquid caused by temperature or pressure changes. It may also be formed by moisture from the air being deposited on a cool surface.

Conductor   Any material or substance that allows current or heat to flow through it.

Continuous assessment   Assessment of competence on every occasion during normal workplace activity. Used for formative assessment and to arrive at a cumulative judgement for final assessment purposes.

Copper acetylide   A spontaneously explosive and inflammable substance which forms when acetylene is passed through a copper tube.

Corrosion   The wearing away or gradual destruction of a substance, e.g. rusting of metal.

Curing   The change of a binder from soluble fusible state to insoluble infusible state by chemical action.

Curing time   The time needed for liquid resin to reach a solid state after the catalyst has been added.

Cutting tip   A torch especially adapted for cutting.

Cylinder   Steel containers used for storage of compressed gases.

Dash panel   A panel attached to the front bulkhead assembly and which provides a mounting for all instruments necessary to check the performance of the vehicle.

Deposited metal   Filler metal from a welding rod or electrode which has been melted by a welding process and applied in the form of a joint or built up.

Diagnosis   The determination, by examination, of the cause of a problem.

Dinging   Straightening damaged metal with spoons, hammers or dollies. In the early days the dingman was the tradesman who worked on completed bodies to remove minor imperfections without injury to the high gloss lacquer or varnish.

Dinging hammer   A special hammer used for dinging or removal of dents.

Direct damage   Primary damage which results from an impact on the area in actual contact with the object causing the damage.

Dolly block   A hand tool, made from special steel, shaped to suit the contour of various panel assemblies and used in conjunction with a planishing hammer to smooth out damaged panel surfaces.

Door skins   Outside door panels.

Door trim   The interior lining of a door.

D-post   The rear standing pillar providing a shut face for the rear door and forming the rear quarter panel area.

Drip moulding   A roof trough to direct water from door openings.

Electrode   The usual term for the filler rod which is deposited when using the electric arc welding process.

Electrolyte   A substance which dissolves in water to give a solution capable of conducting an electric current.

Epoxy   Based on an epoxy resin which is mixed with a hardener.

Evaporation   A change of state from solid or liquid into vapour.

Expansion   The increase in the dimensions of metals due to heat.

Extrude   To draw into lengths.

Fender   American term for wing.

Filler   Inorganic types used to extend low-pressure resins, usually polyesters.

Filler metal   Metal added to a weld in the form of a rod, electrode or coil.

Fillet weld   A weld in which two surfaces at right angles to one another are welded together.

Firewall   Panel dividing engine compartment from interior of the body.

Flange   A reinforcement on the edge of a panel formed at approximately right angles to the panel.

Flashback   Occurs when the flame disappears from the end of the welding tip and the gases burn in the torch.

Flat   A panel is said to be flat when insufficient shaping has caused uneven contours and so flat areas are obvious.

Floor pan   Main floor of the passenger compartment of an underbody assembly.

Flux   A chemical material or gas used to dissolve and prevent the formation of surface oxides when soldering, brazing or welding.

Foams (flexible)   A resin which is often used for cushioning in the automobile industries. These foams are usually urethanes.

Foams (rigid)   A resin with a higher modulus than the flexible foams. These are also normally urethanes and are used in more structural applications such as cores in sandwich constructions.

Four-door   Denotes the type of saloon body having four doors.

Frame gauges   Self-centring alignment gauges which are hung from a car's underbody.

Friction   The resistance to motion that a body meets when moving over another.

Fusion welding   A process in which metals are welded together by bringing them to the molten state at the surface to be joined, with or without the addition of filler metal, and without the application of mechanical pressure or blows.

Gas welding   A fusion welding process which uses a gas flame to provide the welding heat.

Gel   Resin takes on a gel-like consistency (gels) usually within 10–15 minutes of being catalysed. At this point it is impossible to spray, paint or pour. Stored resin which has passed its shelf-life may gel without being catalysed.

Gelcoat   A thixotropic resin normally used without reinforcement and applied first to the mould. It forms the smooth, shiny surface of the finished article.

Glass fibre   Glass filaments drawn together into fibres and treated for use as reinforcement.

Hardener   A chemical curing or hardening agent.

Hardening   Heating to a critical temperature followed by a relatively rapid rate of cooling.

Headlining   The cloth or other material used to cover the inner surface of the car roof.

Heelboard   The vertical board or panel under the rear seat which forms the support for the seat cushion.

Hinge pillar   A pillar on which a door is swung.

Hood   American term for bonnet.

Hydraulic pressure   Pressure transmitted by a liquid.

Hydraulics   The use of pressurized liquid to transfer force.

Impregnated   The particles of one substance infused into that of another.

Independent front suspension   Suspension system in which each wheel is independently supported by a spring.

Indirect damage   Secondary damage found in the area surrounding the damage which caused it.

Inertia   Property of an object by which it continues in its existing state of rest or motion in a straight line, unless that state is changed by an external force.

Insulation   A material which is non-conductive of either heat or electricity.

Integral   A necessary part to complete a whole unit.

Interchangeability   The ability to substitute one part for another.

Kerb weight   The weight of an empty vehicle without passengers and luggage.

Kevlar   A synthetic aramid fibre used as a reinforcement for resins. It is noted for its high impact resistance and is used in racing car bodywork.

Kinetic energy   The energy of motion.

Laminates   A material composed of a number of layers.

Lap joint   A form of joint obtained by overlapping the edges of two pieces of metal. The overlapping parts must be in the same plane.

Latex   A natural rubber used for making flexible moulds. It is a liquid which solidifies on contact with air.

Lay-up   Layers of glass fibres are laid on top of wet resin and then pressed down into the liquid resin.

Learning objectives   A statement of desired or expected achievement on completion of a section or module of a programme of learning.

Leftward welding   This is known as forehand welding.

Mass production   Large-scale, high-speed manufacture.

Metal fatigue   A metal structural failure, resulting from excessive or repeated stress, finally resulting in a crack.

Molecule   A minute particle into which a substance can be divided and retain its properties.

Monomer   A simple molecule capable of combining with itself, or a compatible similar chemical, to form a chain (polymer).

Moulding   The resulting shape of a plastics material when it is removed from its mould.

Mould release   A substance used to coat the mould to prevent sticking of the resin that will be used to make a part. It facilitates the removal of that part from the mould.

National vocational qualification   A vocational qualification accredited by the National Council for Vocational Qualifications, and one that is based on employer led standards of competence.

Near side   The left-hand side of the vehicle as viewed from the driver's seat.

Neutral flame   A balanced flame, indicating perfect combustion of both oxygen and acetylene gases.

Non-ferrous metals   Metals which do not contain any ferrite or iron.

Normalizing   Heating to a high temperature to produce a refinement of the grain structure of a metal or alloy.

Off side   The right-hand side of a vehicle as viewed from the driver's seat.

Original finish   The paint applied at the factory by the vehicle manufacturer.

Oxidation   Chemical reaction between oxygen and some other element resulting in oxides.

Oxidizing flame   A gas welding flame which has an excess of oxygen when burning.

Paddle   A wooden tool shaped for spreading body solder.

Parent metal   The material of a part to be welded.

Penetration   Depth of fusion or weld penetration.

Performance criteria   Statements by which an assessor judges the evidence that an individual can perform the activity specified in a competent element, to a level acceptable in employment.

Pickle   To soak metal in an acid solution in order to free the surface of rust or scale.

Pillar   A vertical support of a body frame.

Pillar face   The front of a pillar visible when the door is opened.

Pinch weld   Two metal flanges butted together and spot welded along the join of the flat surfaces.

Polyurethane   A versatile material used for adhesives, paints, varnishes, resins and foam materials. These are often used in conjunction with polyester-based GRP.

Porosity   The presence of gas pockets or inclusions within a weld.

Prototype   An original model.

Puddle   The small body of molten metal created by the flame of a welding torch.

Quarter light   The window directly above the quarter panel.

Quarter panel   The side panel extending from the door to the rear end of the body (including rear wing).

Range statement Descriptors of the limits within which performance to the identified standard is expected if an individual is to be deemed competent.

Reinforcement Filler material added to plastics (resin) in order to strengthen the finished product.

Resin Resins occur in nature as organic compounds, insoluble in water, e.g. amber, shellac. Synthetic resins have similar properties and are normally converted to solids by polymerization.

Return sweep A reverse curve.

Saloon An enclosed body not having a partition between the front and rear seats.

Scuttle panel The panel between the bonnet and windscreen.

Self-tapping screw A screw that cuts its own threads into a predrilled hole.

Silicone rubbers Used, among other applications, for sealants and flexible mould compounds. They are usually cold curing.

Solvent A chemical fluid which will dissolve, dilute or liquefy another material.

Specifications Information provided by the manufacturer on vehicle data in the form of dimensions.

Squab The rear seat back construction.

Stream lining The shaping of a vehicle body to minimize air resistance.

Subframe Members to which the engine and front-end assembly are attached.

Swage A raised form of moulding pressed into a piece of metal in order to stiffen it.

Swage line A design line on a vehicle body, caused by a crease or step in a panel.

Sweating Uniting two or more metal surfaces by the use of heat and soft solder.

Synthetic A substance produced artificially.

Temperature The measurement, in degrees, of the intensity of heat.

Template A form or pattern made so that other parts can be formed to exactly the same shape.

Tensile strength The resistance to breaking which metal offers when subject to a pulling stress.

Thermoplastic Plastic which can be softened by heating, and which still retains its properties after it has been cooled and hardened. Typical thermoplastics are polythene and PVC.

Thermosetting Plastic which hardens by non-reversible chemical reaction, initiated by heat and/or curing agents. Once hardened, it cannot be melted down without being destroyed.

Thixotropic Generally used to describe substances which have a very high viscosity when stable, but low viscosity when stirred or brushed. 'Non-drip' paint is an obvious example; another is gelcoat resin.

Tunnel A raised floor panel section for driveshaft clearance.

Turret American term for roof.

Underpinning skills and knowledge Identifies the knowledge and skill necessary to perform to the standards identified by the performance criteria in the contexts identified in the range statement.

Validation Tests, checks or assessment to ascertain whether a scheme, programme or package has achieved specified objectives.

Weld bead One single run of an electrode welding rod in manual metal arc welding.

Weld deposit Metal which has been added to a joint by one of the welding processes.

Wheel alignment The adjustment of a vehicle's wheels so that they are positioned to drive correctly.

Wheel arch Panel forming inner housing for rear wheels.

Wheelbase The distance between the centre lines of the front and rear wheels of a vehicle.

INDEX